WESTMINSTER ABBEY RECORD SERIES

VOLUME IX

SURVEYORS OF THE FABRIC
OF WESTMINSTER ABBEY
1906–1973
REPORTS AND LETTERS

WESTMINSTER ABBEY RECORD SERIES

General Editor: Matthew Payne
Keeper of the Muniments, Westminster Abbey

ISSN 1365-4306

Already published

SURVEYORS OF THE FABRIC OF WESTMINSTER ABBEY 1906–1973
REPORTS AND LETTERS

Edited by
CHRISTINE REYNOLDS

With an introduction by
PTOLEMY DEAN

THE BOYDELL PRESS

First published 2019
The Boydell Press, Woodbridge

ISBN 978 1 78327 420 8

The Boydell Press is an imprint of Boydell & Brewer Ltd
PO Box 9, Woodbridge, Suffolk IP12 3DF, UK
and of Boydell & Brewer Inc.
668 Mt Hope Avenue, Rochester, NY 14620–2731, USA
website: www.boydellandbrewer.com

A catalogue record for this book is available
from the British Library

The publisher has no responsibility for the continued existence or accuracy of URLs for
external or third-party internet websites referred to in this book, and does not guarantee that
any content on such websites is, or will remain, accurate or appropriate

This publication is printed on acid-free paper

Typeset by BBR Design, Sheffield

Printed and bound in Great Britain by
TJ International Ltd, Padstow, Cornwall

CONTENTS

The publishers acknowledge the generous financial support of the Marc Fitch Fund in the production of this volume.

GENERAL EDITOR'S PREFACE

This volume forms a continuation of those reports and letters already edited by Christine Reynolds in her earlier edition for the Westminster Abbey Record Series, *Surveyors of the Fabric of Westminster Abbey: Reports and Letters, 1827–1906*. This appeared as volume VI of the series in 2011. The present continuation, extending the story of work done to the abbey up to 1973, is greatly to be welcomed; the reports and letters included in these volumes provide an essential resource for anyone wishing to understand the changes made to the architecture and contents of Westminster Abbey in the modern period. The work of the Surveyors of the Fabric ranged widely, from major restoration programmes to minor refurbishment, from (usually) sensitive interventions into the historical fabric of the building, to designs for its contents. The annual audit reports that successive Surveyors drew up for the Dean and Chapter provide the most detailed record of this work.

Once again, the reports are presented in chronological order. Where appropriate they have been supplemented with supporting material, which, it is hoped, will help to clarify particular references, or to fill apparent gaps, in the reports. Additional notes are appended to some individual reports, labelled **N**, drawing on other sources as appropriate. As with the previous volume, Christine Reynolds's hugely detailed knowledge of both the Abbey's muniments and the fabric of the building enable her to contextualise and support the wide-ranging material presented in the reports themselves. This range of subject matter in the ever-lengthening reports (those for Dykes Bower's twenty-year surveyorship dwarf those of his predecessors) has prompted the editorial decision not to include subject headings in this volume.

It is particularly welcome to have an introduction provided by the present Surveyor of the Fabric to the Dean and Chapter of Westminster, Ptolemy Dean. This is especially significant as he is responsible for the most substantial intervention to the fabric of the building in over 250 years: the design and construction of the Weston Tower outside the Poets' Corner door of the Abbey, built to enable access to the new Queen's Diamond Jubilee Galleries, which were opened by HM Queen Elizabeth II in June 2018.

Profuse thanks must be offered to the Dean and Chapter of Westminster for their unfailing support, not only for this volume, but for the series as a whole. We are also immensely grateful to the Marc Fitch Fund for their financial contribution towards the costs of publication of this volume. Once again, Boydell & Brewer have been exemplary and continuously encouraging publishers who have guided the volume expertly through to publication.

October 2018   *Matthew Payne*

ABBREVIATIONS

SPAB   Society for the Protection of Ancient Buildings
V&A   Victoria and Albert Museum
WAM   Westminster Abbey Muniments
WAM DF   Westminster Abbey Muniments Deanery files
WAM (P)   Westminster Abbey Muniments Plan collection
WAM S   Westminster Abbey Muniments Surveyors papers
WAM SD   Westminster Abbey Muniments Surveyors drawings collection

INTRODUCTION

Ptolemy Dean

Signing off his final report as Surveyor of the Fabric at Westminster Abbey in 1973, Stephen Dykes Bower reflected:

> In concluding, after twenty two years, my last Audit Report I am conscious that, if ever future historians have occasion to delve into them, they may be found to record some information of interest, some seemingly trivial. But in combination these serve to give a picture of one side of the Abbey's life by illuminating, at a particular period in time, the affairs, aims and actions of its Surveyor's department. (**80**)

These words also complete this book, the second volume of Annual Audit Reports, assembled by Christine Reynolds, that cover the work of the four Westminster Abbey Surveyors of the Fabric who spanned the period 1906 to 1973.

The four surveyors covered by this volume are:

William Richard Lethaby (Surveyor of the Fabric 1906–28)
Sir Walter Tapper (Surveyor of the Fabric 1928–35)
Sir Charles Peers (Surveyor of the Fabric 1935–51)
Stephen Dykes Bower (Surveyor of the Fabric 1951–73)

Researchers of Westminster Abbey have indeed been fortunate that every year the Abbey's Surveyor of the Fabric has been obliged to write an annual report on the progress of the Abbey's building works. Each report covers in comprehensive detail the repair and works of alteration not just to the Abbey itself, but also its associated precinct structures. These reports, formally presented to the Dean and Chapter, provide an invaluable and unusually comprehensive record of the attention and upkeep of this remarkable set of buildings. While these are especially valuable to their successors, they also provide a unique insight into the wider history of differing attitudes towards building conservation. In contrast to most published records of building projects, compiled once the works have been completed, these reports are written in instalments as the projects unfold. This means that awkward or uncomfortable details that might normally be edited out of any 'final' summary remain a part of the official account. The reports consequently reveal where hopes are dashed by unexpected changes of circumstance or derailed by controversy. The latter would prove to be a recurring feature of the twentieth-century surveyors.

This collection of reports and letters follows on directly from the earlier volume assembled by Christine Reynolds, which explored the work of the four major nineteenth-century surveyors: Edward Blore, Sir George Gilbert Scott, John Loughborough Pearson and John Micklethwaite.[1] They spanned the period 1827–1906. As Richard Halsey summarises in his introduction to this volume, the nineteenth-century 'restoration' work was also highly controversial.[2] Scott had cause to defend his stonework renewal within the Cloisters, while J.L. Pearson's remaking of the North Transept drew strong public criticism for its substitution of conjectural designs.[3] It was in this context that William Lethaby became the first surveyor appointed in the twentieth century with a 'gentle' repair philosophy that followed the principles set out by the Society for the Protection of Ancient Buildings (SPAB), of which he had been a founding figure. The SPAB had been set up specifically to resist just the sorts of interventionist 'restoration' works that Pearson's re-design of the North Transept had come to represent. The SPAB interpretation of 'restoration' – in other words the replacement of 'old' fabric with 'new', as opposed to 'conservation'; the retention of the old in acceptance of its state of decay – remains the fundamental matter of debate for historic building repair to this day.

The differences of opinion in agreeing the best approach to building repair are expressed passionately in these reports. Just as Scott had openly condemned the restoration work of Wren,[4] which had partly failed within a hundred years, Lethaby would similarly condemn Pearson, as well as the proposed addition of a new vestry (sacristy) to the side of the Islip Chapel in 1927, which he described as 'the greatest disaster the Abbey would have suffered since the restoration of the north transept' (**26**). The cancellation of this project, after a well-organised campaign in the press, vividly illustrates how the challenges and controversies of the twentieth century could be widely and quickly shared in public. Stephen Dykes Bower would find his reputation was severely damaged by public criticism made by Sir Nikolaus Pevsner of his replacement of the high roof timber structures. 'It is a shocking fact that no record of the nave and south transept roofs were made before their reconstruction' was Pevsner's later rebuke.[5] It has been suggested that this controversy may have cost Dykes Bower a knighthood.[6]

Recurring architectural themes emerge within the audit reports that offer insight into the challenges of repairing what remains a technically complex structure. The corrosive atmosphere of London had long caused the Reigate

[1] *Surveyors of the Fabric of Westminster Abbey, 1827–1906: Reports and Letters*, edited by Christine Reynolds, Woodbridge 2011.
[2] Ibid, p. ix.
[3] William Jordan, 'Sir George Gilbert Scott R.A., Surveyor to Westminster Abbey 1849–1878', *Architectural History* 23 (1980), pp. 60–85, 188–90 (p. 76).
[4] Ibid. pp. 75–6.
[5] Nikolaus Pevsner & Simon Bradley, *London 6: Westminster*, New Haven and London 2003, p. 136.
[6] Anthony Symondson, *Stephen Dykes Bower*, London 2011, pp. 143–4.

stone, of which much of the medieval Abbey was built, to dissolve and crumble. Indeed the role of 'Surveyor of the Fabric' had been created as early as 1698 largely to address these problems. In response to the extensive stone replacement works of the previous two centuries, Lethaby's first audit report of 1906 indicates how strongly he valued the remaining medieval masonry. When asked to insert a new door into St Catherine's Chapel, he warned 'it will be a serious wound in the ancient walling' (**1**). Lethaby's approach to the decay of the stone involved the general application of protective limewash. In 1911 he outlined his approach:

> The great doorway facing the eastern walk of the cloister is most distress- ingly decayed on the surface. I have hesitated to recommend dealing with it until we had had long experience of the power of a coating of lime to arrest decay. The experience of many years has now demonstrated that an effort should be made now to save this noble doorway from further decay. (**4**)

Perhaps his clearest statement about the importance of the physical fabric, even in a decayed state, was made in respect of the South Cloister in 1920:

> I trust it will not be soon necessary to renew anymore for I feel that all the old stones, however shapeless from decay, are valuable. We find the appli- cation of lime from time to time a great help in preservation. (**13**)

It comes as a surprise to discover that, in 1928, Lethaby wished to apply limewash to the whole of the Abbey's North Transept where Pearson's relatively newly applied façade of Bath stone was already failing (**26**). In his volume *Westminster Abbey Re-Examined*, published three years earlier in 1925, he had noted: 'Now it is done don't alter it; I would not meddle even with the restoration of a restorer.'[7] This limewash was renewed again in 1935 under Tapper (**40**). The change of repair philosophy back towards physical stone replacement, which is often attributed to Dykes Bower, was in fact first signalled by Sir Charles Peers. In 1939, Peers observed:

> Scott used his shellac 'preservative' on the Chapter House doorway, with disastrous results, and since then the whitewash school have been active … in theory a perfectly sound remedy, but unfortunately not a sufficient one. The decayed stone continued to crumble behind the wash and today neither stone nor whitewash remains … The fact is that since no cure for stone decay is yet devised, the only thing to do is to begin by cutting away all decaying material; no covering up is of any use. (**45**)

The return to the more nineteenth-century 'restoration' philosophy that was practised by Dykes Bower was summarised by remarks made by him in 1965 in respect of the proposed renewal of the Nave floor:

---

[7] W.R. Lethaby, *Westminster Abbey Re-examined*, London 1925, p. 78.

'conservation repair' is completely uneconomic – a drain on the services of our very limited number of masons, when essential and urgent work on the fabric is pressing. Surely to go on replacing what is defective with the same defective material is not merely irrational but actually creating a problem for the future ... Had the existing nave floor either antiquity or outstanding quality, there might be a case for considering its retention. But it is neither old nor a valuable work of art and now that its condition entails problems of maintenance and expenditure, inescapable issues have to be faced. The Purbeck stone of which it consists has proved a failure. (**69**)

The stark contrast in approach to repair taken by Lethaby and Dykes Bower is captured by the treatment of the Feretory canopy, the sixteenth-century timber structure raised over St Edward the Confessor's tomb.[8] In 1926 it had been repaired by Lethaby:

After the removal of the pall over St Edward's Shrine last summer the 16th century upper wooden part of the Shrine was repaired and cleaned revealing some very interesting painted marbling and glass mosaic in the arches and tiny pilasters. A number of broken pieces of the wood and mosaic, which had become detached in [recent] years and had been collected by the Clerk of Works, were refixed in their original position. (**24**)

In 1960 it was repaired again by Dykes Bower:

After two years' absence the wooden feretory [canopy] was brought back and replaced over the Confessor's shrine in February 1960. In its battered condition it had become so unsightly an object that for long it had been concealed under a pall. But its interest as one of the earliest examples of Renaissance design in this country, albeit on a miniature scale, made its proper restoration desirable ... The feretory [canopy] was taken to the works of J Longley & Co Ltd at Crawley, Sussex and ... subjected to minute examination ... Working under the supervision of Mr Eric White, one joiner, Mr H Pavey, and one carver, Mr R Bacon, gradually pieced together the innumerable new sections of woodwork and Mr G Winder of Horsham executed the green and red porphyry marbling, both behind glass and direct on the wood, and the final gilding. The feretory [canopy] has now regained the appearance it must once have presented. (**65**)

Despite all of this effort it is hard to disagree with Lethaby's reflection ('mere trade wood-carving slavishly copying an architect's design is all perfectly dead & worthless') when looking at the result today (**14**).

---

[8] The Feretory 'canopy', which Dykes Bower repeatedly refers to as the 'Feretory'. The Feretory is the receptacle for the relics and the canopy sits over the top. I am grateful to Prof. Warwick Rodwell for his clarification of this and for his other invaluable comments on this Introduction.

The struggle to find a stone best suited to achieve a long-lasting repair of the Abbey is reflected by the large variety of stones on the Abbey exterior. By the later twentieth century, Portland stone, which had first been introduced by Nicholas Hawksmoor and his successor John James for the completion of the West Towers in the early eighteenth century, had come to be accepted – albeit reluctantly. Even Dykes Bower, who from his papers was evidently not sentimental about ancient fabric, reflects on its visual deficiencies:

> Though resistant to the London atmosphere Portland, with its white colour and compact grain, is less suited to Gothic than to classical design: much of the refaced area of the Abbey manifests itself as not original through the scale of the jointing and smooth texture of the stone. But while, with so much old and perished stone to be replaced, its selection was justified and even right, the consequences were prejudicial to the aspect of the building. The exterior of the Abbey is magnificent in mass and composition but its masonry cannot compare with that of, for example, Lincoln where the original stone still remains. Beside it Westminster's would look hard and mechanical. (**75**)

But while the Portland stone had withstood the atmosphere, John James's repair method of attaching the new Portland stone to the older core masonry using iron cramps had already become highly problematic. In 1917 we find Lethaby reporting that

> the two western towers need considerable repairs. The stone used in these is Portland and it has stood very well (since about 1740) but unfortunately iron cramps were used in the construction and these are constantly bursting off fragments of considerable size as they expand in rusting. (**10**)

Accessible iron cramps were removed and replaced in copper, but many were left concealed within the stonework. A surprising revelation from the reports shows Lethaby's creative re-use of second-hand Portland stone salvaged from Smirke's General Post Office on St Martins Le Grand in the City of London, which was being demolished at the same time (**5**). The arguments about the re-use of salvaged stone to reduce building costs are logical enough, but were at variance with the philosophy sometimes expressed by the Society for the Protection of Ancient Buildings, which actively discourages the re-use of building materials. Despite all of this work, a significant campaign of repairs to remove further ironwork would again become necessary during the surveyorship of Donald Buttress in the 1990s.[9] A similar legacy of rusting iron cramps inserted by John James remains to be addressed on the tower of St Margaret's

---

[9] Donald Buttress, Surveyor of the Fabric, who completed these works by 1993.

Church, Westminster, which became a part of the Abbey's jurisdiction by Act of Parliament in 1973 (**78**).[10]

Internally, Scott's 'induration' process of painting crumbling Reigate stone with shellac had darkened the building significantly over time. Scott had acknowledged the darkening effect, but argued that this could be justified as it stabilised the crumbling stone surface and protected it from contact with the polluted London atmosphere – thereby potentially reducing the extent of future stone renewal.[11] Over time the shellac had continued to darken, leading to the aspiration to clean the building. This was expressed by Lethaby as early as 1923: 'It is our hope in the future gradually to clean the whole of the wall surfaces inside the Church and rub up the Purbeck marble shafts etc.' (**20**). Lethaby also suggested the use of a bridge gantry between the Triforium arches to support scaffold, the method that would eventually be used for the internal cleaning by his successors.

Although Lethaby had recommended that the Abbey interior be cleaned, it was Tapper who made a start on this work in 1928, beginning in the South Transept: 'To examine at close quarters the stone work in Henry VII chapel, for instance, shews that something should be done at once to stop the disintegrating effect of the London atmosphere and dirt' (**29**). Two years later the work was proceeding well:

> The stone vaulting, with Wren's gilding and decoration, cleaned compara- tively easily; as also did the walls of the clerestory. The polishing of the marble shafts was really the only troublesome problem, and required a great amount of painstaking labour to accomplish without risk of harming the stone by any of the usual drastic and labour saving methods of cleaning. (**33**)

The work proceeded slowly owing to lack of funds and labour, but by 1934, Tapper was able to promise that the cleaned South Transept 'will be the fairest and most wonderful sight in London' (**39**). Charles Peers was also evidently moved by the visual effect of cleaning which had been 'greatly emphasized' by the Coronation of 1937. He continued: 'As I sat looking at the splendid spectacle, the contrast between the brilliant colours and the grimy masonry was only too evident. However the chords of the new organ brought down from aloft, on to the heads of the distinguished company, an appreciable amount of clotted dust, cobwebs and soot' (**43**). Work continued the following year in the apse. 'Scott's shellac treatment was in evidence and is being removed and the lightening of the vault cells and wall surface will I hope greatly enhance the general effect' (**44**).

---

[10] Works to remove iron cramps from the north side of St Margaret's Church were undertaken by Peter Foster during the 1989 restoration. Further cramp removal from the east end was undertaken in 2016, with major cramp removal works planned for the tower stonework in 2018–19.

[11] Jordan, 'Scott', p. 68.

In his final submitted report, from 1947, Peers pointed the way forward for his successor:

> After centuries of neglect, or smearing with wax and other futilities, a simple process of cleaning has revealed the ancient mercury gilding. This return to cleanliness, small as it is, and needing a world war to bring it about, points the way to the need for a campaign against darkness and dirtiness on a much larger scale ... and nothing could be more salutary and more suggestive of the dawn of a hope of better things than a serious attempt to bring back light and colour. (**54**)

Despite these efforts, when Dykes Bower took up post in 1952

> the tone of the whole interior was brown ... Sir Charles Peers had made a tentative start on cleaning the white surfaces, but they appeared so startling that Dean Foxley Norris had them toned down to what he described as a 'coffee' by the application of wax ... Dykes Bower found the overall effect repulsive.[12]

Dykes Bower's progress was given impetus by the desire to complete the cleaning work ahead of the Abbey's 900th anniversary in 1966 and was made possible by the success of a fund-raising appeal that raised £1 million between 1953 and 1954. In his 1962 Audit Report, Dykes Bower proclaimed:

> Towards the close of 1961 it became possible for the first time to see the high vault throughout the length of the interior much as it must have looked when newly built and it may seem most miraculous that stone which had become so dark should, after 600 years, regain its original colour by the cleansing properties of nothing more than water. (**67**)

In 1966, the pride remained tangible:

> To complete the restoration of the interior in readiness for the 900th anniversary year was the principal aim of work carried out during the last twelve months. Not everything has been achieved that might have been wished; but it may perhaps be claimed that changes and improvements carried out during the period under review have materially enhanced the internal aspect of the Abbey and that no other church of like size in this country is now presented to greater advantage. (**71**)

The extent that the walls of the Abbey had become obscured by wall and other monuments had been a long-standing concern to successive surveyors. As far back as 1852, Scott had proposed a large structure to accommodate all of the Abbey's post-1643 monuments in what he called a 'Campo Santo'.[13] This had not been executed owing to its high cost, but alternatives for re-housing existing

---

[12] Symondson, *Dykes Bower*, p. 37.
[13] Jordan, 'Scott', p. 73.

or future memorials continued to be made throughout the twentieth century. In 1927, Lethaby had advised:

> We have been considering the question of the provision of additional space of a worthy kind for future monuments, and we would suggest that the site of St Katherine's chapel should be considered. The area of the chapel together with the adjoining Canon's house on the north side would offer a site more or less square, on which a building, at once dignified in the interior and unobtrusive without, might be erected. (**25**)

In 1935, Tapper noted: 'Even the effect of overcrowding of the monuments on this wall seems to have almost disappeared in the cleaning, and the west side of the transept, which before was colourless and dreary, now appears spacious and bright and pleasant' (**40**). During that year, he relocated two large memorials that had stood in front of wall paintings on the south wall of the South Transept to the Triforium. In 1932, the very substantial Mansfield monument was dismantled and relocated to a corner of the west aisle of the North Transept. The Craggs monument had already been reduced in size and moved to what is now the St George's Chapel, along with the no less substantial Cornewall memorial, which found itself placed at the cloister entrance (**36**). After much lobbying, Dykes Bower was able to dispatch the substantial memorial to James Watt from St Paul's Chapel to the British Transport Museum in Clapham (**66**). 'This portentous combination of an enormous figure on an enormous pedestal is so grossly out of scale with its surroundings as almost to kill the effect of the chapel and its other monuments,' he wrote in 1953 (**56**). Shortly before its removal its sheer weight had partly collapsed the floor on which it stood.

One unusual solution to the challenge of making extra space for memorials emerged from Peers in 1947 with the suggested re-use of the bomb-damaged church of St John in Smith Square (**54**). Dykes Bower also made similar proposals in 1960, but these were not pursued (**65N**). Undeterred, Dykes Bower continued:

> But there are some memorials whose right to occupy floor and wall space in the Abbey seems so slender as to call for re-examination. It would not be a question of exclusion, but of transferring them to the triforium, which already contains a sufficient number to counter any suggestion that this would be equivalent to banishment. (**64**)

The matter was raised once more in 1964 (**68**), but again not pursued.

Where monuments remained, Dykes Bower redecorated them in bold colours. His philosophy was set out in 1956 in respect of the monument of Queen Elizabeth:

> Its splendour depends on its decoration; but this decoration could not be renewed until the large number of missing features in marble and alabaster, vital to the design, had been supplied … realisation of the

original designer's intention must normally be preferable to perpetual mutilation. (**61**)

But one difficulty with any approach to cleaning and restoration is then determining where to stop. With the Feretory canopy all but renewed in 1960, an unhappy contrast was made with the ancient shrine of Edward the Confessor itself:

> Beneath the colour and glitter of the feretory [canopy] the defacement of the shrine itself is now more than ever obvious. I hope that steps may soon be taken to remedy the mistakes that, in past alterations, have stultified its design and bring back to it something of the beauty it has lost. (**65**)

This captures one of the great dilemmas of the Dykes Bower approach, still embodied by the uncomfortably over-restored Feretory canopy.

Another much larger dilemma of the Dykes Bower legacy is presented in the Abbey's roof spaces, the complete and probably unnecessary destruction of which these reports chronicle in detail. Tapper's works on maintaining the leaded roof structures of St John Chapel had followed a familiar twentieth-century pattern of in-situ repair with proprietary chemicals:

> One of the main beams and many of the joists of this flat were found to be in a bad condition, and these are being strengthened and renewed where necessary, and all the timbers are being treated with Heppel's fluid to destroy the beetle which has caused some damage to this part of the roof. (**33**)

Tapper's treatment of beetle when found in the Library roof in 1931 appears measured:

> I have had this roof re-examined, and although it is true that the beetle is there in small numbers (as is so often the case in ancient timbers), there does not appear to be sufficient damage to necessitate any very drastic work. I have included in next year's budget a small sum to treat the roof timbers with Heppell's fluid. (**35**).

Immediately following his appointment in 1953, Dykes Bower directed a much more interventionalist approach to the repair of the roof structures. While it was clear that the timbers had suffered serious decay over the centuries, Dykes Bower would seemingly not repair structures in situ, particularly if it was felt that their designs could be improved upon, even with the substitution of modern materials. An early foretaste of this approach emerges in the full replacement of the historic oak-framed roofs of the Little Cloister in 1956:

> Removal of the surviving timber in the ceilings of the west and the east walks and reconstruction of these roofs in reinforced concrete has recently been finished ... When dry, the plaster of the ceiling will be whitened so that all four sides correspond. (**61**)

This formerly lead-clad roof was renewed with a mastic asphalt finish, justified on grounds of reduced cost and the wartime damage to adjacent structures. While costs were an undeniably significant restriction in those austere post-war years, the confidence asserted in this matter can be compared with the almost apologetic tone of Tapper's need to renew part of the Cloister roof just over twenty years before:

> Relaying of the lead flat over the west walk of the cloister has been completed. The timbers of this flat roof were found to be in a very decayed condition, and it was necessary for most of them to be replaced by new ones. They were only deal timbers of about 100 years ago. (**40**)

By 1957, work on the renewal of the western section of the Nave roof was already underway. 'Examination and tests have shown that the death watch beetle has penetrated everywhere and that no hopes can be built on any of the woodwork of the roof being immune from its ravages, or only slightly affected,' (**62**) noted Dykes Bower. It is apparent from his annual reports that Dykes Bower considered death watch beetle to be so 'contagious' that chemical treatment was applied even to timbers that had been condemned to be incinerated: 'Badly affected timbers that are incapable of retention are treated before removal and later destroyed,' he wrote in 1954. With little photographic record surviving of the roof timbers that were cleared away it is not possible to know the extent of their decay. It is also all too easy to judge with the benefit of hindsight, especially as there is now much greater understanding of the actions of death watch beetle. This is as summarised by current advice offered by Historic England:

> Spray treatments with insecticides generally have little impact on a death watch beetle population because there is little contact between the insect and the chemical. This means that environmental control is often the most practical option. The deathwatch beetle prefers damp timbers and do not appear to thrive if wood moisture contents remain below 15% throughout the year … The key to deathwatch beetle control is good maintenance so that the building remains dry.[14]

All of this suggests that the ancient roof structures, had they been kept dry, could in all probability have been saved.

While the presence of death watch beetle provided the initial impetus for repair work, as with the Little Cloister roof, there is the sense that the decay also offered the opportunity to 'improve' on the design of the roof structures:

> To save cost, reinforced concrete is being substituted for stone where repairs to the internal face of the wall above the vaulting are necessary; and the spacing of the wooden trusses is being widened slightly to reduce their number. Thus whereas there were 127 of them over the twelve bays

---

[14] English Heritage, *Practical Building Conservation: Timber*, Ashgate 2012, p. 150.

from the west end to the crossing, there will now be 115... The advantage of the roof as altered lies in its simplicity: it has recovered its original form without obstructive central supports, so that conditions both for future inspection of the timbers and for fire-fighting will be easier than before. (**62**)

The willingness to substitute modern materials was also expressed from the outset. Writing in 1953 Chapter were advised: 'The requisite strengthening of the original roof construction could more effectively be provided by steel members framed to give support both to the main roof rafters and the collars' (**57**). Four years later there comes the suggestion to do away with timber altogether: 'it may be expedient to consider whether there should be any further use of oak. The substitution of a steel framed roof ... according to present calculations ... might represent a saving of at least 30% on the cost of oak' (**62**). There is a rare hint of some sense of potential regret to this 'in so far that it would obliterate the original construction which, particularly over the nave, was a remarkable piece of carpentry ...'. To make up for this Dykes Bower proposed: 'if later roofs have to be of steel, one section at least should perpetuate the original construction' – albeit with completely new timbers set to a different spacing from what had originally been found. When news of the replacement roof structures became known, an angry indignance emerges in the lengthy paper prepared for Chapter in defence of the work in 1968: 'Should what is faulty be deemed inviolate because it is the original construction? Does age warrant indefinite perpetuation of error?' The paper concludes with the final thought: 'It is relevant to bear in mind that, being over 100 feet above ground out of sight in the enclosed space above the vaulting and under the outer lead covering, this roof is not accessible to the public and never visited except by the very occasional student' (**74**). One suspects that Lethaby would not have fathomed such a rationale to justify the destruction of the Abbey's primary roof structures.

Uniting all of the surveyors in this volume has been a frustration with the inadequacies of the Abbey's internal workforce. Dykes Bower's reports describe a faltering progress hindered by an in-house works department that was too few in number, too elderly or inflicted by illness and poor attendance: 'until masons are more numerous, spectacular results in restoring the exterior cannot be hoped for', he wrote in 1956 (**61**). This had also been a problem that had inconvenienced Tapper as far back as 1929 (**31**): 'In the last report it was anticipated that work on the south transept would have been started by now but the shortage of labour has not made this possible' (**29**). Tapper's continued frustration with the lack of Abbey works staff was repeated the following year: 'I wish that some special effort could be made to find more money, with which to carry it on faster ... it seems truly amazing that the commencement of so important and necessary a work should have been delayed so long' (**35**). With little progress, the plea was repeated in 1933:

At the present rate of progress on the north transept, it will be years before we are able to attend to the western towers, to mention only the larger areas of outside cleaning, while the deposit of encrusted dirt is allowed to remain on the surface of the stone, disintegration is going on underneath at a very increasing rate. (**38**)

Given his socialist principles, Lethaby was inevitably concerned that the apparent injustice of the Abbey's workforce being paid '17% per hour below the latest standard rate', which he lobbied to change (**16**). Lethaby also offered advice on the eternal difficulty of estimating accurate repair costs, which could equally apply today: 'It is impossible to estimate for works of this kind, which have to be dealt with stone by stone, with any close accuracy and the sums which I have set down are only approximate.' He went on to add:

> Generally speaking it is obvious that the quality of the work must be better under a system which eliminates private business interests. The drastic nature of some restorations of the past has been to a great extent the outcome of the contract system, and in a lesser degree the same objections apply to the system of contract by schedule, owing to the necessity of defining the exact nature of the work in advance. (**16**)

W.R. LETHABY

William Richard Lethaby (1857–1931) had been Chief Clerk in the office of Richard Norman Shaw, and a co-founder of the Art Workers Guild in 1884. An ardent Socialist, he had been appointed Professor of Art at the Royal College of Art in 1901. He would publish two works on the architecture of Westminster Abbey: *Westminster Abbey and the King's Craftsmen* (1906) and *Westminster Abbey Re-Examined* (1925), both of which remain key points of historic reference.

At the heart of all Lethaby's discussions has been the extent to which the ancient fabric of the Abbey was considered to be of importance in its own right, rather than just the overall gothic design that the fabric conveyed. He completed the appendix of his 1925 work with some advice about the 'preservation of the church':

> Whatever we do, much will necessarily decay – paintings, carvings, pavements are quickly fading and wearing away from sight and memory; and a part of any general scheme of preservation must include the recording of all these things … To *restore* these things is to substitute a copy for what remains of an original, but to *copy* it is to preserve a faithful record of it, while leaving the original untouched, which will carry on its interest until it fades to a mere shadow. Which will the next generation thank us for?[15]

---

[15] W.R. Lethaby, *Westminster Abbey and the King's Craftsmen: A Study of Medieval Building*, London 1926, pp. 372–3.

A somewhat unexpected aspect of work to emerge from Lethaby's audit reports concerns his involvement with technical innovation. Full electric lighting was installed into the Abbey for the first time in 1912–13 (**5**). Lethaby's discreet brass fixtures even won favour with his successor Dykes Bower, who carefully relocated them around the various precinct buildings when they came to be displaced in the Abbey by the Guinness chandeliers installed in 1965. Lethaby also undertook the work to renew the Abbey heating system, with a new Portland stone flue tucked in between buttresses on the north side (**16**). Lethaby was also prepared to investigate the use of chemical treatments to stabilise stone, engaging with the Scientific and Research Department for possible silico-fluoride treatments of the stone (**16**).

Lethaby's surveyorship coincided with World War I, and his report of 1916 notes the removal of movable objects such as the Coronation Chair and some of the tomb effigies for safe keeping into the crypt of the Chapter House and the sand-bagging of the Abbey particularly around the Royal Tombs (**8**). A total of 1,630 bags were reportedly used in an operation that would sadly come to be repeated on a much larger scale less than thirty years later by Peers. The Abbey was not damaged during the First War, but Lethaby's 1919 report notes the damage caused by the jubilation that followed its cessation to what is now the Abbey Shop on the Sanctuary: 'Here many of the stones have long been loose and parts were broken away by those who climbed over the railings on the armistice day' (**11**).

SIR WALTER TAPPER

Lethaby's resignation had been forced by ill health (**27**), but his successor, Sir Walter Tapper (1861–1935), had already been involved in the design of what had proved to be a controversial proposal for the addition of a new Sacristy extension adjacent to the Islip Chapel. As the inspecting architect of York Minster, and having trained alongside Ninian Comper in the office of G.F. Bodley, Tapper, a deeply religious man, was a traditionally trained church architect who worked in the gothic style.[16] He had married an assistant at Watts and Co., the church-furnishing company based in Westminster, who had originally supplied Comper and who continue to supply the Abbey with its surplices to this day. Tapper was President of the Royal Institute of British Architects (RIBA) at the time of his appointment, but with the present split between modern 'design' architects and 'historic buildings' or 'conservation' architects, it seems inconceivable that such an appointment could occur today. After the sudden death of his wife in 1931, Tapper had arranged with the Abbey to build a small house for himself at 4A Dean's Yard for use during his lifetime, but he died shortly before its completion so that the Abbey returned a contribution to his executors (**39N**). The house,

---

[16] See, for example, David Dolan and Leigh O'Brien, 'The Life and Work of Sir Walter Tapper', at http://www.sir-walter-tapper-churches.co.uk.

which has a handsome painted plaster reproduction of the Abbey's coat of arms on its first-floor drawing-room ceiling, is now occupied by the Dean's Verger.

Continuity with ongoing repair work at the Abbey was provided by Eric E. Lofting, who had assisted Lethaby since 1921 and continued to serve under Tapper and also Peers after Tapper's death in 1935. A serious matter that occurred in Tapper's time (and something that all the Abbey's Surveyors would no doubt dread) was the fall of a piece of stone from the elaborate stone-vaulted ceiling of the Henry VII Chapel. The incident happened during 1932 just as Tapper's fairly extensive repair of the chapel's exterior stonework, which had included the application of limewash, was coming to a close. The stone fall forced the closure of the Chapel for over two and a half years, while the stone ceiling vault ribs were individually checked and repointed. Pearson's nineteenth-century metal tie bars were retained but adjusted while the ceiling was cleaned and limewashed while access was afforded by scaffolding (**39**). In the roof space itself, every cement patch over the open joints can still be seen to be fastidiously dated '1933'. At the same time Tapper was engaged in the addition of a new reading room, located on an upper floor above the east walk of the Cloister arcade, with an ingenious timber spiral staircase connection to the main library.

While Tapper comes across as measured and reasonable in his various reports, he could evidently be pushed to frustration. In respect of St Faith's Chapel he declared in 1932:

> The existing position of the silver sanctuary lamp is absurd, it is far too high, and should be lowered to a height of about 8 feet from the floor … The oak seats placed on the old stone seat are quite incongruous, and should be removed … The kneelers are thin and poor and quite unworthy. At the west end (south) on the stone seat is a sort of laundry basket, hardly a help to devotion. Opposite is an ugly box, and some shocking candle-sticks, which should be burnt. Kneeling mats are piled on the old stone seat. If orderliness is next to Godliness, as we are told, this should not be … An incongruous board covered with a mauve cloth covers the upper portion [of the door]. It would be comic, were it not in Westminster Abbey … which take away from the dignity of this noble place. (**36**)

Sir Charles Peers

Sir Charles Peers (1868–1952), Tapper's successor, had first consulted at the Abbey in 1930 at the invitation of his predecessor to review foundations that had been uncovered under the Nave floor and which were thought to have been a part of the Confessor's church (**34**). Peers, who was President of the Society of Antiquities, and as much an archaeologist as an architect, had held the post of Chief Inspector of Ancient Monuments from 1913 to 1933.[17] Like Tapper,

---

[17] Nicholas Doggett, 'Peers, Sir Charles Reed (1868–1952)', *Oxford Dictionary of National Biography*, Oxford 2004.

he would also hold the post of inspecting architect to York Minster. Peers had trained under T.G. Jackson from 1893 to 1896, at the time that Rigaud's House for Westminster School in Little Dean's Yard was being rebuilt.[18] Peers had also been instrumental in establishing legislation to protect ancient monuments in 1913, and was closely associated with the period when ancient monuments were acquired by the State for preservation. This enabled buildings to be archaeologically drawn, recorded and cleared of their later 'accretions' to reveal as much as possible their medieval form. They were then labelled to inform visitors and surrounded by open grass for easy maintenance. This systematic approach to the preservation and ordering of ancient monuments would also inform his work at the Abbey.

His first annual report immediately establishes that the pattern of serious archaeological study would characterise his surveyorship. Drawings and recording of wall paintings in the South Transept were commissioned from Professor Ernest W. Tristram, a respected expert who had published a detailed study of the wall paintings at Canterbury Cathedral (**41**). Tristram had also trained under Lethaby at the Royal College of Art and had previously undertaken some careful cleaning of the Crouchback Tomb for Lethaby in 1921 (**15**).[19] 'Accretions', which in the Abbey context took in the form of later eighteenth-century monuments, were dismantled so that the medieval wall paintings could be displayed in the South Transept (see also **42, 44**). The Islip Chapel was returned to its medieval form for worship in 1939 (**45**) through the relocation of the substantial seventeenth-century Hatton Memorial. The memorial was then re-fixed to a new and decidedly utilitarian 'Ministry of Works'-type cement-rendered fletton brick wall supported on a new steel lintel within the north-eastern Triforium.[20] Signage and labelling, an important element of the display of ruins, were added to inform Abbey visitors and staff alike, and even included a list of all the organists from 1560 to the present day being placed on the organ console (**44**). Old glass assembled in the eastern clerestory windows in 1706 was taken out 'for preservation in the Museum' (**44**). The windows were then re-glazed with coloured frosted glass.

At the same time a 'Ministry of Works'-type building repairs specification appears, with the introduction of hard, cement mortars to the stonework of the Deanery (**41**). At the time these hard mortars were seen as 'protective', but being impermeable they soon trapped moisture, causing significant decay to the softer stonework adjacent. Hard cement mortar repairs came to be applied more generally, including on the Jerusalem Chamber parapet in a form known as 'synthetic stone' (**42**). More 'synthetic stone' was applied to the apse of the

---

[18] Pevsner & Bradley, *London 6: Westminster*, p. 206.

[19] For Tristram, see R. Mitchell, 'Tristram, Ernest William (1882–1952)', *Oxford Dictionary of National Biography*, Oxford 2004.

[20] The Hatton Memorial was relocated to the South Transept Triforium in 2017 to enable the Eastern Triforium to be converted into the Queen's Diamond Jubilee Galleries.

Abbey itself in 1939 (**45**). These patterns of repair trapped moisture behind the impermeable cement finish, and like John James's eighteenth-century iron cramps probably caused greater damage to the stone than that which they had sought to address in the first place. Unexpectedly, the application of limewash over some stonework surfaces appears to have continued, perhaps under the influence of Lethaby's assistant Eric Lofting, who was still in post.

In many ways, Peers was the least fortunate of the Surveyors included in this book. In 1936, within only a year of his appointment, Peers would find large parts of the Abbey requisitioned by the Ministry of Works for the erection of additional seating galleries ahead of the Coronation of George VI: 'I look forward with dismay to the prospect that the Abbey staff should necessarily be excluded from the church during the preparations for the Coronation,' he noted somewhat balefully (**41**). These words would echo similar frustrations that would be expressed by Dykes Bower in respect of the coronation of Elizabeth II in 1953 (**56**).

Just three years on, Peers, like Lethaby, would find his work abruptly curtailed by a shortage of staff and funds caused by another World War. By 1940, all efforts had been diverted to undertaking protective measures. These were more extensive than those that had been arranged by Lethaby only 25 years earlier, and included the construction of the windowless reinforced concrete bomb shelter adjacent to the Precinct Wall, which had been intended to serve as a future garage (**46**). The reports made by Peers during the war years provide a vivid record of what must have been a terrifying and dispiriting moment in the Abbey's history. The report of 1942 records in detail the bombing of 11 May 1941, when the supply of water failed, 'so members of the fire fighting squad had to stand by and watch the buildings burn'. Peers continued: 'We must hope to emerge from the present relapse into barbarism with some of our ancient splendours intact' (**48**). The buildings of the Abbey and also of Westminster School were badly damaged by the enemy action of 1941. The crossing tower roof was lost and hastily replaced by a new structure of concrete and asphalt supported on basic steel girders (**49**). This 'temporary' structure survives under new roof leadwork and a painted ceiling to its underside as inserted by Dykes Bower in 1957 (**62**). Peers, with his life-long commitment to public access to ancient places, had successfully argued that the nave of the Abbey should be kept open to visitors regardless of bomb damage, stating: 'But if in the end it proves to have been possible to preserve its continuity of function unbroken, what better record could be desired?' (**50**).

By 1945, when the war was finally over, Peers was already suffering a long-term illness that would mar the last years of his life. There are no Audit Reports for 1945 or 1946, or from 1948 onwards. In 1947 Peers reflected on how the damage of 1941 might have been avoided 'if the National fire-fighting services had been better developed and an adequate supply of water available from the adjacent Thames, we might not now to be deploring the damage to the Deanery and the Little Cloister'. He eventually died in 1952.

Stephen Dykes Bower

The name of Stephen Dykes Bower (1903–1994) had initially been suggested by Lawrence Tanner, the Keeper of the Muniments and author of a number of authoritative books on Westminster Abbey and School. With the uncertain state of Peers's health, the Dean had already suggested that Dykes Bower might be engaged as Deputy Surveyor in 1950 (**54N**). He was formally appointed Surveyor following the resignation of Peers in June 1951. Like his predecessor, Tapper, with whom he had travelled abroad in his youth, Dykes Bower was an established architect in the gothic style.[21] He had trained under Ninian Comper and had become an established authority in the rebuilding of new and bomb-damaged churches and had been responsible for the re-creation of the war-damaged Baldacchino in St Paul's Cathedral.[22]

His biographer Anthony Symondson sums up Dykes Bower's surveyorship at Westminster as follows:

> His 22 years in the position have been overshadowed by controversies, so that the exceptional nature of what he achieved has never been fully recognised. No Surveyor other than George Gilbert Scott did more to unveil the architectural qualities and beautify the abbey's interior, and what we see today is very much what Dykes Bower left.[23]

Dykes Bower's audit reports reveal how his work began with the repair of bomb damage and the reversal of wartime neglect, and it is certainly a tribute to his energy and determination that so much work was carried out in his time. Dykes Bower set about the process of external cleaning and stone renewal, which was not finally completed until the late 1990s under his successors Peter Foster and Donald Buttress. Inevitably he defined the work of his immediate successors.

Nevertheless, posterity continues to judge Dykes Bower with a degree of regret for the amount of ancient fabric that was lost during his tenure. In a letter to Alan Rome he had summed up his philosophy as follows:

> One of the reasons indeed why I view this fashionable word 'conservation' with suspicion is that it is being propounded in some quarters as the proper substitute for Restoration. The latter demands some knowledge and skill; the former is going to give unlimited scope to those who will do the minimum to keep things going, but adding nothing to enable them to make artistic sense.[24]

How the Abbey switched from the 'Restoration' of Pearson, to the 'conservation'

---

[21] Symondson, *Dykes Bower*, p. 7.
[22] Ibid. pp. 25–8.
[23] Ibid. p. 37.
[24] Alan Rome, 'Stephen Dykes Bower', *Churchscape: Annual Review of the Council for the Care of Churches*, 14 (1995).

practised by Lethaby and back again to the 'Restoration' of Dykes Bower is one of the questions that the annual audit papers help to illuminate.

Dykes Bower's detailed and precise audit reports extend to a greater length than all three of his predecessors combined. They provide valuable insight into what appeared to drive his architectural approach. It is difficult to generalise, but a number of key concerns appear to emerge. The first is an undoubted reverence for the design and beauty of Westminster Abbey as a work of architecture. It was the desire to reveal this that drove forward the cleaning programme and, to an extent, the highly controversial scheme to entirely replace the Nave floor, as summarised in 1964:

> I prefer to draw attention to the peculiar place that Westminster occupies as one of the outstanding churches of Christendom. Although the supreme mediaeval embodiment of English genius in architecture, yet it is intimately linked with the greatest achievements of French cathedral buildings and the masterpieces of Rome and northern Italy. This is a privilege never to be forgotten or betrayed. Any new work must, therefore, measure up to the standards they set; and because the nave presents the visitor with his first impression of the Abbey, here, in floor and furnishings, they should be most conspicuously evident. (**68**)

Given the importance of the building, there then emerges a sense that dirt, mess and disorder of all types were unworthy of a building as important as Westminster Abbey. This manifests itself repeatedly in a particular fear of dust. In 1957, there was a desire to throw away items stored in the Triforium:

> After a survey of the objects of every kind that in the course of years have accumulated in the triforium, a considerable number were got rid of as having no value. Even so the quantity that remains is an encumbrance that takes up space and collects dust. (**62**)

A further effort to throw out items was repeated in 1961:

> Following an inspection of the quantity of stone, marble, wood, books, war time paraphernalia and bric a brac of every description that through the years had been consigned to the triforium out of sight, a clearance was made of all that could be classified as rubbish. What remains is not negligible in bulk, but at least there is less to collect dust.

Below the Triforium floor, the presence of yet more dust would be an obvious cause of concern. Writing about the Triforium in 1955, Dykes Bower noted:

> It will still be a necessary precaution to open all parts and, in doing so, to take advantage of the chance to remove from the pockets of the vaulting the deep accumulation of debris, which imposes extra weight on the vaulting ribs and infilling. Over St John's chapel the method adopted was to lift it in long handled scoops, the material then being bagged in sacks and lowered externally down to ground level for carting away in lorries.

The material is sifted before being bagged but, in the varied assortment of objects that came up, nothing of special interest, except an antique chisel, has so far been found. (**60**)

It is fortunate that this work was not completed as, in 2016, a number of dust-filled vault pockets were sifted to reveal 31,000 pieces of glass fragments, most of thirteenth-century date from long-destroyed grisaille windows.[25]

The 1962–3 report makes it apparent that it was the dust created by the erosion of the Abbey's floor that was in part driving the proposal to completely renew the existing nave floor with marble:

It is serious for three reasons: 1. There is the risk of accidents because, particularly for old people whose sight may not be good, uneven paving can be dangerous, 2. Once a hard surface is lost, loose particles of stone dust circulate and make the task of cleaning more difficult ... But if, all the time, fresh dust is being generated as the floor is eroded under people's feet, the process becomes endless and the benefits of cleaning never mature ... The remedy for this state of affairs is a floor that will be durable, easy to keep clean and, of course, appropriate to the building. (**68**)

The fear of dust appears to have lain with a sense that the Abbey, so recently cleaned, would soon become soiled once again. Writing in 1964, Dykes Bower lamented:

As recently indeed as three months ago I felt almost a sense of despair at the state of the interior. Just when the cleaning was drawing to an end, the benefits were being neutralized by layers of dust everywhere so obvious as to fill one with shame. Had the money been spent for nothing? Had the Abbey, after all, no standards to maintain and teach?

He went on to advise:

it may be pertinent to suggest that the problem of dust is aggravated in ways that could surely be avoided. I have in mind a recent occasion when 500 chairs were set out for an occasion at which only 100 proved to be required. And why, I have often asked myself, should it be worthwhile turning blocks of chairs in the east aisle of the south transept to face north west instead of north? Such manoeuvres take time and cannot be executed without just that element of disturbance which creates dust. Is it really necessary? (**68**)

Two years later, it was the creation of dust that caused an expression of concern about the increasing presence of television cameramen in the Abbey:

---

[25] In 2017–18, the fragments of glass found were assembled as a 'donors' window' to light the bridge connecting the Triforium galleries to the stair and lift access tower.

I feel bound to deprecate too the effects on the building that follow from these televised services: not only the damage of some kind that nearly always occurs but also the creation of dust and dirt inseparable from erection and dismantling of such extensive equipment. Our cleaners dust only what they can reach: the great bulk of the dust merely settles out of reach, slowly and imperceptibly undoing the benefits of the internal cleaning so recently finished. (**71**)

In 1968, it was the presence of litter that caused concern:

This report cannot conclude without again drawing attention to the nuisance of litter. Within the church itself it is bad enough; in the cloisters worse; outside Poets' Corner disgusting. All service papers after use, while awaiting removal, are apparently put in a large open container which, piled high with rubbish of every kind, stands within the gates of the masons yard until the next refuse collection. The gates have frequently to be open and in a wind the contents blow about unchecked; even on a still day anyone entering from Old Palace Yard must be revolted by squalid untidiness on the very threshold of the most famous church in the land. There is an abuse here which I think calls for drastic and immediate action. (**72**)

It is important to note that Dykes Bower was working in an era where large high-rise buildings threatened to intrude upon the Abbey's setting. In these areas, he successfully fended off a number of potentially damaging schemes. In 1960, a new building was threatened on Victoria Street, the height of which Dykes Bower was able to have reduced:

When the plans were first prepared, I had negotiations with the Royal Fine Art Commission, the London County Council and the architect, particularly in respect of the height to which it was proposed to build. The architect was sympathetic to my representations and agreed to reduce this from 147 to 107 feet. (**65**)

Dykes Bower also fended off alterations to College Hall proposed by the architects Carden and Godfrey at Westminster School in 1967:

The desirability of improving conditions for the serving of meals would appear now to be a need recognized by the School, although its realization does not make much progress. Mr Carden, the school architect, discussed with me plans he had been asked to prepare for the re-organization of the kitchen offices, but which, since they entailed building a larger brick excrescence in the south west corner of the Deanery courtyard, I did not encourage as acceptable. (**72**)

But Dykes Bower was not always successful. A large underground car park and vent shaft were constructed by Westminster City Council uncomfortably close to the precinct wall along Abingdon Street in 1964, while in 1968:

indignation must be expressed over the erection in Horseferry Road of three monstrous office blocks that architecturally are a disgrace to London and the City of Westminster in particular. Inhuman and endlessly repetitive they have already risen so high as to dwarf everything else in the neighbourhood. College Garden not merely now seems smaller; its charm has been impaired because these horrors intrude upon the skyline. They are even visible from Old Palace Yard. That such an outrage could have been permitted, without a thought for the effect of such high buildings on a vicinity which includes the Abbey and the Houses of Parliament as well as the beautiful 18th century quarter of Smith Square and its adjacent streets, seems as incredible as it is shameful. (**73**)[26]

It is perhaps fitting to end this brief overview of Dykes Bower's papers with his 1972 observations about the prospect of a museum in the Eastern Triforium:

A suggestion now put to me is that one or more of the spaces in the triforium over the apsidal chapels should be fitted up as a museum for classified exhibits (e.g. of carved stone) to which bona fide students could, on application, have access. Though this possibility was referred to in an audit report some years ago as something that might be feasible, in the light of present conditions I feel very hesitant about it. There are more students about and a position could arise in which some might seek entry to explore a part of the Abbey to which the public is not admitted. Unless an attendant accompanied everyone ascending to the triforium and physical barriers were erected to limit the area in which movement were permitted there could be a serious security risk. There is no possibility of a lift to cut out the effort of mounting the newel stairs, which could subject persons with heart trouble to at any rate some strain. Nor is there in the triforium arches protection to restrain anyone with suicidal tendencies.

It is difficult enough to keep the triforium clean: exhibits, unless protected in glass cases, would have to be dusted continually and create a further labour problem. (**79**)

A new gallery was opened in the Triforium in 2018 with a supporting lift and stair access tower. One might wonder what Dykes Bower would have made of that.

[26] The former Department of the Environment towers on Marsham Street were demolished during the 1990s.

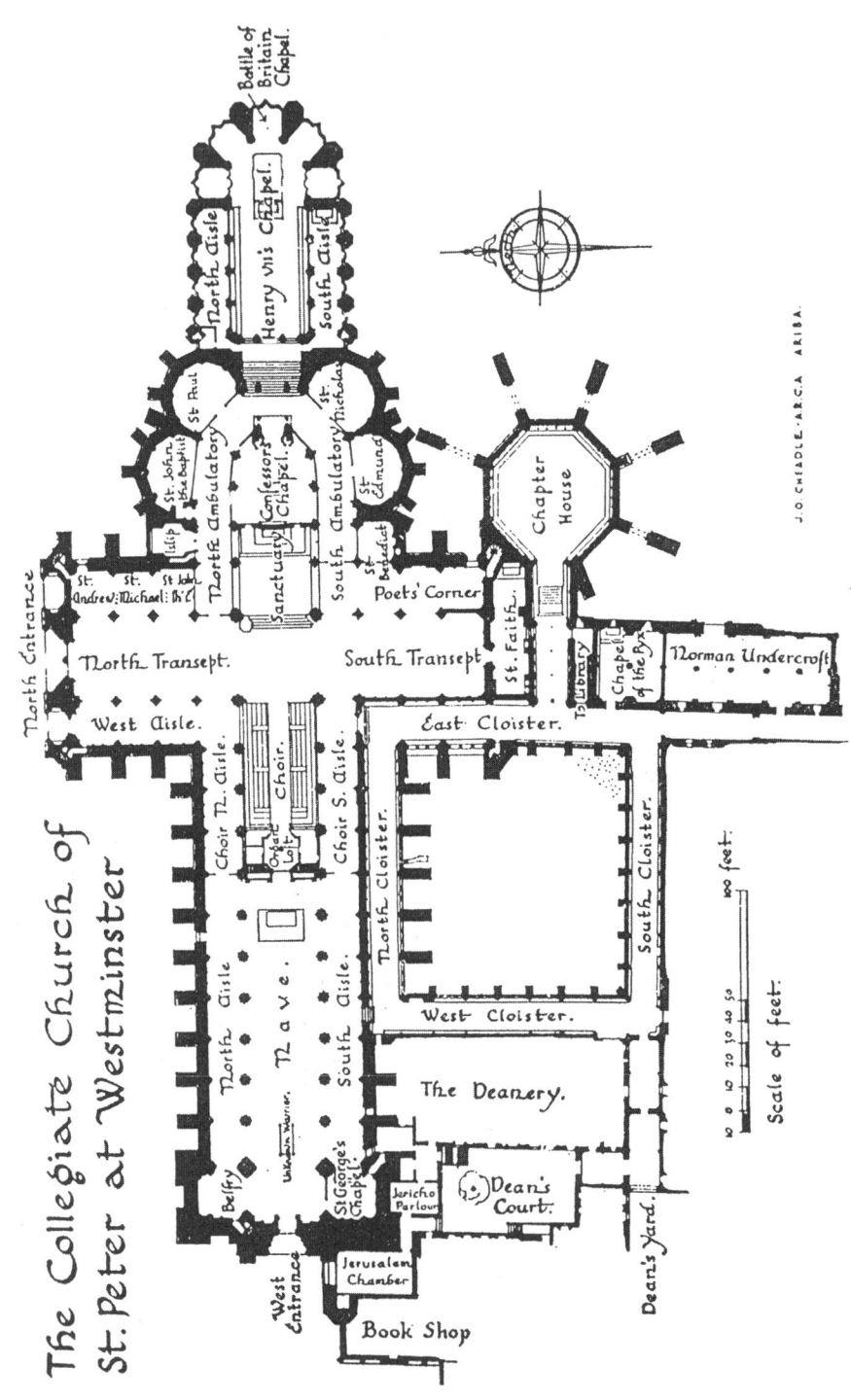

The Collegiate Church of St. Peter at Westminster

Battle of Britain Chapel.

North Aisle

Henry vii's Chapel.

South Aisle

St Paul

St. John Baptist

St. John Baptist

Philip

North Ambulatory

Confessors' Chapel

Sanctuary

South Ambulatory

St Nicholas

St Edmund

St Benedict

St. Andrew

St. Michael

St John Ev'l

North Entrance

North Transept.

West Aisle.

Poets' Corner

South Transept.

St. Faith.

Library

Chapel of the Pyx

Norman Undercroft

Choir N. Aisle

Choir.

Choir S. Aisle

Organ Loft

East Cloister.

Chapter House

North Cloister.

South Cloister.

West Cloister.

North Aisle

Nave.

South Aisle

Lantern Tower

The Deanery.

Belfry

St George's Chapel

Jericho Parlour

Dean's Court.

Dean's Yard.

West Entrance

Jerusalem Chamber

Book Shop

J.O. CHEADLE·A.R.C.A· A.R.I.B.A.

100 feet.

10 0 10 20 30 40 50

Scale of feet.

REPORTS AND PAPERS

WILLIAM RICHARD LETHABY
1906–28

1. Lethaby was appointed at the meeting of the Dean and Chapter on 11 December 1906 at £100 p.a. No reports have so far been found for 1908 and 1913. Those for some years are very short. He published two major works on the Abbey: *Westminster Abbey and the King's Craftsmen* (1906) and *Westminster Abbey Re-Examined* (1925). There are many letters to the Dean WAM 59277–59328, three notebooks c.1905–24 WAM 59328*– 59328*** and plans in WAM (Plans) collection. Various drawings can be found in the CN collection in the Muniments. WAM OA and OS series also contain some letters.

His assistant Arthur G. Wallace was appointed in January 1907 and died in 1917. Some of his plans are in the Surveyor Drawings collection. Assistant Eric E. Lofting was appointed in 1921.

WAM S/1/47

111 Inverness Terrace. W

Feb 7 1907

To the Very Revd. the Dean and the Chapter of Westminster.

Gentlemen,

I have made an examination of the old Hall[1] in the Little Cloisters with special reference to obtaining a better entrance to Canon Beeching's house. Already three doorways exist which have relation to this question, there is the door of access to the Hall itself, there is the door by its side which opens to the passage leading to the Canon's house and there is a corresponding door on the east side of the old hall through which the same passage leads. If still another doorway is made in the west wall of St Catherine's chapel, it will be a serious wound in the ancient wall disturbing one of Abbot Litlington's[2] windows, & it will necessitate a passage encroaching on St Catherine's chapel.[3] Further the access thus gained to the house will be more indirect than at present. If such an alteration were effected and the Hall in use it would probably be found that with its outer door opening directly to it, it would be very draughty, and it might be necessary to put an inner lobby of woodwork to screen this door.

I believe having regard to all these facts, that the best plan would be to put a close screen right across the end of the wall forming a narrow passageway to the Canon's house, and in this same screen putting the door of access to the

Hall which wd. not thus open to the outer air. The second window of the old Hall would be given back to it, and the passage being ceiled over at a low level all the space above it would be included in the air-space of the Hall. With a step ladder and a light balustrade this loft might prove useful for storage. It wd. be like the music gallery in many old Halls. The passage which would thus form common access to the Hall & Canon Beeching's house is lighted by the Norman window of St Catherine's Chapel: with this & a glazed door at the further end it would be amply lighted. This glazed door would be the front-door proper of the Canon's house. The present outer door of the old Hall would be permanently closed.

     W.R. Lethaby.

[1]   Infirmary Hall. Henry Beeching was a Canon of Westminster from 1902 to 1911 and his house was no. 4 Little Cloister.
[2]   Nicholas Litlyngton was Abbot 1362–86.
[3]   The original chapel was built in the twelfth century.

1N.   The Chapter minutes on 9 December 1907 record that he gave a report on the proposed Museum in the Norman Undercroft. Plans were approved on 2 March 1908, the money coming from Ada, sister of the late Surveyor J.T. Micklethwaite as a memorial to him. The Dean's report on a proposal to use the Undercroft and other sites as a chapel for future memorials is inserted in the Minutes of 25 May 1909. WAM OAA/4 is his letter to the Dean in 1908 on cloister limewashing and re-erecting the Muniment Room parapet. At Chapter 8 February 1909 Lethaby recommended that two large-scale measured plans of the Abbey by J.O. Cheadle be acquired. On 8 March 1909 it was noted that some alterations were made to 2 Little Cloister but work on Canons' houses at this period, if money from the Ecclesiastical Commissioners was used, was carried out by their own architect W.D. Caroe.

2.   WAM S/1/48

Westminster Abbey Repairs.

20 May 1909

The very Revd. the Dean & the Chapter of Westminster.

Gentlemen,

   I have examined the under-croft of the Chapter House with a view to its being made of use. It is a very beautiful vaulted chamber about 30 feet across and is dry and well-ventilated. Except for the obstruction caused by a modern door and barrier within the first door, it is perfectly accessible, the steps being easy, wide, & not very many. The first two essentials are to take away the barrier just named, and to bring in the electric light. The latter can be brought on from the Museum along the Gymnasium wall, and in at one of the windows, or a new connection could be made with the supply in Palace Yard. A door should be put at the foot of the ascending turret stair, to shut off access to the triforium. The stairs to the crypt need some repair, and the floor, which at present is of a sort of concrete, and rough, may be paved with tiles like the Museum. Glazed frames should be put in the window openings to keep out dust as well as cold. The works named, with the exception of the electric light, would probably cost between £60 and £70.

The Library and South Transept

The repairs of the west wall of the Library and of the roof[1] are now completed. But the wall on the east side, which is hidden away in a narrow court, requires some patching and pointing, which is being done. The work on the east side of the South Transept is also in progress. While the Library work was in hand the portrait of Dean Williams[2] was taken down, and it was found that wet had long ago run down the wall and damaged it. It is desirable that before it is replaced it should be examined by a picture expert with a view to some little repair.

Front of Jericho Parlour[3] etc.

The masonry facing the entrance to the courtyard of the Deanery is badly decayed on the surface, and needs immediate repair. Some stones must be inserted in cavities and the rest must be pointed, and the surface treated with Baryta.

W.R. Lethaby

[1] Costs for Museum and Library works are set out in the Chapter Book 22 February 1909 and 14 February 1910.
[2] John Williams, Dean 1620–44.
[3] An early sixteenth-century room in the Deanery from which a passage leads to the Jerusalem Chamber.

3. WAM S/1/49

Westminster Abbey Church Repairs

The Very Revd. The Dean & the Chapter.

10 Feb 1910

Gentlemen.

The repairs to the North West tower were completed a few weeks ago. Since that time small repairs necessary to be made to the lower storeys on the West side of the North transept and to the North side of the Eastern bays of the Nave have been begun and it is desirable to continue them for some short time when the whole of the North side of the Church westward of the North doors will have been completely repaired. The Eastern side of the North Transept and the Chapels to the East still remain to be done as well as the South front of the South Transept.

> I am gentlemen
> > Faithfully yours
> > > W.R. Lethaby

3N.   Also included with this is a response from W.D. Caroe – S/1/49A.

4.   WAM S/1/50

Westminster Abbey.

Entrance to the Chapter House.

To the very Revd. the Dean and Chapter.

23 Feb. 1911

The great doorway facing the eastern walk of the cloister is most distressingly decayed on the surface. I have hesitated to recommend dealing with it until we had had long experience of the power of a coating of lime to arrest decay. The experience of many years has now demonstrated that an effort should be made now to save this noble doorway from further decay. I recommend that it be done slowly, a part at a time and that the present dark colour be matched, so that so far as possible no change should be obvious.

> W.R. Lethaby

4N.   WAM 59524* is a letter and report on works September 1912 compiled by Thomas James Wright, Clerk of the Works 1906–28, who succeeded his father Thomas in the post. Their yearly diaries from 1877 to 1928 are WAM WO/O2/01 (1–42) and annual reports 1880–1920 are WAM WO/02/03/001. New stairs and base for the nave pulpit were approved at Chapter on 3 December 1912 and the altar in St Faith's chapel was to be enlarged.

5.   WAM S/1/51

Westminster Abbey.

27 Jan. 1913

Summary of works done year ending Sept. 1912

The South East Apse

The stonework of 4 bays repaired with new window sills & new weatherings & quoins where required to the Buttresses. Also pointing up & making good new caps & bases to columns in Triforium level & all carving made good. Also cuspings to the window.

The Lead Glazing of 5 bays

The windows all taken out & remade with new leadwork, using all the old glass. 3 windows being lengthened by removing old stone slabs. All refixed, stopped & painted including ironwork. The scaffolding erected, taken down & moved as the work proceeded to the last bay by Henry VII chapel.

The North East Apse. Windows only

The lead glazing of 3 bays taken out, remade & refixed, using all the old glass again, refixed, stopped & painted including ironwork.

The College Hall roof

The leadwork taken up, recast & relaid, using 4 tons new Pig lead in recasting sheets.

The South Transept

The scaffold erected to front, the decayed stone on no. 1 buttress cut out, new refixed & 6 courses of new weatherings worked & fixed & facing to 6 courses above.

Henry VII chapel

Scaffold erected from floor to clerestory to repair windows, the work finished and scaffold removed.

Electric Light work

2 projecting scaffolds erected over Lantern for fixing iron supports for new electroliers.[1]

Choir desk & seats

The Lay Vicars & boys seats & desks altered, old seats removed, new ones made in oak, also stall divisions & desks, made & fixed & floors raised.[2]

The limewashing to the east, west and north cloisters, vaulting and walls.

Part of ancient wall in Abbey Garden[3] repaired.

The pavement outside south east or Poets' Corner door, taken up, the drains all relaid & pavement relaid & made good.

     W.R. Lethaby.
     Thos.J. Wright, Clerk of the Works

1   Electric light had been brought in specially for the two coronations in 1902 and 1911 but this was the first attempt to light the whole Abbey with electricity. The electroliers, or chandeliers, in the nave and transepts were replaced in 1965 with crystal chandeliers. Others are still in use.

2   Agreed at Chapter 12 March 1912.

3   The precinct wall was erected in 1375–6.

5N. A sheet of prices is also attached for Portland stone purchased from the Old General Post Office demolition 1912–13. The actual quantity bought was 1379 cubic feet (S/1/51A). The new Abbey Choir School 1912–13 in Dean's Yard was designed by A.G. Wallace (WAM SD.7) and Lethaby was not involved.

6.   WAM S/1/52

Westminster Abbey Repairs

To the Right Revd. the Dean and the Chapter

20 Feb. 1914

The heaviest piece of work now in hand is the repair of the stonework of the south transept, which has been found to have been in a worse condition than any of the other masonry which has been dealt with. These repairs are now well advanced and when they are completed practically the whole of the exterior of the main body of the church will have been attended to within the last eight years. Henry the Seventh's chapel however, has hardly been touched as yet.

Many minor repairs, especially in the east and north walks of the cloister have also been undertaken. In the interior of the church the eastern aisle of the north transept has been put in better condition, the floor has been levelled and a new oak door[1] has been fixed in the doorway which was for so many years boarded up.

A new oak staircase for the nave pulpit is in hand and a number of oak seats in the transepts (those of a better form than the rest) are being altered to make the slopes of the back and seat more comfortable.

W.R. Lethaby

111 Inverness Terrace, W.

1   Design approved at Chapter 5 November 1912. Designs are WAM (P) 389–90. A photo of the old door is in the collection of Thomas Wright (died 1906) in the Library.

6N. On 23 February 1914 Chapter asked him to report on the feasibility of a glass door at the entrance to the Dark Cloister and a wicket at the entrance to Little Dean's Yard from the cloisters (not done).

7. WAM S/1/53

Westminster Abbey Repairs

The Right Revd. the Dean and the Chapter.

13 Feb. 1915

Gentlemen:

The most serious piece of work which has been in hand during the last year has been the repair of the south transept. This was found in a really bad state; much of the casing which was put up in Wren's time[1] was not only badly decayed but it was in many places detached from the backing and in danger of falling. It is being made perfectly sound, but it is a comparatively heavy piece of work to do so, & it is not nearly finished yet.

We have continued to work at the minor repairs of the cloister, and the re-arrangement of some of the wall tablets and cleaning of most of them has put the cloister into better condition than it has been in for a long time.

W.R. Lethaby
Feb 13 1915

[1] Sir Christopher Wren was Surveyor of the Fabric 1698–1723.

8. WAM S/1/54

Report on the Fabric

6 March 1916

The Right Revd. the Dean and the Chapter of Westminster

Gentlemen:

The only important building work in hand during the last year has been the slow continuance of the repair of the south transept. A good deal has been accomplished to the central and upper parts – that on the right hand having been substantially completed before.

The scaffolding is now being removed from the central gable; the left hand portion with its angle turret remains to be done and this is in a bad a condition as any – possibly worse. In many places the thin casing of masonry separated from the wall proper and is in danger of falling. All this work has been necessary and I am thankful that so much has been done without any mishap.

The safe guarding of the tombs and other treasures from air raids has also taken up considerable labour. Separate objects have, as far as possible, been removed[1] and some thousands of sand bags have and are being used to protect the tombs which are in place.

W.R. Lethaby
111 Inverness Terrace

Many moveable items were stored in the Chapter House crypt, such as the Coronation Chair, Henry V funeral armour, Richard II's portrait and moveable tomb effigies, or in the Norman Undercroft. A full report of the precautions and items moved is set out in the Chapter Book 4 February 1919 together with the number of sandbags used (1,630).

9.   WAM S/1/55

Westminster Abbey Report on Fabric

Feb 17 1917

To the Right Revd. the Dean and the Chapter of Westminster

Gentlemen

The main, and indeed almost the only work other than minor repairs, carried out during the last year has been the heavy work of repairing the stonework of the south transept. This is being done by four or five men & I am glad to say that the most dangerous part has now been got through without any accident. Mr Wright has been able by buying good Portland stone from buildings in course of demolition to save considerably under this head. We have found more and more as we went forward that this work was in a really dangerous condition, much of the thin casing having entirely separated from the wall behind.

> W.R. Lethaby
> 111 Inverness Terrace, W.

10.   WAM S/1/56

28 March 1917

Westminster Abbey. Repairs to the Fabric 1917.

To the Right Reverend the Dean and the Chapter of Westminster.

Gentlemen,

I have considered the repairs to the fabric which are most immediately required and beg to report that they are the following. It is impossible to estimate for works of this kind, which have to be dealt with stone by stone, with any close accuracy and the sums which I have set down are only approximate.

1. The completion of the large work of repair to the external stone work of the south transept which had been in hand for two or three years nears completion. The work being dealt with is not mediaeval, as this transept, like most of the exterior, was recased about two centuries ago. This casing is very thin, indeed much of it was only about three inches thick and much of it has come away from the backing, in many parts in a very dangerous way. This work might require from £1500 to £2000.

2. The external stonework of Henry VII's chapel[1] is in many places in a very bad condition, the projecting and carved portions frequently fall off and several of the great octagonal turrets are very badly decayed as is also the upper parapet with its pinnacles. None of this work is really antient and the stone used does not stand the London conditions. The parts renewed should be in good Portland stone like all the more recent works at the Abbey. The work here is of an elaborate and costly kind and ten or twelve thousand pounds might be required to renew the decayed parts in good Portland stone.

3. The stone parapets of the main part of the Church are in some parts in a bad state, but about half is in good repair. To renew the south side of the Nave and the Choir, the east side of the south transept and the north east part of the Apse would cost about £1200.

4. The two western towers need considerable repairs. The stone used in these is Portland and it has stood very well (since about 1740) but unfortunately iron cramps were used in the construction and these are constantly bursting off fragments of considerable size as they expand in rusting. In the repairs copper should be used instead of iron. The southern tower is in worse condition than the other, which has more recently been partially repaired. A great deal of high scaffolding would be required for this work which would thus be costly. Probably five or six thousand pounds will be required for these repairs.

5. The flat lead roofing of the triforium over the north east chapels and in some other parts is in a very bad condition, and some of the timbering is also decayed and will have to be renewed. This should however not cost more than about £400 to make sound.

6. The alteration begun to the seating of the Church a few years ago to make it more suitable for the requirements of the worshippers still requires to be carried out. This might cost from one to two thousand pounds according to the elaboration of the work.

Besides these special works other general repairs are required.

W.R. Lethaby
Surveyor to the Fabric

[1]   Chapter on 7 November 1916 suggested Ketton stone for the re-facing. The chapel exterior had been extensively repaired and restored 1808–22.

11.   WAM S/1/57

111 Inverness Terrace, W.

Feb 8 1918

Westminster Abbey Fabric Report

To the Right Revd the Dean & the Chapter of Westminster

Gentlemen:

The large work of repair on the south transept now draws to its end, and I hope it may be completed in about three months, the work was lately delayed by the frost but again good progress is being made. This has been a serious undertaking as over large areas the thin casing-work put up by Wren had come away and was hanging, as it were, in a most unstable way. This work was absolutely necessary and I am glad it has been done without any accident. On the completion of this work we have finished with the larger schemes which have been in hand for many years, and it is desirable that what should then be done should be considered.

There has again been a considerable fall in the annual expenditure which has been about a 1000£ less this year than before the war; the total spent this year being about 2225£.

I had hoped to have submitted a design for new fittings in St Faith's chapel but a bad eye has prevented my doing any accurate drawing. I hope however soon to be able to do this.

W.R. Lethaby

12.   WAM S/1/58

111 Inverness Terrace, W.

Mar. 31 1919

Dear Mr Knapp Fisher,[1]

I am glad to report that the repairs to the South Transept of the Abbey Church are now so nearly completed that the scaffolding will be begun to be removed this week. In the meantime the repairs of the springing of the vault in the South Cloister is going forward.[2]

The next most pressing matter is now I think the repair of the front of the Offices facing Broad Sanctuary. Here many of the stones have long been loose and parts were broken away by those who climbed over the railings on the armistice day. It requires several new stones, the pointing up of open joints and some extra long spikes to the railing which will prevent any attempt at climbing over in future. I should like at the same time to have the name board repainted with better clearer lettering and to make this little frontage really tidy.

The old stained glass is being refixed in Jerusalem Chamber.[3] The rest I have seen at South Kensington is being dealt with but it will take a long time.

The lettering of some of the inscribed pavement slabs is being recut.

>Yours sincerely
>>W.R. Lethaby

[1]   Edward Knapp-Fisher was Receiver General 1917–38 and also Chapter Clerk.
[2]   Negatives in Library box 16 show the vault uncovered.
[3]   These thirteenth-century panels of glass were displayed in the north window of the chamber until 1987 when they were moved to the Museum. Other stained glass there was later moved to the Muniment Room. At this period the glass from the apse was being cleaned, re-leaded and photographed by the Victoria & Albert Museum at South Kensington, having been taken out for safety during the war.

13.   WAM S/1/59

111 Inverness Terrace, W.

Jan. 24 1920

<u>Westminster Abbey Fabric</u>

To the Right Revd. the Dean and the Chapter

Gentlemen,

Since the completion of the repair to the South Transept only a series of small works have been undertaken. The repair of the front of the Chapter Clerk's office is practically completed.[1]

The stalls of St Faith's chapel, which have been so long in hand, are now well advanced and partly in place.[2]

The wall-pier under the springing of the vault in the S.Cloister, where part of the ribs fell, has now been safely rebuilt. We began at the upper part with the hope of saving some of the lower part, but it was too rotten and had split away from the wall. I trust it will not be soon necessary to renew anymore for I feel that <u>all</u> the old stones, however shapeless from decay, are valuable. We find the application of lime from time to time a great help in preservation.

>I am gentlemen
>>Yours faithfully
>>>W.R. Lethaby, Surveyor.

[1]   The parapet was raised to prevent people gathering on the roof to watch special services. His office at this period was where the Abbey Bookshop is now.
[2]   His recommendation for lighting in the chapel was adopted.

13N.   On 11 October 1920 Chapter reported that Lethaby said that the grille offered by the National Art Collections Fund for the Lady Margaret Beaufort tomb was authentic and could be placed back around the tomb (having been sold in the early nineteenth century along with several other items of ironwork). This was made by Cornelius Symondson in Bilbao iron.

14. WAM S/1/60

Westminster Abbey Fabric

Feb 3 1921

The Right Revd. the Dean and the Chapter

Gentlemen,

The most important piece of general repair executed this year has been the central high gable of the west front which had got into a bad condition.

Repairs of the external walls of Henry VII's Chapel were begun in July last. I have discussed an increase of staff for this work with Mr Wright & he is reporting on it. He has suggested that during the better weather it would be convenient to deal with some of the cappings of the turrets; these are the most decayed of all and a good piece of straightforward work could thus be found. Before much more work is done to the walls generally it will be necessary to decide on some general principles as to dealing with it.

There has recently been a fall of some fragments from the modern work at the N. Transept, so that it is desirable to put up a scaffolding at one corner. There can be no doubt that rapid decay is going forward at this front & I believe it would be wise to undertake a serious experiment here (while this partial scaffolding is up) to try what protective washes will really do.

For the proposed Dean's Chair[1] at the Altar I should like to talk it over with Mr Geo. Jack who is a fine <u>original</u> wood carver & set him to make detailed suggestions & sketches; mere trade wood-carving slavishly copying an architect's design is all perfectly dead & worthless. There is quite too much of it in the church already. Either necessary work should be fairly plain or put into the hands of an artist executant. On the general suggestion that the chair might be of the type with a rounded back, Mr Jack would I have no doubt make a work of real beauty. In regard to the Sub-Dean's stall the same facts apply. It might be a single stall, detached but following <u>the present details</u>, and be done "commercially". It might be a somewhat similar form but omitting the trade carving & such a scheme I should be prepared to see to. Or thirdly it might be done by a competent original carver.

I am gentlemen
Yours faithfully
W.R. Lethaby
111 Inverness Terrace, W.

---

[1] The chair by George Jack is no longer used by the Dean but is in the Abbey collection. The experimental decoration of two of the choir stalls to Jack's design was approved at Chapter 13 December 1921.

15.   WAM S/1/60A

April 30 1921

111 Inverness Terrace, W.

Dear Mr Knapp Fisher,

In the wonderful light of one of these last days I saw the remains of the gilding and colours on the canopy and effigy of the tomb of Crouchback[1] better than ever before. I have little doubt that with careful cleaning much of it could be brought back to sight. It would however require to be done very carefully after the manner of the Sedilia paintings. Do you think Mr Tristram[2] might be asked to make an experiment and report the result? This would require the putting up of some tressels by Wright.

Yours sincerely
W.R. Lethaby

[1]   Edmund Crouchback, Earl of Lancaster (died 1296) whose tomb is on the north side of the High Altar. The tomb was cleaned.
[2]   Ernest William Tristram, wall painting conservator.

16.   WAM S/1/61

Surveyors Report on Labour, costs and repairs.

6 June 1921.

Introduction

The purpose of this report is to suggest the best method of increasing the amount of work in progress and to call attention to matters of immediate importance. It is a short review of the general position, rather than a statement of the condition of the fabric. A further report on repairs and sundry suggested works will be presented for consideration after these urgent general matters have been dealt with.

Labour

There is no doubt that all the works which so far as one can see are likely to become necessary for many years would be better carried out by the Abbey's own staff than by attempting to separate certain parts of the work for execution by an independent contractor. But the staff should be re-organised on a basis which will make it more amenable to periodical fluctuation in number without trade union difficulties and strengthen the authority and control of the Clerk of the Works. This can be done by simply raising wages to the union rate.

Existing conditions

At present the average rate of Abbey wages is 17% per hour below the latest standard rate (May 16th), with holiday advantages reducing it to say 10% below standard rate. The men make a 50 hour week as compared with 44 hours under the unions; the net result being that an individual's weekly wage is about the same as, or even up to 2.5 % more than it would be under union regulations; but he works six hours longer per week.

The danger of these conditions is manifold in that: 1. It is almost impossible to augment the staff except permanently; 2. The whole market of labour, including most of the best class, is not open to the Clerk of Works; 3. There is an implied bargain in the present arrangement for a lower rate of wage in consideration of an easy and permanent job; 4. Trade Union difficulties such as the recent stone-sawing trouble will tend to multiply; 5. The public nature of the new fund lays the existing conditions very open to public criticism.

Recommendations

It is suggested that the wages be raised to the standard rates reducing the hours of work to 44 per week and that the holiday benefits be maintained as existing and made applicable to all men after one years service. The Clerk of Works should be so placed as to be able to capture the best workmen available and Mr Wright concurs in the opinion that it would improve the spirit of the present staff to feel that, excepting as to length of service, they were on the same footing and therefore to some extent in competition with outside workmen.

The monetary loss by this arrangement would only be in the shape of the one hour's work per day before breakfast, and the Clerk of Works would be in a proper position for speeding up the work.

Costs

In considering the comparative merits for the Abbey works of the contract system with those of direct employment the only difficulty in regard to the latter is cost. Generally speaking it is obvious that the quality of the work must be better under a system which eliminates private business interests. The drastic nature of some restorations of the past has been to a great extent the outcome of the contract system, and in a lesser degree the same objections apply to the system of contract by schedule, owing to the necessity of defining the exact nature of the work in advance.

It might be possible in the future to measure certain separable parts of the work after completion for comparison with current building prices so far as they apply. The result would probably show curious variations on both sides, because an exact comparison is hardly possible; and when all was done it could still be said with truth that the real test lay in the quality of the work. After all, the Abbey works do not bear much relation to ordinary building and the requisite patience and painstaking care for their proper execution must be calculated in their cost. Direct employment of labour is undoubtedly the best method of dealing with all such special work, but it cannot be expected in London to compare favourably in cost in all respects with merely business systems.

A piece of work which presents itself immediately as a fair object for comparison (and others will occur) is a proposed stone chimney to the north heating chamber. An estimate of the cost of this could be arrived at by taking out the quantities in detail and pricing them at current rates. And after completion the total cost of labour and materials can be ascertained from the books and a proper percentage added for builder's overhead charges and an assessed allowance made for interruptions, if any, on account of the services in the Church.

Repairs

It is best for the purpose of this report to confine the question of repairs to the three most urgent general headings namely, 1. External stonework of Henry VII's chapel, 2. Alterations to the heating system, and 3. External stonework of the western towers. Repairs of the cloisters, parapets, lead roofs etc. will follow.

The alteration to the heating system must be done at once, if it is to be ready for next winter. If considered especially desirable to do so, both these works could be carried on concurrently with the work in progress on Henry VII's chapel, so soon as the labour question is settled. But it would be doubtful policy to launch out upon too great an increase of work all at once.

We suggest that the heating alterations should be the only other large work to be started immediately, which, with a speeding up of Henry VII chapel, sundry small jobs to be reported later and an improved organisation suggested by Mr Wright for the continuity of certain routine work such as painting, limewhiting, pointing and window and other cleaning, would probably amount eventually to an increase in the building staff of about 30%. The labour from the work in connection with the heating alterations might be available for the western towers in the autumn.

Henry VII chapel

The repair of the external stonework of Henry VII's chapel is proceeding satisfactorily and merely requires a small increase of labour. The stone was re-examined on May 19th by Dr Deach and the experts on stone preservative from the Scientific & Industrial Research Department; and a complete report on the silico-fluoride treatment was promised very shortly. In the meantime the stones which are beyond repair are being cut out and renewed in Portland stone and the remainder of the stonework is being prepared for treatment with such preservative as shall eventually be decided upon.

Alteration to heating system

All the stonework adjacent to the chimneys of the temporary iron flues from the two heating chambers is noticeably decaying more rapidly than elsewhere. Upon examination with a view to planning a better arrangement of the chimneys, the flue on the south side was found to be worn out and even dangerous, and that on the north side was evidently in a leaky condition judged by the sulphur fumes in the effigy room[1] and in the triforium above this room.

Before considering the restoration of the existing flues it seemed advisable to consult the engineers as to the possibility of coupling the two separate heating schemes together and working with new twin boilers entirely from the chamber on the north side. Since the advent of accelerator pumps in connection with low pressure systems almost any length of pipe run is quite feasible; and the use of an accelerator is always expedient with a large scheme because it gives greater heating efficiency with less consumption of fuel.

A copy of the engineers report is attached.[2] They add a suggestion of using boilers which can be fed with either oil or coke. The existing pipes etc. are reported to be in good condition and capable of carrying on indefinitely. The scheme entails a new pipe channel across the nave but this would only be a small closed trench for one pipe with the existing paving replaced on top; and its position (just west of the screen), indicated by Mr Wright, is clear of any recorded graves. An oil tank in the cellars of the old houses which form the north heating chamber ought not to present any serious difficulty if oil proves to be the most satisfactory fuel. The flue to the north chamber should be rebuilt in Portland stone as a proper permanent chimney, hidden so far as possible in the angle of the buttress.

The estimated cost of the engineers work is approximately £4000 and a further £1000 is a rough estimate of Mr Wright's work in connection with the alteration.

Having regard to its many advantages and the fact that the capital outlay will be greatly compensated by economies of working it is recommended that this scheme be put in hand in preference to the alternative of rebuilding the two existing flues.

Western towers

The repair of the external stonework of the western towers presents an entirely different problem to that of Henry VII's chapel. It is a case of comparatively well preserved Portland stone being fractured and burst in places by the rusting of iron cramps used in the original structure (apparently quite unnecessarily) to strengthen the bonding of the stone.

A more detailed report will be made later. As suggested above the extra labour to be employed for work in relation to the heating alteration would be available for the western towers in the autumn. For the present nothing worse can happen than the possible dislodgement of a small piece or two of stone.

Conclusion

It will be seen from the foregoing statement that the affairs of the fabric staff
are nearly at a deadlock pending the settlement of the labour question. The two
matters calling for immediate consideration are 1. The raising of wages to the
standard rates to enable the staff to be increased and 2. A decision in regard to
the heating alteration which requires to be dealt with during the summer.

---

[1] Upper Islip chapel, where the funeral effigy collection was kept. The heating chamber is
just outside the lower Islip chapel. Houses had been built up against this side of the church
and although they were demolished in the late eighteenth century the cellars remained.

[2] Not now attached.

17.   WAM S/1/62

Westminster Abbey Fabric Report

6 March 1922

To the Very Revd. the Dean and the Chapter

Gentlemen.

The external repairs of Henry VIIths chapel are going steadily forward and
stones for the third pinnacle are now being prepared.

The cleaning of the tombs and pavement in the Presbytery has been very
successful. Not only does it reveal beauties of detail which were obscured by
darkened varnish, but I hope that the going over of the surfaces will be beneficial
from the point of view of preservation.

It would be well to carry the work on in the Confessor's Chapel and other
places including the large painted stag in the Muniment Room.[1] During this
coming spring or summer the cloister should be overhauled, cleaned, and
washed with lime. Experience is more and more showing the wholesome effect
of such surface applications. An excellent example is the inner entry of the
Cloister which was done last year. It then seemed a little startling (and hence I
am anxious not to do too much at a time) but it has now toned down and taken
a beautiful colour while the surface is very different from that of the rotting
stone. The entry to the Deanery is another example.

W.R. Lethaby

[note in another hand: Recommendations adopted]

---

[1] The white hart, a badge used by Richard II. The painting was restored.

17N.   Lethaby was asked to examine the ironwork of Queen Eleanor's tomb
and the gates of Henry V Chantry at Chapter on 6 February 1922.

18.   WAM S/1/63

Westminster Abbey

Report of the Surveyor of the Fabric 30 December 1922.

Permission is asked to commence the cleaning and further repair of the Cloisters. The scaling and dropping of small pieces of stone from the vaulting of the Cloisters has increased during the last few months, and it is considered advisable to begin this work forthwith and keep it going (two bays at a time) as continuously as may be practicable without any addition of labour to the staff. It is not anticipated that any new stonework will be required, but all the ribs need careful overhauling and examination and the adjustment of any loose or fractured stones with copper cramps etc. by the masons and the surface of the stonework should be cleaned and treated with limewash preservative. It is noticeable that the surface sealing has completely ceased since the limewash treatment of some 18 months ago in the portion of the Cloisters opposite the Custodian's front door.[1]

The Steward has been asked if two trees (a standard fig and a catalpa) might be planted this winter in the N.E. and N.W. corners of the Cloister garth respectively.[2]

The removal of the unsightly patent chimney pots from the top of Jerusalem Chamber, following the very successful heating of the Chapter Clerk's offices by electricity, is a great improvement in the direction of tidying up: and the resulting elimination of four smoke flues against the Western Towers must be a considerable benefit to the stonework.

After the grass has been sown in March in the Little Cloister garth this will again be a fresh and bright corner of the Abbey buildings, and an example of how much can be done by a little addition, cleaning and orderly arrangement as opposed to reconstruction. I should like to preserve the fountain[3] out of loyalty to those who put it there: it is one of the few Victorian attempts at making the place more delightful. Poor as it may be thought, it represents its time; and it must be 60 or 80 years old. A smart new one might be easily provided, but it would be an alteration and I think the present one has more interest and more "feeling" than any up-to-date thing provided by a designer or contractor could have. I at least would not venture to compete with it and I should not love the work of any man who had the heart to try. When the grass and plants have grown the place will have character; it will be a quiet corner such as an artist might like to draw. I do not think any artist will want to draw a place where there is a new fountain – somehow they don't. We have two or three old marble fragments, from which a new central part above the bowl might be made up, and this would improve the quality of the fountain without importing anything modern. It might of course be removed altogether, but that, I think would be a loss. The present fountain has associations for the ordinary lover of the Little Cloisters.

It is earnestly hoped that the several new stained glass windows recently fixed[4] and being made may be the last; and again we should like to bring to your notice the supreme value of the few remaining windows of white glass. The Victorian windows are not so distressing as the quite modern ones, as, for one thing, we are not responsible for them.

[from Assistant Surveyor E.E. Lofting[5]]
Surveyors Office, Little Cloisters, Westminster Abbey SW1

[1] No. 2 The Cloister. The Custodian was the official who oversaw the vergers' and cleaners' departments at this period.
[2] Chapter agreed to the lime washing and the trees on 2 January 1923. The trees no longer remain.
[3] It is not known who designed this fountain but it was in place by 1871.
[4] Presumably referring to the new series of windows in the nave.
[5] Eric Edward Lofting was assistant surveyor 1921–50.

19.   WAM S/1/63A

Feb 17th 1923

Dear Mr Treasurer,

Tristram Records

It is suggested by Professor Lethaby that a set of records (copies) by Mr Tristram of all the ancient paintings at the Abbey should be gradually collected. Some of them might be framed and hung in certain placed and the remainder kept in a special portfolio in the Library or elsewhere. Such a collection would be of inestimable value to the future.[1]

I understand that the cost of these pictures would vary very much – from about £4 or £5 to even £25 or £30 – according to the time they take, which is of course dependant upon size, subject and detail. I can forsee two to three dozen drawings and more may occur as time goes on. It is difficult to estimate the cost for want of finality – but I suggest the expenditure of say £300 on it during the next two years, progress and schedule to be reported to you.

Yours very truly
E.E. Lofting

[1] E.W. Tristram's reconstruction drawing of the remains of the painting on the base of Queen Eleanor's tomb is now in the Library, as are his reconstructions of two missing Sedilia paintings on the south side. Six large drawings of the Sedilia figures, the White Hart in the Muniment Room and the two wall paintings either side of the altar in the upper Islip chapel were removed from the Samaria chamber in the Deanery to the Library. His drawings of the two south transept wall paintings are in the Library's CN collection.

20.   WAM S/1/64

Westminster Abbey Surveyor's Report [1923]

Henry VII chapel

The repair of the exterior stonework has reached the completion of the fifth pinnacle and all that is needed of new stonework on the sixth pinnacle is worked and carved ready for fixing. If the Chapter is satisfied with the way in which the final treatment of lime preservative on the stone is weathering, we would like to have instructions to proceed with this method of finishing off the work ['Agreed' written against this]

The interior repairs and cleaning of the west window and the vaulting of the Chapel is finished so far as the scaffolding reaches. In view of the coming ceremony of the Order of the Bath[1] this scaffolding will now be removed and a later opportunity sought to proceed with this part of the work. The material from the inside scaffolding will serve to extend the outside scaffold.

The Cloisters

It will have been noticed that the repair of the Cloisters has just been completed for the whole length of the south walk. It is now proposed to work along the West walk from south to north. So far this has been a most satisfactory job and one which has amply repaid the care and patience of the men employed on it. All the loose and fractured stones have been secured and the apex of the vault has been ventilated into the roof-space above in the hope of reducing the effect of condensation. There is one small piece of gilding remaining on one of the bosses and some interesting remains of colour on the ribs in the S.E. corner.

When these repairs have continued round to the earlier work of the North and East walks we propose to clean the old Purbeck marble shafts. It will then only remain to improve the organisation for regular washing, sweeping and dusting of the Cloisters.

When it is remembered that only 18 years ago the wholesale rebuilding of the Cloisters was in serious contemplation and nearly came to be started, the recent work in the South walk becomes especially interesting as an example of what can be done by care in the way of preserving the original ancient work.

Cleaning of ancient painting and tombs

The cleaning of ancient colour decoration has progressed well during the summer. The effect upon the Confessor's shrine and the tomb of Henry III will have been remarked. As an instance of the way in which cleaning alone will reveal the details of the work, the fine realistic carving of the leaves of various trees should be noticed just above the shields on the tomb of Queen Eleanor.

Mr Tristram's assistant has been borrowed for two or three weeks to work on the paintings in Eton College chapel. There is still much work to be done in this department as soon as he returns.

We understand that Mr Tristram has nearly finished the first instalment of his records of ancient painting and decoration in the Abbey which Chapter ordered a few months ago. These could be exhibited if desired at a Chapter meeting in the near future when the framing and hanging of the most interesting of them might be considered. Some small ones, preferably portrait heads, would furnish the splayed window jambs in Jerusalem Chamber and balance the portrait of Henry IV; also a series on the blank east wall of the Lobby might commend itself.

The old tester in the triforium from the Duchess of York's tomb on which there are remains of a painted Trinity and which we have recently cleaned, would probably be well hung and preserved where it could be seen on the south face of the ancient partition in the Muniment Room above the cupboards.[2] ['To be inspected by Chapter' written next to this]

Unemployment

In case the Chapter feel able to help in the movement amongst employers of labour to keep going as much work as possible during the winter, we would like to suggest three works that could be carried on if desired, viz: 1) the cleaning and limewashing of the triforium and the commencement in the South Transept of the cleaning of the walls inside the Church, 2) the relaying of St Margaret's path in stone flags and 3) the building of the permanent Song School.

Cleaning of Triforium etc.

For this work we would want only the addition of about six men to the staff who would work right round the Triforium during the course of the winter. At the same time a bridge could be thrown across the South Transept, close to its south wall, and a commencement made, as an experiment, of the cleaning of the walls of the Church. It is our hope in the future gradually to clean the whole of the wall surfaces inside the Church and rub up the Purbeck marble shafts etc. This is one of the greatest needs of the Abbey at the present time. ['Agreed but no addition to staff' written beside this paragraph]

St Margaret's footpath

The condition of St Margaret's path is more than disreputable: it is becoming almost impassable after rain owing to deep puddles. Could some arrangement be made to enable this work to be taken in hand? and could the opportunity be taken of relaying it in white stone slabs instead of the unsightly cement? About £500 would probably cover the cost of the long length west of the transept door in Portland stone, and this might be made the beginning of the conversion of all these paths into stone by periodical replacement when portions of the cement paths need repair.

['Rector of St Margarets will experiment? these two sections. Ch[apter]. contributing 2/3 not exceeding £300 in any case' written beside this paragraph]

Song School[3]

We think there is no great difficulty in the way of doing this work in winter if it be desired and if some temporary quarters can be found for song practice. Since making the last plan of the new Song School it has seemed advisable for the sake of future developments to move the Lay Vicars from their present position and provide a room for them on top of the new Song School. We think this could be done without much detriment to the practice room as previously planned, and a revised plan can be made if the idea is approved.

Glass roof of cloisters at gymnasium door

We would like to have permission to relay a portion of the paving of the Dark Cloister at the Gymnasium door and re-arrange the gutters and down pipes of the glass roof at this point in a more tidy and efficient manner. In time of rain the water floods right across the pavement owing to the dilapidated condition of the guttering and the subsidence of the stone flagging.

St Faith's chapel

In order to give local light to the reader and if necessary to the congregation as well a deal model of a standard candlestick has been made as an experiment, the design of which has been devised by its lightness to be as inconspicuous as possible. Also a small oak book table is made and placed beside the door, of such a pattern as not to obstruct the passage.

Funeral furniture

A rough deal model of the proposed funeral furniture with turntable has been made so as to try by actual demonstration with the pall whether the design can be improved upon from the point of view of ceremonial drill.

Surveyors Office Westminster Abbey. November 1st 1923.

[1] Henry VII's Lady Chapel has been the chapel of the Most Honourable Order of the Bath since 1725.

[2] The tester was kept in the Library for many years and is now in the Abbey reserve collection. Philippa, Duchess of York died in 1431.

[3] This was in the former Clerk of the Works yard, entered via the old Refectory doorway off the south cloister. In consultation with Lethaby Chapter agreed that plans for the new Song School for choir practice be prepared by Mr [Edward] Warren and excavations be carried out (Chapter 6 January, 3 March and 7 April 1925). The Song School was dedicated 1 November 1925 [Westminster Abbey Chronicle] and was in use as such, with the small Lay Vicars room, until 2015. The area was then converted to provide toilets for visitors.

21. WAM S/1/64A

Letter from E. Lofting Jan 26 1924

Dear Mr Knapp Fisher,

In answer to the Chapter Minute calling for a report on the recent leakages in the roofs of the Archdeacon's and the Custodian's houses:

In the case of the Archdeacon's roof[1] a bad leak was caused on the night of Thursday the 10th just by frozen snow forming a dam in the gutter. I reported personally to the Archdeacon about it at the time. There is no absolute cure. Snow boards might lessen the risk. Two nights previously a very small amount of driving snow got inside the trap door in the rood – but there was no connection between the two accidents. I think the latter can be remedied.

In the case of Mr Westlake's roof[2] there have been no leakages since it was over-hauled last summer. The wall of a WC on the staircase landing is only 4 and a half inches thick and the wet comes right through. I did not discover how thin it was until after the re-decoration. I have had it on my list to stucco the outside of the wall – thought even this could not be guaranteed as a remedy.

Yours sincerely
E.E. Lofting

[1] No. 4 Little Cloister.
[2] No. 2 The Cloister.

22. WAM S/1/65

Protection of Interior Stonework [Nov 1924]

Cleaning and liming the Reredos in Henry V's Chantry was recommended to stay decay. In the cleaning about a bucketful of soot-like corrosive matter which was acting on the stone came away. What has been done has given this delicate work a new lease of existence. The fact that the coating when fresh allows the work to be much better seen is a secondary consideration. I should have recommended the protective coating even if it were thought well to dirty it over so that this rich work would be seen no better than before. The result in this respect can be easily observed from the ambulatory where uncleaned parts next to those cleaned extend over the side entries to Henry VII's chapel. In cleaning and liming nothing whatever should be done which could be seen from the outside.

This Chantry is of especially delicate work in soft stone and I believe it is desirable to extend the protective process all over it. This if sanctioned might be done in instalments. The part completed will very soon "tone down", and when it is thought to be dull enough another part might be undertaken and the new part might be dirtied at once.

The interior of Henry VII chapel is a somewhat similar work and here the west window and part of the vault were cleaned and limed a few years since. I believe it would be well to go over the whole interior in the same way by degrees.

Interiors of the main turret stairs have been limed more than once in the last twenty years and are now in a fairly sound condition. I should like to do as much for the triforium story where not visible from below.

The interior of the main church is a different problem. Here, there is much marble work and any small portion limed and left white would startle people. It is certain, however, that if the church is to last then stone must be kept clean and if possible coated over the surfaces. The whole interior with the exception of the marblework was originally whitened and picked out with colour, and Wren seems to have done much painting of the wall surfaces. I have no doubt that it is desirable that the surfaces should again be coated over, but probably this should wait until the results elsewhere can be appealed to as evidence. In the meantime it would be as well to clean (without liming) special parts like the sculptured spandrels of arches and we should be glad to have permission to do this soon.[1]

W.R. Lethaby 3 November 1924.

[1] Chapter on 10 November 1924 said that no more limewashing should be done without further orders.

23. WAM S/1/66

Westminster Abbey

Surveyors Report 30 Jan. 1925

Henry VII chapel

The repair of the exterior stonework of Henry VII chapel has nearly reached the completion of the south side. During the last few months a very large area has received the final operation of lime preservative and we hope the Chapter will make an inspection of this completed portion as it gives a good idea of what the effect will be when the whole Chapel is finished. This work will proceed much more quickly after the south side is finished because the stonework was more perished on this, the weather, side than it is on the east and north.

The Cloisters

The work of repairing the Cloister vaulting has been much delayed recently owing to Henry VII Chapel having required most of the men available for this kind of work. In the meantime the scaling and droppings from the stone vault of the east walk have increased so much that we would like to deal with the vaulting of this walk at once without waiting for its turn in rotation. We suggest repairing the vaulting only and leaving the walls and the Chapter House doorway to be considered after the north walk has been finished.

Western towers

As stated in the Assistant Surveyor's letter of Oct. 30th last, the stone facing of the Western Towers should probably be the next large masonry work to be tackled after the completion of Henry VII chapel. The trouble with the facing of the Western Towers is that fairly well preserved Portland stone is being fractured and burst in places by the rusting of iron cramps used in the original structure. There is always the possibility of pieces of the stone becoming dislodged and falling before this repair is undertaken, but such a contingency can be greatly obviated by periodical inspection. We propose to arrange for a close overhauling of the outside walls of the Towers during the coming summer by means of the cradle-scaffold.

There is however another matter affecting the Northern Tower to which we ought to call attention namely the vibration of the bell-ringing. We have been watching the effect of this from time to time and although no serious harm may have occurred during the last four years, we think the movement that is evidenced is sufficient to warrant some curtailment of the number of times the bells are rung.

Cleaning inside the Church

A sample of the cleaning of carved and sculptured stonework has been prepared for the Chapter's inspection in Henry V Chantry. Half the west front of the chantry has been only cleaned and the upper part of the east wall of the chantry (the sculptured reredos) has been both cleaned and treated with lime preservative. We would like a decision as to whether the preservative may be applied after cleaning to the whole of the chantry. While it is true that the cleaned half of the west front is a great improvement upon the dirty half, it will be seen (especially viewed from the entrance to St Paul's chapel) that the effect is rather spotty and confusing as compared with the limed east wall, quite apart from the very real practical need of a preservative on the stone.

> W.R. Lethaby
> E.E. Lofting
>   Surveyors Office, Little Cloisters.

24.   WAM S/1/67

Westminster Abbey Surveyors' Report. 29 Jan. 1926

Henry VII chapel

The repair of the stonework of Henry VII chapel is finished on the south side, so far as the masonry is concerned, and is continuing round the east end. There are now two more bays of repaired stonework ready for the final operation of lime preservative which will be applied when the walls are dry in the early part of the summer.

The Cloisters

The cloister repairs have continued to nearly the whole length of the east walk and two more bays of the north walk, including the delicate work of dealing with the elaborate carving of the Chapter House doorway. For the moment in the east walk there is too great a contrast between the cleaned stonework and the as yet uncleaned Purbeck marble shafts of the wall arcading; but this little inharmony will disappear as soon as the marble has been cleaned and wax-polished in the way that may be seen in the westernmost by of the north walk. The furthest boss opposite the Chapter House doorway shows a fine sample of the original gilding, and small patches of the ancient colouring of the ribs may be seen in this bay.

Cleaning the inside of the Church

The west front and south side of Henry V Chantry have been cleaned and left untreated with lime in accordance with the Chapter's order. It is proposed now to erect a small scaffolding to clean the north side of the Chantry in like manner.

All the tombs and monuments in St Edmund's chapel have now been cleaned. This is the first instance of a completely cleaned Chapel (except its walls and vaulting) and the effect is most successful quite apart from the preservative benefit of the work. Some of the coloured 16th and 17th century sculpture and marble work are strikingly beautiful. St Nicholas chapel is now being dealt with systematically in the same way.

St Edward's Shrine

After the removal of the pall[1] over St Edward's Shrine last summer the 16th century upper wooden part of the Shrine was repaired and cleaned revealing some very interesting painted marbling and glass mosaic in the arches and tiny pilasters. A number of broken pieces of the wood and mosaic, which had become detached in [recent] years and had been collected by the Clerk of Works, were refixed in their original position.

Covered way to Little Cloisters

The sunken pavement opposite the School Gymnasium door has been relaid recently to prevent puddles collecting (as ordered over a year ago) and the unsightly manhole and gullies covered with stone slabs, and a stone gutter formed along each side. When the glass roof of this covered way is repaired it is proposed to replace the conspicuously untidy rain water pipes on the archway by lead ones on the side walls where they will not spoil the arched entrance to the Little Cloisters.

Chapel of the Holy Cross[2]

The ancient stone altar slab which has for years reposed against the wall in St Andrew's chapel, has been set up in the newly formed chapel of the Holy

Cross; the old coil of heating pipes being replaced by a new radiator against the screen at the west end of the south aisle of the nave. The bust of Kingsley, Morris [Maurice] and Arnold are temporarily on the south window cill pending the Chapter's decision as to their disposal.[3]

The permission of the Chapter is desired to clean and repair the external stonework of the west window of this chapel, which is original work and is in a dilapidated condition. It may also be found that the stained glass[4] should be overhauled and releaded.

New Lavatories

The proposed new lavatories[5] at the west end of the Church are on the point of being commenced in accordance with the plan which was passed by the Chapter. This work would have been started a month ago but for the unusual pressure of small jobs upon the building staff. The Sanitary Inspector has viewed and approved the proposals.

Refectory wall

The occasion of work at the Deanery has been taken to repair and limewash the Refectory wall above the south walk of the Cloisters, which was in a bad condition. It is one of the few pieces of external wall which have escaped refacing by 'restorers', and is a fine example – Norman work, pierced with large windows, and made up with interesting bits of flint and tile and Roman brick (presumably from early foundations such as are found under the Nave) by Litlyngton.

Norman Undercroft

With the removal of the choir from their temporary practice room in the Norman Undercroft it will now be possible to tidy and re-arrange the Museum.

Surveyors Office, Westminster Abbey.
W.R. Lethaby
E.E. Lofting

---

[1] In 1902 for the coronation of Edward VII a pall was draped over this wooden structure, which had been added in the sixteenth century.

[2] In 1932 this was re-named the Warrior's chapel and in 1944 the chapel was dedicated to St George.

[3] The busts of Charles Kingsley and Frederick D. Maurice were on the west window cill in this chapel but were moved to the ledge of the east aisle of Poets' Corner in 2014. Thomas Arnold was moved to the north-west nave chapel.

[4] The figure in this window is traditionally called the Black Prince and is composed of fragments of old glass.

[5] Presumably those in the Samaria chamber in the Deanery. There is a door into the nave from there.

25. WAM S/1/68

Westminster Abbey Surveyors Report. 11 Feb. 1927

The Cloisters

The work of repairing the cloisters was finished last summer in so far as the walls and vaulting are concerned, and there remains only the polishing of the marble shafts to be completed. This polishing is a very slow process owing to the amount of dirt and sooty deposit to be removed, but the recent cleaning of the marble of the north jamb of the Chapter House doorway gives an idea of the great improvement it will make to the cloisters, especially in the north walk where the marble shafts are so numerous.

Cleaning of tombs

Since last year all the tombs have been cleaned in the chapels of St Nicholas, St Paul and St John the Baptist. A re-polishing lately of the shrine of St Edward, which was cleaned three years ago, shows the benefit of this work and the fine finish that can be obtained after the surface has had some time to harden. Within the last few weeks the uncovering of the blank panel of stone above the old altar of St John the Evangelist has revealed the remains of two carved and decorated spandrils with some well preserved gilding – apparently the Bull and Lamb, symbols of the Evangelists. There is a rough indication of a circular picture or carving on this panel in the drawing on the Islip Roll.[1] The thirteenth century carving in the spandrils of the wall arcading in the chapel of St Andrew is now being cleaned.

Western towers

The piece of stone which fell recently at the west end of the Church was Chilmark stone, part of the restoration of the n.w. corner buttresss by the late Mr Pearson about 1890. The same stone was used in the restoration of the north transept, where it also appears to be rapidly decaying. So far as we can see at present there is no need to alter the original intention in regard to the repair of the Portland stone of the towers after the completion of Henry VII chapel, but we think that the Chilmark stone of the Pearson restoration, both at the west end and the north transept, should be examined by means of light scaffolding for the purpose of removing any crockets, pinnacles and salient parts which may be cracked or broken and likely to fall.

Lavatories and ante-room

The lavatories at the west end and the opening out and reflooring etc. of the ante room are useful works which have been done during the year. It is proposed, with the Chapter's permission, to frame a few more of Mr Tristram's records of paintings to be hung in the ante room.[2] An oak trellis at the end of the Deanery garden would mask the coat hole and lavatory windows as seen from the dining room window of the Deanery.

New boilers

The new wrought steel boilers are working very satisfactorily. When they are not in use during the summer, it would be well to construct a new soot door arrangement in the north heating chamber to facilitate the cleaning of the horizontal flue on that side.

Window cleaning

The cleaning of the church windows is progressing steadily. We hope to devise a way of cleaning the inside of the clerestory windows by means of opening casements at the sill and a cantilever platform erected from the roof outside, the cost of which will be estimated and submitted for approval.

Henry VII chapel

The whole of the stonework repairs on the south side of Henry VII chapel is now completed, and the work on the first bay at the east end of the chapel is well advanced. Progress with this work will be much faster when the repairs have reached the north side, where the stonework is in better condition.

Future memorials

We have been considering the question of the provision of additional space of a worthy kind for future monuments, and we would suggest that the site of St Katherine's chapel should be considered. The area of the chapel together with the adjoining Canon's house on the north side would offer a site more or less square, on which a building, at once dignified in the interior and unobtrusive without, might be erected. The very valuable late Norman arcade would be enclosed and protected by it, and the additional chapel would be entered from, and be an essential part of, the Abbey buildings. Further, the dark cloister and Little Cloisters, and possibly the Museum undercroft, would afford very large accommodation for memorials. At the same time some regularising of monuments and tablets should be considered. The floor spaces here and in the church would be available for inscriptions. To build on the east green would be a great injury to the Abbey in surrounding it with new buildings, and taking up a beautiful garden space. Even the design of such new buildings would open up the difficult question whether they should be sham Gothic or sham Renaissance.[3]

> W.R. Lethaby
> E.E. Lofting
> Surveyors Office, Westminster Abbey.

1   The mortuary roll of Abbot Islip who died in 1532. The roll is kept in the archives. The circular head of Christ, probably by Pietro Torrigiano, originally in this position is now in the Wallace Collection.
2   Samaria room. See 19 f. 1.
3   These plans were never carried out.

26.   WAM S/1/69

Westminster Abbey. Surveyors' Report 5 Nov 1927.

Cloisters

The cleaning and preserving of the stonework in the first bay of the entry to the cloisters, as you approach from Dean's Yard, should be attended to so soon as possible and perhaps it would be well to clean the next bay again (the 'Parlour') at the same time. This first bay is the only part of the cloisters which has not been treated with lime and the surface of the stone is crumbling. There is still a great number of the marble wall-shafts to be cleaned and rubbed up in the north and east walks of the cloisters so soon as more urgent works permit.

Gilbert Crispin effigy

The finest of the Abbots' effigies in the cloister – that of Gilbert Crispin – in black marble, is slowly getting obliterated, although it is partially protected by the stone seat above it. We should like it to be considered whether it would not be wise to set it upright on the seat above its present position. Cleaned and in this position against the wall it would of course be better seen than before, and a good plain slab might take its place.[1]

Western towers and north transept

The western towers and the north transept end have been overhauled by steeplejacks and all broken crockets and finials and other loose stones removed, so as to reduce the risk of falling pieces of stone from above these two public entrances, until such time as repairs with scaffolding can be undertaken. The modern stonework of the north transept and its porches is badly decayed considering that it is only about 35 years old, and its treatment should be taken in hand in the near future.

Parapet on south side

A curious settlement in the upper parapet at the south west corner of the central tower, which has been watched for some time past, has got rapidly worse. The removal of a portion discovered that the mortar in a rubble course of backing at the foot of the parapet below the gutter has disintegrated and allowed the whole parapet to lean over towards the roof. We are arranging to repair this at once, but it is not yet possible to say how much of the parapet may not have to be taken down and refixed.

Lead roof repairs

The re-casting and laying of the lead on the north side of the Presbytery roof will be finished within the next week or two. It became necessary to renew a larger area than was anticipated because some deal packing (counter battens) of about Wren's date on top of the rafters under the battens on which the lead is laid, had completely rotted away and had to be renewed, and this made it necessary to carry on relaying the lead right up to the east face of the central tower. At the same time a new doorway from the gutter into the roof, with lead cheeks and top, has been constructed in place of the old one, and some decayed rafters and collars of the roof repaired and strengthened.

There is a good deal of repairs to lead requiring attention. The gutter along the west side of Jerusalem Chamber is being re-laid at present, as well as the small flat on top of the Jerusalem turret. Also the flat over the Deanery dining room has drawn away from its ridge and let the wet in again. This has been temporarily repaired and permission will be asked to re-lay the whole flat next summer. The large flat above the triforium over St Paul's chapel must also be undertaken before long.

Altar rail

In accordance with the Chapter's order the altar rail which enclosed the Sacrarium, and which had been removed for widening of its gates, will now be stored in the triforium and not be refixed.

Light in Dark Cloister

Perhaps the simplest way of increasing the light at the entrance to Little Cloisters would be to fix an electric point in the wood ceiling opposite the organist's front door, and run from his supply, and make allowance for the little cost of current. A temporary arrangement such as this might be better than disturbing the existing gas lamps, especially in view of the future electrification of the cloister lights which should be considered again sometime.

Sacristy

We hope it may be decided in the end to adopt some composite arrangement for the Sacristy. Every modern structural alteration to the Abbey has been subsequently and rightly condemned, and we would look upon the suggested building of a Sacristy against the Islip chapel as the greatest disaster the Abbey would have suffered since the restoration of the north transept. We do not think that the need for a concentrated sacristy is sufficient to warrant a drastic alteration or addition to the most valuable church in England. The safest course would be to institute an improved composite arrangement. If the wax effigies were moved into the crypt for instance, both the Islip chapels would be available,[2] and there are places in the church and elsewhere, as in the south choir aisle, where large furniture such as new frontal and cope cases could stand.

> W.R. Lethaby
> E.E. Lofting
>   Surveyors' Office

[1] This idea was not carried out. Crispin was Abbot 1085–1117. His effigy, originally in the Norman Abbey, had been in the centre part of the south cloister but was moved to its present position when pipes were laid in 1753.

[2] At this time the collection of wax funeral effigies were displayed in the upper Islip chapel and the idea to house a sacristy here did not go ahead. The crypt of the Chapter House was used for storage. The question of a new exterior sacristy building is discussed in Walter Tapper's reports.

27.   WAM S/1/70

Westminster Abbey Surveyors' Report 13 Feb. 1928

Holy Cross chapel

The repair and cleaning of the vaulting and walls in the chapel of the Holy Cross is practically completed. A number of fractured stones in the vaulting have been secured with copper bands, and a portion of vault-filling which had subsided has been strengthened by means of a copper truss. Part of the south jamb of the west window also required re-setting. All the fractures and settlements appeared to be ancient, probably dating from the building of the western towers when a great additional weight was put upon the original Islip work. There are two notably fine carved bosses in the vaulting, one being the Islip rebus as seen on the Islip chapel screen and elsewhere, and another carved with the letters IHU, which is interesting as being especially peculiar to Islip's time. The old glass in the west window was found to be in very fair repair and is being cleaned in position. When the scaffolding is removed, the wall arcading and Jacobean seat at the floor level of the chapel can be spirit-cleaned like the portion round the door in the south east corner.

South transept

In continuation of the work of cleaning inside the church, we would like to have authority to carry on with the end (south) wall of the South Transept so soon as the chapel of the Holy Cross is finished. It was noticed some years ago when the new rose window was being fixed that there were some small remains of the original gilding and colour on the great censing angels underneath the dirt; and, although these remains would be hardly discernable from the floor of the church, the whole of the stonework of the wall is badly in need of cleaning for the sake of preservation. It would probably be easiest to erect a scaffold from the floor, in which case the patent tubular kind, as used recently at the west end of the church, would be the most suitable, and would cost about £90.

Henry VII chapel

The external repair of Henry VII chapel has reached the two eastern pinnacles, one of which is finished and the other about half-finished in respect of stone repairs. There will shortly be another large area of stonework ready for the final preservative treatment. The effect of this work can now be well seen from a little way along Millbank to the south since the removal of scaffolding at the south east corner of the chapel.

Refectory wall

The Refectory wall on its south face opposite Ashburnham House, and also the remains of the end wall of the Refectory at the side of the school miniature rifle range, have been in need of attention for some time past. This is very valuable ancient work which the decay is getting hold of, and we have tried during recent years to foresee a way of taking it in hand in conjunction with the other works. But there is a large area of it and the men have not been available. Latterly the wet appears to have been getting through the coping with the result that the top course of stone is being disintegrated by damp and frost. We think it would be advisable to arrange for the repair of these walls during the coming summer, even at the expense, if need be, of employing two or three extra men for the purpose.

Henry VII chapel bronze gates and grille

The cleaning of the elaborate bronze gates of Henry VII chapel has taken a long time. Quennell is now at work on the grille of Henry VII tomb. Fred Lane has been detailed as Quennell's understudy and will join him in a week or two, when it is hope this work will be expedited. The cleaned gates and grille will require a certain amount of maintenance and it is proposed to make Forsyth (the painter) and his mate responsible for keeping them rubbed up periodically, so as to leave Quennell and Lane free for the cleaning and upkeep of ancient paintings etc. as before. The stonework round the bronze gates on the inside of the chapel will be cleaned so soon as the grille is finished, which will probably much improve the effect of the cleaned gates.

Abbey prints and drawings

A spare-time job in the joiners shop for a long time has been the making of a drawing chest for the safe keeping of all the Abbey prints and drawings which have been collected from time to time, with good space for future acquisitions. The chest was finished recently and placed in the Library. It has twelve shallow drawers, for easy reference, and doors to the front of the drawers to make it more dust proof.[1] The prints and drawings are being sorted and catalogued by Mr John Carleton in collaboration with the Precentor.

>W.R. Lethaby
>E.E. Lofting
>>Surveyors' office Westminster Abbey.

[1]   This chest was later moved to the Muniment Room and houses what is called the CN collection.

27N.   Lethaby resigned owing to ill health in March 1928 and died on 17 July 1931. At Chapter on 29 July the Dean and Chapter expressed their keen appreciation of his work and devotion to the Abbey. Burial in the west cloister was offered by the Dean but Lethaby had wished to be buried beside his wife in the country. A memorial stone was later unveiled in the west cloister.

SIR WALTER TAPPER
1928–35

28. The Dean nominated Tapper, then President of the Institute of British Architects, to be Surveyor on 24 April 1928 at a salary of £500 per annum plus commission on any new work he supervised. His assistant at the Abbey was Eric E. Lofting. Correspondence with Dean Norris about the proposed new Sacristy is in the WAM collection. Some of his plans are in the Surveyor Drawings and WAM (Plans) collections.

WAM S/1/71

10 Melina Place, St John's Wood, NW

Walter Tapper F.R.I.B.A.
Michael Tapper[1] A.R.I.B.A.
Architects

November 8th 1928

Gentlemen,
    I beg to report as follows:

Henry VII chapel

The repair of the external stonework of Henry VII chapel has reached a point at the east end, from which it is hoped to make faster progress in the future. The condition of the stonework on the north side and at the north east corner appears to be better than was the case on the south side, and it should not be necessary to use so much new stone in the repairs as has been required previously.

Parapet of south transept

The parapet along the east side of the south transept has got into a decayed state and is being repaired. It is probably a restoration in soft stone of 1820 and leans inwards considerably towards the roof. But with care it seems possible to stiffen and repair it, and treat the stonework so that it may harden up to the weather.

St Katherine's chapel

The cracks in the arcade of St Katherine's chapel in the approach to the Archdeacon's house, to which Mrs Charles[2] called attention last spring, appear to be more serious than was at first suspected. The arcade is becoming detached from the body of the wall behind it, owing to wet and frost, and the stone face of the arcade is getting very decayed. These remains of St Katherine's chapel are the most valuable examples of original (Norman transitional) work, and the repair of this arcade ought to be taken in hand without delay.

South transept

The proposal to clean the end (south) wall of the south transept in continuation of the work of cleaning inside the church, was approved by Chapter last February; the pressure of more urgent works has prevented it being started. It will now be possible, however, to commence this work.

Paintings

Professor Tristram's partial reconstruction of the Otho de Grandison painting on the base of Queen Eleanor's tomb, is being framed[3] and will be placed at the foot of the tomb in the same way as the reconstruction of the knights is exhibited at the foot of Crouchback's tomb. In Lethaby's recent paper "Medieval paintings at Westminster" there is a remarkable account of this romantic picture, about which nothing has been hitherto known.

The Office of Works have lately uncovered and cleaned two most interesting panels in the Chapter House on the south east wall, being apparently a fine assembly of the saints grouped in rows, and looking towards the Doom on the east wall.[4]

Transept seating

It would be an advantage if these ugly blocks of seats[5] were removed and chairs substituted, certainly an advantage from a devotional aspect. A centre gangway is also what is needed. There is nothing which gives greater dignity than plenty of floor space and it is easy in the case of a crowded service to increase the chairs as may be necessary.

Choir seating

The removal of the front row[6] of seats and desks in the choir would be an advantage. The floor space here is very cramped and takes away from the dignity of the choir. Chairs for special services could be substituted.

Nave pulpit

The upper portion of this is architecturally good but the base and stairs are modern and are not in keeping with the old. Such pulpits invariably had a centre stem and if this could be arranged the pulpit itself would be worthy of its position.[7]

Henry VII chapel

The iron railings[8] which are close against the chapel on the north side should be removed. They seem to serve no useful purpose and take away from the dignity of this fine building. On the south side as soon as it may be possible the squalid enclosure should be removed.

Paths

The main paths on the north side of the abbey are in a poor state and should be repaved with stone, as also the open space immediately in front of the north transept.

I have the honour to be, Gentlemen,

Yours faithfully

Walter Tapper

[1] Michael was his son.
[2] Wife of Canon Robert Henry Charles.
[3] See 19 f. 1. The original painting may be by Walter of Durham. Sir Otes was a friend of Edward I and went with him to the Holy Land. The painting of the Crouchback knights is probably that by John Carter, which now hangs in the Library.
[4] Referring to the late fourteenth-century wall paintings in the Chapter House.
[5] Presumably referring to the bench pews in the transepts at this period. They were all removed by 1935 (see WAM S/1/84), many being taken to Abbey benefices.
[6] This was later done – see February 1934 report.
[7] Referring to the Jacobean pulpit, later moved to the lantern. A photo of the old base and stairs can be seen in the *RCHM Inventory ... of Westminster Abbey* (1924), plate 22. It was given a new stem and stairs.
[8] These exterior railings stretched along the whole of the north side of the Abbey until the restoration of the north façade in the late nineteenth century. Some were then set back against the wall of the north nave and Henry VII's chapel.

28N.   His plan for a proposed new Sacristy building (two sites were suggested) was reported at Chapter on 23 October 1928 and agreement was given on 28 May 1929. But a long controversy followed, which was chronicled in the Chapter Minutes, and the donor, Mrs Hornby Lewis, eventually withdrew her offer of funds. It was extensively discussed in the newspapers. Some plans are WAM SD/1/629–632. One for the version outside Poets' Corner is WAM(P) 191–196D. There are many papers in the WAM collection. Photos of a mock-up of the building by the north entrance are in the Abbey muniments. 'Hands off the Abbey' by John Physick, *Transactions of the Ancient Monuments Society* vol. 41 (1997), charts the controversy. There was also a small booklet, *Westminster Abbey. The Sacristy and a few thoughts on the Abbey* by 'Thorneya' published at the time. Later it was decided to fit out the crypt of the Chapter House for use as a sacristy (Chapter 23 February 1932 and WAM SD/2/26).

Chapter agreed to the St Katherine's chapel work and Henry VII's railings proposal on 13 November 1928. Improvements to the Jerusalem Chamber were being made this year. WAM(P) 197 is Tapper's plan for the (mock) fireplace there. His plans of no. 2 Abbey Garden, when alterations were to be made, are WAM(P) 183A–C.

29.   WAM S/1/72

10 Melina Place

February 5th 1929

Gentlemen,

I beg to report as follows:

Considerable difficulty is being experienced in keeping pace with the necessary repairs to the Abbey.

In addition to large areas of crumbling stone work which should be taken in hand at once unless they are to get into a state when they will be beyond repair, there are certain buildings which need immediate attention.

The south and east walls of the old Refectory facing Ashburnham House need immediate attention and this work has become urgent.

The external stone work of the Jericho Chamber and the Islip rooms in the Deanery courtyard, in addition to the first two bays of the entrance to the Cloisters are all getting into a very bad state, as well as various valuable remains of ancient masonry in the fabric itself.

Further, a great amount of repair work, such as the north transept end, is also beginning to need attention.

In cleaning and preserving the surface of the walls inside the church there is work for a large staff for a number of years to come. To examine at close quarters the stone work in Henry VII chapel, for instance, shews that something should be done at once to stop the disintegrating effect of the London atmosphere and dirt.

In the last report it was anticipated that work on the south transept would have been started by now but the shortage of labour has not made this possible.

I consider it advisable, therefore, that the staff should be increased in order to cope with all these works which are really quite urgent, for in addition, the inside walls of the church should be cleaned and treated as fast as funds will allow.

It has been brought to my notice that where members of the staff fall sick they are allowed full pay less insurance for a period, I understand, of five weeks. I am inclined to think that this is a bad practice, and one, which though not general, at the same time in isolated cases has been found to be abused, and I would recommend that only half pay be allowed to any workmen who go sick, for a period of four weeks. After that period the case should come up for review when it can be decided if the pay should be continued, or what action should be taken.

I have the honour to be, Gentlemen
Yours faithfully
Walter Tapper

29N. Tapper estimated the cost of gilding and decorating the choirs stalls at about £1,000. Gold from the ingots presented at the 1911 coronation was considered for the gilding.

30. WAM S/1/72A

Assistant Surveyor's Office, Westminster Abbey

4 February 1929

Dear Mr Knapp Fisher

Lighting of Henry VII chapel

In accordance with the instructions of the Ornaments Committee I have considered again the question of the lighting of Henry VII chapel. In regard to the main body of the chapel I must say at once that I think the arrangement and effect of the lighting could not be improved. I am so seldom in Henry VII chapel after dark that I had not fully realised before how very right and beautiful the lighting scheme is. The little standards along the desks, I remember, are small sized models of the original Torrigiani candlesticks of which one exists somewhere in Belgium, and Barkentin and Kraal [Krall] have a copy of it. And the pleasant choir-like arrangement of lights along the desks – the only satisfactory way of lighting a choir – leaving the upper parts of the chapel dim and shadowy, is very graceful. I think it would be a great mistake to go in for any kind of high or general lighting. The row of desk lights requires the upper shadows for its effect.

So much on the score of appearance. Then as to the practical point of getting more light, I think if necessary the desk standards could have a branch at each side, so as to get three lights instead of one on each standard; and I suggest that the recent experiment of temporary lighting be adopted as a regular thing for the few special occasions when a choir is needed behind the altar.

The aisles of the chapel, you remember, were lighted only three or four years ago, as simply as possible, to enable the vergers to carry on showing parties round on a dark day. I still think it is the best and most inconspicuous way of getting a little light in the aisles for this purpose; and it avoids the introduction of distracting modern fittings. But in the case of St [Lady] Margaret's chapel, which may come into use for occasional services, the number of lights might perhaps be increased to three, and possibly a stronger arm could be devised if desired with some kind of simple pendant fitting at the end instead of the naked lamp. I am not sure that this would be an improvement because the tombs are in the way and to make the lights more conspicuous might only be confusing. At present they are not noticed unless one looks for them, and then their severe avoidance of anything like an aesthetic effect seems to reflect the right attitude of a modern necessity in an ancient chapel. I can see no way of getting the lights on to the other side, in between the windows, without being ornamental, and to that extent out of place. The vaulting bosses are not pierced. Evidently the original lighting was a range of candle brackets along the south side of which the fixing plugs still exist.

Yours sincerely
E.E. Lofting

31.   WAM S/1/73

Report, unsigned and undated, presumed to be 22 November 1929. (This was mentioned at Chapter on 10 December.)

Henry VII chapel

The repairs of the stonework on Henry VII chapel are completed across the whole of the east end, and another large section of scaffolding has been removed. This work is now turning the corner to continue along the north side.

St Katherine's chapel

The work of repairing the remains of the south arcade of St Katherine's chapel in the approach to the Archdeacon's house is all but finished. It has been a slow and intricate job to bond the facing to the wall behind with copper ties, and make the structure solid with grouting, only removing and replacing a stone here and there to get at the heart of the wall. A larger amount of modern brickwork has been removed from the top of the wall, to reduce the weight on the arcade arches; and the weathering, re-formed at a lower level, will be covered with lead to ensure a dry wall in the future.

Refectory wall

Repointing and making good of the south side of the old Refectory wall is being started immediately, commencing from its west end over the Song School. There is a great length of this wall, and the work will take a considerable time. The intention is to do as much as possible of it this summer, and then leave it till the spring, if the winter should be too hard to make good progress with this kind of work.

Winter and summer work

Mr Bishop[1] is trying to organise the various repairs to the fabric so as to concentrate on inside work during the winter and outside during the summer. In so far as this is possible, it must of course make for greater speed and economy, and it should save a certain amount of sickness during the winter among the workmen.

Lightning conductors

The whole system of lightning conductors is being renewed and improved in accordance with Messrs. Cutting's report and the recent order of the Chapter.

Records

A full size drawing in reconstruction of the Chaucer inscription has been made by Miss Walker and a reduced photograph of the drawing will be framed and placed on the tomb to match the other inscriptions on monuments.

Choir stalls

A portion of the choir stalls has been gilded for the Chapter's approval.

¹ William Bishop was Clerk of the Works from 5 September 1928 to 1955.

32. WAM S/1/73A

Assistant Surveyor's Office

6 February 1930

Dear Mr Treasurer

Collegiate Houses

In regard to the repairs of the houses I have first to explain that as the electric lighting at 3 Little Cloister requires to be re-wired and the work at this house will in consequence take longer than was expected, Canon Donaldson is willing to let the bulk of the repairs wait until next year. From the point of view of labour and cost we would be glad of a reduction in the amount of work on the houses for the years and Canon Donaldson suggests that if the outside painting and the decoration of the hall and dining room and best bedroom were done this year, the remainder might wait until next year. In the following list therefore I have only included an estimate of £159 for this house to cover these items.

The estimates requiring Chapter approval are:

21 Dean's Yard	£593.19.3
3 Little Cloister	159.0.0
5 Little Cloister	664.0.0
6 Little Cloister	762.5.0
	£2179.4.3
Choir School	157.0.0

If we add (to the total for houses) the sum of £295 already sanctioned for 2 The Cloisters, the amount to be expended on the houses for the year is

£2474.4.3, exclusive of any small works at the Deanery of 17 Dean's Yard which may possibly be required later, and exclusive also of the usual little emergency repairs and the cleaning of gutters and flushing of drains &c.

Budget

The total forecast of expenditure by the Clerk of Works department for the year ending 29 September 1930 comes to £12,089.0.0. This includes all works on the fabric and houses and choir school, so far as can be foreseen, and it includes also the watching and heating and lighting of the fabric. It is almost exactly the same total as the actual cost last year (£3 in excess to be exact), and within a margin of £500 for contingencies, I think it could safely be said that it need not be exceeded. But it will be seen that <u>any</u> contingences must bring this total in excess of last year's expenditure, and, as was reported last Audit Chapel, it should be anticipated that the cost of fabric repairs will tend to increase during the next few years.

The probable cost of the houses this year, and their actual cost last year (£3,164) is still rather high; but I think that after another two or three years (when all the houses have been overhauled twice) the average yearly cost of their maintenance will begin to fall considerably. But the gradual increase of expenditure required by the fabric is likely to be more than this expected saving in the average cost of the houses.

Yours sincerely
E.E. Lofting
Rev. Canon V.F. Storr

33.   WAM S/1/74

July 2nd 1930

Gentlemen,

I beg to report as follows:

Henry VII chapel

The repair of the stonework of Henry VII chapel has reached a point about the middle of the north side, and the final treatment with lime preservative will be completed up to this point by the autumn. There are now remaining four bays to be repaired, two of which should be finished in respect of masons' work before the winter, so that there would seem to be a fair possibility of getting this work completed by the autumn of next year.

Refectory wall

Repair of the south side of the old refectory wall has progressed very well considering the intricate nature of the work. The Norman arcading has been opened up wherever it remained, and a few of the wall-shafts of this arcading are now visible, supported by copper bands and cramps. The whole length of this wall will be finished by the end of the summer. The east end wall of the refectory, in which there are the remains of an elaborate later wall-arcading, is in even worse condition than was the north wall. But with a covered scaffolding it will be possible to carry on preparing this end wall in the winter, so as to enable the whole of this work to be finished next spring.[1]

Cleaning south transept

The internal cleaning of the south end of the south transept was finished in April down to the bottom of the triforium storey. The stone vaulting, with Wren's gilding and decoration, cleaned comparatively easily; as also did the walls of the clerestory. The polishing of the marble shafts was really the only troublesome problem, and required a great amount of painstaking labour to accomplish without risk of harming the stone by any of the usual drastic and labour saving methods of cleaning. There is a great deal of the original painted decoration remaining on the censing angels, and some on the two central figures. And these four sculptured figures have been finished with a protecting film of wax, in the same way that Professor Tristram has treated the other paintings in the Abbey.

The Chapter is asked to authorise the continuance of this cleaning operation during next winter, to extend to the other three bays of the south transept.

The suggestion is to clean the remaining three bays next winter, so that the whole of the upper part of this transept will be done, down to the horizontal line of the string course below the triforium. Then in the following winter it might be possible to bring the work down into the main arcade of the transept and into its aisles, finishing so far as possible to straight lines in order to avoid a patchy effect.

Lead roofs

The re-casting and re-laying of lead roofs is being continued this summer over the large flat above St John's chapel. One of the main beams and many of the joists of this flat were found to be in a bad condition, and these are being strengthened and renewed where necessary, and all the timbers are being treated with Heppel's fluid to destroy the beetle which has caused some damage to this part of the roof.

> Believe me, Gentlemen,
> Yours faithfully
> Walter Tapper

[1] This went ahead (Chapter 21 July 1930). Photos of the south side before later buildings were erected in front of it are in the Library collection as well as photos of tiles found under the soil. A full survey with notes of the stone types used was done during the 2008 cleaning and repair.

34.   WAM S/1/75

Surveyor's Report November 7 1930

Henry VII chapel

The repairs of the stone work of Henry VII chapel have been to some extent delayed during the summer owing to the urgency of the builders' work in connection with the re-organisation of the heating scheme. There are three bays remaining to be done, and probably my forecast of last July, when it was hoped that this work would be finished by the autumn of next year, should be extended a little.

Refectory Wall

The long length of the north wall of the Refectory has been finished, and work has been commenced on the east end wall. The missing portion of the wall arcading of this end wall has been discovered behind some modern brickwork. It is in a dilapidated condition, but it will be possible to uncover and repair it, so as to show the whole length of the lower part of the east wall of the Refectory. The class room of the school, built on top of this wall will be treated to harmonise better with the old wall underneath, and arrangements have been made with the School to pay their share of the work. When finished it will be a good work of improvement and tidying up, apart from the necessary preservation of the ancient wall; and it if might lead to the removal of the miniature rifle range to some more suitable position, it would be all to the good, and would help to make one end of the old Refectory site into a pleasant and worthy place.

Lead Roofs

Part of the large flat over the triforium about St John's chapel has been re-laid. The area covered this summer was disappointing, owing to the work being held up by a large amount of repairs of roof timbers under the lead flat, referred to in my last report.

Cleaning of South Transept

During the winter months the inside cleaning of the south transept will be carried on in accordance with the Chapter order of last July. Bridges of trussed beams are being made, upon which to erect the scaffolding, which should be in position by about the end of the month. It will be remembered that the portion to be tackled this winter is the remaining three bays of the transept, from the vaulting down to the level of the triforium floor.

The platform across the south end bay has been left in position all the summer, and a number of people have enjoyed the opportunity of getting a near view of the censing angels. These are the most beautiful and stylish examples of mediaeval sculpture that exist; wonderfully and strangely perfect when compared with other contemporary work, such as the Annunciation in the Chapter House. Arrangements were made for good photographs to be taken by Mr Hull of the South Kensington Museum – the plates of which will be deposited in the Abbey collection; and Professor Tristram has undertaken to make a drawing reconstructing the complete decoration of the figures. Also some of the best of the sculptured heads and masks round the south east corner of the triforium were cleaned and photographed.

Heating

The heating system has been completely re-arranged. The old heating pipes[1] remain unaltered but the two separate systems have been coupled together by means of a flow pipe at the triforium level in the wall passage of the south transept, and a return pipe across the nave underneath the floor. The heating chamber near the west cloister door has been abandoned, and the whole of the Abbey heating will now be worked from the north chamber by three new oil driven boilers and accelerating pumps.

Foundations discovered in nave

During the construction of a trench for the new heating pipe across the nave some very interesting foundations were discovered immediately under the floor. What there is to be seen without digging deep is perhaps rather too late in feeling to belong to the Confessor's church; and the way in which some oblong bases are cut into square ones, seems to indicate either a change of mind or subsequent alterations. Some remains of tiled floors are above the level of the chamfers on the bases, and therefore presumably later than these bases. Part of a return northwards on the easternmost pier of those uncovered which at first seemed to be the west wall of the early church is probably the first composite pier of the nave. At the moment and until further excavations are undertaken one can say nothing very definite. I am having accurate plans with dimensions and photographs made of all there is to be seen before covering up. We propose to make further excavations after Armistice Day. Mr Peers,[2] President of the Society of Antiquaries, is giving us his valuable assistance in the matter.

Ancient stone coffin

During the redecoration and repairs of no 5 Little Cloisters, the Sacrist's house, an ancient stone coffin was found under the floor of the Farmerer's Hall. The coffin was empty and was lying north and south in the centre of the south end of the Hall. Its date would be early 14th century. It has a simple floriated cross on the cover stone, and a double hollow chamfer round the edge. From the facts of its north and south position and being empty and barely three feet under ground, it would appear to have been previously found somewhere and re-buried. It has been taken up and placed in the museum.[3]

I should like to conclude by reminding the Chapter of the improvements I suggested in my former reports, such as the removal of the front row of the choir stalls, the substitution of chairs for the present incongruous seats in the transepts, and the decoration of the organ case.

sgd. Walter Tapper
10 Melina Place, NW8

[1] Tapper recommended Messrs Haden who had attended to the heating since 1860 (Chapter 13 May 1930). Temperature recorders were placed in the Abbey (25 November 1930).
[2] Sir Charles Peers, who later became Surveyor of the Fabric at the Abbey.
[3] The coffin lid now stands in the Dark Cloister against the east wall. The coffin itself may be one of those now placed in a corner of the cloister garth.

34N.   At Chapter 10 November 1930 Tapper explained his views on a proposed Rood Screen and he was to send sketches. A temporary screen, with a Calvary, was tried out above the organ loft and the High Altar in April 1931, at night in secret. But the newspapers reported it and the fact caused some controversy. A screen over the High Altar is depicted in the 1532 mortuary roll of Abbot Islip, preserved at the Abbey. The idea was dropped as too expensive (Chapter 14 July 1931).

A report of 19 December 1930 (mentioned at Chapter on 24 December) is not extant.

35.   WAM S/1/76

Surveyor's Report 1931.

Henry VII chapel

The work on the outside of Henry VII chapel has progressed very slowly owing to shortage of labour. There are nearly two whole bays still remaining to be finished. Following on the masonry repairs, the finishing operations of this work are done by the same workmen, who have been doing the cleaning inside the south transept; and will probably take until next summer to finally complete these repairs of Henry VII chapel.

North transept

Reviewing the future continuation of outside stonework repairs generally, I have again considered the comparative urgency of the north transept and the western towers, and I have decided that the north transept is the more urgent of the two. I have therefore allowed in next year's budget for commencing the repairs of the external stonework of the north transept as being the next large work of this kind which is most pressing, after the work on Henry VII chapel has been finished.

Refectory wall

Since my last report the east end wall of the refectory has been finished, and the modern school building above it has been tidied up and made to harmonize with the old work. This repair and preservation of the Refectory walls is a work which had been pressing for many years and its completion is very gratifying and successful as an example of careful repair. I hope that the School may be persuaded to find another place for the miniature rifle range.

Cleaning of south transept

The cleaning of the inside of the south transept is getting on slowly. As in the case of Henry VII chapel, there is not a sufficient number of men employed to make good progress possible. Practically three out of the four bays of the transept are now cleaned, down to the level of the triforium floor. The further this work progresses the more impressed I become by its importance and beauty, and by its necessity for the preservation of the carved and sculptured stonework; and I wish that some special effort could be made to find more money, with which to carry it on faster. Now that there is a large area of the cleaned surface to be seen, if one stands at the north end of the platform supporting the scaffolding and compares the cleaned work with the other parts of the church, it seems truly amazing that the commencement of so important and necessary a work should have been delayed so long.

Professor Tristram is getting on with his drawings showing a reconstruction of the decorated sculpture on the south wall. And the question has been raised by Canon Woodward as to whether casts of the censing angels should not be made while the opportunity is afforded by the scaffolding. With the Chapter's permission I would ask the Victoria & Albert Museum whether they would like to make casts.

Lead roofs

The recasting and relaying of the lead flats on the north side of the chevet has been carried on to the completion of the flat over the Islip chapel and is being continued eastward.

Library roof

It will be remembered that there was reason to believe that the death watch beetle was causing some damage in the Library roof. I have had this roof re-examined, and although it is true that the beetle is there in small numbers (as is so often the case in ancient timbers), there does not appear to be sufficient damage to necessitate any very drastic work. I have included in next year's budget a small sum to treat the roof timbers with Heppell's fluid, and at the same time to distemper the walls and clean the book cases.

Parapet of south transept

Work on the east parapet of the south transept has been held up for want of labour. About one third of its length was repaired two years ago, and the making good of the remainder, which is in a very bad condition, has now been commenced. It is a difficult job and will require a certain amount of restoration with new stone, owing to its having been allowed to go so are in decay before being taken in hand.

Heating chamber

The roof of the heating chamber is being waterproofed, and extra ventilation provided, and a second exit from the chamber is being formed by means of an iron ladder which was asked for by the fire inspector.

Transept seating

As I have said in previous reports, it would be of immense value to the devotional aspect of the Abbey if the transepts could have chairs substituted for the existing incongruous seats.

Choir stalls

I understand that the removal of the front row of the stalls, which would give dignity to the choir, depends on the re-arranging of the Mansfield monument,[1] now under the Chapter's consideration. It has occurred to me that if the choir were transferred to the organ gallery, the accommodation which the front row now provides could be arranged in the existing choir seats. The Chapter may wish to consider this suggestion.

Signed Walter Tapper, 1931.

[1] Lord Mansfield's monument was moved to the north end of the west aisle of the north transept (it was originally between the pillars next to the Three Captains monument).

35N.   At Chapter 23 March 1931 Tapper was to report on the question of the re-erection of the James Cornewall and James Craggs monuments. This was in order to set up the Warriors or Holy Cross chapel (designed by J.N. Comper) in the south-west nave chapel. Craggs had a large monument against the eastern part of the screen facing into the nave and Cornewall was on the north side. Craggs was reduced in size and the figure put on the window sill of the chapel. Cornewall was moved to the cloister entrance (permissions sought to move this are recorded in the Chapter Minutes 14 July 1931).

On 9 June he was asked to take up various questions from Chapter with Sir Herbert Baker who was designing a new Church House building in Dean's

Yard. Letters concerning this are in Sir Charles Peers files WAM S/2/VI and VIa. Funds for use of the Fabric were discussed at the 30 June 1931 meeting.

36.   WAM S/1/77

10 Melina Place, St John's Wood, NW

4 February 1932

Dear Mr Dean and Gentlemen,

<u>Westminster Abbey</u>

HENRY VII CHAPEL. The last section of the repairs of the outside stonework of Henry VII chapel is now nearing completion. All the sooty deposit on the stone of this last section has been removed down to ground level, and the work of making good the decayed stones, and raking out and repointing the jointing of the old masonry is well advanced. The application of the lime preservative will be proceeded with as soon as weather conditions are suitable for it, and it is hoped to have this work finished and the scaffolding removed early in the summer.

CLEANING OF S. TRANSEPT. The cleaning of the interior of the south transept has been continued during the winter months. Work is now in progress on the last bay, and in a few weeks time, the whole of the upper part of this transept will have been cleaned down to the level of the triforium floor. The next portion of this work to be taken in hand will be to carry the cleaning of the south wall of the transept down to the floor of the church. For this purpose a scaffolding is about to be erected against the south wall, and the boarded platform across the triforium will be removed in sections, commencing at the south end. The cleaning process will then have to be suspended until October next, as we shall have expended the amount provided for this purpose in this year's budget. In October we shall hope to proceed with the cleaning of the west arcade and the west aisle of the transept.

Professor Tristram has nearly finished his drawing of the censing angels and the two central figures, and a cast of the angel in the south west corner has been made by the Victoria and Albert Museum. An old cast of the angel in the other corner was also found, and bought by the Museum.

It is suggested that the copy of the new cast which has been given to the Abbey by the Victoria and Albert Museum and which is now in the Abbey Museum, should be coloured and decorated by Professor Tristram in reconstruction of the original colouring and he has been asked to estimate the probable cost of doing this.[1]

NORTH TRANSEPT. It is intended, in the spring, to make a start with the erection of the scaffolding to the outside of the north transept, in order to carry on with the repairs of the stonework of this transept, following the completion of Henry VII chapel, as foreshadowed in my report of last June.

LIBRARY ROOF. The Library roof has been thoroughly overhauled and cleaned, and treated with Heppell's fluid to destroy the Death Watch Beetle. Very little serious damage had been done by the beetle, only one of the curved braces of one of the principal trusses having to be renewed. The walls of the Library were washed down and distempered, and the woodwork repainted and the bookcases carefully cleaned and repaired. If it could be arranged that the regular dusting and cleaning of the Library and its bookcases should be done more frequently, it would be a great improvement. It appears to have suffered to some extent from neglect, and a great deal could be done by regular use of a vacuum cleaner and rubbing up of the woodwork.

LEAD ROOFS. Another section of the lead flat roof over the north east triforium has been stripped and repaired, and the lead re-cast and relaid. A few of the oak joists in this section had to be replaced by new ones, and all the old timbers were treated with beetle-destroying fluid. The work on this lead flat is now in abeyance until the weather becomes more favourable in the spring, when the next section eastwards will be commenced.

HEATING. The work on the heating chamber mentioned in my last report has been finished. Since the beginning of this winter the new oil fuel installation has been working very satisfactorily, maintaining an average temperature of 60° in the church.

PARAPET OF SOUTH TRANSEPT. A number of new stones have been worked in preparation for the repair of the east parapet of the south transept, but it has not been possible for want of labour to continue this work any further. It must be carried on during the coming summer, even at the expense of some delay in the other necessary repairs of external stonework.

CLEANING OF MONUMENTS. The cleaning of the monuments in the church is being proceeded with systematically. All the monuments in St Paul's chapel have re-appeared with wonderful freshness and interest under their recent cleaning and the old banners in this chapel, and St John's, which were in a very tattered condition, have been taken down and repaired and re-hung in their original positions.[2]

Two important items of general cleaning and repair I would like to mention have been the choir screen and the screen behind the High Altar. Both these screens have been overhauled and cleaned and all loose fragments secured with very great improvement to their appearance and preservation.

ELECTRIC LIGHTING. As recommended in Messrs Belshaw's last report, an extra 2½ inch copper conduit pipe has been fixed from the main fuse board under the organ up to the Nave roof. The wires have now been divided into two sections which will greatly facilitate fault-finding in the future, and make it possible to withdraw an individual wire in the proper way.

ANCIENT FOUNDATIONS UNDER NAVE. I would like to put on record on my report, and recommend for reference, Mr Tanner's and Mr Clapham's very excellent papers[3] on the foundations of the Confessor's church, recently discovered under the Nave floor, read to the Society of Antiquaries on December 3rd. Copies of my plan of these foundations have been made, and deposited with the Assistant Keeper of Muniments.

TRANSEPTS. I should be glad if the Chapter would bear in mind my previous recommendation to substitute chairs for the existing incongruous seats. It would greatly add to the dignity of the building.

CHOIR. Also, the removal of the two front rows of seats, so getting a wider gangway, so essential to the dignity of the choir.

ST FAITH'S CHAPEL. Some little time since, the Clerk of Works informed me that the chapter wished the lighting improved. I found, on going into the matter, that the existing electroliers were hung far too high, and I had them lowered, as far as the chains permitted. They could, with advantage, be lowered still further, both from an aesthetic and practical point of view.

I understand that such lowering is supposed to adversely affect the picture on the east wall. I may say at once that this is not the case, and even if it were, there are other things to be thought of, of equal, or even more importance, such as, for instance, the chapel itself, which is strikingly beautiful.

The disposition of any fittings needs very careful thought and care so as to emphasize this beauty. The proportions of the chapel are tall and narrow, something like three to one, and the Old Masters, in hanging any electroliers or lamps, took care to emphasize such by making the chains as long as possible, as may be seen to this day in many of the great churches abroad, especially in Spain, where lamps are suspended just above the height of a man. The idea that such interfere with the view of this, that, or the other feature was of secondary importance, for it simply meant moving a foot or two one way or the other.

It was one of the principles of Gothic building to see, as it were, one thing behind another, and it gave a sense of mystery. This can be understood at the Abbey as well as anywhere else in the world, and it is just the difference between it and a classic building such as St Paul's.

And now, may I make a few suggestions which would improve the devotional sense of St Faith's.

The existing position of the silver sanctuary lamp is absurd, it is far too high, and should be lowered to a height of about 8 feet from the floor, "pace" the picture.

The oak seats placed on the old stone seat are quite incongruous, and should be removed. All that is required here is a velvet cushion on the stone seat and a silk brocade wall hanging, or perhaps the tapestries[1] which are at present stupidly arranged could be hung in this position. This is a matter which I could consider later.

The kneelers are thin and poor and quite unworthy. At the west end (south) on the stone seat is a sort of laundry basket, hardly a help to devotion. Opposite is an ugly box, and some shocking candlesticks, which should be burnt. Kneeling mats are piled on the old stone seat. If orderliness is next to Godliness, as we are told, this should not be. At all events, Orderliness is one of the essentials in good architecture.

The door from the chapel to the transept has been a good one, and with very little effort could and should be repaired. An incongruous board covered with a mauve cloth covers the upper portion. It would be comic, were it not in Westminster Abbey, which makes it otherwise. A cupboard in one of the recesses is quite unworthy, and there is an untidy board behind the grille of the safe.

The majority of the items I have mentioned can be improved at very little cost, as it means getting rid of ugly things, which is hardly a question of ways and means, but simply a real desire to get rid of unworthy things, which take away from the dignity of this noble place.

And now, may I plead generally for a better administration in matters concerning the Abbey. On my periodical visits, I find quite unworthy things being done, such as the stupid cupboard in the Islip chapel, and on enquiry, I am told that it is the desire of some one individual who gives instructions to some other individual, and your Surveyor, who is responsible personally, has not even been consulted. I mention this, not from any personal point of view, for I have lived long enough to know that this is a very small matter, but I do resent this great building being treated in this sort of fashion. There is not a thing, no matter how small, which does not require your Surveyor's personal attention, thought and care, and nothing should be done without his knowledge. If the Chapter would in all cases instruct the Chapter Clerk to convey their wishes to him, he would, as you well know, be only too pleased to give them his personal attention. Nothing concerning the Abbey is too much trouble. I do indeed plead for this consideration, on behalf of this noble building.

> And remain,
> Yours very faithfully,
> Sgd. Walter Tapper

---

[1] This was done and the cast is in the Abbey collection.
[2] These were removed at the time of cleaning of the interior in the later 1950s.

3   *Archaeologia* vol. LXXXIII, 'Recent discoveries in the nave of Westminster Abbey'. His plan is WAM SD/1/54. An outline of the area of the foundations was cut on the nave floor and can still be seen today. Photos of the excavations are in the Abbey collection.

4   These were either side of the wall painting and both are now in Cheyneygates. The larger one depicts the expulsion of Hagar and the smaller one was a section of vase and flower tapestry.

37.   WAM S/1/78

10 Melina Place, St John's Wood, NW

20 July 1932

Gentlemen:

Westminster Abbey
Surveyor's Report

Henry VII's chapel

The repairs of the outside stonework of Henry VII's chapel are now completed. The finishing treatment of the surface of the stone is a good example of the use of limewash as a stone preservative, properly prepared and applied in the right way. The extreme whiteness goes off within a month or two, leaving only the appearance of cleaned stonework, which brings to light the beauty of line and detail in the ancient work.

North transept

The scaffolding has been erected to the upper part of the north transept, and the work in repair of the stonework is about to be commenced. When the stonework above the great rose window has been finished, it is proposed, as the work proceeds downwards, to clean and repair the glass of the rose window. At the bicentenary commemoration of Dean Atterbury[1] a small fund was raised towards the repair of this window, which will enable a light cantilever scaffold to be put up on the inside, so as to get at both sides of it and do all that may be necessary to the glass.

Cleaning of s. transept

The cleaning inside the south transept is in abeyance during the summer months, and will be recommenced in October. Since the opening to view of the cleaned vaulting and triforium by removal of the boarded platform, the work has been much admired, and I would like to remind the Chapter again that a special fund should be raised to enable it to be carried on faster. About half of the south wall has been done, and when this has been finished down to the floor it is proposed to work along the west arcade including the Muniment Room.

Professor Tristram has finished his drawings of the sculptured Confessor and Pilgrim and the censing angels, and is commencing the decoration of the cast of the censing angel in the museum.

The Crypt

The heating of the crypt for use as a sacristy has been done by an extension from the existing hot water system in the church, and the wiring for electric light has been rearranged. The windows are being glazed to suit the old iron grilles, and the walls and vaulting are being repaired and cleaned in preparation for the fixing of the oak cases which Mr Laurence Turner is making.

Lead roofs

Recasting and relaying of the lead flat over the north east triforium is being carried on, another large section having just been completed. It is becoming urgently necessary to make more progress with these lead roofs, because the aisle roofs of Henry VII's chapel and the flat over the west walk of the cloister must be dealt with in the near future.

Parapet of s. transept

It has been found necessary to restore this parapet completely in new stone, the old work being too far gone for repair and strengthening in the way I had first intended. It would appear to have been built about 1800 in a very soft stone, none of which can be re-used with safety in its restoration.

South wall of Deanery

The ancient stone-faced south wall of the Deanery is urgently in need of repair and preservation, in continuation of the work done recently to the Refectory wall, of which it forms part. I have included a small sum for this in next year's estimates, and propose to put the work in hand next summer.

I am, yours very faithfully
(Sgd) Walter Tapper

[1]   Francis Atterbury had been responsible for inserting the glass in the north rose window in 1722.

38.   WAM S/1/79.

10 Melina Place

6 February 1933

Gentlemen,

Westminster Abbey

North transept

Since my last report it has not been possible to make any progress with the repairs of the outside stonework of the North Transept, for want of a bigger staff of workmen. There is a very great area of stone to be dealt with in this work, and I am getting anxious that the work may be seriously delayed unless some more men can be employed, which is not possible without increasing the total expenditure allowed for the year. The scaffolding of the upper part of the transept was erected six months ago, and since then the Clerk of the Works has not been able to spare even two men to get one with the work.

Cleaning of S. Transept

It was hoped to start again on the inside cleaning of the south transept in October and to keep it going through the winter months; but here again the work has been held up for want of men. It was not until about a fortnight ago that we were at last able to recommence this work, in a small way, on the south wall of the transept.

I suggested in my last report that a special fund should be raised to enable this urgent work of inside cleaning to be carried on faster. It is immensely important as preservation, and it is also looked upon as the most satisfactory work that has been done at the Abbey in modern times. A very great amount of experimental work was required before it could be made practicable. And now that it is fairly launched, with the upper part of the south transept finished as an example of what can be done, I feel very strongly that a great effort should be made to continue it on a much larger scale than is possible with the present allowance of funds.

The Crypt

The glazing of the windows of the Crypt and the repairs and cleaning of its walls and vaulting have all been finished. The fixing of the oak cases will be commenced next week. The extension of the hot water heating to the Crypt has been very successful, in spite of the depth to which the pipe had to drop and return. As high a temperature, as in the church itself, is maintained.

Lead Roofs

Relaying of the lead flat over the N.E. triforium has been carried on almost continuously since last July, with only one interruption when the plumbers were required to relay the gutter behind the new parapet on the east side of the south transept. The oak beams and rafters of this triforium roof, in the last section repaired, were in better conditions than in some earlier sections, but treatment of them with the beetle-killing fluid is being continued. In about six months, at the present rate of progress, this triforium roof should be finished up to its east end, and either the aisle roofs of Henry VII chapel or the flat over the west walk of the cloisters may be commenced.

Parapet of s. transept

The work of restoring the east parapet of the south transept in Portland stone has now been completed, and the lead gutter behind the parapet has been relaid.

Muniment Room

The walls and vaulting of the Muniment Room was in course of being repaired and cleaned, and its heating and lighting re-arranged, all in conjunction with the scheme in progress of putting the Muniment Room in communication with the Library.

Professor Tristram is working on the cleaning of the large painting on plaster of Richard II's white hart. This painting had become very indistinct, except upon close inspection, by the application many years ago of a preservative solution which made the surface of the plaster extraordinarily hard and very dark in colour. The hardness of the surface makes the cleaning operation very difficult without risk of damaging the paint underneath, but by working right through to the plaster on the unpainted ground the figure will be to some extent silhouetted, and the details inside the painting will become more apparent, when cleaned so far as possible, on a lighter ground.

There are some interesting remains of ancient colour on the mutilated boss in the south end bay of the vaulting, and also on the fine bosses in the groined reveal of the south window.

Library

The remodelling of the Library to connect it to the Muniment Room, and the formation of an Annexe to it in the roof space over the east walk of the cloister, is progressing well. The steel and concrete carcase of the Annexe is all in position, and when this has been screeded and asphalted on top, the covering of it with tiles will commence in about a month's time. The alteration of direction in the stone staircase of the Library makes a greatly improved entrance to it from the cloister.[1] I am hopeful of getting this work completed by about the end of May.

Henry VII chapel

It is over two months since I presented my report on the condition of the vaulting of Henry VII chapel, and as the work will take two and a half years to do, it is becoming urgent that a start should be made as soon as possible. The two main points to be borne in mind in regard to this work are, that the chapel cannot be reopened till the repairs are done, and that these repairs could not be done in less time than two years and will probably take longer.

In view of the great number of cusps alone, that are jointed in exactly the same faulty way as the one which fell, I could not be responsible for a reopening of the chapel before the work is done, even if the District Surveyor would allow it, which is most unlikely. And as I explained in my report of November 17th, the raking out and refilling of joints of ribs and panels can only be done, like underpinning, in small sections at a time for fear of causing movement.

[Mansfield monument]

The removal of the Mansfield monument to the north end of the west aisle [of the north transept] is being undertaken.

Increase of Staff

May I conclude this report with a reminder that more funds are needed to expedite the work on the outside of the north transept and the cleaning and preservation of the original stonework inside the church. At the present rate of progress on the north transept, it will be years before we are able to attend to the western towers, to mention only the larger areas of outside cleaning, while the deposit of encrusted dirt is allowed to remain on the surface of the stone, disintegration is going on underneath at an ever increasing rate.

> I am, Yours faithfully,
> Walter Tapper
> Surveyor to Westminster Abbey.

[1] The new stone stairway was made to turn to the right rather than leading straight up into the room. Tapper took away the seventeenth-century gallery on the north wall and put a wooden spiral staircase in the north-west corner leading to a gallery over the roof of the east cloister to make a working space, with frosted glass domes (since replaced with plain perspex) above and windows overlooking the cloister garth. This leads into the Muniment room (the previous entry to this being via the door and turret stair from the cloister below). Money was provided by The Pilgrim Trust. Photos of the Library before conversion are in the Abbey collection and also the White Hart painting before restoration.

38N.   A letter from Tapper set out in the Chapter Minutes of 11 April 1933 stated that he would report again on Henry VII's chapel in six months' time; the western towers were not, in his opinion, in bad condition but repair to the parapet was advised; the re-conditioning of the Museum was to go ahead. On 24 October his plans for protection of the Unknown Warrior's grave were not approved. On 5 February 1934 his plan for the decoration and restoration of Henry VII's chapel was submitted to the Great Master of the Order of the Bath, and gilding of the bosses would be paid for out of money received from the sale of the gold coronation ingots.

He did not attend at the opening of the urn said to contain the bones of the Princes in the Tower in July 1933.

39.   WAM S/1/80

4 Dean's Yard, Westminster.

16 February 1934

Gentlemen,

Westminster Abbey

Henry VII chapel

Good progress has been made with the repairs of the vaulting of Henry VII chapel. Raking out and refilling all the joints from the roof space above the vaulting has made a very sound and successful work, and has greatly strengthened the vault. All the jointing of the cusps has been renewed and strengthened with copper bands, and the fractures in the spandrils have been stitched with copper, and the fixings of the pendant bosses have been secured. The ends of the tie rods, which were fixed during the surveyorship of Mr Pearson, have been rearranged to relieve the masonry of any pressure or vibration. Almost all the works of structural repair of the main vault have been finished, and the cleaning has been commenced.

Cleaning of S. transept

Following the completion of the Muniment Room, the cleaning of the south wall of the transept was continued down to the level of the string course, above the doorway to St Faith's chapel. During this winter, the arcade on the west side of the transept, opening into the Muniment Room, has been cleaned. I would like to call special attention to this cleaning of a part of the main arcade of the Abbey because the effect is extraordinarily beautiful. The lines and details of the arcade, arches, and carved spandrils, have never before been seen since medieval times. A comparison of this cleaned portion with the rest of the main arches gives some idea of the great importance of this work.

It is hoped to finish the area of wall below the Muniment Room, down to the floor level, before having to suspend operations in favour of outside work, during the summer months, and to carry on with the completion of this transept next winter by cleaning its east arcade and aisle. Then the south transept of the Abbey will be the fairest and most wonderful sight in London.

Library and Muniment Room

I ought to put it on record that since my last report, the remodelling of the Library and Muniment Room has been finished, and the two rooms put into direct communication by construction of the gallery extension to the Library in the roof space over the east wall of the cloister. This was a most successful and gratifying work, the importance and future significance of which has been expressed by all who have seen it.

North transept

The stonework of the upper part of the north transept, namely the pinnacles and gable end, was overhauled and repaired during the summer and autumn, and good progress was made considering the small number of men that could be spared. The greater urgency of the masonry repairs in Henry VII chapel tended to hold up the work on the north transept. The men at present employed in the south transept will be available to carry one with the north transept repairs, when the weather is favourable for the work.

The Cloister

The north walk of the cloister was overhauled and treated with lime in the summer, and it is intended to deal with another section, during the coming summer. I have been anxious for the stonework of the cloister to be cleaned and treated again as soon as possible. It can only be done in summer because the stone is not dry enough in winter for this kind of work, and with so much other work in hand it is difficult to do more than a little at a time. But by doing a portion every summer, for the next four or five years, it should be possible to get round the whole length of it. In a case like the cloister, where the stone has suffered greatly from condensation, and has been allowed to go too far in decay, it is necessary, especially in the first few years of its treatment, to overhaul and clean it periodically.

Museum

The scheme of improvement and reorganisation of the Museum was begun in November, and is now practically finished and ready for the exhibits to be arranged. The walls and piers and vaulting have been repaired and cleaned and a new system of electric lighting installed and the Museum has been very successfully heated by electric tubular radiators. The new furniture for display of exhibits includes a good oak table for the models, and oak racks in tiers for the collection of ancient stones, and some fine metal glazed and electrically lighted exhibition cases, made by Mr Bainbridge Reynolds.[1]

South wall of Deanery

The old stonework of the south wall of the Deanery was repaired and pointed and limewashed in the summer. It is the continuation westward of the Refectory wall and was in a bad state of repair, and its preservation entailed a good deal of work. At the same time an improved arrangement of outlets and gutters for the water from the Deanery roof was fixed, with heads and downpipes all in lead.

Lead roofs

Relaying of the lead flats over the north east triforium has been completed and it is intended to proceed next with the lead flat over the west walk of the cloister.

Also the worn out iron rain water pipes on the north side of the Church are being replaced by cast lead pipes, as the necessity arises.

Sacristy

The formation of a Sacristy in the crypt is working well, and a recent improvement in its ventilation appears to have obviated the fear of damp. Some inventive tidying of the small sacristy and plate safe in St Faith's chapel has been done, including candle racks, linen chest and shelving, and a closed trolley has been made for the transport of the plate.

Choir stalls

The added front row of the Choir stalls, a very unworthy and cramping extension of the stalls in Victorian times, has at last been removed. The gain in spaciousness and dignity is enormous. I am considering what would be the best rearrangement of the choir desks, and the lighting of them, and I hope very shortly to get this matter approved and put in hand.

Choir [north transept] seating

The removal of the existing benches and the seating of the north transept with chairs will be finished in the course of a few days.[2]

Wax effigies

The wax effigies in the upper Islip Chapel are being cleaned,[3] and set up again by the Victoria & Albert Museum, and their cases are being made dust proof. I am having some experiments made to try to improve the lighting of the effigies.

[Pulpit]

The temporary sound board over the pulpit was placed and I should be glad to know whether it improved the acoustics, and if so, whether a permanent one can be made?

>   I have the honour to be,
>   Yours very faithfully,
>   Walter Tapper
>   Surveyor to Westminster Abbey

[1] One of these showcases was later used in the Library after all were removed from the Museum, but this in turn was disposed of.
[2] His plan for transepts seating is WAM(P) III.
[3] See 'On some later funeral effigies in Westminster Abbey' by L.E. Tanner and J.L. Nevinson, *Archaeologia* vol. LXXXV (1936).

39N. On 24 April and 8 May 1934 Chapter discussed the proposal by Tapper to build a house for himself (for use in his lifetime only) on the site of the Dean's

Stables (west side of Dean's Yard, now called 4B and 5). On 3 July they accepted his new plans and terms were set out at the meetings on 10 and 24 July. He spent quite a lot of his own money on the building, and at his death Chapter agreed to pay a certain amount to his estate to reflect this (26 November 1935).

Also on 3 July his letter about works at College Hall is set down. On 30 October his design for a new pulpit was approved but this was never done as the existing ones were utilised.

40. WAM S/1/81

4 Dean's Yard, Westminster

14 February 1935

Gentlemen,

Westminster Abbey

Henry VII chapel

The work on Henry VII chapel since my last report has been largely concerned with surface repairs and cleaning of the inside walls. The structural repairs of the main vault have already been reported upon, and following these repairs the vaulting of the five radiating side chapels at the east end has been consolidated in the same way as the main vault was done, by cutting out the disintegrated joints of all the stone panels separately, and refilling and grouting them by working from the roof space above the vaulting as well as from below.

The cleaning and final treatment of the walls internally of the chapel has been a long and intricate job, owing to the great area of masonry to be dealt with in such elaborate work. The finished result is an extraordinary interesting example in modern times of the use of limewash (specially prepared and refined) as the final treatment after internal surface repairs and cleaning. And it is exactly the same method of cleaning and preserving of all undecorated stonework which was customary and periodical with medieval builders; but which somehow lapsed and became forgotten in later times, until at last dirt and decay came to be looked upon as inevitable so far as stonework was concerned.

The beautiful range of statuary[1] below the windows has come to life in a wonderful way, each figure having been taken out of its niche and carefully cleaned and treated. And the opportunity was taken to get some good photographs of some of the best of them.

The fine stepped and barrel vaulted entrance to the chapel has been repaired and cleaned and renovated like the chapel itself, and the ceiling of the entrance has been decorated in gold and colour. I hope it may be possible to finish both the aisles of the chapel next winter. These aisles are completely separated visually from the chapel and its entrance but the structural repairs of the chapel will not be finished until the aisles and their vaulting are also done.

The stalls and their canopies are being cleaned and waxed, and the making of the new altar, in reconstruction so far as possible of Torrigiani's altar, is well advanced.[2]

South transept internal cleaning

The cleaning of the inside of the south transept is being continued. Since my last report the west wall, below the parapet of the Muniment Room, has been done with all its monuments and mural tablets. This was almost as great a revelation of the advantage and importance of this work as was the cleaning of the arcade on the same side, about a year ago. Even the effect of overcrowding of the monuments on this wall seems to have almost disappeared in the cleaning, and the west side of the transept, which before was colourless and dreary, now appears spacious and bright and pleasant.

The lower part of the south wall of the transept, completing the cleaning of the whole of this wall, has also been done. Here in the lowest stage of wall arcading, which ranges with the doorway of St Faith's chapel, were found some very important remains of ancient decoration in colour. And in each of the two bays on the east side of the doorway very remarkable paintings have come to light, of about the same date as those on the Sedilia (AD 1308). The face of these two arched recesses had been covered with thin dark marble, as a sort of background to the respective monuments in front; and the mortar (putty) bedding of this marble facing has yet to be carefully removed by Professor Tristram from the surface of the paintings.

So far as can be seen at present, the picture in the recess nearest to St Faith's doorway is St Christopher on a green ground, with an inscription only partly decipherable. And the other picture appears likely to be a figure of Our Lord, after the Resurrection, on a red ground spotted with fleurs-de-lys, but only part of the head of this picture can be seen so far.[3]

The work of uncovering these two paintings was interrupted by the Royal Wedding, when the scaffolding had to be removed; so temporary screens were fitted into the two recesses. And it now seems best to keep them covered up for another few weeks, till the work on the eastern arcade of the transept, in the corner above them, has been finished. There were no remains to be found of the ancient decoration in the corresponding two recesses of the wall arcading on the west side of St Faith's doorway, although it is almost certain that originally there were also paintings here as part of the same scheme; and painted decoration can be seen behind the Goldsmith monument, which fills the upper part of the doorway itself.

Work is now in progress on the eastern arcade of the transept, with its arcade piers, and will be completed this winter; and the cleaning of the east aisle of the transept will be carried on next winter. The uncovering, cleaning and preserving of the two paintings will be recommenced within the next two months.

North transept exterior

Repair of the outside stonework of the north transept is being continued. During last summer the upper part, above the rose window, was repaired and lime preservative applied on the surface of the stone. Since the lime treatment cannot be carried on in the winter months, work was concentrated on the repairs and pointing of the lower part, preparing the stone for the preservative treatment, which will be done this coming summer. By the end of the summer it is hoped to have the whole of the north front finished down to the gabled roofs of the porches.

The glass of the great rose window (Dean Atterbury window) was also cleaned inside, as provided for some time ago at the bicentenary commemoration of Dean Atterbury. The glass was in good condition, but had been painted over with a film of yellow tinting on the inside when the north front was restored about thirty five years ago.[4]

Repairs of the parapets

To keep abreast of the repairs of the parapets all round the building I have adopted the principle of making a separate item in the budget estimates each year for this purpose. The upper parapet all round the east end of the church, east of the transepts, has now been repaired, and work is being continued along the west side of the south transept and along the south side of the nave.

Western Towers

The parapets and the remaining three unrepaired pinnacles of the western towers have also to be dealt with, in advance of the proposed general repairs of the stonework of these towers. Part of the parapet of the north west tower has been re-set, with copper cramps and dowels in place of the rusted iron ones, and these repairs will also be carried on further during the summer.

The Cloister

The west walk of the cloister has now been overhauled and treated with lime, in accordance with the programme of doing one section each year, which I suggested in my last report of progress. The south walk will be the next to be done.

Lead Roofs

Relaying of the lead flat over the west walk of the cloister has been completed. The timbers of this flat roof were found to be in a very decayed condition, and it was necessary for most of them to be replaced by new ones. They were only deal timbers of about 100 years ago.

Choir Stalls

The alterations to the choir stalls have now been finished, with the addition of new metal book rests for the choir and a new arrangement of lighting.

Choir [transept and lantern] seating

The heavy and ugly benches have now all been removed from the transepts and crossing, and replaced by chairs. This is a very great improvement.

Wax effigies

The cleaning and repairing of the wax effigies in the upper Islip chapel are being continued by the Victoria & Albert Museum, one figure at a time being taken away to be dealt with at the Museum. There are three now remaining to be done.

Pulpit

The Victorian marble pulpit[5] has been removed and it will be replaced by the ancient oak pulpit which formerly stood in the nave. A new base has to be made for the ancient oak pulpit, which I hope will be ready for the pulpit to be fixed by Easter.

New Pulpit [should be New Notices]

A general tidying up and improvement of all the notices in the church has been done in accordance with the order of Chapter. Most of the old printed notices were unsightly and distracting as well as untidy. The new scheme is based upon the principle of each notice being separately designed to fit its position, and being written in good lettering. And, more than this, the ground of each notice is coloured to tone with its surroundings; or with the wall against which it is placed – and the lettering is then written in black or light [?white]. This avoids the distracting spottiness of notices, which is so commonly seen.

[Robert] Stephenson window

The Stephenson window,[6] which had been stored in the triforium for some years, has been refixed in the north choir aisle. Its dark borders and grounds have been omitted and substituted by clear and slightly tinted glass, which has greatly improved the design of the window and solved the old difficulty of its having been so very obstructive of light.

College Hall

Alterations and working improvements of the kitchens and service quarters of College Hall were carried out during the summer vacation by the School, with the sanction of the Dean & Chapter. The ancient beams of the Hall floor were overhauled by the Abbey staff and treated with beetle destroying fluid; and gas heating of the Hall was installed, and some other minor works done, at the expense of the Abbey. It was also agreed that the Abbey should redecorate the Hall as soon as this can be conveniently arranged.

I have the honour to be,

Yours faithfully,

Walter Tapper.

[1]   Statues of saints and philosophers.

[2]   Tapper designed the altar and work was carried out by Laurence Turner. The Order of the Bath paid for it. It incorporates two pillars from the Renaissance altar designed by Pietro Torrigiano.

[3]   The figures show St Christopher carrying the Christ Child, with two inscriptions, and the risen Christ with St Thomas, which has no remaining inscription. Tristram's drawings are in the Abbey collection. He wrote an article in the *Burlington Magazine*, May 1937.

[4]   The feet of the figures had been cut off and other alterations had been made by J.L. Pearson.

[5]   This was in the lantern, and made by Samuel Cundy to a design by Sir Gilbert Scott. It was given to All Saints, Bendigo in Australia (Chapter 12 December 1934). The seventeenth-century pulpit was put in that position, having been moved from the nave. The sixteenth-century linen-fold ('Cranmer') pulpit was moved from Henry VII's chapel to serve the nave.

[6]   This window, designed by William Wailes, had been installed in 1862 in the nave where Stephenson is buried. The order of the medallions was changed when it was re-erected.

40N.   An undated coloured design for hangings and ornaments for the altar in Henry V's Chantry is WAM (P) 399.

Sir Walter had been knighted and elected to the Royal Academy in 1935 but died at 4A Dean's Yard on 21 Sept 1935. His funeral was held at the Abbey and his ashes buried in the west cloister.

SIR CHARLES PEERS
1935–51

41. The Chapter Minutes of 8 October 1935 record the appointment of Sir Charles Peers CBE as Surveyor and his acceptance letter (which is WAM 61936). His retaining fee would be £300 (suggested by Peers himself) plus out-of-pocket expenses. His assistant at the Abbey until his death in January 1950 was E.E. Lofting. Peers deposited all his Abbey files (WAM S/2) in the Muniments (plus some on works he did elsewhere including Charterhouse, Durham, Eton and York). Other correspondence is in the main WAM collection, including his letters in 1929 about the proposed new Sacristy building. There are also letters in the Lawrence Tanner collection at the Abbey (LM/06/04/011–12). No reports were given in 1945–46 or 1948–51 owing to his illness. His resignation letter of 5 June 1951 is in WAM DF.3.

WAM S/1/82

18 February 1936

It is three and a half months since I became Surveyor to the Fabric, and though for the sake of continuity I am attempting a record of all that has been done in the past 12 months, I can only speak from first hand knowledge of the work carried out since the beginning of November 1935. This I propose to take first.

I. I found two principal works in progress, both of internal cleaning and repair, one in the east aisle of the S. transept, the other in the south aisle of Henry VII chapel.

South Transept and St Benedict's chapel

In the S. transept the wall faces are of Reigate stone, the vaulting has Reigate ribs and a filling of chalk with bands of Reigate, and the window mullions are of Reigate, with tracery in the heads of Doulting or some kindred limestone. The pillars of the arcades with their capitals, and the jamb shafts of the windows are of Purbeck marble; the main arches are of Reigate, having in some case their springers and a few of the lower voussoirs of Caen. The Reigate stone, generally speaking, is in excellent condition, showing the original tooling, and where its surface has been at all affected the damage has been due to damp air, in the days before the church was properly warmed. The coating of dirt which has till now disfigured the fine ashlar masonry has had less effect on the Reigate than it has on the marble. This latter, originally polished, is always apt to corrode if the surface is allowed to become rough and dirty, and a good deal of the marble work in the transept has in fact lost its surface from this cause. The purbeck capitals have been run with lead, a common practice with medieval builders, but the large extent of the bed to be covered with molten lead made it expedient to run the metal in at a very high temperature, and as a consequence the neckings of the capitals have split off in places, the damage being made good in plaster. This, and a little surface flaking which may be due to pressure, is the extent of the damage sustained by the fabric, except where the wall arcades have been cut away for the fixing of monuments. Cleaning of stone and re-polishing of marble is practically all that is needed.

The windows retain their original arrangements for glazing, having in the main lights wooden frames to which the glass is secured; the frames being held in place by stout iron bars built into the masonry of the window, and from their position being clearly part of the 13th century work. The ends of the bars, as usual, show some evidence of rust and consequent splitting of the stonework. In the tracery of the heads of the windows the glass is set in a groove in the stonework, a practice which superseded the wooden frames in the latter part of the 13th century. These Westminster windows are earlier examples of the glass groove, by some 20 years, than anything else I know in Britain.

Of the monuments in this aisle and in St Benedict's chapel, the repair of which is being undertaken at the same time, it need only be said that they are in need of the same cleaning of stone and polishing of marble as the walls and pillars. They have lost pieces of ornamental detail from time to time, and there is little prospect that any of these can be recovered; but what remains is being carefully secured.

South aisle Henry VII chapel

The south, or Lady Margaret's, aisle of Henry VII's chapel shows in its fan vaulting the same evidences of initial settlements that were seen in the main vault of the chapel. As a rebuilding to the true lines would have been needless and very costly, the dislocated masonry has been grouted and pointed up as it is, and there is no reason to fear any further movement. For the rest, the stonework of the aisle, where it has not been damaged by the ladders of cleaners, is in wonderful preservation. The lower parts of the east wall were begun in Reigate stone, but all the rest is in Bath stone, full of delicate and sharply cut detail. It has been freed from its encrusted dirt, and the statues of St Katherine and St Margaret, with their canopies above and the frieze of angels below them, are very beautiful in the golden brown stone.

I have attached some photographs to this report showing the effect of cleaning here.

In the window bays some delightful royal beasts, lions, dragons and greyhounds, hitherto practically invisible and black with dirt, can now be seen just below the panelled ceilings of the bays. The glass, with its crowned initials of King Henry in silver stain, is in good repair, but certain quarries which had been set inside out have been replaced in their proper position.

I shall propose to follow up the work here with the cleaning of the monuments. During the cleaning of the roof over Queen Mary of Scots' monument a painted inscription – I S 1614 – came to light, and may have been put there while the tomb was being set up by King James I. The record of the burials in her tomb is very insufficiently set forth by the slab in the floor put in by Dean Stanley, and I propose to have a list prepared and hung on the north side of the chapel abreast of the monument.

The lead roof of this aisle is in a poor state, and will be renewed and re-laid when the weather is more favourable.

Paintings in S Transept

The painting of St Christopher, behind Gay's monument, is being treated by Prof. Tristram, and has not been exposed to its full extent, the upper part of Gay's monument having been removed for the purpose. When Prof. Tristram has finished his treatment and made a copy of the painting the monument will be replaced.

In the next bay of the wall arcade to the north [i.e. east], behind Thomson's [i.e. N Rowe] monument, part of a figure of Christ, on a red ground has been uncovered. He holds a cross-staff, which suggests a Harrowing of Hell or a Resurrection scene, but till more has been revealed the subject is uncertain.[1]

These paintings are of quite exceptional interest, from the style of their drawing, and belong I imagine to the end of the 13th century.

II. Work done before my appointment: ie. from Feb to Nov 1935

[Lofting prepared a draft in February 1936 (WAM S/2/XIX), which Peers did not use, but this includes more detail on treatment of the courtyard wall.]

North transept exterior

The whole of the north front of this transept has been treated down to the ground level. Loose, broken and cracked stones were removed or secured with copper, the decayed joints cut out and made good, and the surface cleaned and whitewashed. No new stone was used in these repairs.

Western towers

The Portland stone parapets and pinnacles of the NW tower have been made good; the rusty iron cramps cut out and the stones renewed where necessary. On the SW tower one pinnacle, which was in worse condition than the rest, has been similarly repaired.

Parapets

The upper parapets all round the church have now been repaired and repointed.

Deanery courtyard

The north wall of the courtyard has had its joints deeply raked out and re-bedded in cement mortar with two inches of lime mortar as pointing in front of the cement. The stonework was cleaned and treated with lime water and the whole subsequently whitewashed. The east wall of College Hall was treated in the same way and the west wall of the Deanery repaired and distempered over the stucco.

College Hall

Internal redecorations were carried out during the summer vacation.[2]

III. Future work

The Wax Effigies

The cleaning and repair of these figures is now finished; most skilfully carried out by the Victoria & Albert Museum; and I am considering whether a better system of lighting them can be devised. The stone steps up to the chamber where they are to be seen – really the chantry chapel of Abbot Islip – are getting dangerously worn by the many visitors, and I am arranging to protect them with oak steps and rubber treads, which will be noiseless and easy to repair. The handrail, now too high, is being lowered to a convenient level.

Bohun tomb

This beautiful little arcaded tomb in St John Baptist's chapel, which is said to have been formerly in the Confessor's chapel, is now partly buried in the wall, and being perfectly preserved on all sides, ought to be brought out and set up where it can be properly seen. There is room in St John's chapel for this, but a base for the Purbeck marble tomb will have to be devised.[3]

St Faith's chapel

When the work in the south aisle of Henry VII's chapel is complete, as it should be in some seven weeks, I should propose to start the cleaning of the walls of St Faith's chapel. This, when the preparations for next year's coronation are begun, will have to be used for the daily services, and it is essential that it should look clean and decent; at present its walls are black with dust.

The Coronation

I look forward with dismay to the prospect that the Abbey staff should necessarily be excluded from the church during the preparations for the coronation. Not only will our work be vexatiously delayed but it will mean the dismissal of an appreciable number of our staff. I cannot see why the work of cleaning the north aisle of Henry VII's chapel (Queen Elizabeth's aisle) or for the matter of that the cleaning of the chapels in the Chevet e.g. St Edmund's and St Nicholas' should not proceed while the Abbey is in the hands of the Office of Works.

Further, it seems to me most undesirable that the Surveyor of the Fabric should be shut out of the Abbey while it is being fitted up for the coronation. I am told that the decorations of the Abbey for the coronation of King Edward VII were supervised by Lord Esher and Mr Micklethwaite, the then Surveyor. This, if it is a fact, makes a valuable precedent which should not be allowed to lapse.

Staff

I should not like my first Report to end without a record of the high opinion I have formed of the capacity of the Abbey staff, under he most competent direction of the Clerk of Works, Mr Bishop.[4] I judge them to be entirely competent to carry out any work which they may be called upon to perform.

Charles Peers

Feb 18 1936

[1] The monuments to John Gay and Nicholas Rowe were not replaced and were moved to the south-east triforium in 1938 to allow the thirteenth-century wall paintings to be seen. Christ and Doubting Thomas were the figures behind Rowe.

[2] His correspondence with A.L.N. Russell, Westminster School architect, on School works in Little Dean's Yard and at 17 Dean's Yard is WAM S/2/VIb.

[3] The tomb of Humphrey and Mary de Bohun (died 1304 and 1305 respectively), children of Humphrey de Bohun, Earl of Hereford was originally in St Nicholas's chapel and moved to St John the Baptist chapel at some date between 1532 and 1600. See an article about opening the Bohun tomb in Peers and Tanner, 'On some recent discoveries in Westminster Abbey', *Archaeologia* vol. XCIII (1949). Negatives taken by R.P. Howgrave Graham of the coffins are in the Library collection.

[4] William Bishop was Clerk of the Works 1928–55. He died in 1962 and his ashes are buried in the west cloister.

41N.   At Chapter on 26 May 1936 Peers's recommendation for a railing and ropes to protect the Lady Chapel altar was approved, as was his design for a credence table there. This was made by Laurence Turner. Correspondence between Peers and Turner on various Abbey works and works elsewhere 1936–45 is WAM S/2/XXI. The Surveyor and others were appointed to a committee to deal with matters arising in connection with the forthcoming coronation of George VI. He received three of the 100 shillings that were offered for the redemption of the Sword at this ceremony – a few of these were distributed among the Abbey clergy and officials. On 8 December he was asked to prepare a rough plan of the finished appearance of the organ that was being restored (WAM S/2/XVI). He was to proceed with enquiries regarding the building of a Canons' garage in College Garden (WAM S/2/XIX(5). On 22 December Chapter asked him to draw up plans. Details of annual expenditure on the fabric is WAM S/2/I.

42.   WAM S/1/83

February 1937

In presenting my report as Surveyor to the Fabric for the period February 1936–
February 1937, I think it proper to preface what I have to say with some reference
to the preparations for the Coronation and its effect on the normal programme
of work. The requirements of the Abbey Church and of the other buildings
in the precincts remain unaffected, and it has seemed to me essential that they
should be attended to in precisely the same way as in ordinary years. This it has
been possible to arrange, and while the Abbey Church has been handed over to
the Commissioners of Works as from January 4th, the Abbey staff have not been
shut out, but have carried on the programme of work on the interior of the
building as contemplated, and will continue to do so. Mr Bishop's appointment
as part time Clerk of the Works on behalf of the Commissioners of Works does
not prevent his fulfilling his usual duties, due provision having been made to
relieve him of certain routine functions which he normally performs.

Henry VII's chapel

In Henry VII's chapel the cleaning and repair of the south or Lady Margaret's
aisle has been continued, the whole of the interior stonework having now been
treated. The three consecration crosses on the south wall are now clearly visible.
The monument of Mary Queen of Scots has, as proposed in my last report,
been thoroughly cleaned, so that the black and white marbles now appear in
their proper contrast, while such colour and gilding as yet remains is once more
visible. The inscriptions on the base of the tomb had lost the white filling of their
letters, and this has been renewed and the lettering on the tablets at either end
of the canopy has been re-gilt. The alabaster unicorns on the top of the tomb
had with one exception lost their horns, these have been replaced in oak, the
material of the one old specimen. A list of all the burials in this tomb has been
fixed to the panelling opposite the monument, and side by side with it a copy
of King James' order for the removal of his mother's body from Peterborough.

The white marble monuments of General Monk and Horace Walpole's
mother [Lady Catherine] have been cleaned and lightly waxed and the paving
of the altar pace, with the records of the royal burials (Charles II, William and
Mary, Anne and Prince George of Denmark) in the vault below, have been
similarly treated.

The cutting in half of the canopies of the stalls, to provide material for the
new stalls set up at the installation of the Order of the Bath by George I, left
their mutilated backs exposed in three bays of the south aisle. I have designed
and set up an openwork oak screen on the top of the old panelling in one of the
three bays to mask these mutilations, and propose to treat the other two bays in
the same way.

In the north or Queen Elizabeth's aisle a start has been made with cleaning
and repair. The stonework here is even dirtier than that in the south aisle was,

because of the stove in the vestry at the west end of the aisle. This though now out of use and to be removed, has coated everything with a crust of soot, which it is to be hoped can be removed without leaving any discolouration behind it.

The dislocation of the vaulting, like that of the south aisle, is much in evidence, but more severe than the rest, some of the stonework having dropped as much as four inches, while the fan vaulting springing from the pendants is nearly falling outwards on the north side. What has happened is that the thrust of the high vault transmitted by the flying buttresses has pushed out the top of the north wall of the aisle, and everything suggests that this was an initial settlement. No serious repair has ever been made, but the worst cracks and splintering have been filled in with rough plaster and no signs of subsequent movement are to be seen. The date 1817 on the stonework records such a repair. What has now to be done is to run the open joints with cement from the back of the vault, and to secure loose stonework where necessary. A few of the most marked dislocations can be modified by resetting, but no attempt to restore the original profile need be made.

For purposes of record I add that in the main chapel a credence, at the east end of the southern stalls, and a set of wrought iron standards round the altar, have been made and set up from my designs.

St Benedict's chapel and the South Transept

The whole of the east aisle of the south transept, with its vaulting, except the southern bay, has been finished, together with St Benedict's chapel at the junction of the transept with the south ambulatory.

The process of cleaning and repair was fully detailed in my last report and need not be again described. In the course of the work all monuments set against the walls have been dealt with in detail, loose parts being securely fixed, marble and alabaster cleaned and polished, and colour and gilding revealed but in no case renewed. The monument of Frances, Countess of Hertford against the east wall of the chapel conceals a good deal of medieval painting, with fleurs de lys on a red ground like those in the newly uncovered painting of the Incredulity of St Thomas, and doubtless of the same date. One of the carved spandrils of the wall arcade on the south wall has a pattern of green leaves and red berries, and the Purbeck marble string above it has also been coloured. The original piscina recess now contains the kneeling figure of Dean Goodman, 1601: the jambs and back are of the 13th century, but the arch of the 17th, with the arms of Westminster impaling Goodman in the head. At the back of the recess, almost hidden by the effigy, is a purbeck marble frame, rebated for a shutter, through which by a splayed opening through the wall anyone standing outside the chapel could see the altar of St Benedict. The blocked doorway immediately to the west of the piscina is clearly associated with this, and there must have been a small external chamber here in the angle between the chapel and the transept. It looks as if this was the living place of one of the Westminster anchorites.[1]

In the east aisle of the transept a patch of old colour shows above Cowley's monument, but the design is not to be identified.

Chaucer's tomb is a second hand monument of Purbeck marble c.1500, set up by Nicholas Brigham in 1556. In its original place, wherever that may have been, it stood against a south wall, probably in the south east angle of a chancel or chapel, and on its altar tomb were three metal shields of arms, the rivet holes for which still exist, but the Chaucer arms have been cut on the marble backings. The marble panel at the back is of poor quality, and much perished by damp. The lettering on it has been picked out in black and the two Chaucer shields coloured.

In the south end of the transept the painting uncovered by Dr Tristram has turned out to represent the Incredulity of St Thomas and is more perfect than that of St Christopher. It is of admirable quality and very well preserved. It was hidden by the monument of Nicholas Rowe, Poet Laureate (d.1718), with a bust by Rysbrack and an inscription by Pope. Some other place must be found for this as well as for Gay's monument in the arcade which contains the St Christopher painting. Nothing can of course be done till after the Coronation.

St Faith's Chapel

This chapel has been cleaned throughout, its ventilation improved, and the bosses of its vault coloured. Cleaning and the better light have helped to emphasize the artistry of the notable collection of corbels which carry the springers of the vault, dating from the middle of the 13th century.[2]

Bohun tomb in St Edmund's chapel [actually St John the Baptist's chapel]

This tomb, as proposed, has been removed from the wall in which it was half buried, and has been set on a marble base. It contains two small wooden coffins, which may be assumed to be those of the two grandchildren of Edward I, John [actually Humphrey] and Mary de Bohun, who died in 1304. The marble tomb itself is, however, some forty years older than this.

The Wax Effigies

A new system of lighting with strip lights on the cases has been installed and has done away with the reflections on the glass.

In connection with the preparations for the coronation I have carried out two pieces of work.

1. The Lantern over the crossing has been cleaned and re-coloured, and the glass in the eight windows of the lantern has had its backgrounds modified to improve the lighting. The structure of the lantern is due to Wren, who ceiled it with a plaster vault. This was destroyed in the fire of 1803 and the present plaster vault is dated 1804 on the central boss. It is constructed on a system of centreing, suspended from the tiebeams of the roof. I opened the roof, to which

there is no direct access, to examine the timbers, and found them, as far as could be ascertained, in sound condition. The glass windows were given by Lord John Thynne[3] in 1859 and at the same time Scott added certain Gothic details to Wren's windows and doorways. Access to the leads is by a stair at the s.e. angle of the lantern. This stair is open to the weather at the top, and I am fitting a wooden hatch, which will not show above the parapet, at the stair head to protect it.

2. The west doorway of the nave and its flanking niches, that is, so much as will be seen in the Annexe to be constructed at the west end of the church, has been cleaned, and it appears that much of the stonework is original, of the time of Abbot Litlyngton. It is in very fair condition, though a good deal renewed in Doulting stone by Scott about 1871. The vault of the doorway and its panelled splays are in Reigate stone, much decayed and showing the remains of a coat of whitewash, which had been quite useless as a preservative. This, with the loose stone, has been brushed off and its further treatment left till after the Coronation. The yellow stone of Litlyngton's work is being repaired where necessary in synthetic stone.

The north end of the Jerusalem Chamber, abutting on the west front of the church, is largely built of Kentish rag, with parapets of Chilmark stone added by Scott in 1870. The whole is in fair condition, and has now been cleaned and repointed, and the parapets repaired in synthetic stone.

This completes the record of what has been done in the past twelve months, and the works immediately in view will be the treatment of the north aisle of Henry VII's chapel and of the chapel of St Edmund and St Thomas, in the south ambulatory, in continuation of the work on St Benedict's chapel. These works can continue throughout the preparations for the Coronation, our men entering the church by the door in the south aisle of Henry VII's chapel.

The remodelling of Pearson's organ cases – which it must be remembered were set up as a memorial to Purcell[4] – can proceed as soon as convenient, and it will be possible to retain the greater part of Pearson's woodwork. The arrangement of the new pipes will, however, make certain alterations necessary. The new console on the screen is being cased in oak panelling to my design.

The memorial to King George V

Plans for this are as yet far from being settled, but whatever is done cannot fail to affect the Abbey.[5] The rather untidy little masons' yard along the south side of Henry VII's chapel, which is all the storage room we possess, must almost certainly be cleared away, but there is no other spot available. What we ought to have is the space now occupied by the School gymnasium, and if alternative accommodation for this could be provided on the west side of Little Dean's Yard, at the back of the house lately occupied by Canon Carnegie, this very urgent matter might find a reasonable solution. It must be faced sooner or later, and surely the sooner the better. It is not for me, in the limits of this report, to enlarge on a matter which must always be in the minds of the Abbey authorities.

[1]   See 'On some recent discoveries …' by Peers and Tanner regarding the Anchorite's cell.
[2]   St Faith's chapel plans WAM SD/1/61–63.
[3]   Thynne was Sub-Dean of the Abbey. The stained glass was damaged by blast in late 1940 and the whole vault destroyed by a firebomb in May 1941. For the history of this area, see *The Lantern Tower of Westminster Abbey 1060–2010* by Warwick Rodwell (Oxford: Oxbow Books, 2010).
[4]   The Henry Purcell musical commemoration was held in 1895 to raise funds for a suitable organ casing, designed by the Surveyor J.L. Pearson.
[5]   Placed in the open space near the Chapter House and Henry VII's chapel, facing Parliament. The gym area remained with the School.

43.   WAM S/1/84

Estimates for the year 1937–8

In submitting the estimates for 1937–8 I wish at the risk, in the first place, of repeating myself, and in the second of forestalling my next year's Report, to lay stress on one matter concerning the fabric. Both this year and last certain additional sums have been available, for what is to my mind the most important item in the estimate, that is the internal cleaning of the Abbey church. In 1936–7 a sum of £700 remained over from the special fund for the treatment of the interior of Henry VII's chapel, and in 1937–8 the occupation of the Abbey church by the Office of Works has relieved us of much of the annual cost of heating and lighting, allowing me to transfer to internal cleaning an appreciable sum from these items. But ever with these aids the work proceeds slowly, and its importance has been greatly emphasized by the Coronation. As I sat looking at the splendid spectacle, the contrast between the brilliant colours and the grimy masonry was only too evident. However the chords of the new organ brought down from aloft, on to the heads of the distinguished company, an appreciable amount of clotted dust, cobwebs and soot. I should like to follow up the work now proceeding in St Edmund's chapel with the scaffolding and cleaning of the main span of the church from the eastern arch of the crossing to the apse.

The fabric fund, as stated to me on my appointment, amounts to some £13,500 that is £9,000 from the Ryle[1] fund, and £4,500 from other sources. My estimates for the present year and for last year have been a little under £10,000, the various items, some 25 in number, being pretty closely calculated by Mr Bishop from his expert knowledge of the requirements. No material reduction in any item is practicable, and more money is needed, in the absence of windfalls on which I cannot calculate. I should like to frame the estimates for the coming year on a basis of £11,500, in order to make it possible to get a substantial amount of work done. It must be remembered that once done there will be no need to consider a renewal of this work for at least a century, so that it cannot be classed as recurring expenditure.

[1]   This fabric restoration fund was launched by Dean Ryle in 1920.

44.   WAM S/1/85

Report of the Surveyor to the Fabric

February 1938

This report includes the period taken up by the preparation for the coronation of HM King George VI, the coronation itself, and the removal of the coronation seats and fittings. It should be placed on record that all the necessary work was done with the greatest care and skill by the Office of Works, and when the Abbey church was returned to the Chapter in September it was possible to certify that no damage whatever had been done to anything within its walls or to the structure itself.

However, as recorded in my last year's report, the progress of our work on the interior of the church was in no way hindered by the preparations for the coronation, but followed the lines already contemplated.

Henry VII's chapel

The cleaning and repair of the north or Queen Elizabeth's aisle, begun last season, is now finished. All stonework is cleaned, including that of the vestry, from which a thick coating of soot had been successfully removed. The vaulting has been made secure, as proposed, and may be considered sound. The glass in the west window of the aisle, which was in part loose and incomplete, is now in good order. During the cleaning of the Savile monument some of the original openwork cresting of the wood panelling at the back of the stalls was discovered. This is the only remaining piece and it has been repaired, without any addition of new work, and set up in its correct place in the next bay to the east, where it can be seen. Queen Elizabeth's monument has been cleaned and the loose portions re-fixed. The black marble columns have been re-polished and the inscriptions on the upper panels re-gilt. Those on the base of the tomb, which are in white paint on black marble, and were in clumsy lettering, certainly not original, have been renewed in good letters, following the old setting out in every particular.

With regard to the vestry in this aisle, now that the obsolete heating apparatus which stood here has been removed, I would suggest to the Chapter that there is here a place which, while not sufficient to take all the vestments and hangings now in the presses in the north transept, could house a considerable proportion of them. Furthermore, if certain difficulties of access can be overcome, the turret stair leading from this vestry might be made to communicate with the space above the vestibule of Henry VII's chapel, where an ample room,[1] quite invisible from outside, could be constructed to serve as additional to the existing sacristy in the crypt of the Chapter House.

The chapel of St Edmund and St Thomas

The work in St Benedict's chapel being finished, this chapel, next to it on the east, has been taken in hand. It was found that Scott's shellac treatment, considered by him as a stone preservative, had been most thoroughly applied here not only to all wall surfaces, but also to the vault and the monuments, and this added to modern application of wax over the old dirt had given a dark and gloomy appearance to the chapel, in spite of its large windows of clear glass. The shellac was difficult to remove, but when this was done the original 13th century tool marks appeared on the Reigate stone masonry, showing that it was in no need of any protective covering.

The Purbeck marble shafts have been cleaned and polished, as in St Benedict's chapel, and the monuments, of which this chapel has a particularly splendid series, have been taken in detail, and are nearly all finished. Minute descriptions of the work on each monument might prove tedious, and a few notes must suffice. The gilt and enamelled copper effigy of William de Valence, 1296, half brother to Henry III, having been freed of its coverings of dirt, shellac and wax, has revealed a good deal of its gilding – apparently mercury gilding – and where this had been worn off the exposed copper is being treated with colourless lacquer as a protection. The copper plating which covered all the oak chest on which the effigy lies is now only represented by a few small patches, and the thirty enamelled figures of "weepers" with the arcades in which they stood, and the inscription running round the upper edge of the chest, have long since been torn off and taken away. Only a few enamelled shields on the lower edge of the chest, preserved because they were on the side towards the screen which closes in the chapel, are still in place. These I propose to fix in a corresponding position on the south side of the tomb, where they can be seen, but under proper protection from the public. The alabaster effigy of John of Eltham, 1337, second son of Edward II, lost its splendid canopy in the 18th century, but is otherwise well preserved, though showing no traces of colour. The alabaster figures of "weepers" – here shown as kings and queens – on the base of the tomb are set against a dark background which proves on examination to be made of thin slabs of dark shale, perhaps an economical substitute for black marble. On the monument of Sir Richard Pecksall, 1571, the design and sculpture of which are of very notable excellence, the cleaning of the columns and panels has shown them to be of a greenish marble resembling Purbeck, and probably from Bethersden.

The masonry backing to the wall monuments of Katherine Knollys, 1568, and Jane Seymour, 1560, in the s.e. bay of the chapel, proved to consist of pieces of the 13th century wall arcades destroyed when these monuments were put up. A good deal of colour remained on these fragments and they have been taken to the museum for preservation.

The Confessor's Chapel [*and clerestory windows*]

A start has been made with the cleaning of the high vault, the clearstory and the triforium over this chapel. The gilding and painting on the vault were part of Wren's work in the early years of the 18th century, and it is instructive to notice that cracks in the pointings at the junction of vault and walls show that since

Wren's time the side walls here have gone out some 1.5 inches on each side. This I imagine to be due to the decay of the flying buttresses, which have since been repaired – no signs of recent movement being visible. Scott's shellac treatment was in evidence and is being removed and the lightening of the vault cells and wall surface will I hope greatly enhance the general effect.

[*Apse windows*]

The three eastern windows of the clearstory are filled with old glass collected from different parts of the church in 1706 – the glazier's name Thomas Drew, and the date, are scratched on the shield of St Peter in the head of the central window. Many fragments of inscriptions, and bits of 13th and 14th century grisaille, are glazed in with the rest, and the best of these, together with some pieces of 13th century crowns on yellow glass and a few little pieces of 13th century drapery, I have taken out, putting clouded glass in their place, for preservation in the museum where they can be examined. In each of the six main lights is a large standing figure, mainly of early 16th century date: the two figures in the middle window are of the Confessor and the pilgrim, with 17th century heads replacing the originals. Over each figure is an ogee canopy enclosing a shield, three of which are of Henry III's date, having the arms of England, Provence and Cornwall. Shields with these arms are recorded to have been in the windows of St Edmund's chapel in 1686, and it may well be that Wren moved them thence to the clearstory. They are being taken down, modern substitutes being put in their place, and they will be glazed into the white glass in St Edmund's chapel, where they can be clearly seen, being the oldest surviving heraldic glass in England. At the same time the quarterly shield of England in the tracery of the n.e. clearstory window is being taken down and replaced by a copy. The leopards in the third quarter of the shield are of Henry III's time, cut down to fit their place, the rest of the shield being of Tudor date.[2]

The south transept

In my last report I referred to the need to find places for two monuments in Poets' Corner, which have been dismantled to reveal the paintings in the wall arcades behind them. Clearly they cannot be put back in front of these paintings, and it seems to me that the only place in which they can be set up is the triforium, where there is ample space. The two monuments are those of Gay and Nicholas Rowe, and if they are placed at the south end of the east triforium of the south transept they will be as near as possible to their original place and can be well seen by anyone who climbs the stair in the s.e. angle of the transept.

The same solution suggests itself in the case of the monument of Esther de la Tour de Gouvernet, formerly in the north ambulatory, and partly overlapping the tomb of Queen Eleanor of Castile. A place has to be found for it and it is out of the question that it should once more disfigure the Queen's tomb. It would be easy to find a place for it in the triforium.[3]

Organ cases and pulpitum

The replacement and adaptation of Pearson's organ cases must be taken in hand at no distant date, but what is equally important in this connexion is the rearrangement of the loft over the entrance to the choir, to accommodate in the first place the choir, when it is convenient that they should sit there, and in the second place the music books for which Dr Bullock has no room. I shall hope to submit a scheme for this, including a second staircase of access on the north side, balancing that on the south, so that the choir walking in procession can divide right and left and reach the loft with no difficulty or delay.

In this connexion it may be recorded that a list of all the organists from 1560 to the present day is being put on the new organ console.

External masonry

The cleaning and repointing of the west wall of the Jerusalem Chamber has been continued, and the west wall of the College Hall has been similarly treated. The rest of this elevation, up to the late Chapter Clerk's house, is now to be taken in hand.

The s.w. tower has been scaffolded for examination and a part of its Portland facings, beginning from below the cornice under the round windows, has been treated. The cutting out of iron cramps, which have rusted and split the stone, and the cleaning off of the accumulations of soot, are the matters here dealt with; the problem of stone decay, so urgent elsewhere in the church, does not arise here, though there is some considerable weathering.

Work in prospect

The above report gives sufficient indication of the progress of work and of what it is hoped to do in the course of this season. On finishing the cleaning of the high vaults and triforium over St Edward's chapel, I should propose to continue this work on the two bays of the presbytery, up to the eastern arch of the crossing: this work might start in the autumn when outside repairs become impossible.

The treatment of the eastern cloister door, on which I have been asked to report, has been considered, and I am submitting a report and design. A vestibule to this door in view of the narrowness of the south aisle, needs careful planning, but I shall devise a scheme as well as I can.[4]

11th March 1938.

[1]   Chapter decided against a room here on 24 May 1938.
[2]   This roundel is now in Muniment Room. The small items of glass removed no longer exist in the Museum collection and may have been re-used in various composite windows, with war-damaged glass, in the 1950s.
[3]   The monument to Esther Gouvernet, Lady Eland, by sculptor Nadauld, is in two sections, the relief and the inscription panel. The inscription had been placed in St John the Baptist's chapel, over the inner doorway of the chapel of the Pew. Both were moved to the triforium.

⁴ His designs for ironwork on this door (and the Islip chapel door) are WAM(P) 807–9. For
   the vault and floor plan see SD/1/57–59. The report is WAM S/2/XIV (3).

44N.   On 12 April 1938 Peers was asked to submit designs for wooden candlesticks in St Faith's chapel. On 22 November he was asked to prepare a scale
model for removeable Communion rails (which was approved on 14 February
1939). On 13 December it was decided not to raise up the gravestone of the
Unknown Warrior to help protect it or provide a lamp there (WAM S/2/XIV
and XXIV). On 7 March 1938 he conducted Queen Mary and Princesses
Elizabeth and Margaret on a tour of the Abbey (recorded in the journal kept by
Lawrence E. Tanner, Keeper of the Muniments. This is an unpublished volume
in the Abbey Library.)

45.   WAM S/1/86

Report of the Surveyor to the Fabric

February 1939

This report, as being one of a series, is intended to be read in sequence with
my former reports, and its arrangement is dictated by them as far as they are
relevant to present work.

Henry VII's chapel, north aisle

The suggestion to make use of the vestry at the west end of this aisle has been
followed, and it has been fitted with drawers and hanging places, though not to
its full capacity.

The chapel of St Edmund and St Thomas

The work here is finished and the chapel reopened to the public. Every part of
the masonry and all the monuments have been dealt with in turn, as described
in last year's report, and the chapel, being larger and better lighted than
St Benedict's chapel, may be taken as an example of the effect which the present
treatment aims to produce. All surfaces were cleaned, whether gilded, painted
or plain, and while the process of cleaning has revealed many traces of colour
hitherto unseen, no attempt to restore lost colour or gilding has been made. But
I hope that this work will chiefly serve as a demonstration of the real value of
coloured marbles, which depend on a polished surface for their effect, and give
to a building life and splendour which can be obtained in no other way.

     In certain cases, as on the Talbot and Pecksall monuments, inscriptions have
been re gilt for the sake of legibility, and the brass of Bishop Ferne of Chester,
1662, which was being worn away by the feet of visitors, has been raised on a
low marble base, as was previously done to Archbishop Waldeby's brass, for the
sake of protection.

The three shields of 13th century glass, removed from the clearstory windows of the apse above the Confessor's chapel where they were placed by Wren about 1706, have been glazed into the south east window here, one over the other, and can now be seen at close range, as their unique interest deserves. Shields of this sort formed part of the original glazing of St Edmund's chapel, and were still there in 1686, and I should like to believe that these are the identical specimens, but of course that can never be proved. The shield of England is perfect, but the other two had been altered, probably in 1706, the white ground of Cornwall being replaced by blue glass, and the pallets of Provence wrongly leaded up, giving a counterchanged arrangement. These two shields have been correctly repaired by Mr Kruger Gray,[1] the blue glass in Cornwall being replaced by white, and the pallets of Provence put in their proper order.

The Confessor's chapel

Work here is completed from the crown of the vaulting down to the Purbeck marble string at the base of the triforium, and a beginning has thus been made to a treatment which I hope my now be regularly followed through the transepts into the nave. The contrast with the two western bays of the presbytery, which still bear the grime of many years, is sufficiently instructive; the value of the marble shafts in emphasizing the soaring lines of the building is now apparent, and the gilding on the vault ribs – a renewal by Wren of older gold – carries the eye upwards as it was meant to do. It is reasonable to suppose that the diaper patterns in the triforium must have been painted, but there is not a trace of colour now; all stonework here was covered with Scott's shellac 'preservative', and this may have accounted for any lingering evidences. In the triforium the labels of the arches are stopped on dripstones carved as human heads of admirable style; but it is curious to note how some of these have been replaced by small blocks of chalk, while one has cracked off and the broken stone has been clumsily recut into a parody of the 13th century detail. There may also be seen in the bay over the altar screen the scars made by the rood beam which spanned the church here at triforium level, carrying two seraphs in addition to the rood with Our Lady and St John, as the Islip Roll[2] shows.

[Apse windows]

The glass in the clearstory windows is dealt with in my last year's report, but it may be recorded that ventilating panes have been set in the head of each window, where previously no outlet for air existed. I should like to add that the stuffiness often complained of may be considered due in an appreciable degree to the dirtiness of the wall surfaces, and will be lessened as the cleaning proceeds. In a small way St Faith's chapel is a good example of this; it is much fresher since its cleaning a few years ago.

The south transept

The monuments of Gay and Rowe have been removed to the east triforium of the transept and set up against the south wall, their weight being taken by steel joists, so that the vaulting of the east aisle of the transept bears no part of the load. The wall in this bay of the triforium are being cleaned, and it is obvious that if this part of the church were to be properly cared for, it might be made most attractive, though never, I fear, very easy of access.

I am considering a scheme for the clearing and fitting up of the whole triforium east of the crossing, and among other things panelled wood ceilings below the rough common rafters seem to suggest themselves; I should like to try the effect in the bay now cleaned, when circumstances permit.

[Dr Johnson bust]

A bust of Dr Johnson by Nollekens having been given to the Abbey, I have designed a white marble panel to provide a setting for it, and this will shortly be placed on the screen wall near Johnson's grave at the south end of the transept, the monument of Mrs Pritchard[3] being moved to the triforium to make room for it.

[Wall paintings]

In cleaning the wall against which the lower part of Gay's monument stood, an inscription has been revealed below the painting of St Christopher;[4] it is the couplet commonly used with this subject.

SANCTI XPOFORI SPECIEM QUICUMQUE TUETUR
ILLA NEMPE DIE NULLO LANGUORE TENETUR

The stone benching cut away for the Rowe and Gay monuments has been made good and a panel set in the seating in each bay to record the removal of the two monuments to the triforium in November 1938.

[Edmund Spenser grave search]

In connexion with the south transept a reference is here made to the search for Spenser's grave,[5] on which I have already made a report to Chapter. Further investigation has shown that the solid foundation exists over the whole area of the two southern bays of the aisle, and with the help of a plan made by Mr Wright, preserved among the Abbey papers [muniments], it is possible to lay down a complete scheme of the burials in this part of the church. It remains to add that the bones removed in the process of clearing the grave of Matthew Prior (?) have been put in a wooden box, with a brass plate to serve as identification, and buried over the place whence they were taken.

Other works

The new doors for the eastern cloister doorway are now finished and it is hoped to put them in position shortly.

I have prepared a design for new movable altar rails, a model of which has been set up and approved, but its execution must wait till funds are available.

I have also prepared sketches for the fitting up of Abbot Islip's tomb chapel,[6] and I am getting estimates for the details of this work, which will include an altar with frontal and dossal, gilt wood cresting and heraldry on the east wall over it, silver altar cross and candlesticks, a new door to the chapel, lighting pendants and a carpet. The stonework of the chapel will have to be cleaned, and the Hatton[7] monument removed to the east triforium of the north transept, where a suitable place exists.

To commemorate the fourth centenary of William Tyndale, and his translation of the Bible, an alabaster marble slab has been set up in the south aisle of the nave [i.e. choir aisle] on the back of the wall enclosing the choir; this entailed moving the tablet of Sir Thomas Trigge and refixing it some feet higher on the wall.

Lists of consecrations [of bishops] in the Abbey are being put up in the choir entry [under organ loft] on the south side, the work being done by Miss Styles: it is intended to put similar lists of Abbots and Deans of Westminster on the north side of the entry.

A set of seven banners of the Mother Country and the Dominions[8] has been hung in the Warrior's Chapel.

The portrait of King Richard the Second[9] has been set up against the north east pier of the south west tower, with excellent effect; and its temporary supports will now be replaced by permanent fittings.

In the matter of the organ cases and the pulpitum, matters remain as in my last year's report, to which I should like to refer. Much of the woodwork of the organ case is in Mr Laurence Turner's workshops, and is insured by him with other contents of his premises.[10]

Work in prospect

The work in the upper stories of the apse being now finished, it is proposed to undertake the treatment of St Nicholas' chapel, on the same lines as the chapel of St Edmund and St Thomas. This, with what is necessary in the Islip chapel, will be the substantive internal work for the coming year.

Outside work

Surface repairs to the buttresses on the north side of the clearstory of the apse have been in progress, synthetic stone (or new stone where necessary) having been employed. A series of experiments has also been made by the officers of the Building Research Station on the cleaning of our external stonework by means of a water spray. Such work has been carried out recently on the

Admiralty screen in Whitehall, and at Buckingham Palace, and has proved quite effective on limestones, but not on sandstones. It involves the use of a great deal of water and appreciable pressure. Applied to the exterior of the north aisle of the nave, just west of the north transept, from the string below the windowsills downwards, it cleaned the stone very successfully, but whether it has any good effect on checking stone decay it is not possible to say.

On the south west tower the cutting out of iron cramps and repair of the fractures caused by them in the Portland stone facing has proceeded.

The work on the west wall of the College Hall has been continued and carried on southwards up to the north wall of no. 21 Dean's Yard.

The treatment of the vaulting and the inner walls of the cloister is no new question, but sooner or later – better sooner than later – it must be seriously considered. Our records show that stone decay had made very extensive progress in the last hundred years, and that no treatment hitherto adopted has been effective to stay its ravages. Scott used his shellac 'preservative' on the Chapter House doorway, with disastrous results, and since then the whitewash school have been active. I think that I am correct in saying that Mr Micklethwaite began this: at any rate I remember going round with him to see his results, and among other places to the Blackstole Tower,[11] where he had whitewashed the ribbed vault of the entry, the Reigate stone ribs of which were crumbling away. He had protected them from the London atmosphere by a thick coat of whitewash, in theory a perfectly sound remedy, but unfortunately not a sufficient one. The decayed stone continued to crumble behind the wash and today neither stone nor whitewash remains, the ribs having decayed back to the line of the filling of the vault.

This is what is happening in the cloister. In the south walk, which was the first to be treated thus, the decay is everywhere to be seen: in the north walk, the next to be done, it is obvious, and in the west walk, the last to be limewashed, an examination shows that decay is proceeding steadily behind the yellow covering. The fact is that since no cure for stone decay is yet devised, the only thing to do is to begin by cutting away all decaying material; no covering up is of any use. When the cutting away is done, it remains to decide whether to leave the broken lines as they are, or to bring back the original profile, either in a new stone or in plastic stone. The latter is I consider preferable, as entailing less cutting away of old material, and not giving a new and hard appearance to the repaired work.

All the window tracery in the cloister is now new, more's the pity; this may have been necessary, but nobody today can judge of that; and since there is no necessity to use new stone in the vaulting ribs at present, I am in favour of making plastic repairs. Decay having gone very far, there will alas be plenty to do, but in the next few years I think it ought to be undertaken.

Charles Peers, 20 February 1939

<hr>

[1]   He etched his name and date in the glass. See Peers and Tanner, 'On some recent discoveries …'.

2 The mortuary roll of Abbot John Islip 1532 is preserved in the Abbey Muniments. The roll was flattened out ready for display in the new Queen's Jubilee Galleries in the triforium of the Abbey, 2018.

3 Hannah Pritchard was a famous actress who died in 1768. Her tablet is by Richard Hayward.

4 For details of the upper and lower inscriptions associated with this painting, see Peers and Tanner 'On some recent discoveries …'.

5 This took place on 24 October 1938 but nothing conclusive came of it. Negatives of the items found, taken by R.P. Howgrave Graham, are in the Library collection.

6 See WAM 62101–28 and Peers papers WAM S/2/II.

7 The large monument to Sir Christopher Hatton (died 1619) took up the place of the original altar. A tablet to his wife Alice was on the wall to the south of this, which was also moved to the triforium.

8 The flags of St George for England, Canada, New Zealand, South Africa, Australia, India and Newfoundland. See Peers files WAM S/2/XXIV. These were later joined by the Union Flag or Padre's flag used at the burial of the Unknown Warrior, which originally hung over that grave.

9 The portrait was originally hung in the Quire. Later it was moved to the Jerusalem Chamber (within the Deanery) and, before being moved to the nave, had been displayed on the south side of the Sacrarium. Correspondence with Sir Kenneth Clark of the National Gallery in 1944 about cleaning away modern re-painting is WAM S/2/VII (10).

10 At Chapter on 28 May 1941 a letter was read about the storage of the cases when he asked to be relieved of the responsibility. It was agreed he should retain them and be paid his expenses. See the March 1942 report for removal of woodwork to the Bishop's Manor, Southwell.

11 On the east side of Dean's Yard just to the south of no. 20. Originally part of the monastic cellarer's department it was where black bread (low-grade loaves) was distributed to servants of the church. The spiral stair within the tower still remains.

45N.   At Chapter on 28 March 1939 (and 23 May and 4 July) discussions took place about estimates for cleaning work and how they should be adhered to by the Surveyor. Also at the March meeting work on the new bomb-proof shelter for 160 persons in College Garden was discussed and that the structure should meet with Peers's satisfaction. On 25 April his suggestion to make a columbarium, for burials of ashes, under the floor of the Islip chapel was approved in principle. This vault is still in use.

46.   WAM S/1/87

Report of the Surveyor to the Fabric

February 1940

In this year's report space must regretfully be given to an account of the measures taken to protect from possible enemy action the most precious of the Abbey's possessions.[1]

What has been done differs in some respects from the measure adopted in 1914–18, which are recorded in the acts of a Chapter held on Tuesday February 4th 1919. Without going into detail it may be sufficient to recall that everything then moved from the church was stored in the crypt of the Chapter House except the effigy of Queen Eleanor and the wooden superstructure of the Confessor's tomb, which were put in the Norman Undercroft.

On the present occasion the practical impossibility of providing within the Abbey precincts bombproof shelters large enough to take everything that we wished to place in safety, led to the adoption of an expedient which had long been in preparation, as a result of experience gained in the war of 1914–18: namely the removal from London (or any other presumable danger points) of all such objects as could safely be transported to places which, by reason of their remoteness or lack of military importance, were unlikely to be attacked.

A list of such places, and their allocation to various bodies, had been drawn up, and to the British Museum there had been assigned (inter alia) Boughton House in Northamptonshire, placed at the disposal of the Government by its owner the Duke of Buccleuch. The authorities of the Museum readily granted the request of the Chapter to be allowed space at Boughton House for such of their possessions as could conveniently be removed thither, and by the end of May 1939 all arrangements for transport had been worked out and agreed upon. When the outbreak of war became imminent action was taken and on August 30th and 31st there were despatched to Boughton the following:

The effigies of:

  Bronze: King Henry III
  Queen Eleanor of Castile
  King Edward III
  King Richard II and his Queen
  Lady Margaret Beaufort

  Copper: William de Valence

  Wood: King Henry V
  The portrait of Richard II
  The 13th century Retable
  The 13th century glass shields of England, Provence and Cornwall.
  The Italian painting from the altar in Henry VII's chapel [by Vivarini]
  Painting of the Order of the Bath (from Deanery) [by Canaletto]

In addition a number of metal boxes containing documents from the Abbey muniment room and library were sent to Boughton.

In the case of the Coronation Chair and the copy of it made for the coronation of Queen Mary II in 1688 [1689 coronation] the Chair was sent to Winchester and the copy to Gloucester (August 25th). The Stone of Scone was taken from the Coronation Chair and put in a place of safety.[2]

It remained to protect, as far as that could be done by means of sandbags and timber, such things as it was considered inexpedient or impossible to remove from the Abbey Church:

  The Confessor's Shrine and wooden upper part
  Queen Philippa, effigy and tomb

King Henry VII and his queen, effigies and tomb[3]
Queen Elizabeth, effigy
Queen Mary of Scots, effigy
John of Eltham, effigy and tomb
Edmund Crouchback, ditto
Aymer de Valence, ditto
Aveline of Lancaster, ditto
King Henry III's tomb
King Edward III's tomb
Richard II's tomb
Queen Eleanor of Castile's tomb

The sedilia on the s. side of the High Altar and the paintings of St Christopher and the Incredulity of St Thomas in the s. transept were also cased in with boarding.

The mosaic floor in front of the High Altar was covered with 3 inch planking, and the brasses of Eleanor de Bohun and Archbishop Waldeby in St Edmund's chapel were similarly protected.

It was decided to leave the glass in the clerestory windows of the apse in position but to make wooden framings, which could be fitted to the outside of the windows: the same was done for the windows in the west walls of the n.w. and s.w. towers of the nave.

In the crypt of the Chapter House there were stored:

(5) bronze canopies from the tombs [effigies] of Eleanor of Castile, Edward III, Richard II and his queen and Lady Margaret Beaufort.
(3) bronze cushions from the tombs of Edward III and Richard II and his queen.
Six bronze angels from the tomb of Henry VII.
Roundel bust of Sir Thomas Lovell.
Sword and shield (Edward III) from Confessor's chapel.
Helm, shield and saddle from Henry V's tomb.
Panel of 13th century grisaille glass from w. aisle of n. transept.
13th century glass from Jerusalem Chamber, n window.
Glass from s. window of Jericho Parlour.
Old glass, various dates, taken in 1938 from windows of the apse and kept in Library.

and of modern and recent dates:

Two parcels of Ackermann books [R. Ackermann's two-volume history of the Abbey (1812) presented by George V and Queen Mary].
Crucifix and two shields from Confessor's Shrine.
Mantles and crests from stalls, Henry VII's chapel.
Three tapestries from n. aisle, Henry VII's chapel [Henry III, St Edward & Pilgrim]
Various copies of carvings etc. by Prof. Tristram.

In the Pyx Chapel were stored:

The oak chest from William de Valence's tomb.
The banners from the stalls, Henry VII's chapel
Ackermann case and table [used to display the volumes mentioned above].
The helms from the stalls in Henry VII's chapel are placed within the sandbag protections round Henry VII's tomb.

External protection by sandbags:

W. windows, Jerusalem Chamber
N. window, Islip chapel
Windows of crypt of Chapter House
Rising main, n. chapels of ambulatory
East doorway, n. transept
Wall between gymnasium and Undercroft.

Air Raid Protection etc.

In the Infirmary Garden, against the 14th century east wall, a concrete shelter has been built, and fitted with light, water and air conditioning plant. It is so constructed that in future it may serve as a garage.[4]

In the Undercroft a first aid post has been installed, with sanitation, hot water supply, emergency lighting, heating and ventilation.

The Pyx Chapel has been taken over from the HM Office of Works for the duration of the war, and connected with the first aid post by a doorway through the blocking wall on the south side. It is to serve as a Gas Air Lock, and dressing and equipment room for firemen.

Fire Fighting Organisation

The Fire Fighting and Protective System is carried out by the Surveyor's staff. The staff is divided into three sections ie. Day section (who carry on with their normal duties); Evening section; and the Night section. The two last mentioned sections change over at the end of each week. The hours of duty are as follows:

> Day section 7.30am to 4.30 pm
> Evening section: 4.30pm to 11 pm
> Night section 11 pm to 7.30 am

Every member of the staff has gone through a course of fire drill. After the Abbey is closed, the evening and night sections go through periodical drills, making them conversant with the use of the hose, and lowering men from the triforium with the life line. No water is being used at these drills. The roof and triforium telephones are tested several times nightly to make sure they are kept in working order. Every fireman has been fully equipped with clothing, helmet and respirator.

The system has been brought up to A.R.P. requirements, including water containers, stirrup pump and three quarter inch hose attached to all hydrants.

The London Fire Brigade made their six monthly inspection of the apparatus on 27th January 1940 and no complaints or suggestions were made by them regarding the efficiency of the arrangements.

A temporary bridge has been erected at the west end of the nave at triforium level to facilitate operations in case of fire. In the N and S transepts and nave platforms and lowering tackle have been erected for lowering casualties if required.

The programme of work, as detailed in my last year's report, has been inevitably cut short, but the story can be carried on.

St Nicholas' chapel

St Edmund's chapel being finished, a start was made on St Nicholas' chapel, next to it eastward, and the vault and upper parts of the walls have been cleaned, the work proceeding more quickly because Scott's shellac treatment has not been applied here.

Islip chapel

More progress has been made with Islip's chapel: the work here being now in measurable distance of completion. The preliminaries entailed the removal of the Hatton monument to the triforium of the north transept, the cleaning of all stonework, and the rearrangement of the floor levels. The Islip badges in the vaulted ceiling now appear in their old colours, untouched except for a little cleaning, while the Abbot's name repeated many times among the badges has had its original gilding renewed. The lines of the vaulting ribs have been gilded, but the mutilated keystone of the vault remains as the iconoclasts left it.

The refitting of the chapel is well advance and should be complete by Whitsuntide. The cresting of the gilt and burnished wood, with the IHS monogram and the arms of the Abbey and Abbot Islip, is in position over the altar; the dossal and frontal are being fitted, and the silver altar cross and candlesticks are ready. The design of the floor, in Hopton Wood and Purbeck, is settled and the marble is being worked and will shortly be ready. On the lozenges of Hopton Wood it is proposed to inlay in lead letters the names of those already buried in the chapel, and all future burials can be similarly recorded. The space below the floor of the chapel, excavated some 200 years ago to supply more room for burials in the Abbey but for some reason or other hardly used at all, has now been fitted with stone loculi which will take some seventy cremations, and more space is available after this.

One result of these excavations is worthy of record. It is clear that in the excavation of this chapel in the 18th century the grave of Abbot Islip was destroyed, except for its west wall whose brickwork remains intact, showing evidences of a flat brick arch over the grave. Islip's coffin is nowhere to be seen:

it may have been removed to another chapel, for it is hard to believe that it was broken up and thrown away. But at present we are entirely at a loss; an inscription recording his burial will be cut in the new pavement, but it is sad that in the restoration of the chapel to its proper purpose the remains of the man who built it can no longer occupy the place in which they were laid in 1532.

With the reopening of the original doorway to the chapel, and the renewal in stone of that part of the screen on the south side which has hitherto served to give access to the chapel, the structural repairs will be completed.[5] It remains to consider the glazing of the north window, for which a sketch has been prepared by Mr Kruger Gray, and perhaps the glazing of the southern screen also, with silverstain quarries used sparingly among plain glass, like the glazing in the chapel at King's Cambridge.[6] What remains of the monument of Islip, a black marble slab on four bronze pillars, will be set up in the north bay of the chapel as it has been since the 18th century alterations.[7]

The upper story of Islip's chapel, the original chantry chapel, has for long been used to contain the wax effigies. The trampling of innumerable visitors, which mattered little when the tomb chapel was used only for storage, will be most inappropriate in future, and the time has come to consider whether these effigies cannot now join their dilapidated elders in the Museum in the Undercroft.[8]

South transept

In the south transept a small tablet commemorating the three Bronte sisters has been set up below Thomson's monument, at the cost of the Bronte Society. A proposal to put up a memorial to Keats has not matured.

Cloister

A start has been made with the repair of the cloister vaulting, two bays at the east end of the south walk being scaffolded. But beyond a little preliminary cleaning nothing has been done, and this much needed and difficult work must I fear remain in suspense for the present.

Triforium

I referred in last year's report to a scheme for the clearing and fitting up of the whole triforium east of the crossing. Events have given a new turn to this proposal, and I am now working on a plan which shall in due course be submitted to the Chapter. A rather ambitious plan, it must be admitted; but it makes possible the realization of an idea which is not new, the finding of space for chapels of the Dominions within the Abbey. There is just as much floor space in the triforium as there is in the ambulatory and the ring of chapels round the Confessor's Chapel – though not, of course, as much height – and it needs little effort of imagination to see the four principal radiating chapels fitted up and allotted to Asia, Africa, America and Australia. Access is, of course, the difficulty, but it seems to me that a scheme which is reasonably sufficient can be devised.[9]

[*Elkan bronze candelabrum*]

I must add the record of the presentation[10] to the Abbey of a bronze cande-labrum, the work of Mr Benno Alkan [Elkan], representing the Old Testament story, which has been set up at the west end of the south aisle of the nave. Suitable lighting for it, and the filling of the openings in Islip's screen behind it with a light fabric, against which the lines of the bronze work will show to advantage, are now being considered.

sgd. Charles Peers
16 February 1940

Appendix – Materials used in protection work on tombs, monuments etc.

16,200 sandbags
325 cubic yards sand
5,503 lineal feet 3 x 9 inch deals
7,707 square feet 1 x 9 inch boarding
175 lineal feet 2 x 3 inch battens
2,240 square feet Paramount board
1,856 square feet asbestos sheeting
7 rolls ruberoid felt
36 rolls soft padding felt
67 dust bins for water containers

Allowing for use and waste it is expected that all the above materials can be of use after dismantling.

[1] Correspondence regarding war removals and protection is in Peers's files WAM S/2/II, V, IX, X and XIV.

[2] A map giving the secret location of the burial of the Stone was sent to the Prime Minister of Canada in case of invasion (WAM 61368–75). The Stone was put in the vault of the Islip chapel.

[3] In 1941 the bronze screen around this tomb was dismantled and removed to Mentmore. Each piece was stamped with a number to facilitate re-erection after the war (WAM S/1/XIII (17)).

[4] At this date there was a lane on the other side of the precinct wall where a car could access the garage, which was provided with a turntable mechanism.

[5] The old door is still preserved in the triforium. The alterations to this chapel were paid for by members of the Wilberforce family.

[6] The south screen was not glazed. The north window was filled with glass given by Dean Don after the war with a figure of St Margaret, designed by Hugh Easton. A sixteenth-century panel with the Islip rebus is incorporated in this.

[7] In 1950 the slab and pillars were used as an altar in the new Nurses Memorial chapel in the upper chantry.

[8] After war evacuation the wax effigies were displayed in the Museum. The earlier funeral effigies had been on show there since the display opened in 1908.

9   This scheme came to nothing.
10 An anonymous gift of Lord Lee of Fareham and his wife (one showing New Testament scenes was also given by them later). After their deaths plaques were put on the bases of each, recording their names. Correspondence with Elkan is in WAM S/2/XI.

47.   WAM S/1/88

Report of the Surveyor to the Fabric March 1941

Another year almost a blank as regards constructive work has to be recorded. To the long list of precautionary measures undertaken in 1939–40 there are additions, and a new chapter, that of war damage, has been opened. To the list of protected monuments are now to be added the following:

> The Duchess of Suffolk
> Edward III's children [presumably John of Eltham and small tomb of Blanche and William of Windsor]
> Archbishop Langham
> Sir Lewis Robsart
> Sir Richard Pecksall
> William Thynne
> Richard Busby
> Geoffrey Chaucer
> John Dryden

and from Henry VII's chapel seventy three statues have been taken from the line of the canopied niches below the clearstory windows, and placed in the Undercroft.[1]

Our experience of enemy air raids began in September. At 12.30am on the night of September 12th–13th a loud explosion outside the west end of the church was heard and a good deal of the 18th century glass in the great west window was broken. The plain glass in Jerusalem Chamber and the Chapter Office also suffered, but the 13th century panels from the n. window of Jerusalem had of course been removed long before, and the mediaeval glass in the west windows of the n.w. and s.w. towers, being protected by boarding, survived without harm. A small crater just outside the iron gates, a foot deep by two and a half feet across, showing where the missile had fallen; it seems more likely to have been one of our own shells than a German bomb.

A 9.45pm on September 13th serious damage was done to the Abbey Choir School on the west side of Deans Yard by a H.E. [high explosive] bomb, which fell on the west half of the building, breaking through the roof and concrete floors as far as the first floor, where it exploded and blew out a large piece of brick masonry, dislocating much more and destroying windows and window frames. The building however did not collapse, being modern and soundly constructed, but interior partitions and fittings were blasted down and destroyed.

The A.F.S. [Auxiliary Fire Service] were in occupation at the time and suffered five slight casualties.

At the same time an oil bomb was dropped in front of the doorway of 4B Deans Yard, starting a fire which was soon put out by the Fire Brigade and the Abbey firemen. The damage was not serious, the door being scorched, some glass broken and brickwork and paving slabs damaged.

At 1.45pm on September 19th a very large bomb fell on County Hall on the other side of the river, shaking all buildings in the neighbourhood. Many windows in the east end of the Abbey church were blown in and in particular the Chaucer[2] window in the east aisle of the s. transept, in spite of its apparently sheltered position, was shattered.

A 12.45am on September 25th the south front of no. 6 Little Cloister was damaged by an oil bomb which fell in its garden; glass, woodwork and furniture were broken and displaced, and a brick pier of the arcade on the garden front had to be taken down and rebuilt.

About the same time an oil bomb fell on the n. aisle of St Margaret's church, starting a fire which was dealt with by the Abbey firemen until the Fire Brigade arrived.

At 12.15am on September 27th a heavy bomb fell in Old Palace Yard, just outside the s. gable of Westminster Hall, and due east of Henry VII's chapel. This blew out nearly all the glass in the chapel windows, except for that in the tracery of the clearstory, and the masonry at the e. end of the chapel was battered with flying stones, so that parts of the window tracery were knocked out and the openwork parapets over the e. ambulatory chapel were splintered and blown off their beds. No doubt the whole chapel was considerably shaken, but except for the fall of two pendants from the roof no trace of serious movement is at present to be seen.

In the N.E. ambulatory chapel the figure of St Sebastian, broken and mended some time ago, was again broken and had to be taken out and repaired, while in the S.E. chapel the figure of St Dorothy was much injured by a missile which came through the window and destroyed the feet and pedestal of the statue. For the rest some of the canopies of the stalls were blown out of place, the wood carving over the new altar broken, some of the statuary on the Duke of Buckingham's monument thrown down, and the nose of Dean Stanley's effigy splintered.

In the church itself, all windows in the eastern chapel,[3] and the clearstories of the east arm and the east side of the transepts were shattered, as well as most of those in the lantern over the crossing. In the north transept and to a less extent on the north side of the nave, the effects of the shock were to be seen in broken windows, but on the south side of the church there was no damage to speak of. The three eastern windows in the clearstory of the main apse, over the Confessor's chapel, had been boarded in to protect the old glass which they contained, and except for slight injuries they survived.

Damage to the external stonework of the church, though not conspicuous, may well prove to be appreciable: pinnacles, buttresses and parapets must have been shaken and weakened, to an extent which only time can show. Obvious casualties include the window over the door in Poets' Corner, where the central mullion was almost knocked inwards by a flying stone, the marble shaft on its inner face being thrown off and splintered.

The Chapter House and the Canons' houses on the north side of Little Cloister (nos. 1, 2, and 3) suffered in windows and roofs, but without serious structural harm.

The next attack was on October 9th when at 10.30 am three incendiary bombs fell on no. 1 Little Dean's Yard, on the north green of the Abbey church, and in Broad Sanctuary. The Abbey firemen put them out and no harm was done.

On October 14th two heavy bombs fell at 7.55pm. One seriously damaged the recently completed Church House on the south side of Dean's Yard, six people being killed, while the second fell in Great Smith Street, and damaged the roof and windows of 4B and 5 Dean's Yard, and the office and workshops of the Abbey Clerk of Works.

On October 19th at 8.50pm an incendiary bomb fell on the Jerusalem Chamber and another on Henry VII's chapel: but both were promptly put out by the Abbey staff and the AFS, with only slight damage to the roofs. At the same time a H.E. bomb fell on the Busby Library [at Westminster School], smashing the roof and the fine plasterwork of the ceiling, and breaking through the ancient sub vault of the monastic reredorter and the coverings of the channel of the drain. A second bomb fell in Abbey Garden outside nos. 4 and 5 Little Cloister, blowing in the windows and dislocating woodwork.

On October 20th the concrete shelter built against the e. wall of the Abbey Garden, and noticed in my last report, was tested by the fall of two bombs in College Mews, within a few feet of the shelter. This was at 2.10 am when thirty people were in the shelter but they fortunately escaped with a severe shaking: the building itself was unharmed.

On November 16th at 1.30am three incendiary bombs fell, one on the roof of the s. aisle of the nave, one on the School Gymnasium, and one on the roadway in Dean's Yard. Small holes in the roofs were the only damage.

On January 11th 1941 an incendiary bomb fell on the pavement outside Poets' Corner door at 7.45pm doing no damage.

On March 8th at 9.10pm fifteen small incendiary bombs fell; one on the south west tower of the church, one on the roof of the west walk of the Great Cloister, one in the Cloister garth, one outside Poets' Corner, one on the roof of 4B Dean's Yard, one behind the Choir School, six in Dean's Yard and three near St Margaret's Church. Of all these, that on the sw tower came nearest to doing serious damage; by the rest only slight holes in the roof of the west cloister walk and of 4B Dean's Yard were caused.

So for the moment ends this hateful and degrading record.

For all these things temporary repair only can be effected. The windows have been filled in with opaque materials, and Henry VII's chapel shut off from the rest of the church.

A temporary altar has been set up in the nave, in the position once occupied by the medieval nave altar against the rood screen, one bay west of the pulpitum.

The programme of work, normally the important part of these annual reports, is practically a blank.

[*Islip chapel*]

The work in the Islip chapel, which in my last report was to have been finished by Whitsuntide 1940, was in fact carried on to completion, except for the treatment of the glass in its north window. The marble floor was laid down and polished, the remains of Islip's monument set up under the north window, its marble slab and four bronze pillars being cleaned and polished, the wooden part of the screen towards the ambulatory renewed in stone, and the doorway at the s.w. reopened and fitted with a curtain of green and gold brocade. A tablet in commemoration of the Wilberforce family was fixed to the new screen work at the s.e. corner of the chapel. Though no formal consecration of the new work has taken place, the chapel has been used for services; and the ashes of one member of the capitular body placed in the reconstructed vault: but now the chapel is dismantled and unused.

It is futile to attempt any reference to future work.

Charles Peers
1 April 1941

1 Plans for war removals and notes of positions of statues on Henry V Chantry and in Henry VII's chapel are WAM SD/1/66–70.
2 This window had been erected in 1868.
3 This included most of the remaining Tudor glass in Henry VII's chapel (some quarries were collected together after the war and are in a window of the side aisle). Also Lady Augusta Stanley's nineteenth-century memorial window in the same chapel. The window in the east triforium given by Archdeacon Bentinck and a memorial window to Dean Ireland above Henry V's chantry were lost. The Ashanti war and Vincent Novello windows were lost from the east aisle of the north transept.

47N. At Chapter on 26 January 1942 a credence table for the chapel of the Holy Name (i.e. Islip's chapel) designed by the Surveyor was approved. This was carried out by carver Robert Thompson of Yorkshire (the 'mouse man').

48. WAM S/1/89

Westminster Abbey. Repairs to damaged buildings Sept 1941

In the air raid on the night of May 11th 1941 incendiary bombs were showered on the Abbey and its precincts and the supply of water failed. So the members of the fire fighting squad had to stand by and watch the buildings burn.

In the church the early 19th century roof of the lantern over the crossing was destroyed, with its plaster vault, and the burning ruins fell into the church. The Jacobean pulpit at the n.e. crossing pier was damaged, and some of the marble pavement in the crossing smashed, but there was nothing more serious. The roof of the Library next to the south transept caught fire, but this was dealt with by bringing a hose through the rose window in the gable wall of the transept and put out with no serious damage to the roof; but many of the books were drenched with water and covered with ashes and have since been under skilled treatment by the Public Record Office, with Mr Hilary Jenkinson as our advisor.

The Deanery suffered far worse things, its principal rooms being practically burnt out. The range set against the church, containing Jericho parlour, Samaria and Jerusalem Chamber, with the 17th century additions, escaped with little damage, as did the College Hall and kitchen on the west side of the Deanery courtyard, but the rest, including all the principal rooms of the Deanery, Library, Study, Drawing room, Dining room, bedrooms, kitchen and offices, were burnt out. The stonework of Litlyngton's time and earlier has survived with little harm beyond partial discolourations, but the woodwork and all 17th and 18th century additions have proved to be only fit to be cleared away as beyond repair.

The complete destruction of the great timber roof of Westminster School exposed the vaults of the Norman Undercroft of the Abbey dormitory to the weather and rain has been soaking into the haunches of the vaults ever since, but the most extensive damage to our possessions is to be seen in the Little Cloister. Of the seven houses surrounding the cloister, no. 6 is quite destroyed, no. 2 is only fit to be pulled down, and nos. 3 and 7 are mere shells. No. 1 though much shaken is capable of reinstatement as far as the ground and first floors are concerned, and nos. 4 and 5 escaped the fire entirely. As in the Deanery, the medieval stonework, being part of the buildings which stood round the Infirmary cloister, has survived without serious loss, and the late 17th century cloister arcades on all four sides need only minor repairs. Litlyngton's Tower [no 8] in the angle between the Abbey dormitory and the rere-dorter has lost roof and floors, but its stonework is reasonably sound as far as can be seen from below.

The making good after all these calamities falls under two heads, by the provisions of the War Damage Act 1941. The first of these, comprising clearing and temporary repair, for safety and protection from weather, is termed First Aid, and the cost of the necessary works, which are done with the approval of the local authority and of the Ministry of Works and Public Buildings, is repayable from public funds on completion. These works are now in progress, and need not be further described here. The second head, covering the final reinstatement of all damaged buildings, cannot be dealt with until the end of the war, but full schemes of the work to done must be prepared for submission to the authorities, so that as far as is at present possible, their extent and probably cost may be known.

I am therefore submitting a preliminary scheme for the buildings of the Little

Cloister,[1] not worked out in full detail, but showing the general treatment which seems indicated.

With the exception of nos. 3 and 7 the houses round the cloister were of later 17th century brickwork incorporating the remains of the 14th century Infirmary. A good deal of original detail remained, in staircases, fireplaces, and plasterwork, but the casement windows had been replaced by sashes in nearly every case. Fortunately there survived a few specimens of the original casements on the north side of no. 1 in which house the preservation of the first floor elevation on the south side must be taken to rule the general character of the rebuilding.

I have worked out the plans on a scale of accommodation, which provides three sitting rooms and five bedrooms, besides kitchens, bathrooms etc. for each house. Two stories and an attic suffice for this, except in no. 7, where there are three stories. Roofs and floors should be of fireproof construction. Separate hotwater systems for each house, with hot and cold water basins to each bedroom, gas cookers and fires, radiators or ceiling heating, and labour-saving appliances generally. Electric lighting and plug points for lamps, kettles etc.

The only alteration in the layout of the site is that I have planned for two houses on the site of no. 6 and I have left the question of the rebuilding of no. 3 for further consideration. No. 7, which is tall and narrow, could be made into two flats instead of one house, if such accommodation were to be found convenient.

Charles Peers, 16th September 1941.

[1]   See WAM SD/3/5–9. Chapter on 23 September 1941 recorded that these plans were the Surveyor's own initiative and they would be free to choose the final architect for the rebuilding work.

49.   WAM S/1/90

Report of the Surveyor to the Fabric – March 1942

Since the date of my last report, which was largely a record of air raids, there has been only one serious attack on the Abbey buildings, namely the incendiary raid on the night of May 10–11 1941. This was fully described by me in connexion with a scheme for ultimate reconstruction of the houses in Little Cloister, submitted on September 16th and need not be repeated here. Since that date I have made a set of drawings to show how the Deanery[1] might be re-planned and have also set out a design for a new vault to the Lantern over the crossing,[2] in order that a scale model may be made. Occasion has been taken to improve the lighting, providing sixteen windows in place of the present eight.

The roof of the Lantern over the crossing, destroyed on May 10–11 has been reconstructed in permanent form. This was obviously the economical method, because the provision of a fire proof covering was essential, and to construct this over a wide span of 35 feet demanded steel of definite scantlings, where no light temporary substitutes would meet the case – precast concrete slabs have been used for the coverings and finished with a coat of asphalte – it is hoped that eventually a copper roof will be added.

Certain additions have been made to the ARP outfit, such as the covering of the roofs of the western towers with sandbags, and of the roof of the south triforium of the nave over the organ pipes. More sandbags, water containers and stirrup pumps have also been provided in various parts of the church.

A grant of £5,000 having been made from Government funds, it has been possible to continue the work of removing the contents of the church to 'places of safety' outside London. Accommodation having been provided at Mentmore, the list of what has been moved thither is as follows:

From Henry VII's chapel.

> The effigies of Henry VII and Elizabeth of York.
> The four putti from the angels of the tomb (from the Undercroft)
> The bronze screens round the tomb (except the base courses)
> The bronze plated gates at the west of the chapel.
> Seventy three stone statues from niches above the arcades (from the Undercroft)
> All stone statues from the radial chapels and from the Elizabeth and Beaufort aisles.

From Henry V's tomb chapel.

> All moveable statues, large and small

Iron work

> The 13th century screen from Eleanor of Castile's tomb.
> The gate and screen from Henry V's chantry

Woodwork

> The wooden tester over Eleanor of Castile's tomb.
> The canopies, seats and book rests from Henry VII's chapel
> In addition to these there were sent to Mentmore:
> A number of pieces of the Abbey plate, packed in wooden boxes and sealed.
> A box of plate from St John's church Smith Square.

There were also removed from Boughton to Mentmore, on October 17–23, the effigies of:

> King Henry III
> Queen Eleanor of Castile
> King Edward III
> King Richard II and his Queen
> Margaret, Countess of Richmond
> William de Valence
> and the headless wooden effigy of King Henry V

The following were removed and stored in the crypt of the Chapter House:

> The stall plates of the Knights of the Bath from Henry VII's chapel.
> The marble busts of Johnson, Camden and Barrow from the south transept.
>
> The wax effigies from Abbot Islip's chantry chapel, namely:
> King Charles II
> Queen Elizabeth
> King William III and Queen Mary II
> Queen Anne
> Lord Nelson
> Lord Chatham
> Duchess of Buckingham
> Duchess of Richmond
> Duke of Buckingham

were removed to a disused part of the Piccadilly tube station assigned to the London Museum. In the process it was discovered that the clothes of four of the effigies were attacked by moth; so they were taken to the Victoria and Albert Museum for treatment, and in due course stored with the other figures in the Piccadilly tube.

The woodwork of the organ cases, which had been removed during the preparations for the coronation of King George VI and Queen Elizabeth, and stored by Mr Laurence Turner in his workshop, were in part exposed to damage by the destruction of adjacent buildings in air raids. By the kindness of Bishop Barry this woodwork, except for certain plain framing retained in the Abbey precincts, has been stored at Southwell [Minster].

In the case of monuments which are not suitable for removal, protection by sandbags is being continued as the labour at the Chapter's disposal permits. What has been hitherto done has been to pick out special monuments here and there, but in this year in view of the money now available from outside sources, it has been decided to taken the chapels systematically, and beginning with St Edmund's chapel to work from s. to n. round the apse. In this way St Edmunds and St Nicholas chapels are now fully protected, and work is proceeding in St John's and St Paul's. At the same time St Benedict's chapel, where the Langham and Dryden monuments were dealt with last year, is being taken in hand.

Into this year's record also fall the additions to the protection of the tombs of Queen Elizabeth and Queen Mary of Scots, the protection of the tombs of the children of King James I [Princesses Sophia and Mary], and of King Richard II's badge of the white hart on a plastered petition in the Muniment Room in the s. transept.

It remains to mention certain repairs consequent on the air raid of May 10–11 1941. The first aid treatment of damage done to the houses in the Little Cloister was completed in February 1942 and certain minor repairs to the choir stalls and renewals of the marble pavement under the Lantern are also completed.

The destruction of the great roof of Upper School exposed the vaulting of the Norman Undercroft to the weather, and a serious amount of water soaked into the springings of the vaults. The floor area of Upper School has now been made water proof by the School Authorities at their expense, and the gradual drying of the vaults is proceeding.

Looking at the year's records as a whole, it will be seen that we have patched up our War damage and made large additions to the list of evacuated and protected monuments. General maintenance must gradually fall in arrear as time goes on but that is the common fate. We must hope to emerge from the present relapse into barbarism with some of our ancient splendours intact.

If it is permissible to look forward to the time of reconstruction one point is well worth consideration, and that is whether the bureaucrats can be brought to see that the gradual accumulation by us and others like us of building materials, which every one will urgently need when the time comes might not with advantage be authorized now, as occasion serves. I am thinking specially of stone, which the quarries would be glad to supply, and which is not a directly war winning commodity (unless in addition to the bows and arrows recommended by high military authority, we revert to catapults). In repairs to the arcades of Little Cloister and in the new Deanery, an appreciable quantity of ashlar will be wanted.

Signed C. Peers. March 1942.

[1] See WAM SD/5 folder of drawings. The architects chosen to re-build the cloister houses, the Deanery and Cheyneygates were Seely & Paget [John Seely, later Lord Mottistone, and Paul Paget]. A wooden representation of Peers's head, together with seventeen others of Abbey officials and those concerned in the reconstruction, were attached to the roof of the inner room of Cheyneygates in 1951. A statue of St Catherine was later unveiled above 3 Little Cloister as a memorial to Lord Mottistone. Their drawings are also in the SD collection.

[2] Letters and plans regarding the repair of the lantern roof including the columns and plumb lines are WAM S/2/XIV (16) and WAM SD/1/635–640.

49N. Peers offered to store certain treasures at his country home, Chiselhampton House, Stadhampton, and this was accepted at Chapter on 12 May 1942.

50. WAM S/1/91

Westminster Abbey. Report of the Surveyor to the Fabric

March 1942–April 1943

In the past twelve months no addition to our air raid history has to be chronicled.

In the matter of protection and removal it will be simple to record with regard to removal, that a complete statement of what has been done is contained in the Schedule of War Removals compiled by Miss Powell[1] by direction of the

Dean, bringing the story down to the end of 1942. The work of protection, made possible by the grant of £5,000 from Government funds, has proceeded and the grant is now exhausted. It must be understood that the cost of removals and storage in 'places of safety' is also charged to this grant. The work of sandbag protection to the chapels round the apse, begun in 1941–2, has now been carried to completion, working from south to north, and including the east chapels of the north transept, where the Norris[2] monument has been protected by brick walling and its upper part taken down and stored. In addition to this, the sandbag protection to the royal tombs around the Confessor's chapel has been greatly strengthened and the screen wall at the west of the chapel has been also protected on its east side.

The question of further protection ie. in the transepts and nave, is now to be decided, and involves a consideration which has not so are had to be taken into account. The eastern parts of the Abbey church have been withdrawn from the public and will so remain till better times, but the nave and transepts, being in constant use, have a vitally important part to play. Westminster Abbey, a place of pilgrimage for thousands in peace time, is of even more significance in war. As far as may be, in should appear to all who have come from overseas in its normal condition, not encumbered and blinded by boarding and sandbags and with its altars and furniture not less but if possible more splendid than hitherto. Its priceless fabric can be protected only from fire, there is no escape from the heavy bombs which might at any time descend upon it. But if in the end it proves to have been possible to preserve its continuity of function unbroken, what better record could be desired?

On this question of fire protection, a new development has to be recorded. Our experience of the past few years has shown that much more ought to be done before we can look forward with any confidence to dealing with enemy action if or when it may again take place. We have therefore called the National Fire Service into our counsels and the officers of no. 34 Fire Area with members of the Regional Commissioner's staff, after a preliminary inspection, drew up a report which was fully discussed on Dec 8 1942 at a conference in the Chapter Office, attended by myself and the Clerk of Works on behalf of the Abbey, and by Messrs. Croad, Pudsey and Clark of the Regional Commissioner's staff and from the Fire Force Commanders Kerr and Benton with three colleagues. The scheme outlined in the report was fully discussed and generally approved and need not be given in detail here, as reports of the conference have been drawn up both by myself and by the N.F.S. The practical outcome is that part of the new installation will be provided and paid for by the NFS, while the rest will be chargeable to Chapter funds. The NFS provide two new pipe lines from the river, one to the green north of the church and one to Poets' Corner, with the necessary tanks for static water, while the Chapter are responsible for everything attached to the church, the principal expense being in connexion with the dry risers and the outside staircases from ground level to the high roofs.

This arrangement was confirmed by the Dean and Chapter in the Dean's letter of Jan 4th and it has since been arranged that Mr Pudsey is to undertake on our behalf the provision and erection of the material necessary for the carrying out of the Scheme. The work has already begun and will be proceeded with.

Within the last few months a start has been made on normal maintenance work, with the scaffolding and cleaning of Islip's upper chapel. A close examination of the masonry shows that certain small repairs in Caen stone date from the time of Abbot Islip, and a few details of the carefully obliterated paintings of the Crucifixion, the Last Judgment on the east wall have appeared. A more curious feature is to be seen in the north window, where two of the three foliate capitals of the marble shafts date from Wren's time and are well intentioned imitations of 13th century work. For the lower chapel I have designed a credence table, which is now in position and for the nave altar two standing candlesticks of gilt oak, which were given in memory of HMS Barham, sunk in the Mediterranean 25 Nov 1941.[3]

The closing of Henry VII's chapel has made it possible to make an inspection of the Hanoverian vault[4] which underlies the western part of its marble pavement and had not been seen for a number of years. The result of the inspection was to satisfy ourselves of the soundness of the structure and it appeared that the damp from which the wood of the coffins and their velvet coverings had suffered was not now a serious matter. No question of repair to the coffins, or to the marble sarcophagus of George II and his queen, seems appropriate for the present at any rate.

C. Peers, 5 April 1943

[1]   WAM 63099A–B. Dorothy Powell was an assistant in the Muniment Room.
[2]   The large cenotaph to Henry, Lord Norris in St Andrew's chapel.
[3]   Made by Robert Thompson of Kilburn in Yorkshire. Correspondence is in WAM S/2/XIII (2).
[4]   Constructed in 1737 for the burial of Queen Caroline and used for the burials of George II and his family. An account of the opening on 15 January 1943 is recorded in Lawrence Tanner's unpublished Journal.

51.   WAM S/1/92

Meeting held in Jerusalem Chamber Feb 29 1944

Present: The Dean, Sir Charles Peers, E.E. Lofting [assistant surveyor], Mayor V. Rogers, W. Bishop [clerk of works], T. Hebron [chapter clerk], A.J.D. Woods, assistant secretary to War Damage Commission and J.R. Macdonald, senior technical adviser to War Damage Commission.

The Dean opened the proceedings by thanking Mr Woods and Mr Macdonald for their attendance. He explained that in order to avoid unnecessary complications it appeared desirable to have the views and advice of the War Damage Commission before the formulation of any claims in respect of the repair of the Abbey and the rebuilding of official houses etc. Sir Charles Peers reviewed the damage the Abbey and official houses had sustained and the various works of repair and rebuilding it was proposed to carry out.

Conclusions:

Stained glass. Mr Woods said that as regards churches generally the proposal was that where the east or other principal window was in stained glass it should if desired be replaced in stained glass and where a church had a number of stained glass windows, that a reasonable measure of replacement in proportion to the loss should be provided. Windows erected privately as memorials should not be replaced at the Commission's expense merely because they were memorial windows. This proposal of course is intended as a general rule and would not necessarily be applied to special important churches such as the Abbey. On the other hand it might be that the Abbey Authorities themselves would not think it either necessary or even desirable to replace every stained glass window. Mr Woods suggested that the Dean and Chapter should make up its mind what it would wish to do and in due course discuss its proposals with the Commission.

Lantern roof. This to be a 'cost of works' payment. The Commission would pay for reinstating the roof and vaulting as before the damage, any additional cost over and above the original work would have to be borne by the Dean and Chapter.

Henry VII's chapel. Cost of erecting scaffolding for the purpose of examining the vaulting of Henry VII's chapel would only be paid by the Commission if it was found that repairs due to war damage were necessary.

The Deanery. When the Deanery is rebuilt it is proposed to carry out considerable alterations and it would therefore be necessary to ascertain the "permissible amount" (this is the maximum amount payable by way of a cost of works payment and represents what it would cost if the Deanery were reinstated exactly in its pre-damaged form, omitting any valueless parts). It was agreed that the "permissible amount" should be based on the cube rate and it was suggested that the procedure to be adopted here should be as follows:

    a. Plan of original building to be produced
    b. Agree "permissible amount" first with War Damage Commission
    c. Give details of cube figures
    d. Terms of building contract to be produced

Little Cloisters. Sir Charles Peers explained the medieval work and the suggested proposals of the rebuilding. Mr Woods while not wishing to be too definite until after further consideration, was of opinion that the houses in Little Cloisters could be treated as part of the same unit as the Abbey so that they might be expected to quality for a cost of works payment.

<u>Choir School and Dean's Yard houses etc</u>. Each property to be a separate unit and either a cost of works payment or a value payment made, as may prove to be appropriate, in respect of each property.

<u>Busby Library</u>. Either the Dean and Chapter of the Governors of the School to make a claim for the whole work.

Generally:

The general principle should be that "permissible amount" should be worked out in conjunction with the Technical Officers of the Commission. For convenience this might be done on the basis of 1939 costs which could be adjusted by a percentage addition to take account of subsequent increases in prices. If comparative estimates were also obtained for the work it was proposed to carry out (which may include improvements in relation to the original building or buildings) the Dean and Chapter would be able to obtain an approximate estimate at any rate of the financial position.

52.   WAM S/1/93

Westminster Abbey Report of the Surveyor to the Fabric

April 1943–April 1944

For another year, though bombs have fallen at no great distance from the abbey precincts, no actual damage to the fabric has to be recorded.

In my last report the policy of extending sand bag protection to the transepts and nave was mentioned. But the advantages of keeping these parts of the church open and unencumbered have carried the day and as a result the surroundings of the nave altar have received attentions to which they have long been strangers. The pavement here and throughout the nave is laid in lozenges of Purbeck stone, which by constant wear have acquired a rough greyish surface. This pavement was put down in Islip's time early in the 16th century and like all other marbles was meant to be polished.[1] The whole area of the second and third bays west of the pulpitum is now in process of being brought back to its former seemliness, and appears in various shades – of brown ranging from cream colour to amber, while the Victorian grave slabs set in it are acquiring a dignity which they had lost of late. Certain additions to the fittings – a pair of gilt oak altar candlesticks, of a set with the standing candlesticks given last year, and a faldstool sent from Plymouth dockyard[2] but a good deal refashioned in our own workshops – are now in position and the whole space roped off to protect the newly polished floor.

What memorials the war may require is yet uncertain, but one is already in preparation. The eastern chapel in Henry VII's chapel has been assigned to be the memorial chapel for those airmen who fell in the Battle of Britain,[3] and its arrangement are now being discussed between the Dean and the memorial committee, with Lord Trenchard as their chairman, and backed by ample funds. Descriptions of what is intended must wait till the designs now in preparation are more advances and have been approved; and of course there is no certainty about the time when the materials needed will be forthcoming.

During the past twelve months conversations have taken place between the War Damage Commission and ourselves, with highly encouraging results, so that a liberal treatment of our liabilities, when the time comes, may be reckoned with. I hope that I shall not be thought unduly optimistic to believe that this time is now not far distant, and that the treatment of the Deanery and of the Little Cloisters will soon become a matter of practical politics.

Charles Peers July 1944.

[1]   The nave floor was re-laid in 1834 with many of the original gravestones being taken away, to be replaced by names and dates on small lozenge stones. It is not certain how much of the original marble floor was re-used at this time.

[2]   Presented by the Royal Navy Shipwrights.

[3]   Correspondence is in Peers's file WAM S/2/XXIV and WAM 62153–62235, 62314–24 and WAM OA/2/10 series. The chapel was unveiled by the King on 10 July 1947.

52N.   At Chapter on 13 April 1943 his designs for a nave lectern were approved.

53.   It seems no reports were given for 1945 or 1946 as he was ill.

Correspondence about the tablet to Admiral Robert Blake 1942–44 by Gilbert Ledward is WAM S/2/VII (13). At Chapter on 10 July 1945 the case he designed to house the Civilian War Dead memorial books in the nave was inspected. See WAM S/2/VI and XXIII. The case was made by Robert Thompson.

54.   WAM S/1/94

Surveyor's Report for the year ended April 1, 1947

The aftermath of war takes the form of a series of inhibitions; the shortage of staff and materials and the abundance of official restrictions, tempered by occasional evidences of goodwill, make any attempt to overtake arrears of maintenance or to envisage any programme, as in pre war years, a fruitless labour. So that for the twelve months under review the gradual replacement of such things as could be removed out of London for greater safety seems the most important work which has been undertaken. When this has been done there will at least be the satisfaction of knowing that all such things are clean, sound and in good order. Perhaps it is not yet too late to record the wonderful escape of the Abbey Church from serious structural disaster: indeed our chief peril came from incendiary bombs, which were not beyond our power to deal with as regards the Church itself. And if the National fire-fighting services had been better developed and an adequate supply of water available from the adjacent Thames, we might not now to be deploring the damage to the Deanery and the Little Cloister, which seem likely to remain incomplete for years to come.

[*Henry VII's chapel*]

Of such works as are now in progress the reinstatement of Henry VII's chapel is the most important. If we could get 4 more carpenters and 2 more masons we could make a better show; but in spite of many enquiries these tradesmen are not to be found or likely to be found as things now are. But the prospects are that all damage to the masonry, chiefly caused by the blast of the heavy bomb which fell in Old Palace Yard, will be dealt with by the end of this summer. The high vaults, contrary to what one would expect, stood the shock well, though the fall of the carved ends of two of the great pendants – one of them directly above the royal tomb – shows what the concussion must have been. The range of statues below the clearstory windows had been taken away and stored in the country and are now back in their places, unharmed, and of the larger statues in the radial chapels only one, that of St Dorothy in the s.e. chapel, was damaged by a flying stone coming through the window. The principal damage was to the glass. In the clearstory a good proportion of the original glazing remained in the tracery heads and still survives, owing to the protection of the stonework, but the most important panel, a 'messenger' in the middle light of the eastern window, was blown to pieces, and not a trace of it is now to be found. The main lights of the clearstory were filled with white glass, and will be so filled again. Crown glass would be the most effective material, but it is unobtainable and we must be content with sheet. The royal effigies in their bronze chapel are once more in their place, and an appreciable quantity of the wooden stalls and their canopies will be in place by the date of the opening of the Battle of Britain chapel by the King.

In the church the replacement of the gilt bronze effigies of the Kings and Queens in the Confessor's chapel is completed. After centuries of neglect, or smearing with wax and other futilities, a simple process of cleaning[1] has revealed the ancient mercury gilding. This return to cleanliness, small as it is, and needing a world war to bring it about, points the way to the need for a campaign against darkness and dirtiness on a much larger scale. From 1935 for a few years a systematic cleaning of masonry and monuments was put in hand, and by the outbreak of war the radial chapels on the south of the apse were completed and a start made on those on the north side. Now, the blocking of broken windows and the unavoidable suspension of all cleaning since 1940 has thrown back into gloom, and nothing could be more salutary and more suggestive of the dawn of a hope of better things than a serious attempt to bring back light and colour. Of the cloister and external masonry generally it seems hopeless to speak. The neglect and crumbling stonework, which in living memory retained some of its ancient surface and contours, remains to witness to the supineness of its guardians. That the process is one of long continuance is no apology for its continuance.

[*Apse windows*]

On one other point some progress may happily be noted, namely in the repair of such old glass as remains in the church. The three clearstory windows of the apse, which were boarded up during the war and escaped with a shaking, have now been made good as far as that can be done, and the 18th century glass of the west window of the nave, as well as the partly medieval west windows of the aisles, are being or have been reset, with some patching as seemed necessary.

[*Nurses memorial chapel*]

The proposal to make the upper Islip chapel into a Nurses' chapel – one of the war memorials – is being taken up and Mr Comper[2] has designed glass for its north window – the lower Islip chapel is to receive a north window designed by Mr Hugh Easton.

[*War memorials*]

The addition to existing 1914–18 memorials of references to 1939–45[3] has produced some problems which need much ingenuity to overcome – but good hopes are entertained of ultimate success.

Certain proposals for new memorials, on our overcrowded walls, must be considered, but need not be dealt with here. Such things are always with us. In this connexion the proposal that the now parochially disused church of St John[4] in Smith Square should be brought within our control is of much interest.

Charles Peers, April 1947.

[1] A 1945 report on the cleaning of the royal gilt bronze effigies (i.e. Henry III, Eleanor of Castile, Edward III, Richard II and Anne of Bohemia, Henry VII and Elizabeth of York and Lady Margaret Beaufort) and the wooden effigies of William de Valence and Henry V, in the Undercroft while awaiting re-instatement, is included with Peers's reports. This was written by H. Maryon and H.J. Plenderleith. They published an article, 'The Royal Bronze Effigies in Westminster Abbey', in the *Antiquaries Journal* vol. XXXIX (1959). Photos, including back views of the bronze figures, are at the Victoria & Albert Museum. An exhibition of many evacuated effigies and treasures was held at the V&A in November 1945.
[2] The window here was also designed by Hugh Easton, although the rest of the chapel was Sebastian Comper's design.
[3] These included the Million War Dead memorial in St George's chapel and the RAMC memorial window.
[4] The Dean and Chapter did not take over the administration of this war-damaged church.

54N.   At Chapter on 9 November 1948 Peers's advice was sought in connection with the design for the Keats and Shelley memorial tablets. On 11 January 1949 the question of stalls for use of the Dean and Canons either side of the nave altar was discussed, and the Dean was to consult the Surveyor. On 25 July 1950 the Dean referred to Peers's failing health and put forward the suggestion that Stephen Dykes Bower should be approached to be deputy surveyor with a view to his succeeding Peers in due course. Peers's resignation was recorded at Chapter on 12 June 1951, and he died 16 on November 1952. His ashes are interred in the vault below the lower Islip chapel.

STEPHEN DYKES BOWER
1951–73

55. At a meeting of the Dean and Chapter on 25 July 1950 the Dean suggested that Stephen Dykes Bower should be approached to become deputy surveyor with a view to succeed Peers in due course. On 13 February 1951 a retaining fee was to be paid to him until a new Surveyor was appointed. On 8 May the Chapter Books record that he was suggesting various works that should be done. On 12 June 1951 he was appointed Surveyor at £600 per annum with the customary commission to be paid for supervising any new work, plus expenses. This was confirmed at Chapter on 26 June. It was stipulated that architects Seely & Paget would continue their work on re-building the war-damaged Deanery and official houses and be subject directly to the Dean and Chapter and not the Surveyor (WAM DF.3). Dykes Bower deposited all his Abbey files in the Muniments, WAM S/3/1–64, and some of his drawings for projects and proposed projects during his time are in the WAM Surveyor Drawings (SD) collection. Various articles, lectures and talks by him are in WAM S/3/1.

WAM S/1/95

Report of the Surveyor of the Fabric March 1952

The comprehensive report on the fabric, which is in course of preparation, I hope to submit shortly. For the purpose of the Chapter Audit I propose to follow the practice of my predecessors in the Surveyorship and make this statement a record of the past year's activities.

[Norman Undercroft Museum]

The most important constructive task of the year was the conversion of the Norman undercroft into a museum and exhibition room for the display of the wax effigies.[1] The walls and vaulting have been lime-washed, the lighting and electric heating improved, the woodwork of the show cases for the wax effigies toned to a uniform colour and the bronze display cases cleaned and re-conditioned.[2] From the large number of objects formerly set out, a selection has been made of those of most value and likely to be of interest to the general public: the rest have been transferred to the triforium of the choir until a proper home can be found for them. As re-arranged the museum appears more spacious and attractive, while the architectural quality of its setting can be better appreciated. That it has proved popular is attested by the number of people – nearly

80,000 – who have visited it since the opening; in twelve months this figure may have risen to 100,000. Since some of the expenditure was recoverable from the War Damage Commission, the actual cost was comparatively small and may be considered to have been well spent since there is every prospect that the museum will continue to be an appreciable financial asset.

[*Funeral Effigies display*]

A further improvement, which should enhance its appeal, will shortly become possible. Now that the two full-length effigies and busts of various Queens, together with the bust of King Henry VII, have been cleaned and restored by Mr Howgrave Graham,[3] their removal from the library is expedient because following a descriptive article in 'Country Life', a considerable number of visitors apply to see them. Clearly they ought to be in the museum and it is proposed to place the two effigies in the spare bronze case, for which a new wooden plinth is being made to lift it off the floor and ensure protection from damp, and to display the busts in new showcases, to be made by the Abbey staff and designed to suit the proportions of each. These cases would stand on pedestals and be placed in front of the piers of the arches, four on the east side and two on the west.

[*Cleaning monuments and stonework of chapels*]

From a visual point of view, as affecting the aspect of the Abbey, the other chief work of the year had been the progress in the cleaning of the monuments. Except for those in the chapels of St Paul and St John the Baptist, which I hope it will be possible to tackle very shortly, all the monuments have now been cleaned with results that, in some cases at any rate, must temper the criticisms even of those who decry them. The process of cleaning cannot of course be regarded as one that will not have to be repeated, for the London atmosphere all too quickly leaves its mark and it is only necessary to compare the monuments cleaned first with those recently finished (e.g. in the west by of the north aisle of the nave) to see that some degree of labour will have to be applied to this task almost continuously. But the general condition of the monuments is now very good and many of them reveal beauties that were largely obscured before.

In the execution of the work however I have instituted one change of policy. When the cleaning of the monuments was first started, none of the actual walling of the building had been cleaned: the whole tone of the interior was the brown, which is still indeed predominant, but which, since the upper part of the apse was cleansed under Sir Charles Peers, can now be seen not to be the natural colour of the stone but only the discolouration of centuries of dust and dirt, aggravated by Sir Gilbert Scott's application to the stonework of a coating of shellac. Against this drab background the marble monuments, when newly cleansed, appeared startling in their whiteness and Dean Foxley Norris ordained that they should be toned to a 'coffee' colour, which was achieved by the liberal use of wax.

Whatever its justification at the time, to continue this treatment today would, I am sure, be unwise. The recovery of the natural colour of the stone throughout the interior is one of the paramount needs of the building and, if it can be achieved, the monuments would appear more congruous if, instead of being artificially subdued, they displayed the natural brightness of their materials. The 'coffee' finish has not improved with time, because even in some twenty years, it has darkened further and some of those monuments that exemplify it, look already as though they had hardly been cleaned at all.

In the cleaning that is now being carried out, the aim is to restore the marble as far as possible to its original condition and to let the monuments appear as fresh as when they were installed. The results are self-evident and I hope the process may gradually embrace all those that will soon be due for cleaning a second time.

In the two chapels already mentioned – St Paul and St John the Baptist – I am anxious that the walls and vaulting should be cleaned at the same time as the monuments. This would bring the mural treatment of all the apsidal chapels into harmony and is a task that would enable some of the Abbey staff to continue at work in the building during the months before the Coronation after the public are excluded. It could be carried out without affecting the preparations that the Ministry of Works undertakes in the nave, choir and transepts.

[Clerestory & other windows]

The third important work of the past year has been the progress in re-glazing the clerestory windows. Those in both transepts are now finished and the whole of the clerestory in the eastern section of the building has recovered its former lighting. Preparatory work is going on to enable the glazing of the choir and transept triforium windows to be inserted during the summer months, and when these are finished, a notable stage will have been reached in restoring to that part of the interior in which the central ceremonies of the Coronation take place, its natural illumination. I would however press for an early decision on the glazing of the two large 2-light windows in the eastern aisles of the transepts.

That in the south transept – known as the Chaucer window – contained stained glass which, following war damage, was removed to the triforium. In the north transept window stained glass remains in situ, very badly damaged and impossible to appraise owing to the temporary protective filling placed outside it. It commemorates officers and man who fell in the Ashanti war 1873–4 and from such examination as I have been able to make, it would appear to be by Clayton and Bell, though not as good as much of their work. I doubt if its repair would be feasible or worth while.[4]

The Chaucer glass I have inspected. Each of the two lights contains three scenes set in grisaille with coloured borders. The topmost scene is set too high in the pointed head of each light and none of the scenes, in design and colour, are very happy. The glass is capable of repair, but whether re-instatement is desirable may be doubted. On the other hand, the grisaille and coloured borders are good and should certainly be kept for re-use elsewhere – a matter on which my full report will contain some definite suggestions.

I do not myself think that, now that it has been displaced, this window has sufficient intrinsic merit to justify a claim to the important position it occupied. The Abbey has suffered much from the haphazard glazing of its windows with glass of indifferent quality and the benefit to architectural effect and the balance of light which would accrue from continuation of the clear glazing, which is now almost consistent east of the lantern, outweighs in my judgement, whatever case for restoration there may be on other grounds (Chaucer, it may be noted, is not dependant on this window for commemoration, since his tomb is below it).

[*Henry VII's chapel*]

The glazing of Henry VII's chapel has made disappointingly slow progress and the firm hitherto employed have, at my suggestion, agreed to the major part of the remaining work being entrusted to the glaziers who are already engaged on the rest of the Abbey windows. The latter's estimate has been submitted and, if the licence allowance permits its acceptance, the work can be completed this year.

In preparation for the installation service of the Order of the Bath, the joiners of the Abbey staff carried out with great skill the intricate and difficult re-assembling of the canopies on the south side. But the continuation of this task on the north side would make disproportionate demands on their time, and since it is clearly desirable to synchronize so far as possible the completion of the glazing and the restoration of the woodwork, an outside firm, Messrs. J. Longley & Co. Ltd., have been invited to submit an approximate estimate for restoring the canopies of the stalls in this chapel – three on the south side and all on the north side.

The Chapter will now have received their figures for consideration and it may be noted that, if accepted, the work will take about twelve months to carry out. Since all of it except the fixing will proceed at the firm's workshops, the final restoration of King Henry VII's chapel should be virtually complete when the Abbey is re-opened after the Coronation next year.

[*Exterior*]

During the year the masons have been chiefly engaged on the reparation of buttresses and pinnacles on the east side of the north transept and north side of the choir. They have also carried out re-pointing and minor repairs where necessary to the stone cusps of those windows that have been reglazed. A good deal of work has been done in pointing the masonry portions of the new Deanery, which it was arranged should be carried out by the Abbey staff, trained in the method of 'Ancient Monuments' pointing.

On the exterior of the west walk of the cloisters Messrs. Dove Bros., the contractors for the Deanery, have renewed a length of the coping facing the cloister garth. It would however be desirable to renew also some of the coping opposite, ie. over looking the Dean's garden, for which the South Western Stone Company could supply the stone. The fixing could be undertaken by the Abbey masons.

[Interior, miscellaneous]

Such other works as call for comment concern the interior. The Jacobean panelling in St George's chapel is being restored as a memorial to the Abbey staff.[5] The Brunel window, formerly on the north side of the nave, is being slightly reduced in size and replaced on the south side. The window in King Henry V's chantry is being filled with glass by Burlison and Grylls, formerly in the eastern aisle of the south transept.[6] Two wrought iron candelabra, presented by Lord Hinchinbrooke for use in St Faith's chapel, are being cleaned and restored by Messrs. Bainbridge Reynolds. Since these may all be in position by the time this report is presented, the results will already be evident.

To conceal the organ console, which was unduly prominent in the view looking west down the choir, curtains have been provided to the organ loft. A new Lenten array has been made for the Islip chapel; and from a length of very fine cloth of gold, presented privately, it is hoped to make a festival frontal for its altar.[7]

[1] The wax effigies had previously been displayed in the upper Islip Chapel. Files on the Museum for 1952–73 are WAM S/3/52.
[2] Put in the Museum in 1934 and designed by Bainbridge Reynolds (Lethaby report).
[3] R.P. Howgrave Graham, assistant Keeper of the Muniments 1948–59, also published other articles on the effigies including 'The Earlier Royal Funeral Effigies – new light on portraiture in Westminster Abbey', *Archaeologia* vol. XCVIII (1961). His conservation diary is WAM 64922.
[4] This window, in the eastern aisle of this transept, was not kept. Nor was that to Chaucer reinstated. Files on windows from 1952 to 1962 are in WAM S/3/30.
[5] Staff or former choristers who died during the war.
[6] The St Edward window. The work on this, and the adapting of the Brunel window, was done by Edward Woore.
[7] Files on furnishings from 1952 to 1973 are in WAM S/3/35–36.

55N. At Chapter on 26 February 1952 the Surveyor was to consult on the disposal of the Joseph Locke window, which had been taken down from the nave about 35 years previously. This was later taken to Barnsley. Also at this meeting and that on 25 March it was noted that the Coronation Stone had been replaced in the Coronation Chair but the question of its protection by a screen once it was returned to St Edward's chapel should be discussed with the Surveyor – the Stone had been stolen on Christmas Eve 1950 and returned in April 1951. It had been subsequently kept in the vault of the Islip chapel until it was replaced in the Chair. Letters about its authenticity are in WAM S/3/22. On 27 May 1952 the Surveyor was to discuss with the representation of the Ministry of Works the preparations of the Church for the forthcoming coronation. Letters on this subject are in WAM S/3/64.

56.   WAM S/1/96

Report by the Surveyor of the Fabric 1953

Preparations for the Coronation have necessarily restricted the amount of work that could be undertaken on the fabric during the last twelve months; and since it will presumably be another six months before the building is fully restored to its normal form, only twelve months work will have been accomplished in two years. In view of the pressing need to tackle much major repair, this lends still greater urgency to the Abbey Appeal and in particular to its objective of securing sufficient funds for an increase in the maintenance staff. Unless enough men can be employed to permit of more progress and greater speed, the main preoccupation in care of the fabric will be, not so much its preservation in sound condition, as a continual attempt to arrest its deterioration.

Stone work

The masons have been occupied during the year chiefly on work to the pinnacles and buttresses over the triforium apse and north transept, and on repairs to the jambs, cusping etc. of those clerestory windows and windows of Henry VII's chapel and its aisle that have been reglazed.

In the west cloister the wall has been built up solid where formerly there was a window opposite the foot of the main staircase in the Deanery.[1] The pointing of the masonry to the Langham and Litlyngton rooms has been finished.[2]

In the 'pit' between the apse and Henry VII's chapel, badly fractured stones in the parapet and elsewhere have been renewed and the scaffolding has been left in position to enable the walls, lime-washed during Lethaby's surveyorship, to be lime-washed again. This will improve the effect, viewed from within, of the glass in the west window of Henry VII's chapel and the stained glass in Henry V's Chantry.

Much of the external stonework of the west door of the nave is soft and flaking badly, though less urgently in need of attention than other stonework elsewhere. As a temporary measure loose, scaling portions have been removed and the stone brushed back to a hard surface. To the procession entering at the Coronation it would otherwise have presented a very unseemly aspect.

Glazing

Recent changes mark a notable stage forwards in freeing the building from some of its war time disfigurements. The windows throughout the whole of Henry VII's chapel, including the aisles, have been reglazed, bringing back to the interior its former lightness. The diamond quarries of medieval glass, bearing the letters H and R and which were formerly hardly noticed owing to being mixed with plain glass, have now been collected and re-set in the centre lights of the west window of each aisle.[3]

Equally welcome is the change wrought in the appearance of the nave and choir by the substitution of clear glass, matching that in the rest of the clerestory, for the dark 19th century stained glass[4] in the six war damaged windows immediately west of the crossing on the south side. For the first time for almost a hundred years an even balance of light throughout the nave, transepts and apse has been achieved. Through these great clerestory windows there now pours in a radiant flood of light, and the old glass in the three apse windows gains by being the only stained glass at this level.

[*Henry VII chapel*] *Woodwork*

In the last few weeks about half the stall canopies on the north side of Henry VII's chapel have been re-erected, following restoration by James Longley & Company Limited at Crawley: the remainder will be fixed after the Coronation. Having at intervals inspected the work in execution at one of the firm's joinery shops, which was set aside exclusively for the use of three selected craftsmen, I can testify to the skill and patience expended on it. Now that the canopies are once again in place, it is difficult to realise that a few months ago this woodwork was a collection of hundreds, if not thousands, of pieces, many of them so minute in size that it might have seemed impossible to re-assemble them. All were carefully examined, sorted and repaired where necessary, before being brought together again. This fine woodwork, necessarily fragile because of its intricacy, and smallness of scale, is probably now stronger than it has been for a very long time.

Structurally, therefore, Henry VII's chapel is, or shortly will be, fully restored and, after the Abbey is handed back by the Ministry of Works, the chief need here will be to clean all those parts that can be reached with the vacuum cleaner. When the stall canopies were removed the discolouration of the stonework above the heating grates behind them revealed only too clearly how much dirt, in a London building, is circulation all the time in the air.

Cleaning

A start was made some months ago on the cleaning of St Paul's chapel, but so far only the vaulting and the upper part of the walls have been finished. A return has been made here to the practice instituted by the late Sir Charles Peers and demonstrated in the triforium and clerestory of the apse – of polishing, rather than merely waxing the surface of the Purbeck marble shafts. It is necessarily a slow and laborious process, but, as Lethaby[5] pointed out, had the Purbeck always been kept polished it would not have deteriorated to the degree now reached when the distinctive quality of the material can hardly be recognised.

As a result of cleaning, a curious two-headed boss in the vault – practically invisible before owing to grime – can now be clearly seen from below, and a band of medieval painting has come to light on the east wall. This probably formed the top of an ornamental frame to a much larger painting, obliterated when the monument to Lord Cottington was built against this wall in 1678/9.

The boss has been photographed by Mr Howgrave Graham[6] and I am taking advice on the best means of preserving the wall painting.

The portion of this chapel now cleaned displays more clearly than ever what the whole of the interior of the Abbey could be like, and therefore deserves the notice of every visitor. But the time expended on just this small section has provided a salutory reminder that, if a quicker rate cannot be established when cleaning has to be tackled on a far bigger scale, half the benefits of the process will be nullified. By the time one end is finished, the other will be dirty again.

It is true that only two or three men were at work simultaneously on St Paul's chapel, and constantly they were having to be taken off the job to tackle something else, which no doubt the dislocation caused by the Coronation preparations made inevitable. But again it is worth pointing to the moral that a far larger regular staff is needed, so that the wasteful practice of switching men from one occupation to another can be avoided. There should be sufficient resources of men to enable the jobs of real importance to go steadily forward without interruption.

In my report of a year ago I expressed the hope that it would be possible to carry through the cleaning of St Paul's and St John's chapels while the Abbey was in the hands of the Ministry of Works. In the event it has taken six months to do one half of the chapel.

[*Watt statue*]

It is pertinent here to refer to the statue of James Watt. This portentous combination of an enormous figure on an enormous pedestal is so grossly out of scale with its surroundings as almost to kill the effect of the chapel and its other monuments. If there is the least hope of another home for it being found, the sooner this can be settled the better. If, after the cleaning of the chapel were finished, it then became necessary to take the Watt statue out,[7] the upheaval would be so great as to cause fresh dust and dirt to settle on everything.

Monuments

Cleaning of the monuments was proceeding steadily until the Ministry of Works took possession of the building; since then it has only been possible to deal with those monuments that are still exposed to view, such as the statues of various statesmen in the north transept.[8]

The choir stalls were cleaned by means of the vacuum cleaner.

Reredos [*High Altar*]

A lesser job of cleaning has been carried out to the reredos in preparation for the Coronation, chiefly to remedy the blackening of the cornice by smoke from the altar candles. Examination of the reredos from ladders showed a surprising number of breakages among the crockets, pinnacles and carved ornament generally, and I hope that opportunity will arise in the future to renew the missing fragments. Still more desirable would be an alteration comparatively simple and inexpensive to carry out. The appearance of the reredos would be immeasurably improved if the plate glass were removed from the two doors and oak panels substituted.[9] Glass in such doors is an architectural anachronism of the worst kind that, in the Abbey of all places, should not be tolerated.

Jerusalem Chamber

To make the Jerusalem Chamber more seemly for the reception of the Regalia before the Coronation the painted ceiling has had a preliminary cleaning and application of Rentokil and the panelling and tapestries have been vacuum cleaned. Getting rid of a great deal of dust has already improved its appearance, but much more work must follow. Examination of the roof from scaffolding has shown that the death watch beetle is present in many of the roof timbers and further treatment with Rentokil injected into the holes with a pressure gun will be necessary to ensure its eradication. The painting on the timbers can then receive the more thorough cleaning that it badly needs. The wall behind the existing painted frieze[10] which extends around three sides above the panelling and is already flaking, will then be made good and painted white. The plaster on either side of the north window, and the stone jambs and mullions to this and the two west windows, will be painted white to match.

I should be inclined to advocate the clearance of the large radiator enclosure[11] in the south west corner of the room. It takes up space, serves no purpose, and is a perpetual dust trap which has lately harboured dead rats.

New works

The closet formerly sited in the sacristy north of the vestibule to Henry VII's chapel has been replaced by a new one formed at the foot of the staircase on the south side opposite.

During the course of the year a stone tablet commemorating Cecil Rhodes was fixed on the west wall of the south aisle of Henry VII's chapel, and a new floor slab over the grave of Thomas Telford in the nave.

A walnut table to carry the duplicate copy of the Battle of Britain Roll of Honour is being made to replace the shelf now attached to the end of the stalls on the south side of Henry VII's chapel. Three new oak cases are being made for the Museum.

In St Faith's chapel new electric heating has been installed.

The four light window of the altar in Henry V's Chantry has been filled with stained glass representing Henry III, Edward I, Edward III and Henry VII, these four figures being part of the Burlison and Grylls glass formerly in the Hora window in the east aisle of the south transept.[12]

The Brunel window formerly on the north side of the nave was refixed after slight adaptation and re-arrangement in the south aisle opposite, only to be removed again to make an exit from the Coronation stands.

1   This was where the old monastic water tank had been situated, which received piped water from Hyde Park.
2   The two rooms in Cheyneygates that received bomb damage in 1941. The rebuilding divided these rooms from the main Deanery, and a wooden staircase was rebuilt. A door halfway up the stairs leads into the Deanery.
3   The glass is actually Tudor with the initials H and R for Henry VII Rex, with symbols of dragons and crowns.
4   The subjects here represented prophets and were by Thomas Ward. Installed in 1856 they were part of a larger scheme (not completed) for filling the clerestory windows with stained glass. There were also at least two in the west clerestory of the south transept and one on the east of this transept, also removed.
5   W.R. Lethaby was Surveyor from 1906 to 1928.
6   Howgrave Graham's negatives are in the Abbey Library collection.
7   It was finally removed in 1960 and a small plaster bust substituted (north choir aisle). The inscription on the statue was copied onto a stone in the floor of the chapel.
8   Correspondence about monuments and stones from 1952 to 1967 is in WAM S/3/41–46.
9   This was done and the panels were painted with various designs.
10 This was added by Dean Stanley in his restoration of the room in the 1870s and showed scenes from the history of the chamber. It is thought to remain underneath the white paint. The work was by Clayton & Bell.
11 This, based on the design on the gates of Henry VII's chapel, was put in store and still exists in the Abbey collection.
12 Other figures from this war-damaged window were installed in the inner room of Cheyneygates. The original window, with a figure of St Edward, had been presented by James Hora in 1903.

56N. At Chapter on 28 October 1952 the Surveyor was asked to design a new blue altar frontal for use at the coronation. This was not to cost more than £500 (Chapter 23 March 1954). In fact this was not completed in time for the ceremony. At the meeting on 8 December 1953 Dykes Bower's plans for the conversion of the Chapter Office to a new bookshop were discussed. He suggested raising the floor level to avoid having to go down as many as four steps into the shop. The two bottom steps of the staircase into the Jerusalem Chamber would also then be covered to make more room. He attended the 22 December meeting and fabric repairs were detailed. Expenditure reports from 1953 to 1968 are in WAM S/3/5.

57.   WAM S/1/97

Report 1954

For the greater part of the twelve months of which this annual report is a retrospect, work on the fabric had virtually to be suspended while the Abbey was in the occupation of the Ministry of Works before and after the Coronation. The success, however, of the Appeal for one million pounds,[1] which became evident as the term of its duration drew to a close, enabled a start to be made on many pressing tasks and, within a comparatively short period, a good deal has been done.

[*Stonework and decay*]

The attempt to overtake accelerating decay in the external stonework continues to be the chief and perennial concern, but the prospect of being able to undertake repairs on a much larger scale than has hitherto been possible is encouraging and a start has been made with the removal of Blore's parapets along the south side of the nave and the west side of the south transept, where the Bath stone had so deteriorated as to become dangerous. The purchase of additional scaffolding and an electric hoist now permits the simultaneous rebuilding of these parapets – totalling in length nearly 300 feet – in Portland stone, matching the corresponding parapet on the north side which was renewed earlier in the century. The substitution of battlements for pierced quatrefoils will restore the parapet to its original form and give it greater durability.

Repair of the pinnacles and flying buttresses above the triforium, between the north transept and the apse, has continued. The fractured parapets of the well between the apse and Henry VII's chapel have been reconstructed, and other masonry repairs to the walls below them completed. All the stonework of this well has been lime washed.

In connection with the reglazing of various windows in the triforium and elsewhere, opportunity has been taken to replace decayed cusping with new stone, and the Chaucer window has recently been scaffolded to permit of the renewal of the central mullion.

[*Cloisters*]

As a precaution following small intermittent falls of stone, the vaulting of the cloisters was examined from a travelling scaffold and the surface brushed free of loose and scaling material. On the north side of the nave splints were fixed to one of the pinnacles of which the spire was insecure.

A chemical investigation has been carried out by Professor Whittard in the science department of Bristol University, into the cause of stone failure in the cloisters. A full report has been received from him, together with the results of tests into the properties of certain kinds of stone, submitted for trial to ascertain their suitability for use in the restoration of the cloisters.

[*Lead roofs*]

In August 1953 a detailed survey was begun of the condition of all lead roofs on the fabric and adjacent buildings. The more obviously defective parts were already known, but now that the survey is finished the general condition of the lead has been found to be worse than was realised. The only satisfactory roofs are those which were re-cast and re-laid by Mr Corse from about 1925 to 1935; everywhere else there are defects that, if not rectified, will give trouble in the future. Some of these can be deferred for a few years, but others are urgent and the order had already been given for the largest of them – the re-covering of the nave roof, together with the roofs of the two western towers.

This work it was hoped to start in the spring of 1954 but when the stone parapet and some of the masonry in the courses immediately below were removed, the feet of the main roof rafters were revealed and found to have suffered badly from attack by death watch beetle, as well as wet and some dry rot. The lead gutters proved to be laid on an unsatisfactory system of wooden supports in similar condition. To leave timber so affected in position would clearly be unwise, and reconstruction of the top of the wall will now be necessary.

Inspection of the roof showed, moreover, other weaknesses. That these had become evident at some former time may be deduced from the addition to the original roof formation of king post trusses between the level of the collar and the main tie beam across the base. The intention was to add strength, but in fact the weight of the king post exerted on the tie beam at its centre has caused deflection as deep as nine inches. The king post trusses are now doing harm rather than good and would be better removed. The requisite strengthening of the original roof construction could more effectively be provided by steel members framed to give support both to the main roof rafters and the collars.

This however will necessitate much extra and unforeseen work that will take a considerable time to complete. Stripping of the lead here, prior to recasting and re-laying, must therefore be postponed until the roof is secure and meanwhile, in order not to lose the summer months, I recommend that priority be given to the repair of the lead roofs on the triforium of Henry VII's chapel, the western towers, the Jerusalem Chamber and the Chapter Office.

[*Cleaning*]

The main work in the interior has been the cleaning of St Paul's Chapel, now finished, and St John's chapel, still in progress. This has entailed the washing of the vaulting and walls, the polishing of the marble is in itself a slow progress, but in St John's chapel much time has also had to be spent in removing the shellac which was applied – it is believed by Sir Gilbert Scott – as a protective coat on the stonework, and which had darkened its colour. In the course of the work various interesting details came to light – in St Paul's chapel the roof boss of a two-headed man and a band of mural painting above the Cottington monument, the former hitherto almost invisible and the latter unknown. Much original painted decoration on the monuments can now be seen, faded but still distinct enough to indicate the intended colouring. On the other hand cleaning has shown how severely the surface of the many choice marbles, used in these monuments, has suffered from the corrosive acids in the atmosphere owing to failure to keep them polished, as also from extensive damage resulting in the mutilation or loss of portions of their design. A decision will soon have to be taken on how far such damage should be made good and whether it would be desirable to restore original colouring where it can clearly be recognised, before time finally obliterates all trace of it.

[Other cleaning including Jerusalem Chamber]

Many lesser cleaning jobs – to the reredos, the tombs on the north side of the sanctuary and elsewhere – were carried out as part of the preparations for the coronation. The cleaning of the Jerusalem Chamber was carried only so far as to make it more seemly for the reception of the regalia on the night before the ceremony. From scaffolding now about to be erected the painted ceiling will be treated for the extermination of death watch beetle; and, when that has been done, the frieze, lime washed only on the north end last summer, will be lime washed on all four sides. I hope that at the same time it will be possible to install better lighting fittings, to have the tapestries cleaned, and to remove the stove in the south west corner, which is never used, takes up much space, and harbours dirt and dust.

[Henry VII's chapel]

In Henry VII's chapel replacement of the stall canopies after restoration has been completed in accordance with the contract. Seeing now the richer effect of those on the north side, I think it would be desirable to make good various missing pieces to certain canopies on the south side that were refixed by the Abbey staff, but without any attempt to supply members that had been lost.

The reglazed west window is at last free of the scaffolding which, during the coronation period when it could not be employed for structural repair of the fabric, had to be stored in the well, obscuring light and spoiling the appearance of the glass.

The altar ornaments and standard candlesticks in the Battle of Britain chapel, owing to failure of the lacquer on the silver, have now been silver gilt. The altar rails are at present being treated to match. A new linen altar frontal has been provided for use in Lent.

The duplicate copy of the Battle of Britain Roll of Honour formerly lodged on a small shelf at the east end of the row of stalls on the south side, is now carried on a walnut table, made and presented for the purpose.[2]

[Courtenay grave discovered]

Shortly before the Abbey was re-opened to the public at the end of November 1953, a small hole was noticed in the floor of the Confessor's Chapel. Probing showed that there was a cavity of some size below and it was deemed advisable to investigate further. This led to the discovery of the hitherto unknown tomb of Bishop Courtenay, whose skeleton was found together with the remains of a wooden crozier and a fine gold ring, set with a large ruby. Full notes, measurements and photographs were taken before the tomb was sealed over and I recorded for the archives a detailed account of the proceedings. Although the finding of the ring was not disclosed, the event secured considerable notice in the press and aroused much interest.[3]

[*Coronation Chair*]

Wide publicity was also given to the cleaning of the Coronation Chair and the new light thrown on its history as a result of research by Mr Percival Prescott of the Ministry of Works. An illustrated booklet, issued by the Stationery Office, summarized his conclusions and a fuller report, in a limited edition, will be available shortly.[4] X-ray photographs of the Chair showed that its existing decoration superseded an earlier scheme of painting, of which a few remains are just visible; but the treatment of the Chair was confined to careful cleaning and the only alterations made in its appearance were the removal of one or two crude wooden strengthening members of 19th century date, and the substitution of new velvet covered arm rests for the previous upholstered ones that were themselves an incongruous addition before the Jubilee service of Queen Victoria.

[*Organ cases*]

With a view to the restoration of the Pearson organ cases, discussions have been proceeding between Sir William McKie, Messrs Harrison and Harrison and myself for the replanning of the instrument to fit them. An estimate for this work has now been received and I shall shortly be putting forward definite proposals.

[*New works*]

Among new works may be mentioned four new oak show cases for the museum and the five coronation copes, made of specially woven silk damask. The wrought iron grille to surround the Coronation Chair is now being made to my design. The wrought iron gates in the entrance to the cloisters from Dean's Yard have been repainted in red and gold.

[*21 Dean's Yard*]

Passing now to the house, no. 21 Dean's Yard has been adapted to become the Chapter Office with a flat on the top floor. Plans have been prepared and estimates will shortly be ready for converting the north end of the former Chapter Office[5] into a bookshop to take the place of the book stall in the south transept.

[*Choir and Song schools*]

In the Choir School a new central heating boiler was installed and a new domestic boiler has been ordered. The front and back staircases were repainted.

A new asphalte roof has been laid on the Song School, which has been redecorated inside.

[*Houses*]

The restoration of 4B Dean's Yard after war damage was completed and the house brought into occupation.

In no. 20 Dean's Yard the main bedroom, dressing room, spare bedroom and one bathroom were redecorated.[6] A cork floor was laid in the dining room and other small jobs carried out. Among further works needed are the provision of new windows to the drawing room, removal of the canvas lining to its walls, plastering and redecoration, the redecoration of the hall and waiting room, and the demolition of the unused room at the east end of the garden.

Following an inspection of no. 2 The Cloisters, proposals have been made for remodelling the basement and ground floors, which would reduce the size of the house and make it more convenient. Others needs are renewal of the electric wiring, the installation of central heating and remodelling of the plumbing and general redecoration. It has not so far been possible to proceed with any of this work.

In no. 1 Little Cloisters where trouble had been experienced through the presence of too large an air pocket behind the heater and cooker flues, causing reduction of the effective draught, the flues have now been reduced to 6" diameter and carried into one outlet. Damp in the kitchen floor and walls requires attention and a good deal of redecoration to all floors is due. The house was last decorated in 1947.

On no. 4 Little Cloisters the roof needs re-tiling and the lead gutter re-forming. In No. 5 the hall is very damp and the size of the room makes it difficult to heat. A scheme is in preparation for separating it from the rest of the house and putting it to some appropriate use. A new front entrance will be formed from the forecourt of No. 4.

External painting is being carried out on nos. 4 and 5. It is also required on nos. 1 and 2, where I recommend that the same choice of colour – white – should be adopted.

S.E. Dykes Bower, Surveyor of the Fabric.

[1] The appeal for the restoration of the fabric and interior cleaning was launched in the Jerusalem Chamber by the Prime Minister, Winston Churchill, on 30 January 1953. Correspondence is in WAM S/3/8. See also WAM 65048–51, 65095 and volumes for The American Fund for Westminster Abbey in the muniment collection. The target sum was reached on 24 May 1954.

[2] The table and also a Lenten frontal for this altar were designed by the Surveyor (Chapter 26 January 1954). The duplicate copy of the book now resides with the Dean's Verger.

[3] Richard Courtenay, bishop of Norwich, died in 1415 and was buried in the Abbey by the express command of Henry V. The ring was not re-buried and is on display in the Queen's Diamond Jubilee Galleries at the Abbey. Photos by R.P. Howgrave Graham of the grave are in the Abbey Library, the plan of the site is WAM (P) 828 and a typescript by the Surveyor is in WAM S/3/1.

[4] Copies are in the Library. A full conservation and cleaning programme was carried out in 2011–13 with the addition of a new front tracery panel, in order that the Chair could be displayed under a new canopy in St George's chapel.

⁵   This house was formerly the Chapter Clerk's residence, designed by Edward Blore in
    1847–8 and built by William Cubitt & Co, with a passage linking to his office facing Broad
    Sanctuary in front of Jerusalem Chamber (now the Bookshop, opened in 1956). It had
    been used as two flats from 1939 (one being called 21A), initially for use by a minor canon
    or the choir school headmaster but they were used by Abbey Registrar Tom Hebron and
    later by Canon Frederic Donaldson after his house had been blitzed during the war –
    WAM OA/03/42 (4–5). The flat known as 21A was incorporated into the main Chapter
    Office in 1958 (Chapter 22 July). In 1977 the Chapter Office moved to the renovated 20
    Dean's Yard. After being leased out for some years the Abbey later re-occupied no. 21 for
    more offices.
⁶   This was a Canon's house until the 1970s. Files on houses in the precincts from 1951 to
    1973 are in WAM S/3/49.

57N.   At Chapter on 27 April 1954 it was noted that the Surveyor was to prepare
a design for the case to house the sword of George VI, recently presented by
The Queen and The Queen Mother for display in Henry VII's chapel.

58.   WAM S/1/98

Westminster Abbey Restoration

Progress report by the Surveyor of the Fabric

[undated but 1954]

The Nave roof

Work began on the nave roof[1] early this year with the removal of the stone
parapets on the south side of the nave and the west side of the south transept. In
the process of lifting the lead gutters to enable the lower courses of stone to be
taken out, the feet of the main roof timbers were revealed and a serious state of
affairs disclosed. Almost all of them, also the wall plates, were found to be badly
decayed as a result of wet rot and attack by death watch beetle. This rendered
necessary further close investigation of the whole woodwork of the nave roof
and examination showed that death watch beetle was present in all but a few
timbers. A major task of the last few months and one which will continue for
some time ahead has been the treatment of this roof to exterminate the beetle
and protect the wood against further attack. This is being done first from inside
and then, as the lead is lifted bay by bay, will also be carried on from outside.
It was found that most of the roof rafters were cut from oak trees about 60–80
years old, not as often, from trees 200 to 250 years old. Thus there is sap wood
on both sides, which is readily subject to attack, though after it has been cut
away enough strength remains in the heart of the timber to obviate replacement
except in a few cases. Where however new oak has to be supplied or scarfed on
to existing members, it is being specially selected and either sprayed or steeped
in sodium pentchlorophenate.

Badly affected timbers that are incapable of retention are treated before removal and later destroyed.

It is interesting to note that the roof rafters, which are roughly 4 by 7 inches and laid with their widest side horizontally, are spaced at approximately 16 inches centres which is the standard for similar timber construction today. Where larger baulks of timber occur the span is widened.

While priority has thus had to be given to the woodwork of the roof, the progress in rebuilding the parapet has necessarily been slower than was hoped, but some of the new stonework is now in position in the western bays and a reserve of worked stone is on the site awaiting fixing. Fresh deliveries will arrive from the quarry when this had been used up.

Similarly the stripping of the lead has been deferred until the treatment of the timbers from inside has been completed. In general, the opening up of those parts that have hitherto been invisible has shown the state of the structure to be worse than was already known and the scope of the remedial work necessary is proving larger than had been anticipated. Investigation of the wooden roofs over the vaulting in other parts of the building has confirmed that the death watch beetle is active to a serious extent and if as much work has to be done elsewhere as it now in progress on the nave roof, there will be a large programme of this work for the next few years.

Jerusalem Chamber

For some months the Jerusalem Chamber has been undergoing restoration and it will probably be brought back into use about the beginning of 1955. The samples of wood here exhibited show the nature of the damage to the roof which has been caused by death watch beetle. They demonstrate how serious would have been the consequences had the damage not been discovered in time. When scaffolding was erected and close examination became possible, the oak was found to be riddled with death watch beetle, live grubs being discovered in timbers that were already almost completely perforated. Although there was nothing from below to indicate the grave damage, ultimate collapse of the roof would have been inevitable.

The lead work has been stripped and the timbers treated both externally and internally, though as a precaution treatment will be repeated at intervals of twelve months for the next three or four years. The lead is being recast and will shortly be re-laid. After dismantling of the internal scaffolding the floor will be uncovered since trouble has been discovered in the cellars which extend beneath this room and the College Hall.

The Cloisters

In the cloisters a start has been made with washing the traceried windows and walls on the south and west walks. The stonework here, renewed about a hundred years ago, was beginning to show signs of succumbing to attack by acids in the atmosphere and, in so far as washing frees the surface of corrosive deposits, the life of the stone should thereby be prolonged. The improvement in its appearance is very noticeable.

Glazing of the upper part of the windows has begun and this, by keeping the weather out, will help to arrest deterioration of the vaulting.

Tests of various kinds of stone have been proceeding with a view to ascertaining their durability in London conditions. The results are now being considered but it is unlikely that a start will be made on a large scale restoration of the cloisters until stone repairs on the higher portions of the main building have reached a more advanced stage.

Interior cleaning

Internally the cleaning of St Paul's chapel and St John's chapel, the first items in the general cleaning of stonework, have been finished and are instructive in showing how the original colour of the stone can be recovered once the overlay of dirt and grime is removed. Cleaning has now been started on the Confessor's chapel and should be finished before the end of the year. Steel beams will then be placed across the presbytery at triforium level and scaffolding built up on top to enable the two western bays of the presbytery from the triforium up to the vaulting to be cleaned. When this is finished, cleaning of the arches and pillars below will follow.

The cleaning of St Paul's and St John's chapels included the cleaning of the exceptionally fine monuments, though some repair work is still in progress where they have suffered from damage or neglect in the past.

Repair of windows broken as a result of bomb damage during the war is continuing: the two largest now in hand are the Chaucer window and its equivalent in the north transept. In the Chaucer window considerable repair of stonework has been necessary.

[1]   Photos of beetle damage and correspondence regarding this roof are in WAM S/3/17.

59.   WAM S/1/99

Progress Report on Restoration. Dec 15 1954

Now that the cleaning of the Confessor's chapel is almost finished and the scaffolding available for use elsewhere, it may be useful that I should state the order in which other portions of the east end should be cleaned and the estimates for carrying out each stage of the work.

It was agreed some time ago that as soon as the apse was finished, the vaulting, clerestory and triforium in the two bays west of it should be cleaned. But the scaffolding for this will be erected on a bridge spanning the presbytery and this bridge is not to be erected till after the Epiphany next year. Since polishing of the Purbeck marble pillars is now the only job awaiting completion in the Confessor's chapel, it became necessary to transfer to other work the men who have been engaged on stone washing, so that they can be kept in continuous occupation. I therefore arranged for them to move to the triforium of the apse and presbytery, where the roof timbers are being treated against death watch and lyctus beetle. This process, which involves cutting away infected sap wood, inevitably brings down a good deal of wood dust and dirt and therefore makes cleaning expedient. After the timbers in each bay have been treated, stone cleaning will follow.

Only a limited number of men, however, can be employed in the space of one triforium bay and it was desirable to provide work for the rest and to put to use the scaffolding which, in the triforium, is not required. This has now been erected in the portion of the north ambulatory between the Confessor's chapel and the chapels of St Paul and St John, where the contrast of cleaned and uncleaned stone is more obvious. The scaffolding can be so disposed that the use of the ambulatory for processions at Christmas will not be impeded, and screens will be provided to keep dirt from soiling the above mentioned chapels.

The time schedule for cleaning that part of the triforium eastward of the line of the reredos of the chancel is six weeks; for the part west of it (ie. two bays on each side) four weeks. One of the radiating chapels has already been done and the next started, so that, allowing for the Christmas holiday, the eastward section should be about finished by the time the bridge is in position. The other section it will be more convenient to undertake as the cleaning of the two west bays of the presbytery comes down to triforium level.

The time schedule for the north ambulatory, from Henry V's chantry (which is being cleaned by our own men and will, I hope, be finished by Christmas) to the line of the reredos, is twelve weeks. Here however, apart from the vaulting and arches of the arcade, there is comparatively little stone to be washed: the chief work will be polishing the Purbeck marble pillars. Therefore, since the job will begin with the vaulting and arches, it may be assume d that the stone washers will be available to move to the presbytery just about the time when the scaffolding there is ready for them. The marble polishers will come later.

Four months was the period first estimated by the London Stone Cleaning Company[1] for the cleaning of the west bays of the presbytery down to triforium floor level. In the light of experience gained in the Confessor's chapel, they now hope that they may be able to reduce it. But if the scaffolding cannot all be moved by Easter, the bulk of it should be gone. The next stage, cleaning the arcade from triforium level down to the sanctuary floor, should take from two to three months: but I have deferred consideration of this because various problems in connection with the use of the sanctuary will need to be discussed.

Again deployment of available manpower must influence the sequence of work. The stages of the presbytery cleaning – vaulting, clerestory, triforium – will not, by themselves, give scope for all the men who can profitably be kept busy and it should, I think, be possible to undertake concurrently some cleaning elsewhere. Thus while the presbytery cleaning proceeds, I would suggest tackling that portion of the south ambulatory from Henry V's chantry to the line of the reredos, which should take eight weeks, and at the same time to vacuum clean the two chapels – to bring them up to the same finish as the north chapels – which should also take eight weeks. Concurrently also with the cleaning of the presbytery from triforium down to sanctuary floor should be undertaken cleaning the remainder of the north and south ambulatories, which would require eight and six weeks respectively.

These proposals and their cost may now be set out thus:

Cleaning	Start	End (approx)	Cost
Triforium, east of reredos	Dec 1st 1954	Jan 15th 1955	£ 750
North ambulatory, " "	Dec 15 1954	Mar 5th 1955	1650
Presbytery – above triforium	Jan 10 1955	Apr 30 1955	2480
South chapels St Nicholas	Mar 6 1955	Apr 2 1955	232
St Edmund	Apr 4 1955	Apr 30	442
Triforium, west of reredos	May 2 1955	May 28	400
S.Ambulatory, east " "	May 2	May 28	443
Presbytery, below triforium	May 30	Sep 10 say	2000
N.Ambulatory, west of reredos	May 30	Jul 23	1000
S. Ambulatory, " "	Jul 25	Sep 30	700

Total cost £10,097.

Naturally this represents an ideal time chart, to which for one reason or another it may not prove possible to adhere: the dismantling and erection of scaffolding, for example, may interpose delays between different items of work. It might also be well to cut into the programme in the spring to interpose the washing of the east and north walls of the cloisters, which would take eight weeks each and cost £900 and £1250 respectively. The greater cost over the south and west walls is accounted for by the greater height of the parapets to which cleaning would have to be extended.

But with three month's recovery margin, this programme indicates what I judge to be the amount of work that could be carried out in 1955. Cleaning of the interior east of the crossing would be finished.

In 1956 it should be possible to complete the cleaning of the north transept with which would be coupled the repair of the glass in the rose window and inserting new stained glass in the lancets below. The cost of this glazing would be recoverable from the War Damage Commission.

In 1957 a start could be made on the choir, the four bays of which (ie. including the bay occupied by the organ screen) would require a year. That entails consideration of the organ. If the organ cases are to be reinstated, it will be necessary to synchronise the unavoidable alteration of the instrument with the cleaning of the arches in which it is set. And since the organ builder will probably require at least a year's notice of the period in which he will be able to operate, a decision about the organ ought to be taken by the end of 1955.

By the end of 1958 I should hope that cleaning would have extended to the western termination of Henry III's work and to have included replacement of the temporary roof over the lantern by a permanent roof, the reglazing of the eight windows in the lantern – both recoverable charges from the War Damage Commission – and cleaning of the crossing. It might also include the polishing of those pillars in the south transept that were left undone before the war, the completion of its cleaning and going over the walling generally with a vacuum cleaner to freshen its colour.

Even if unforeseen delays intervened and the work so far outlined ended only in 1960, there would still be five years in which to tackle the cleaning of the nave and its aisles. That should be enough to ensure the transformation of the interior by 1965, the 900th anniversary of the founding.

If the total cost of cleaning the eastern arm of the crossing with its radiating chapels, be put at £15,000 and estimating a like sum for the north transept the choir and for each of the four bays of the nave, the cost would be £75,000–£20,000. Allowing for contingencies and work to the monuments £100,000 – a figure below that finally given in the appeal – would be about right.

Turning now to the work on the roofs, the first months of this year were occupied with opening up, examination of the extent of the damage to the timbers and preparation of a scheme for overcoming the structural weaknesses disclosed. This was finally settled in the summer and work started about August. Since then nine new steel tie-beams have been placed in position over the three western bays of the nave, of which that between the towers is wider than the others. Further beams are on order and due for delivery at any time. Now that some of the initial difficulties have been faced, the rate of progress ought to be accelerated, though the irregularity of the nave roof causes no two bays to be quite identical in dimensions so that the job can never be one of straightforward repetition. I hope however that the steel should be fixed in at least a further six bays by the end of 1955.

As soon as a sufficient length of roof is set free by the engineers, the lead workers can commence stripping the outer covering for recasting and the masons with fixing the new stone in the parapets. The lead could in fact be stripped between the towers now, but as it would be inadvisable to do so in the winter, this will be deferred till the spring. As soon as the lead is removed, the roof timbers will be treated from above, as well as from below, against death watch beetle.

At present some additional work is being carried out in underpinning the south east angle of the north west tower at its junction with the north wall of the nave at parapet level. A serious weakness came to light here and it has proved necessary to replace with reinforced concrete some of the interior walling that was composed of no more than loose rubble. This will occupy attention for some little time.

If another year and a half or two years are required to complete the nave roof, probably four years should suffice for the roofs of the transepts, presbytery and apse.

Over the roof of Henry VII's chapel, where the presence of the long horn beetle has been found in the roof timbers, which are of soft wood not oak, scaffolding is now being erected to make possible remedial treatment which it would be too hazardous to undertake from the top of the vaulting: it should be fixed before Christmas so that work can begin in the new year. Since the long horn beetle is even more difficult to eradicate than the death watch, this scaffolding may have to be kept in position for some years, to permit periodic inspections and fresh applications of insecticide.

Apart from the leadwork and masonry, for which estimates have already been obtained and given in previous reports, it is impossible to predict with accuracy the cost of the structural work to the roof. The extent of what is required in any one portion varies according to the state of what is found. When however more has been done and a clearer picture can be gained of what may be expected as average conditions, there may be a better basis on which to form an idea of approximate expenditure.

By 1965 the aim should be to have completed all the work to the roofs – steel, timber, leadwork and masonry – so that their safety should be ensured. Thereafter the main tasks would be confined to masonry – the restoration of the north west tower and the cloisters, if these cannot be started before, and the continuous replacement, all over the fabric, of decaying stone with new. This latter process must necessarily last for years because some deterioration cannot be avoided so long as the conditions which cause it persist.

At present one mason is working full time in the nave roof and the others are pointing up open joints in Henry V's Chantry and the triforium of the apse.

A survey has now been made of the Infirmary Hall so that drawings can be prepared for the internal repairs needed to fit it for use as a room for occasional meetings and a vestry for the Brotherhoods of St Edward and St Peter.[2] Preliminary inspection of the roof has shown that death watch beetle is present in the timbers of the roof and a more thorough examination will be made before Christmas, when some of the plaster between the puncheons will be cut out to reveal the state of the wall plates now invisible.

In the cloisters two painters have been employed in painting the wrought iron grilles in the windows of the south walk. They are now working on the 18th century grille and gates in the east walk and will continue on the similar one in the west walk. All this iron work was suffering badly from rust and the loss of missing parts, to the distortion of the design. These missing parts are being made by Bainbridge Reynolds & Company and will be fixed when ready.

Later on, when all the houses in the Little Cloister are finished, it would be advisable to re-paint the 18th century ironwork in the arches to the garden and to wash their stonework, as a protection against decay.

The oval windows in the Dark Entry, looking into the garden of Ashburnham House, will be glazed as soon as the masons have carried out the necessary repairs to the stonework. These and the long window south of them, now in poor condition, will be fitted with specially thick glass to deaden noise from the shooting range.

When this has been done, so that at least some draught and dust are excluded, it would be desirable to repair the plaster vaulting, clean the mural tablets and stonework and then limewash the walls, here and in the passage to the Little Cloister. I would suggest that the provision of glazed swing doors at the south end of the Dark Entry[3] ie. to Little Dean's Yard, should be considered. So long as the ends are open, it will be difficult to prevent this passage being a tunnel and again getting as dirty as it is now.

There has been an enforced pause in the work in the Jerusalem Chamber while waiting for new oak of the exceptional size required for the main principal to be replaced. This has now arrived and, after impregnation against death watch beetle attack, will be placed in position. It will then be possible to finish such work as remains to the roof so that the new lead covering can be laid. Norman & Underwood, the firm who are to do this, should be able to proceed to it straight from the roof of the former Chapter Office which, as part of the alterations in converting it to be the new bookstall, is to be tackled first.

The internal scaffolding in Jerusalem must remain until the frieze has been limewashed and the new oak principal painted. A decision will have to be taken however about the entire painting of the roof. Though this may be assumed to preserve the pattern and colouring of the original medieval decoration, most if not all of it is a 19th century repainting that has faded badly. What for example was intended to be white or ivory has become a drab cream and there has been a corresponding loss in the strength of the red and greens.

If this were the original decoration it would be reasonable only to paint the new principal and any other new oak to match the rest. As it is not, I think it would be preferable to repaint all those portions that have clearly lost their intended tones.

Arrangements have now been made for the large quantity of stained glass from bomb damaged 19th century windows, now stored loose or in boxes in the triforium, to be removed by the glaziers, Goddard & Gibbs Limited, to their workshop in Shoreditch. They have undertaken to store them and in due course to lay the glass out for inspection. None of the figure work would be suitable for re-use, but some of the medallions, borders and grisaille are too good to discard. I would like to reserve them for the eight lights of the lantern, which will have to be reglazed, when the present broken glass has been removed. At that height the glass might look very well and have much the appearance of old glass.

In St John's chapel the painting of the Hunsdon monument and shields on other memorials is finished. The only work remaining here is the restoration of the Exeter tomb which starts on December 20th.

To ensure that, when this is done, we shall be able to retain the services of Mr Butchart, who painted the Hunsdon monument, I should like to employ him on the monuments in St Paul's chapel. The two cleaners on the Abbey staff are at present working on Queen Elizabeth's monument in the north aisle of Henry VII's chapel and when they have done the bulk of this Mr Butchart could repaint the heraldry with which it is abundantly adorned. But it would not be possible for him to undertake the fine monuments in St Paul's chapel until their marble, which is badly perished, has been made good and polished, and other missing ornaments supplied. I propose therefore to obtain from Earp & Hobbs Limited, who did the work on the Hunsdon monument, estimates for what is needed in St Paul's chapel so that, if these are approved, there shall be no break in their employment after the Exeter monument is completed.

In this connection it may be opportune to mention the desirability of removing the statue of James Watt. If there is any chance of a home for it being found in Scotland, the sooner it can be transferred the better.

It remains to report that a start on the Abbey bookstall[4] has been made with the structural alterations to be carried out by Dove Bros., and that the improvements to the heating of the Song School have been finished by Drake & Gorham.

S.E. Dykes Bower, Surveyor of the Fabric, December 15th 1954.

[1]   An album of photos taken of their work is in the Abbey Library.
[2]   These groups act as servers and cross bearers in Abbey festival and Communion services. Those in the Brotherhood of St Edward are old choristers of the Abbey.
[3]   This was not done.
[4]   Files on the Bookshop and its later extensions are in WAM S/3/57–59.

59N.   Chapter also recorded items in this report, the money for repairs to come from the Abbey Appeal fund (8 June and 27 July 1954).

60.   WAM S/1/100

Report by the Surveyor of the Fabric 1955

As I submitted a statement earlier this year on the general progress of the restoration work, it is not necessary in this report to add much about items that were so recently described.

Nave roof

A temporary roof of steel has now been constructed and is in position over the western bays of the nave. This will enable the lead to be stripped, and the roof timbers to be examined and treated from above. While there is thus protection from the weather the aim is to carry out all the remaining work required, chiefly the replacement of defective timbers and to complete this section of roof so that the masons can build the first length of the south parapet. The temporary roof will then be re-erected over the next bays and the process will be continued throughout the length of the nave.

Much time had to be spent on underpinning the south east corner of the north west tower, but this job has been completed and I hope it will henceforward be possible to concentrate on the roof itself, since it will probably be at least three years or more before the nave is finished.

Henry VII's chapel

The area between the outer roof and the vault has been scaffolded and the timbers examined and treated with insecticide. The scaffolding must remain in position for a long time ahead, since successive applications will be needed and the timbers kept under observation to ensure that the long horn beetle, which is even more insidious than the death watch and difficult to detect, has been eradicated.

Interior cleaning

Progress with this has been good and the time schedules have been adhered to and in some instances improved upon. The Confessor's chapel, the four radial chapels, and the north ambulatory with the exception of its two western bays are finished. Work is now proceeding on the eastern bay of the north ambulatory and the upper part of the two bays of the presbytery.

When scaffolding made possible an examination of the vaulting, a great number of fractures were found in the infilling and at the junction of the vaulting with the side walls over the clerestory windows. They proved to be less serious than a first view suggested and have now been made good by the masons. I am told by Mr Bishop that similar fractures were found when the apse was cleaned before the last war and it is interesting to recall that Wren, in a report to Dean Atterbury in 1713 wrote 'the vaulting now covering the Quire, tho' it be more adorned and gilded, is without due care in the masonry, and is the worst performed of all done before'. He added 'this is now amended with all care, and I dare promise it shall be much stronger and securer than ever the first builders left it'.

The original decoration of the vault was then re-painted – a curious attempt to reproduce the medieval pattern in the manner of Wren's time though effective when seen from floor level. As much of the paint has flaked off it is being retouched where necessary. The same was done in the apse and care is being taken to preserve consistency with the work there.

I hope that the scaffolding will be taken down at the end of June, when the bridge can be re-erected in the two bays of the north transept next to the crossing. Cleaning will then begin on the arcades of the presbytery.

In Henry V's Chantry the washing of the reredos and newel staircases has been carried out by the Abbey staff. Save for some repairs to the floor, the interior of the Chantry is nearly finished. The next work is the cleaning of the fronts to the ambulatories.

Monuments

In St John's chapel all the monuments, with the exception of the medieval tombs of Abbot Fascet and Bishop Ruthall, have been cleaned and their heraldry repainted. The large Exeter tomb in the centre was in a poor state of neglect, many of the features of its architectural design being loose or missing. These have been made good but no attempt has been made to restore missing parts of the sculpture e.g. the hands of the two recumbent figures.

The Hunsdon monument is now an exemplar of what monuments of its period should be – the marble re-polished and the ornament gilded and coloured. I hope it may be possible to treat the similar, though smaller monuments in the other chapels in the same way.

The tomb of Queen Elizabeth in the north aisle of Henry VII's chapel has been partially cleaned and polished. But so many parts of its design are missing and need to be supplied that, until a decision can be taken on its proper restoration and painting, I have transferred the cleaners on to the two Halifax monuments close by.

Glazing

The Chaucer window in the south transept and the corresponding window in the north have been re-glazed with clear glass and repairs carried out to the stonework and ironwork. This work was paid for by the War Damage Commission, with whom a claim has been negotiated for the repair of the stained glass in the rose window of the north transept and the triforium windows in the south wall of the south transept.

The Triforium

Washing of the stonework has been completed throughout the triforium of the presbytery and eastern sides of both transepts, but the marble shafts have not yet been polished. A great deal of repointing to the walls has been carried out by the masons. The roof timbers have been carefully inspected and, after cutting away of all rotten sapwood, have been treated with insecticide. Timbers that have been badly attacked by death watch beetle and will have to be cut out, have been marked for replacement as soon as the joiners can tackle this job.

To ascertain the condition of the supporting timbers under the floor boarding, a first examination took place in the space over St John's chapel. Wood worm was found in the underside of much of the boarding but the general condition of the main supporting members appeared fairly good, with practically no sign of death watch beetle. The floor joists have however inadequate bearing on the wall plate, which accounts for a certain springiness in the floor and a means of stiffening them is now being considered.

The condition of the floor in this section affords, of course, no guarantee that it will be the same elsewhere. But it is at least satisfactory that a second opening of the floor – this time on the south side – showed nothing worse or very different. It will still be a necessary precaution to open all parts and, in doing so, to take advantage of the chance to remove from the pockets of the vaulting the deep accumulation of debris, which imposes extra weight on the vaulting ribs and infilling. Over St John's chapel the method adopted was to lift it in long handled scoops, the material then being bagged in sacks and lowered externally down to ground level for carting away in lorries. The material is sifted before being bagged but, in the varied assortment of objects that came up, nothing of special interest, except an antique chisel, has so far been found.

All timbers, whether sound or not, will be treated with insecticide. I have not yet decided how far the floor boarding, infected with wood worm, should be replaced by new because, thought this might be desirable, it is impossible to compute the cost until the extent of the defective areas is known.

For many years the triforium has been a store for a growing collection of fragments of stone, woodwork, metalwork, glass, books, pictures and many other things. After inspection by the Dean, Canon Carpenter, the Clerk of Works and myself, a start was made on clearing these objects that either had no value or were never likely to be used. The stonework was sorted and pieces of no value have been removed for breaking up. What has been kept is either of interest or suitable for sale as souvenir fragments. Some of the woodwork has been disposed of to the London Diocesan Fund for use in bombed churches that are to be rebuilt. The glass has all been removed by the firm of glaziers who have worked on the Abbey windows and has now been sorted and laid out in their shops for my inspection. I hope shortly to go through it to decide what might be of use in the reglazing of the eight windows of the lantern.

New works / additions

A memorial slab to William Herschel was laid in the north aisle of the nave and a tablet commemorating the setting up of Caxton's printing press and the assistance given by the press to the Abbey Appeal, was fixed in the wall outside Poets' Corner door. Memorial stones to Canon Donaldson and Sir Charles Peers were set in the floor of the Islip chapel, and to Mrs Marriott in the north wall of the Little Cloister.[1]

A new grille, the gift of a private donor, was placed round the Coronation Chair enclosure in the Confessor's chapel, and a new case made to display the sword and scabbard of King George VI, close to the Sovereign's stall in King Henry VII's chapel. This is now in position.

The two shields on the wall of the south aisle of the nave, above the door to Samaria, were re-painted at the expense of a private donor.[2]

The super frontal of the new frontal for the high alar, the Queen's coronation gift, has been embroidered and the design for the rest of the work, which has been submitted to the Ornaments Committee, awaits approval.

The addition of further volumes, inscribed with the names of the civilian dead of the last war, has necessitated slight alteration of the case which houses them. These were agreed with the Imperial War Graves Commission and are being carried out by the Abbey joiners.

Concealed lighting has been installed in Henry V's chantry.

The stone coffin which had at some time been placed on the steps of the Hunsdon monument in St John's chapel was moved into the north aisle of the presbytery and set east to west. Occasion was taken to open the coffin and the remains found seemed to confirm the tradition that it is the tomb of Abbot Millyng.[3]

In view of another tradition – that the front panel of the monument to Colonel Popham and his wife, also in St John's chapel, had been turned back to front and that the hidden face bore an inscription – it was decided to test its authenticity when the monument was being cleaned. The stone was removed but the back was found to be plain.

In the floor on the south side of the Confessor's Shrine the existence of a small hinged stone had for long been a mystery. On the supposition that it might contain a relic, the decision was made to open it but nothing was found.

Measured drawings have been made of the wooden feretory placed by Abbot Feckenham on top of the Confessor's Shrine, which is in need of proper restoration. Careful examination has been made of fragments of mosaic and glass with which it was decorated and these have been analysed to ascertain their composition. The mosaic could be made today, but so far it has proved impossible to find any glassmaker who can repeat the blue glass used in the pilasters of the upper storey. Enquiries and trials are still proceeding.

Heating

After the failure of one of the boilers early this year proposals and an estimate of approximately £6,000 were received from G.N. Haden & Sons for such repairs as would be possible in time for next winter. It was subsequently decided to seek a comprehensive report from a consulting heating engineer on the system as a whole. Mr Goddard, whom I invited to undertake this work, has met me and discussed the problem on the site. His conclusions are now awaited.

The Cloisters

During the summer of 1954 a start was made on washing the stonework of the cloister windows and the south and west sides were finished in the autumn. Work was suspended during the winter because of the risk of frost, the action of which on wet stone would be to cause disintegration. It has not been resumed on the east side and will shortly continue on the north.

The south and west sides, rebuilt by Blore, were in fairly good condition, though the stone was beginning to deteriorate in places. Now that it has been freed from the acid deposits that were the cause of decay, and providing that these are not allowed to accumulate again, it should last for a long time. The stone has recovered its natural colour and the architectural detail shows to better advantage.

On the east side there will have to be a little stone replacement in the parapet, the walling above the windows, and the base course. But the more elaborate moulded work in the windows themselves is sound and opportunity is being taken to polish the marble shafts that occur only here and on the north side.

So long as the electric hoist is in use and the north east corner of the cloister remains enclosed as a small builder's yard, it may be difficult to clean the entire cloisters. But the greater part of the north side and the short bay in the west side that was built by Wren, not Blore, should be finished during this summer.

Although no glass was inserted at the time of the mid 19th century restoration, Blore provided grooves for it in the tracery, having no doubt noted their existence in the original stonework. The south and west sides have now been glazed, and the glass is prepared for fitting on the east side. Templates have been taken of the window on the north side and the glass is being worked in readiness, but here glazing grooves will have to be re-cut by the Abbey masons.

The insertion of glass in the upper part of these windows will help to exclude driving rain and wind and afford at least some protection to the cloister vaulting.

The wrought iron grilles[4] in the main lights of the windows on the south side have been repainted and the missing portions of the scroll work are being supplied by Bainbridge Reynolds Limited and should shortly be ready for fixing.

The fine late 18th century Gothic grilles at the south entrance to the east and west walks of the cloister, designed by Keene, Surveyor of the Fabric at the time, have also been repainted, though the gilding of certain portions has to await re-fitting of many missing features. Some of those have recently been fixed and the remainder are being made.

The wrought iron grille at the entrance to the cloisters from Dean's Yard has been redecorated in gold and colour.

The Dark Cloister

The need to repair the broken glass in the long 12 light window looking into the garden of Ashburnham House led to examination first of its wooden frame and then of the wooden ceiling joists resting upon it. Their condition was sufficiently bad to make opening up of the roof advisable, since the plaster ceiling concealed the timbers and the poor state of the lead flat above them suggested that damp might have been penetrating to the enclosed space in which they were embedded. They proved in fact to have been so badly attacked by death watch beetle and wet rot as to be rotten, and this roof is now being reconstructed with new timbers and its lead covering recast and relaid.

The window is being re-glazed with special thick glass and similar glass is being provided for the two oval windows hitherto open. The oak frames in which this will be put are made and will be fitted as soon as the masons have dressed the stone openings. The glass has been selected to reduce noise from the school shooting range and will mitigate draught and the entry of dust and dirt.

Drawings are being prepared for glazed swing doors in the inner arch at the entrance to Little Dean's Yard, so that this Dark Cloister shall not be open to the wind at both ends.[5]

So far only preliminary inspection has been possible of the state of the roof south of the section that is now being reconstructed. In those places where the plaster has been removed, the joists appear fairly good and, if further opening up shows nothing different, it may not be necessary to disturb it.

The final task will be to brush down the walls, remove defective plaster renderings, repoint the masonry where necessary and limewash the stone and plaster ceiling.

Farmerer's [Infirmary] Hall

After separation of this room from no. 5 Little Cloister, for which a new entrance has now been provided, scaffolding was erected to permit close examination of the roof, signs of death watch beetle having been detected in a preliminary inspection from ladders. Although some rafters and purlins have been badly attacked and will have to be renewed or spliced, most of the timbers are sound. As a protective measure they were all treated with insecticide while the scaffolding was available. But it would have been too costly to keep this on hire until the new timbers have been worked and are ready for fixing; the room will therefore be scaffolded afresh later on, when any changes in the electric lighting can be effected at the same time.

Measured drawings of the hall have been made and plans are being prepared for its furnishing and equipment as a vestry for the Brotherhoods of St Edward and St Peter. When, however, the roof repairs have been completed, other essential works will have to be undertaken – the removal of the unsightly corner fireplace & the installation of new electric heating, the provision of a new wood block floor in place of the present floor partly stone paved (the existing stone flags will be useful elsewhere – possibly in the passage to the College Garden), partly boarded; cutting out defective plaster and redecoration.

Mention may be made of one change which would be specially desirable. The proportions of the hall are at present vitiated by the passage, formed with it, giving access to the courtyard in front of nos. 4 and 5 Little Cloisters. However there is no staircase to the gallery above it, which thus remains a useless dust trap. If there is to be adequate accommodation for the members of the Brotherhoods, as well as for such large pieces of furniture as the cope chest, now in the east aisle of the north transept, together with a table, cupboards, wardrobes etc., the room will need to recover its original size. I therefore recommend the following changes. 1. The entrance to the Farmerer's Hall should be the door in the Little Cloister which now opens into the passage to the courtyard in front of nos. 4 and 5. 2. The existing entrance to the hall should be built up and door re-used in a new opening to be formed where there is now a window looking into St Katherine's chapel. 3. The approach to the courtyard should be a stone paved path adjacent to, but outside the north wall of the Farmerer's Hall. The blank wall which at present connects the north east corner of the hall with the south nave arcade of St Katherine's chapel should be pulled down.

[*St Katherine's chapel*]

Such a change must necessarily be considered in relation to the future treatment of St Katherine's chapel. But if it may be assumed that, after no. 3 Little Cloister has been built, St Katherine's chapel will be laid out as a garden, the proposed passage would not conflict with this larger scheme and could be designed as a first instalment of it. While however there must be some interval of time before St Katherine's chapel can be dealt with as a whole, a decision about this passage in the Farmerer's Hall ought to be taken soon, since it must affect the work to be carried out in flooring, redecoration and furnishing.

The Little Cloister

In the east walk death watch beetle is present in the oak ceiling rafters and wall plate, which are in poor condition. As the cost of repair and renewal of the worst affected parts would be considerable and since the roofs of the south walk and half of the west walk are being constructed, as part of the war damage repairs, in concrete with a plaster finish like that of the north walk, I recommend that this treatment, which is more suitable to the 18th century character of the cloister, should be adopted throughout. The northern half of the west walk, which is of timber, is late 19th century work, but the oak is already infected with wood worm and would have to receive protective treatment. Setting the cost of this against that of reconstruction in a permanent material, it would clearly be better to replace the timber with concrete and avoid the incongruity of one half of one side being different to all the rest.

Jerusalem Chamber

The work of restoration has proceeded less quickly than I had hoped, chiefly because the state of the roof proved to be even worse than was at first apparent, some of the most important structural members, in particular the two main principals, having to be completely renewed. It took some time to obtain oak of the requisite size for these, and bringing them in through the narrow door from the former Chapter Office and hoisting them into position while the floor space was encumbered with scaffolding, was a difficult operation. The larger part of the work however has now been done and when relaying of the lead roof, now in progress, is finished, the new timbers will be painted and the existing decoration of the ceiling touched up as necessary. The frieze will be limewashed and the scaffolding can then be removed. The next step will be to lift the floor and examine the joists below, the condition of which, being invisible cannot yet be known. It is impossible therefore to say when this room can be re-opened for use, but it is unlikely to be before the end of 1955.

College Hall

The stone floor is supported upon a substructure of oak which is partly visible from the cellars below. The timbers, although of large size, have been so eaten by death watch beetle that they are now too weak to carry the considerable weight of the paving, increased as it is by the heavy tables and benches that stand upon it. The paving has in fact sagged in places and seeing that the hall is used daily by 150 boys at a time, there is some risk of its collapse. Measured drawings of the building have been made and a scheme is now being completed for eliminating all the timber substructure and substituting a new reinforced concrete floor. The main weight of this would not be taken by the existing walls, thick as these are, but by stancheons, close to but independent of them. The existing paving would be re-laid on this new floor, though many of the square stones are cracked and new ones will be required.

The aim is to get the work carried out during the summer holidays, but I have warned the Bursar of Westminster School[6] that completion cannot be guaranteed within that period and that, however inconvenient, other arrangements may have to be made for the school meals at the start of the autumn term.

College Hall kitchen

Following some cases of food poisoning, subsequently traced to other causes, the kitchen and kitchen offices were inspected by the Medical Officer of Health and the Sanitary Inspector for the City of Westminster. Their report referred to 'unsatisfactory conditions' in respect of the kitchen itself, criticism being made of the redundant pipework, conduits, casings etc. which harbour dirt, and of the loose and flaking plaster of the walls. It was further stipulated that a wash hand basin should be provided in or adjacent to the kitchen and that the male staff lavatory should be re-sited to secure aerial disconnection between the water closet and the kitchen.

Proposals are being submitted to the Medical Officer of Health which it is hoped will satisfy the latter requirements. A wash basin can be provided without difficulty, but it is less easy to re-site the WC. Aerial disconnection can, however, be secured by the provision of a door between the entrance to the lavatory and the kitchen passage and, if this is agreed, the work can be put in hand.

The criticism of the kitchen is, in my opinion, reasonable, the network of pipes is impossible to keep clean and some are almost certainly obsolete. The kitchen needs redecoration, but it would be useless to attempt it until the intricacies of the plumbing have been sorted out. The question arises however of whether this is the responsibility of the Dean and Chapter or of the School.

Abbey bookstall [*shop*]

Plans for the conversion of the former chapter office into a bookstall were approved in 1954 and the work is now in progress. When the old floor was taken up some old foundations were discovered and a measured drawing made for record purposes. From the appearance of the brickwork I should judge these remains to date from the 17th or 18th centuries and they probably belonged to small houses pulled down when the present building was erected.

The alterations were timely in revealing serious decay in the ceiling joists, which have had to be cut out and replaced with new. The lead roof is being recast and relaid and the shop fittings will be fixed as soon as all structural work is finished.

When the reduced estimate for showcases, counter etc. was accepted, the best method of displaying post cards, of which the sale is very large, was still under consideration. In company with the Registrar, I visited the headquarters of Valentine & Company and saw the types of fitting evolved and made by them for their own use. The design and finish of these would not be suitable for the Abbey bookstall, but George Parnall & Company who are making the other fittings have now given an estimate for two fittings and special lighting on a design which incorporates the working arrangements of Valentine's model. Their figure is £349.11.0d and, if the fittings are to be ready in time for the opening of the bookstall, which I hope will be in the late summer of this year, it would be desirable to accept this as soon as possible so that the work can be put in hand.

[*West entrance paving*]

The granite setts which are to replace the grass on the right hand side of the approach to the west door of the Abbey are on the site and Dove Bros. will lay them and carry out the adjustment to the railings and entrance gates to bring these centrally onto the axis of the west door and the monument in the Sanctuary.

Song School

Improvements to the heating were carried out by Drake & Gorham Limited and are proving satisfactory.

Abbey Choir School

Designs have been prepared for the installation of a passenger lift and the estimate by Marryatt & Scott for supplying this accepted. Estimates for the builder's work are now being obtained and these will include the cost of the war damage repairs. Negotiations have proceeded satisfactorily with the War Damage Commission and the District Surveyor.

I am preparing a design for a school honours board, which is being presented by Miss Donaldson in memory of her father.[7]

21 Dean's Yard

The alterations to this house, to connect it with the chapter office behind and provide additional accommodation, as well as a flat for the Registrar, were completed during the year.

20 Dean's Yard

Cork flooring was laid in the dining room and other small repairs and improvements were carried out during August and September 1954.

2 The Cloisters

The condition of this house[8] has for some time been unsatisfactory; the electric wiring is bad, some of the rooms are damp and the basement kitchen and offices are inconvenient. I was asked to consider what could be done to remedy these defects but formed the conclusion that, while the house remains in its existing form, any expenditure could at best be only a palliative and would certainly be recurrent. The main structure – the front half facing Dean's Yard medieval, the back half late 17th century – was added to in the 19th century in such a way that its character has been impaired and its upkeep rendered difficult owing to the complicated form of the roofs.

Having measured up the house I am convinced that the right course would be to remove all the 19th century additions leaving only the original core. This would have three advantages: it would make the house smaller, though still of adequate size and much easier to work; it would enable the space now occupied by the portions to be pulled down to become a small garden; and it would give opportunity to deal with those structural defects that are bound to cause intermittent trouble.

My plans are now being priced and when approximate costs are known will be submitted for consideration.

1 Little Cloister

A new floor was laid in the kitchen, where rising damp had been persistent. Cracked panelling in the drawing room was removed and new panels inserted. Several minor repairs were executed and most of the house redecorated. Some small further work is necessary to the flue from the Aga cooker.

The exterior, and those of nos. 2, 4 and 5, were repainted to a uniform shade of white with different colours for the doors.

Building work is now in progress in nos. 6, 7 and 8 as part of the War Damage repairs.

General Observations

A review of the fire protection arrangements for the Abbey has taken place recently and although tests have shown these to be reasonably satisfactory, certain proposals have been put forward by the Chief Officer of the London Fire Brigade. He has agreed to the removal of the water tank in the south west tower, which it would be desirable to dispense with because of the danger of flooding if at any time a leak occurred in it, and because of the great weight, amounting to thirty tons or more. He has also approved the installation of an automatic warning system throughout the building, which should be a surer safeguard for quick detection of a fire than patrol by a night watchman who, having to traverse the floor, triforium and roofs, might, at the moment of danger, be far from the scene of it. This matter is still under review.

Restoration of the Jewel Tower and its opening shortly as a museum has brought at any rate a stage nearer the Ministry of Works plan for removal of the house property, which at present conceals the Jewel Tower from Old Palace Yard, and laying out the ground so cleared as lawn. As this would expose to view part of the precinct wall and be beneficial in many ways to the Abbey, I asked to be informed of what was proposed and attended a meeting of the Ministry of Works when the plans were shown to me. For financial reasons their realisation may not be immediate, though a start may be made on one part of it. The Ministry will accept responsibility for tidying up the east wall of no. 4 Little Cloister where buildings, now demolished, adjoined it and for any repointing and repairs to the precinct wall exposed as a result of their excavations in lowering the ground to the level of the former moat between the wall and the Jewel Tower.

Later on, when the wall is exposed to view, it would be desirable to take off the unsightly brick addition, which raised its height, between no. 4 and the future no. 3 Little Cloisters.

I took the opportunity to raise the future of the site, now owned by the Commissioners of Crown Lands, lying parallel with the College garden, and to express the hope that this would not be used for an office block, shutting out the fine view of the Abbey from across the river. The Ministry of Works, while pointing out that they have no control over this site, agreed that they would welcome its retention as an open space, which would indeed complement and greatly enhance their own scheme. They gave me to understand that there was no imminent risk of the offices being built; but it is clear that this situation will need watching.[9]

[Mr Bishop's retirement]

Mr Bishop announced his desire to retire from the position of Clerk of the Works in 1954 and the vacancy was advertised in October that year. A fair number of applications were received and five candidates were interviewed. Mr H. Carter, a mason by trade, has now been appointed and is to take up his duties in September.

S.E. Dykes Bower.

[1]   The Surveyor designed the Herschel stone. Mrs Marriott's ashes were later moved to the Islip vault to join those of her husband, Canon Stephen Marriott.
[2]   The Balliol shield and Venables shield.
[3]   This is just east of Bishop Duppa's large stone.
[4]   By Thomas Potter.
[5]   There are wooden doors there.
[6]   Files on works at Westminster School from 1951 to 1972 are in WAM S/3/61. Files about College Hall from 1955 to 1972 are WAM S/3/56. See also WAM SD/5.

7   Frederic Donaldson, Canon 1924–51. Designed by the Surveyor.
8   Files on this house are in WAM S/3/54. See also WAM SD/2 and SD/6.
9   The area remained an open space.

60N.   The Surveyor's salary was increased to £1,000 per annum plus a further £2,000 per annum in respect of the ongoing restoration works (Chapter 12 April 1955).

61.   WAM S/1/101

Report of the Surveyor of the Fabric 1956

The work of the past twelve months, which this report summarizes, has expanded in scope and variety. So many separate items have to be recorded that a brief account must suffice for each.

Nave roof

As the work of cutting out defective roof trusses continues, the cloister garth has had to become a workshop for the carpenters engaged in the making of new trusses and the repair of existing ones capable of re-use. By the end of March eleven new ones had been fixed in position and three more, with one old one, were ready for erection.

The spacing of the trusses is being increased from 1 foot 9 inches to 2 feet centre to centre, which will have the effect of slightly reducing their number and helping to keep down costs. It will not affect the structural strength of the roof or change its character, since the spacing is irregular and already 2 feet in places.

Between the west towers, where the condition of the roof was particularly bad, all the old trusses have been removed and three new stone corbels have been fixed by the masons to carry a new oak wall plate.

Fixing of the new steel ties has progressed so much in advance of the timber repairs that until the time lag between the two is reduced, it has been temporarily suspended.

To secure greater expedition by employment of a larger labour force, some re-organization of the work took place earlier this year, entailing more use of the services of Dove Bros. After a few initial difficulties the results have proved satisfactory and will be kept under observation.

Throughout the presbytery, apse, transept roofs and that part of the nave roof which structural repairs will not reach for a year or two, the procedure is to examine the timbers, mark those that are defective, cut away all sapwood, which contributes nothing to the strength of the wood but may harbour beetle, and treat all with a preliminary application of insecticide.

Already this examination has shown that the apse roof is in very bad condition and that of the south transept not much better.

Apse

The top parapet round the apse built, like that already taken down from the south side of the nave, of Bath stone which has succumbed to the London atmosphere, is badly fractured in several places and now too precarious to remain with safety. It will have to be rebuilt in Portland stone like the sections of parapet west of it, renewed in the surveyorship of Sir Walter Tapper.[1]

Scaffolding is about to be erected for its dismantling and the apse will have to remain without a parapet until new stone is worked and ready for fixing.

Interior cleaning

Throughout the whole eastern arm of the interior ie. presbytery, sanctuary, ambulatory and the apsidal chapels, cleaning of the stonework and polishing of the marble has been finished, together with repair of masonry cracks in the vaulting and touching up of the gilding and painted decoration of the vault ribs and bosses.

Cleaning of the clerestory and triforium of the two bays of the north transept nearest the crossing is also finished and has commenced in the other two. The scaffolding recently removed from the ambulatory and pillars of the presbytery will now be erected to permit cleaning of the north transept aisles.

King Henry V's Chantry chapel and the newel staircases leading to it have been cleaned. Concealed lighting has been installed, part of the floor renewed in marble and the tops of the newel turrets sealed over. The chapel now awaits furnishing – a dorsal to fit the recess over the altar that must once have contained a painted retabulum, suitable altar ornaments, a small carpet and cushions for the stone benches.

The fan vault under this chantry was found to be very defective and has required extensive repointing. This is finished, excepting the crown which forms the central boss. Polishing of the marble shafts is almost complete.

Glazing

The scaffolding in the north transept has enabled a closer examination to be made of the glass in its rose window. More breakages have been found than could be detected previously and I have submitted a revised claim to the War Damage Commission, formal acceptance of which (given verbally) is now awaited. The glaziers will start the repair shortly, as the requisite external scaffolding is almost ready. The cost of both repairs and scaffolding will be borne by the War Damage Commission, who have also agreed the claim for the eight damaged windows of the lantern. Scaffolding for these will be erected above the crown of the arches of the crossing and the glass is already prepared in the shops ready for fixing.

As no charge will accrue to the Dean and Chapter for this work and it is to the advantage of the War Damage Commission that the work should be executed before costs rise further, it will be of mutual benefit to re-open these windows which have remained blocked for so long.

A claim for small repairs to the Burlison & Grylls glass in the window below the south transept rose was agreed some time ago and the glaziers will carry out the work at the same time as the larger work mentioned above.

In the cloisters two windows under the muniment room remain to be glazed and I have for some time been considering their treatment. Their 18th century Gothic tracery, much larger in scale than that of the other windows, presents special problems and my recommendations will be submitted this summer.

Triforium

New boarded floors have been laid in two of the apses of the chevet and the old rotten boarding is now being removed on another section. Some delay was experienced through having to reject delivery of timber unsatisfactory in quality.

Monuments

During the past twelve months the cleaning of the monuments by the Abbey staff has continued in the chapels of St Nicholas, St Edmund and in both aisles of the chapel of Henry VII. The larger and more elaborate monuments, which need restoration of decayed marble and making good of missing pieces, as well as re-decoration, demand expert treatment; our resources of skill and labour admit only of cleaning and polishing the smaller ones that are still in fairly good condition. The two Halifax monuments in the north aisle of Henry VII's chapel demonstrate the kind of work that our men can usefully tackle: only the painting of the arms and letting of the inscription on one of them required outside assistance from Mr Butchart.[2]

The monument of Queen Elizabeth, the most important undertaken this year, exemplified the type that we cannot tackle unaided. Its splendour depends on its decoration; but this decoration could not be renewed until the large number of missing features in marble and alabaster, vital to the design, had been supplied. Even now the full effect is marred because some are lacking: the Queen's effigy lacks its crown, collar and sceptre;[3] the emblem – crowned lion – that, on the south side, should balance the thistle surmounting the north, and several coronets over royal and ducal arms are absent.

The treatment of this tomb has aroused much public interest and, in correspondence which reaches me on the subject, the wish is frequently expressed that, so much having been done, restoration should be consummated by supplying the remaining omissions. Drawing on the pictorial evidence of old prints as well as the knowledge of those versed in heraldry, it should not be difficult to do so; architecturally, too, realisation of the original designer's intention must normally be preferable to perpetual mutilation.

In the south aisle of Henry VII's chapel, work to the tomb of the Countess of Lennox has proceeded as far as our cleaners can carry it. The next stage is for specialist marble workers to make good missing pieces and Mr Butchart will carry out the re-decoration. Before the end of the financial year in September, it will not be possible to undertake any other major work; but thereafter I hope that the tomb of Mary, Queen of Scots, on which preparatory work has been in progress, will be treated in the same manner as that of Queen Elizabeth.

[*Cleaning*]

When the tombs in these two aisles are finished a return can be made to the apsidal chapels. It would be premature to do anything in St Paul's chapel, if there is a chance of the statue of James Watt being transferred to Scotland; I have therefore obtained estimates in readiness for tackling the monuments in St Nicholas chapel, which contains some of the finest of the large 17th century examples.

Since my last report Mr Butchart has coloured the arms on the Exeter monument in St John's chapel. The result shows what could be accomplished on the not dissimilar Villiers tomb by Nicholas Stone in St Nicholas chapel, which is in perfect condition and has now been cleaned.[4]

Coronation Chair

The Coronation Chair was returned to its place in the Confessor's chapel before Christmas and in future will be inspected by the Clerk of Works and myself every four months. In view of suggestions that its decoration was deteriorating, the Ministry of Works, who undertook preservative treatment before the coronation, were invited to make an examination. Their report confirmed that, apart from the flaking off of minute fragments of gesso, the condition of the chair had in no way changed.

Heating

The heating consultant, Mr H.G. Goddard, submitted his proposals for improvement of the heating system, and drawings and a specification have been prepared. These have been sent to six firms, whose tenders will be received shortly. If the work can be started in the early summer, the new scheme should come into operation next winter. It has been designed to extend to the Library and Chapter House and, in respect of the latter, agreement has been reached with the Ministry of Works whereby that Department will make payment to the Dean and Chapter for its share of the running costs.

Two oil fired boilers will be substituted for the existing three and the existing heating ducts will be left unaltered, except that, from most of their length, the iron gratings will be removed. Stone paving will be laid to match the rest of the paving and all the heat at ground level will issue from fan convectors, spaced at regular intervals. The only structural work entailed will be in excavating deeper pits to accommodate them.

On the triforium floor the batteries of pipes, which are not merely impossible to keep clean but an agency for circulating polluted warm air, will give place to similar fan convectors. These occupy little space and should obviate discolouration of the newly cleaned walls.

Each convector will be fitted with an automatic thermostat and Mr Goddard is confident that the system should ensure avoidance of waste heat with greater overall efficiency.

Other works

In the chapel of Henry VII, the sword and scabbard of King George VI have been placed in a bronze case, fitted with burglar-proof glass and set on a marble pedestal with incised and gilded lettering.

At the west end of the nave the oak case containing the Civilian Roll of Honour has been reconstructed to accommodate additional books, entailing slight changes in its design.

The inscription on the grave of Richard Brinsley Sheridan in the south transept has been re-cut at the expense of a private donor.

A memorial slab is being designed to be placed over the grave of Lord Trenchard in the RAF chapel, now marked by a temporary stone.

Work on the Queen's frontal for the high altar has continued and should be finished in time for the translation of St Edward the Confessor.

A new alms box for the north transept, incorporating some carved 17th century woodwork, and a new chest for the frontals of the altar in Henry VII's chapel are being made in the joinery shops.

Wire guards have been fixed in the windows of the north west tower to keep birds out of the belfry. New lighting has been fitted over the chime boards which have been refixed in correct order.

Jerusalem Chamber

Restoration came to an end early in 1956. The ceiling has been entirely re-painted, the frieze whitened, the tapestries cleaned and the glazing of the two windows repaired. The gift of two crystal chandeliers[5] permitted a notable improvement in the lighting and a plaque, fixed under the north window, commemorates the launching of the Abbey Appeal. The room was re-opened at a ceremony on February 13th. Jericho and Samaria were re-painted in time for this.

College Hall

During August and September 1955 the work of reconstructing the floor of College Hall was carried out, except for replacement of the stone flags and their renewal where necessary. These are to be laid on the dais during April 1956 and in the rest of the hall during the summer holiday.

The condition of the floor had become dangerous as a result of death watch beetle attack in the timbers in the cellar below. So advanced was their decay that it was fortunate that they had not collapsed under the weight of the stone floor and the heavy tables and forms upon it.

All timber has now been eliminated. The floor is carried upon a substructure of reinforced concrete and the cellar opened out to form much needed storage room which is already proving useful.

During the summer scaffolding will be erected to permit examination of the roof of College Hall, and floors in the flat over the kitchen will be lifted to reveal the woodwork of the kitchen ceiling. This is plastered on the underside and there is no other means of ascertaining its condition.

Abbey Bookstall

The conversion of the former Chapter Office into the new Abbey bookstall, which had been in progress during the year, was completed in March 1956. The roof, which was found to be very defective, has been reconstructed and a new lead covering laid on the whole of the one-storey range. With the introduction of new electric lighting and heating the existing system was overhauled and a new control room formed to accommodate the switch boards; the shop has been equipped with specially designed furnishings and display windows; the turret chamber, off the stairs to the Jerusalem Chamber, fitted up for storage; and the new paving of granite setts laid outside the north entrance to match the rest of the forecourt to the west door of the Abbey.

Song School

A piece of stone and an inscribed brass plate, presented by the Canadian choir which sang in the Abbey two years ago, was fixed in the wall on the right hand side of the entrance.

The Cloisters

Cleaning and glazing of the walls facing into the garth is finished, with the exception of the two bays in the east walk behind the electric hoist.

New stone treads were fixed in the steps to the nave door at the north end of the west walk.

Following examination from a travelling scaffold recently assembled in the east walk, an experimental repair is being made on the vaulting. The primary reason for the failure of so much stonework in the cloisters is the incompatibility of the materials used. Limestone in juxtaposition with sandstone can, in certain conditions, injure the latter by chemical action. Thus the chalk blocks in the vaulting, although they themselves are sound, have caused the ornamental bands and vaulting ribs of Reigate sandstone to crumble. As we have available in our yard some limestone which, used in place of Reigate, should form bands of suitable colour, this is being inserted in one bay for trial, and if the result viz. that it is not affected like the sandstone is successful, the rest of the east and north walks could be tackled with a considerable saving of expense.

The Dark Cloister

The former timber roof has been entirely renewed, covered with lead outside and plastered beneath. New lead gutters and down pipes have been fixed and a new oak window inserted, glazed with thick glass to mitigate noise from the shooting range.[6] Some preliminary brushing down of the walls has been carried out and lime washing will begin this summer.

The Little Cloister

Removal of the surviving timber in the ceilings of the west and the east walks and reconstruction of these roofs in reinforced concrete has recently been finished. At the same time decayed lengths of the stone cornice have been cut out and renewed in Clipsham stone. When dry, the plaster of the ceiling will be whitened so that all four sides correspond.

The roof on the east side, when opened up, was found to be very weak and has had to be re-formed. To save expense its lead covering has not been relaid, but the flat has been formed in asphalte. Enforced rebuilding of the parapets has given opportunity to tidy up some unsightly patchwork on the east side, though final completion here will be carried out by our staff not the contractors.

Infirmary Hall

The repair of the timber roof is complete. New oak members have been inserted to replace those that were too decayed to remain and all the woodwork has been treated with insecticide. An unsightly strut, added some years ago to strengthen the construction, has been dispensed with and the oak cornices, which had got out of place, properly aligned. The tiles, which had to be stripped to give access to the rafters from above, have been relaid and, internally, the space between the rafters plastered. The glazing of the two side windows has been repaired and the system of electrical heating settled. The next stage will be the removal of the passage and building up both of the east doorway and the former front door of no. 5 Little Cloister. The west door to the passage will became the entrance to the Hall and the window adjacent to it must be removed to make way for a doorway leading to a new external walk to the courtyard in front of nos. 4 and 5. This will entail removal of the wall linking the north east corner of the Infirmary Hall to the arches of St Katherine's chapel and raising the ground to bring the new walk to the level of the Little Cloisters and the courtyard.

My proposals for the treatment of this walk and its roof will be submitted for consideration shortly. The work could be carried out by the Abbey building staff using surplus stone and timber for the facing of the retaining wall and a simple roof.

When the alteration of the doors is finished, removal of the fireplace, laying of a wood block floor, replastering and decoration of the walls in the Infirmary Hall can proceed. The room will then be ready for furnishing in whatever manner is decided.

College Garden

Now that the frontage of the new houses on the south side of Little Cloister is freed of scaffolding, it is desirable to tidy up as quickly as possible the area of garden that has for so long been a builder's yard. The work can be carried out by our own labour, as soon as Dove Bros. have evened out the mounds formed by building debris. But I would advocate one afterthought to the scheme shown on my drawing: that the walled enclosure in front of the end of the Busby library should become part of the garden and form a continuation of the proposed low terrace. The gardener's potting shed, which is concealed in it, could be erected elsewhere.

Precinct wall

As restoration of the Jewel Tower by the Ministry of Works has advanced, discussions have been held with the Ancient Monuments branch on the treatment of the ground lying between the Tower and the precinct wall. The former moat has been excavated and may be filled with water, and a grass terrace will be laid out adjacent to the wall. The Ministry is carrying out repairs to the wall, where buildings that formally abutted on it have been demolished. Various patches of decayed brickwork are being rebuilt in stone and other larger areas of 18th century brickwork repointed. This will improve both the condition and appearance of the wall and expose to view a section of it that has hitherto been invisible to the public.

The Ministry is defraying the cost of opening out a blocked up postern gate in the wall and providing an oak door, that will lead from the new Jewel Tower garden up four steps to the garden terrace of no. 4 Little Cloister.

Our staff are concurrently rebedding and pointing the brick coping on the section of the precinct wall that forms the south west angle of this Jewel Tower garden and have replaced in stone some unsightly and decayed wooden cills in the east front of no. 4. Repair of the rubble walling of the precinct wall remains to be finished.

The new lay out round the Jewel Tower represents the first instalment of a larger scheme for a lawn extending northwards to join the existing lawn round the statue of King George V. This will expose the whole east side of the precinct wall and greatly enhance the surroundings of the Abbey. I hope it will be possible, when no. 3 Little Cloister is built if not before, to complement what the Ministry has already done by removing from the top of that section of the wall east of St Katherine's chapel the ugly brick additions, which mar its appearance and falsify its height.

Abbey Choir School

Work on the installation of the passenger lift and restoration of the war damage is due to begin in the middle of April and to end in time for the opening of the autumn term. Three tenders were obtained and that of Dove Bros. accepted, their figure being approximately £1500 lower than the other two.[7]

Repairs have been carried out to the stained glass in the bay window of the dining room and school Honours Board, to be fixed in this room and given as a memorial to the late Canon Donaldson is now being made.

Decoration has commenced in no. 3B [Dean's Yard] and repairs completed to the windows, floors and electrical installation.

Houses

No. 1 Little Cloister. The chimney containing the kitchen flue was heightened and is now proving satisfactory.

No. 2. On the first and second floors the end rooms to the east have been blocked off for adaptation to a flat and guest suite when no. 3 is built. The rest of the house was redecorated.

No. 4A. A new domestic heating boiler was fixed earlier this year.

No. 6. Building is still in progress

Nos. 7 & 8. These houses came into occupation in November 1955 and April 1956 respectively.

Clerk of the Works office. Work is still in progress

No. 2 The Cloister. Plans for the conversion of this into a smaller and more convenient house were approved and the bill of quantities is now ready for pricing.

No. 21 Dean's Yard. An old lean-to shed in the garden has been removed and a brick retaining wall built round the basement steps.

General Observations

(a) A new stone cutting machine was purchased in November 1955 and is proving most useful in operation.

(b) Mr Carter,[8] the new Clerk of Works, took up his duties in September 1955 and has already demonstrated ability and energy in supervising the multifarious tasks that fall to his lot. There has been a perceptible speeding-up of work in all the different trades and in the promptness with which any new calls are met.

(c) I would comment in conclusion on two general questions. With any old building of the size of the Abbey, there can never come a time when repair work of some sort will not be necessary. To have a time limit in view for certain operations, such as the repair of the roofs and the interior cleaning, is desirable and necessary because without a sense of urgency progress may too easily flag. But in some trades output is directly governed by the amount of labour available. Repair of the stonework, for example, will continue to be slow while the shortage of masons, general throughout the country, persists. Even is every part of the fabric in need of restoration could be scaffolded, large scale works on the exterior would not be feasible at present. Restoration must consist at present in doing whatever will best contribute to soundness of the essential structure.

Thereafter it will gradually merge into maintenance, when the vital need will be to ensure that sufficient work can be undertaken yearly to prevent decay out-stripping repairs. The rate of decay in London demands particular vigilance. But until masons are more numerous, spectacular results in restoring the exterior cannot be hoped for.

Meanwhile the practical policy is to try to anticipate trouble before it develops too far, and to complete one job properly, rather than to leave it half done and then switch labour back to it later.

There are many relatively unimportant places where a little expenditure now would save much greater expense later. The Jerusalem Chamber, College Hall, Infirmary Hall, the bookstall, the Little Cloister, the Dark Cloister and the houses have had in varying degree to make demands on our resources that are not yet at an end, although a great deal has now been accomplished. The aim must now be to get all this unavoidable work to buildings, outside the fabric proper, thoroughly finished as soon as possible so that energy can be fully concentrated where it is so much needed – on the care of the Abbey itself.

S.E. Dykes Bower,

Surveyor of the Fabric. 9th April 1956.

1 Surveyor 1928–35.
2 William John Butchart, eminent church decorator who had worked for J.N. Comper. He also worked on gilding the choir stalls and organ case as well as many monuments; he died in 1969.
3 The collar and sceptre head, and also the cross on the orb, were not added to the effigy until the 1970s and the crown in the 1980s. New railings around the tomb were designed and added in 1983.
4 Sir George Villiers. The heraldry on this was not coloured.
5 Given by Guy Wellby. They were replaced in 2012 by circular metal chandeliers.
6 Westminster School range, which was in Ashburnham garden.
7 Files on the Choir and Song Schools 1956–72 are WAM S/3/60.
8 Harry Carter, who held the post until his death in 1966. His ashes lie in the west cloister.

62.   WAM S/1/102

Report of the Surveyor of the Fabric 1957

During the past twelve months it has become possible to see more of the results of the work that has been going on in the three years since restoration began. Visual evidence of this work, much of which is continuous and some of it by its nature slow, only unfolds gradually: but those changes in the appearance of the building which are now becoming noticeable serve a useful purpose in enabling the public to view the first fruits of the appeal. As in previous reports, an outline of what has been going on in different parts of the fabric may best be given under separate headings.

Nave roof

Reconstruction of the timber roof and other repairs above the vaulting in the three western bays (ie. a quarter of the nave) is complete. The temporary roof of corrugated iron now covers the next three bays where progress, if never so fast as could be wished, is at any rate satisfactory and quicker than on the first three. The employment of an outside contractor has been dispensed with and the job is being carried out by our own staff, now working each day till 6pm to see whether, economically and on a time basis, this is advantageous. To save cost, reinforced concrete is being substituted for stone where repairs to the internal face of the wall above the vaulting are necessary; and the spacing of the wooden trusses is being widened slightly to reduce their number. Thus whereas there were 127 of them over the twelve bays from the west end to the crossing, there will not be 115, of which 39 have so far been made and fixed, leaving 76 to be dealt with. If the present rate of progress remains constant, the twelve bays should be finished by the end of 1959.

The advantage of the roof as altered lies in its simplicity: it has recovered its original form without obstructive central supports, so that conditions both for future inspection of the timbers and for fire fighting will be easier than before.

What is disappointing is to find that the poor condition of the existing timbers is more or less consistent throughout. In the three western bays they were extremely bad; but those further east at least looked as though they might be better. Examination and tests have shown that the death watch beetle has penetrated everywhere and that no hopes can be built on any of the woodwork of the roof being immune from its ravages, or only slightly affected.

The transepts and apse cannot be dealt with until the nave is finished. But when the time comes to start on them, it may be expedient to consider whether there should be any further use of oak. The substitution of a steel framed roof would be regrettable in so far that it would obliterate the original construction which, particularly over the nave, was a remarkable piece of carpentry. Steel moreover is not without its disadvantages, in that it must be continually protected against rust and being rigid, lacks the flexibility of timber. On the other hand, according to present calculations, its use might represent a saving of at least 30% on the cost of oak.

I do not meanwhile advocate a change to steel on the nave roof, because it would seem to me right that, if later roofs have to be of steel, one section at least should perpetuate the original construction.

Leadwork

The new lead covering on the western three bays of the nave was completed and releading on the next three bays has now begun. In carrying out this work provision is being made for ventilation openings to ensure a cross current of air in the roof space over the vaulting. This will further be stimulated by the provision of stone louvres in the west window of the gable surmounting the west front.

As the leadworkers complete the gutters at the base of the roofs, the masons follow with the rebuilding of the parapet, the worked stone for which have been on the site for over a year.

A gift of £30,000 by the Commonwealth Mining Companies of Broken Hill, New South Wales, and the Consolidated Mining and Smelting Company of Canada to ensure that lead shall continue to be used for all those roofs of the Abbey that need renewal was at once a welcome act of generosity and a token of the interest that its restoration has inspired.

The apse

The dangerous parapet, referred to in my last report, was removed but its eventual rebuilding in Portland stone will have to be deferred until the roof has been repaired.

Internal Cleaning

The programme for this has been fairly well adhered to and by the end of the year the aim is to have both transepts finished and the bridge erected in the two eastern bays of the choir. What began as the desirable and necessary task of cleaning the walls of their coating of dirt has turned out in fact to be an important and major repair job. In every bay without exception fractures in the vaulting – mostly the re-opening of earlier cracks – have kept our masons busy and enabled trouble to be remedied in time.

In the western aisle of the north transept one roof boss was found to retain some of its original colour, which is being preserved. Photographs of all bosses and details of interest have been taken by Mr Howgrave Graham while the scaffolding has made this possible.[1]

As cleaning and polishing of the marble proceeds further, the majestic beauty of the Abbey interior reveals itself more clearly and there is no need to enlarge on an undertaking which, it is to be hoped, will in 1965 reach a glorious culmination.

The Lantern

A fall of stone about eleven months ago from the stone cornice above the arches of the crossing made necessary the hasty erection of scaffolding to enable the interior of the lantern – inaccessible otherwise – to be examined. Several loose pieces of stone and plaster were found and for a time services in the choir had to be suspended. Scaffolding round the four piers of the crossing would in any case have been erected for the polishing of their marble shafts and it was decided to synchronize this task with the repair of the walling above. Now that both are done, the lantern has been bridged across with a temporary floor at the level of the stone cornice, on which concealed scaffolding has been built to enable to remains of Bernasconi's plaster vault to be removed and the new flat ceiling, which will be decorated,[2] to be substituted. This work – a War Damage liability – is now in progress.

Monuments

The tomb of Lady Margaret Beaufort in the south aisle and the monuments in the apsidal chapels of Henry VII's chapel have been cleaned by our two men, who were now beginning on the monuments in the eastern aisle of the north transept.

The main work however has been the restoration of the monuments to the Countess of Lennox and Mary Queen of Scots. The first stage was cleaning, carried out by our men; the second making good of missing features of the design, carved by Earp & Hobbs; the third the decoration in colour by Mr Butchart. Mr Scott Giles has advised throughout on heraldry and many other details.

In such work the final result must depend largely on the painting and, in so far as these two monuments display again the unique artistry of Mr Butchart, I would express the hope that it will be possible to employ him further on work of the same nature. There is now, I think, sufficient proof that the finest of these monuments, treated in the right way, could be one of the distinctive glories of the Abbey. But Mr Butchart is getting old and may not be able after many more years to undertake work that cannot be hurried. If the decoration of the 17th century monuments in the apsidal chapels and elsewhere, cannot be completed by him, it is doubtful whether anyone else will be found capable of emulating his standards.

Triforium

Spraying of the roof timbers with insecticide has continued but is not yet finished in the nave aisles. The re-flooring of the apsidal chapels is complete.

After a survey of the objects of every kind that in the course of years have accumulated in the triforium, a considerable number were got rid of as having no value. Even so the quantity that remains is an encumbrance that takes up space and collects dust. There must always, no doubt, be certain things that cannot be destroyed or given away and have to be stored somewhere; an example is the fine woodwork of the Schrider organ case, for which it is to be hoped a use will some time be found. Others, of which the brass lectern that used to stand in the choir is an example, are never likely to be required. This lectern, which at present merely stands covered in a dust sheet, might be very acceptable to some colonial cathedral or a church and, if a suitable opportunity occurred to dispose of it, I should not press of its retention.

Glazing

Two undertakings of special interest have been completed in the last year: the glazing of the eight windows of the Lantern with broken 19th century glass from war damaged windows, arranged as grisaille, and the repair and cleaning of the rose window of the north transept. Seen 120 feet above the floor, the effect of the lantern windows resembles that of old glass and suggests that it was less the colour and craftsmanship than the design and figure drawing of much 19th century glass that made so many windows of that period unpleasing.

The painted glass in the rose window proved, on close inspection from scaffolding to be more badly damaged than had been realised. It was taken out in sections, repaired, cleaned, and missing portions made good. Now that it has been reset and the stonework of its tracery washed, the quality of the glass shows to much greater advantage than before and, so far from being heavy and coarse, appears bright and translucent. The addition of leadwork, resulting from leading over cracks, has also improved its scale by breaking down the size of some over-large pieces of glass.

Below this window the six lancets remain to be filled with stained glass, designs for which are being prepared by Mr Brian Thomas. They should be ready for submission this summer. The single light windows[3] on the north end of the east and west transept aisles are being glazed with clear glass, to enable more of the War Damage money to be allocated to the six lights in the transept itself.

The west window of the south aisle of the nave,[4] containing old glass, was damaged in a gale in the summer of last year. It was subsequently found to be in a precarious state and had to be taken out and thoroughly repaired.

Heating

The first of two new boilers was installed and brought into operation before the winter; the second followed about the end of the year. Like the three old boilers they supersede these are oil fired but a test showed that each was capable of giving 7% more heat singly than two of the old together.

Immediately after Easter the second phase of the new heating scheme will start with the removal of the batteries of pipes in the triforium and the substitution of fan convectors. As warm air is distributed by the latter horizontally, the new system should obviate the staining of the walls by convection, which is inevitable wherever exposed pipes are near a wall.

Hitherto it has been impossible to open up the wooden floor of the triforium itself (as distinct from the apsidal chapels) because the coils of heating pipes are fixed upon it. As soon as they come out, the same procedure will be followed as in the chapels ie. the vault pockets cleaned out, the joists and boarding examined and cither repaired or renewed as necessary.

At ground floor level the iron gratings in the nave aisles will be replaced with stone covers and the only open ducts will be over convectors, one to each bay, fixed in slightly deeper pits.

In the choir and Henry VII's chapel heating pipes will run under the stalls and pews with new ducts in the risers of the steps.

The new system has been designed to include the Library and Chapter House and terms have been agreed with the Ministry of works whereby their liability in respect of the latter can be assessed.

About six months are likely to be required for the completion of the work so that the whole should be ready for the next heating season.

Furnishings

A new chest to contain the frontals of the altar in Henry VII's chapel was designed to harmonize with the existing chests in the Sacristy and made by our joiners. It has been placed in front of the central pillar opposite the entrance door.

A new alms box for the north transept has also been made in our joinery shops, but will not be put in position until the stone cleaning is finished. The alms box incorporates some 17th century carved oak consoles which have been lying unused for years.

A number of framed notices, asking the public not to touch the monuments, have been made for fixing in suitable positions.

The kneeling stools in the choir have been re-upholstered and the crosses and emblems of the ends of the banner poles are being re-gilded.

In the ringing chamber in the north west tower the chime [peal] boards have been re-arranged and a new one, inscribed by Miss George, added. Wire guards to keep out birds have been fixed in the windows of the belfry.

A memorial stone has been placed in the Battle of Britain chapel over the grave of Lord Trenchard.

Periodical examination of the Coronation Chair continues but no sign of any deterioration in its condition has been detected.

A new frontal for the High Altar, representing the Queen's coronation offering, was used for the first time on the Feast of the Translation of St Edward the Confessor. Elaborately embroidered on a specially woven blue silk damask, it was made by Watts & Co. of Dacre Street, Westminster and took almost two years to work.

The Cloisters

The experimental repair of the vaulting in the east walk of the cloisters, which was described in my report of last year, has been continued by our masons at intervals when it has been possible to spare them from more urgent work elsewhere. All the stonework of the vaulting and walls has been brushed down and limewashed with results that, in addition to their practical value, may commend themselves as aesthetically pleasing.

The east walk is almost finished and during the summer I hope it will be possible to tackle the north walk, where this treatment should conserve the existing stone without any need for such extensive renewal as, in the south and west walks, will be unavoidable.

The Dark Cloister

The ladders formerly kept here on brackets were removed and the walls pointed and limewashed. The 19th century rafters in the ceiling were also limed, with great improvement to their appearance.

The Little Cloisters

The masons carried out renewal of the jambs to windows and doors in the south walk and a marble cherub, which for some time has been stored in the triforium, was placed in the niche adjoining the front door of no. 7.[5]

The roof over the east walk was rebuilt and covered with asphalte; the ceilings to the east, south and west walks plastered and whitened after rebuilding in reinforced concrete; the masonry of the inner walls washed and the railings re-painted.

Infirmary Hall

Completion of the repairs to the roof was recorded in my last report. The corner fireplace – an ugly modern intrusion – has since been cut out, but laying the new floor and re-plastering the walls cannot proceed until the electrical work necessitated by changing the installation in the hall itself, as well as in nos. 4 and 5, from D.C. to A.C. has been completed. Arrangements for this have recently been concluded with the supply company and the electrical contractors (Drake & Gorham), and the job should start very shortly.

College Garden

The iron spikes on the precinct wall, damaged during tree felling operations were removed. They had long been rusty and useless, as well as unsightly.

The re-opening of the blocked doorway from the terrace of no. 4 to the Jewel Tower garden was finished by the Ministry of Works, old bricks and tile being used to make up the jambs where the original stone had perished. The coping of the precinct wall in this corner was re-bedded by our staff.

The ground in front of nos. 6 and 7 was finally cleaned up of builder's debris in the autumn and laid out as a formal garden in front of the Surveyor's Office, with a private garden in front of no. 7. A new gardener's hut erected in the south east corner of the garden took the place of that which stood within a small enclosed yard below the south end of the Busby Library and the space this yard occupied has now been thrown into the garden of no. 7. Although the paving of the paths and the turfing of the lawns is completed, the brick walls still await their stone copings. The wrought iron gates too, that are being made for the garden doorway from the Little Cloister, are not yet ready for fixing.

A major improvement has been the narrowing of the central path and the abolition of the transverse east to west path and central circle. The larger area of turf makes the garden seem more spacious as well as more beautiful and, by getting rid of a waste of untidy soil and gravel, should facilitate its upkeep. It would not be desirable to carry out the simple reform of aligning the flower beds with the new path; at present their parallelism with the old one is painfully obvious but to anyone not knowing the reason for it would appear inexplicable.[6]

Choir School

Restoration of this building after war damage, the installation of a passenger lift and internal redecoration started in April 1956 but could not be completed as was hoped before the autumn term. This was largely because the extent of concealed war damage proved much greater than showed outwardly. The job lasted, in fact, eleven months and entailed the virtual rebuilding of a portion of the west elevation and the renewal of a large proportion of the metal windows, as well as the rewiring of the electrical system.

A substantial part of the cost will be borne by the War Damage Commission, but the non-recoverable expenditure will still be heavy because, after a long period of years during which it would appear that not much had been spent on it, the building has now had to be reconditioned throughout. Careful maintenance in the future will be essential to avoid such an oversight as that which allowed the windows to rust beyond repair for lack of regular painting.

New wash basins, which have been awaited for weeks, are now being fixed so that the boys will be able to return during April.

The stained glass of the organists' window in the dining hall was repaired and the list of names is being brought up to date.

A new honours board for the dining hall, given as a memorial to the late Canon Donaldson, was made some months ago but could not be finished until agreement had been reached with the donors' family on its treatment and colour. Now that this has been settled, work can be resumed and the board should be fixed this summer.

Dean's Yard

The unsightly pale fencing[7] which had for some years enclosed the grass area was replaced by concrete posts and chains. While this has done something to mitigate the deplorable aspect of what must once have been an attractive enclosure, the condition of Dean's Yard in general continues to evoke – and to deserve – the astonished criticism of visitors. What ought to be a lawn is a barren waste of trodden soil, on which the only green growth is that of weeds; the stone curbing round it is broken and uneven and the whole lay out as dull and unattractive as it could possibly be. That this should be tolerated as a foreground to the chief church of the land would be incredible if it were not true.

College Hall

The marble paving was laid during the summer vacation in time for re-assembly of the school at the start of the autumn term. This completed the reconstruction of the floor, which had become dangerous because death watch beetle had weakened its wooden structure. In its new form the floor contains no timber and will henceforth be immune from this trouble.

Bookstall

Draught excluders were fitted to the doors and have proved satisfactory. An electric bell has been provided for emergency use by those serving in the shop.

Houses

a. The Deanery. The frame of the Canaletto painting in the drawing room, damaged after loan to an exhibition, has been carefully restored and the picture is now back in place.

b. No. 2 The Cloister. The alterations to this house were deferred to permit its temporary use by the Choir School during the winter and spring. They will begin after the boys vacate it in April.

c. No. 20 Dean's Yard. The house has been redecorated, except for certain rooms not required for use. A new stone coping was fixed on the elevation facing Dean's Yard.

d. No. 2 Little Cloister. The first and second floor rooms at the east end have been walled off for inclusion in the building works of no. 3.

e. No. 4 & 4a Little Cloister. The electric installation was found to be dangerous and re-wiring is now in progress. A broken ceiling joist has made it necessary to take down and re-plaster the ceiling in one room; this has entailed an external scaffold for removal of the debris. Two rooms are being decorated in 4a and an extractor fan installed in the kitchen.

f. No. 6 Little Cloister. This house and the Surveyor's office adjoining were completed and brought into occupation in the late summer.

The Clerk of Works office came into use at the same time.

S.E. Dykes Bower, April 8 1957.

[1]   These negatives are in the Abbey Library collection. The colouring may not be original.
[2]   Designed by James Wyatt and executed by Francis Bernasconi after a fire in 1803 destroyed the Hawksmoor ceiling. The lantern roof was hit by an incendiary in May 1941 and destroyed. The new ceiling design was designed by the Surveyor.
[3]   The west aisle previously had a window to Adrian Hope, part of the Indian Mutiny series, and the east aisle had a memorial window to Vincent Novello, both nineteenth century and blown out or damaged by blast.
[4]   Traditionally known as the Black Prince window.
[5]   This came from the Gilbert Lort memorial in the Abbey, which had been reduced in size in the nineteenth century.

6   Westminster School had proposed that, in return for a site in the Garden to accommodate
    new laboratories and a music school, they would make the garden of Ashburnham House
    available to the Dean and Chapter. The Surveyor expressed his views on this in February
    1957 (see S/3/61). This was not done.
7   The railings had been removed for scrap metal after 1941.

63. WAM S/1/103

Report by the Surveyor of the Fabric March 28 1958

Roofs

Nothing new can be added to what has been said about this work in the reports
of the last few years but its progress can be gauged by a few statistics. Out of a
total of 115 new oak trusses for the length of roof between the west end and the
Lantern, 65 have been made. Four more steel beams have been fixed, bringing
the number in position to 14, with 10 more to come. Of the timber bays, 6
have now received their new lead covering and the temporary roof has lately
been erected over the next three. Thus the half way mark has been passed and
completion may reasonably be anticipated in 1959.

The masons have been occupied chiefly with fixing new pad stones in the
walls to support the ends of the steel beams and with building the parapet over
the south clerestory. Although the worked stone has been on the site for two
years or more, its used had to await the re-forming and re-leading of the gutters
which was itself a sequel to the reconstruction of the main roof structure.

The apse and transept roofs are being kept under observation and a check
is made each month to record any signs of movement. One beam in the apse,
which bears a great loading strain and on which a deflection of one quarter inch
was registered in November 1957, is the subject of weekly watch.

Some two years ago one of the king post trusses in the south transept was
found to have sunk and to be touching the crown of the vaulting. To prevent
any weight being transmitted to the latter, it was strapped up and has not moved
since. But the other tie beams of the king posts were in September last also
noted as resting, or appearing to rest, on the vaulting. Mr Paton, the consulting
engineer, who was asked to examine them advised that, though there was not,
in his opinion, any present danger, regular records should be kept to ascertain
whether movement was taking place. This has been done and so far there is no
evidence of it.

The Lantern

The decision to replace Bernasconi's plaster vault by a flat ceiling was referred
to in my last report. While this was under construction during the months
April to August, the design and full size working drawings for the decoration
were prepared and in September the setting out was started. The whole work,

which finished in March 1958, has been carried out by our own painters, with assistance from Mr Butchart on the gilding.

Mahogany boards, one inch thick, form the surface on which the painting has been carried out. Above is a three-quarter inch layer of insulation board fixed to 11 x 2 inch wooden joists which run between the steel beams spanning the 35 feet lantern opening. All this construction is new, but the steel members inserted after the war to support the low-pitched external roof are retained. Over the asphalt, put on there as a temporary covering, battens bolted down to the concrete roof will be laid to receive lead, which will be the permanent external covering. Entrance from parapet level will be provided by a low door on the east face to the space under this pitched roof and above the flat ceiling.

The lanterns of several cathedrals have flat wooden ceilings, either fully or partially decorated in colour. At Norwich, for example, where the ceiling is divided by moulded ribs into square panels, only the ribs are painted. At Ely the surface is unbroken and the whole of it painted with one design filling the square. That of the Abbey is comparable, but the decoration is non-pictorial being designed in the Westminster tradition of geometric pattern and executed in the full range of Gothic colour. This, by day, will be tempered by the light that comes through the grisaille glass of the lantern windows. At night it will be illuminated in a soft glow thrown by permanent electric light fittings fixed just inside the openings from the roof space above the nave, presbytery and transepts.

Internal cleaning

The main task in the past twelve months has been the cleaning of the two transepts. The north is entirely finished, but in the south the one open bay of the west arcade remains to be done, together with the wall and mural tablets in the other three bays. The vault, clerestory and triforium of the two east bays of the choir are finished and the bridge is now being assembled in the two next bays ie. over the west end of the stalls and organ loft.

To keep as many as possible of the team of men who have been engaged on this work in occupation while scaffolding is erected on the bridge, the platform for the future temporary organ in the north choir aisle was put up in advance to facilitate – with the aid of additional scaffolding – cleaning of this aisle bay. The one east of it has already been cleaned and since, once the temporary organ is installed, it will be impossible to tackle this second bay for another twelve months, the arrangement has proved convenient.

Heating

The new boilers have already been brought into operation when my last report was written. Since then the second stage of the installation has been in progress with laying the new heating pipes in the existing ducts at floor level, which the masons have subsequently been covering with stone paving in place of iron gratings. Fan convectors have been placed in the triforium, under the organ loft and at the ends of the choir stalls where they are incorporated in extended platforms, that will shortly be enclosed with surplus portions of Blore's woodwork,[1] hitherto stored in the triforium, to match the choir stalls.

As in the choir, heating pipes have been taken under the raised floors of the stalls in Henry VII's chapel and the stairs up to them have been made detachable to give access to the pipe runs.

The Library and Chapter House have been connected to the new heating system through St Faith's chapel.

During the past winter some trouble has been experienced with uneven temperatures in the building for which, since there is no lack of heating surfaces it is hard to assign a cause. During the restoration of the Lantern ceiling however the steel doors opening from the roof spaces above the nave transepts and apse have had to remain open in connection with the construction of the scaffolding. This may have contributed to draughts, though no doubt only partially. The defects are being investigated by the heating consultant and the engineers responsible for the work and should be remedied before next winter.

A new chimney to the flue from the boilers which is much needed to improve their draught and to discharge exhaust at a higher level cannot be fitted until after this heating system is over. Other improvements still remain to be done and their combined effect should be beneficial.

Fire Prevention

A new dry riser to the nave roof has been installed and Merryweathers Ltd are now fixing the automatic fire alarms. This work will take some time but when finished should prove an economy by making the services of night watchmen redundant.

I feel some concern over the possible condition of the electric wiring in the upper library which is presumably at least twenty years old and might constitute a possible fire risk. It would be advisable to have it tested and I hope that there may be less need in future to run electric heaters off lighting points.

The triforium

Spraying of the timbers with insecticide has continued on both sides of the nave. This completes the first application to the wooden roofs at this level.

Glazing

War damage repair to the Burlison & Grylls glass in one of the two light windows below the rose window in the south transept has been carried out; also to the two clerestory windows on the north side of the choir, during the cleaning of the eastern bays.

Designs by Mr Brian Thomas for new stained glass in the six lancets below the rose window in the north transept were approved and the work should be

finished in time for the Lambeth Conference service on August 10th. The corresponding lancet in lights at the ends of the aisles was glazed with clear glass to
enable more of the money recoverable from the War Damage Commission to
be spent on the centre six.[2]

Monuments

Early in the past year the railings round the tomb of Mary Queen of Scots were
re-fixed and the missing sceptre fixed to the lion at the foot of the effigy.

On the adjacent tomb of the Countess of Lennox a new crown was added to
the head of the figure and small finishing touches carried out to the decoration.

In Queen Elizabeth's aisle the painting of the two tombs of the daughters
of James I was restored by Mr Butchart, who also cleaned and gilded where
necessary the monument to the Princes in the Tower. No other work has been
carried out by Mr Butchart to the monuments during the past year, as for much
of the time he has been engaged on gilding the ceiling in the Lantern.

Our two cleaners have continued their work on those monuments that, never
having been decorated, are suitable for ordinary washing. They have completed
those in the apsidal chapels of Henry VII's chapel, the east and west aisles of
the north transept and some in the east aisle of the south transept.

Memorials

A new bronze bust of William Blake on a pedestal of Belgium black marble was
designed by Sir Jacob Epstein and unveiled in November 1957. It is attached to a
pillar of the east arcade of the south transept. In the floor almost opposite to it
has been set a memorial stone commemorating Gilbert Murray.

In the nave an inscribed stone has been laid over the grave of Mrs Carnegie,
immediately east of that of her husband [Canon Carnegie].

A new marble slab, having the same inscription as the old one, has been laid
on the grave of Mary Illingworth in the north transept. The cost was met by
relatives.

To record the services of the Crown in India, a tablet of Roman stone on a
background of black Belgian fossil marble was erected in the west walk of the
cloisters and unveiled by the Queen in March 1958. It bears the Royal Arms and
the decorations of the Star of India and the Indian Empire carved in stone and
coloured.[3]

Abbey Furniture

The new alms box, incorporating four 17th century carved consoles that had
long lain unused, was brought into use in the north transept in the autumn of
1957. Of the original position and purpose of these consoles nothing seems to
be known.[4]

Over the upper part of the entrance doors to the north transept, ie. above the
top of the inner porch, curtains have been hung to conceal the poor appearance

of the timber and to reduce draught. They have been made out of existing material obtained, it is said, in the time of Dean Stanley and still, after cleaning, in good condition.

In the chapel of Henry VII cushions have been made for the desks to the top row of stalls out of the red velvet obtained for the exhibition of Abbey treasures in St James's Palace a few years ago [1953].

After treatment by experts in the Armoury at the Tower of London the helmet, the shield and saddle of Henry V have been replaced on the tie beam in the west arch of his chantry chapel.[5]

The tapestry on the south side of the Sanctuary was returned after cleaning and is again in position.

Two Persian carpets were bequeathed under the will of the late Mrs Carnegie and are now in use.

The wooden feretory over the Confessor's Shrine has recently been removed for repair and restoration by the firm of J. Longley & Co. Ltd. who a few years ago undertook the repair of the stall canopies on the north side in Henry VII's chapel. The work has been made possible by a private donation of £1500.

The Organ

The woodwork of the Pearson organ cases, that has for years been scattered along the triforium, was collected and carefully sorted. The two fronts have now been set out on the floors of the north apsidal chapels and after Easter two joiners are to be sent by the contractors, who will undertake re-erection of the cases, to work at a bench set up for them here and piece the whole together. Much of the elaborate oak carving is undamaged and very little is missing. But a good deal of patience and skill will be needed to repair the breakages and, out of the boxes of small pieces, to find the right one to go back in its intended position.

After the Lambeth Conference service on August 10th, the organ builders will dismantle the north half of the instrument and cleaning of the stonework will follow. The casework will then be installed, while dismantling and cleaning proceed on the southern half. While subsequently the casework on this side is fitted up, re-building of the organ will begin opposite. The aim is to have the instrument, or at least a part of it, available for use in time for the Purcell tercentenary celebration in June 1959. As one of the cases was given in memory of Purcell, its reinstatement before that event is particularly appropriate.

The Cloisters

Brushing down the loose surface of the stonework and lime washing the walls and vaulting of the east walk was finished in the summer of 1957; brushing down was also carried out at the end of February 1958 in the south and west walks as a safety precaution. One tablet, from which the inscription had entirely perished, was removed in the east walk.

On the slate slab in memory of the Reverend J. Lupton the inscription was re-cut at the cost of the family.

The laying of a new electric cable to the houses in the Little Cloister necessitated some excavation both in the cloister garth, the south walk and the Dark Entry. The grass and paving that had to be lifted have now been fully replaced.

Infirmary Hall

The structural repair of the roof was finished some time ago and the plaster between the rafters has now been whitened. The walls have also been re-plastered and whitened, with notable improvement to the natural lighting of what was previously rather a dark room. New electrical wiring has been installed and as soon as the fittings are in place and the new floor laid the room will be ready for use.

Although the pseudo gallery has been retained, I still hope that this may soon be removed as the extra space in the hall would not merely improve its proportions but may prove to be needed for the accommodation of the furnishings required.

Houses

There has been less work to report on the houses than in the past few years. Redecoration of the interior of 20 Dean's Yard and of two rooms in 4a Little Cloister was finished in April 1957. Renewal of the electrical installation in nos. 4 and 4a Little Cloister was completed in April 1957 and of that in 5 Little Cloister in November.

In the Deanery redecoration of the Langham and Litlyngton rooms [Cheyneygates] and the staircase up to them is now in progress. It is proposed to hang on their walls various pictures, chiefly portraits of 17th and 18th century Deans, the two tapestries now in St Faith's chapel[6] and the four heraldic embroideries hung in the sanctuary at the coronation and on permanent loan from the Ministry of Works. They have had to be stored for four years and will now be framed and protected by glass. Various good tables and chairs will be brought together from different places to form a nucleus of furniture.

The alteration of 2 The Cloisters began in May 1957 and has continued throughout the succeeding twelve months. The house will be ready for occupation after Easter 1958, though tidying and paving of the garden and repair of its east and south walls will last some weeks longer. The house has been reduced in size by demolition of various additions to the east and the original block has been largely reconstructed. On the front to Dean's Yard the battlements and the cusped heads to the second floor windows have been removed, a new plain parapet at a lower level substituted and the windows re-glazed with leaded lights. On the east front a new front door has been designed to harmonize with the 18th century sash windows. The entrance from the cloisters has been remodelled and the three light window above, which was in a very bad condition, rebuilt slightly higher in the wall. A paved terrace has been made along the front of the house, with two steps down to the garden. Internally the lowest flight of the old staircase, which was lost in previous alterations, has been restored and a new window made to match the existing one higher up.

Although much more compact than before the house has been remodelled without the sacrifice of any of its best rooms and should be both easier to run and pleasanter to live in.

The completion of the north range of the Little Cloisters has been in progress during the last six months. The end house, no 3, should be ready for occupation by May, together with the guest rooms and flat being made in rooms hitherto part of no. 2.[7]

College Garden

The stone coping and balls to the new retaining walls in front of 6 and 7 were fixed and the parterre planted with flowers in time for the summer of 1957.

Wrought iron gates, designed by Seely and Paget, were placed in the outer doorway from the Little Cloister.

In February 1958 a strip of lawn adjacent to the dormitory and an enclosure in front of the precinct wall to Great College Street were fenced off to give the builders engaged on the restoration of Big School [Hall] facilities for bringing in materials. The ground should be freed and re-sown with grass before the summer of 1959.

St Catherine's chapel

With the approaching completion of no. 3 and removal of builders' materials, a start is now being made with clearing the ground so that it can be laid out as a garden. The level of the soil within the former nave has been lowered to expose the plinths of the Norman pillars and to show whether any of the original paving remains hidden. So far none has been found.

As soon as levelling is finished and the site freed of debris, the first steps can be taken to lay out the space as a garden. But the state of the Norman masonry in pillars and walls is bad and much repair will be needed to prevent further deterioration. The work, which could be done by our masons when not engaged upon more essential jobs on the Abbey itself, ought not to be delayed too long.

Discussions were held with the Ancient Monuments Branch of the Ministry of Works on the treatment of the precinct wall of the east end of St Catherine's chapel and it was agreed that the top portion of brick, which is not part of the original stone structure, would be better taken off. This would reduce the height of the wall by about 3 feet and improve its appearance alike from St Catherine's chapel and the Jewel Tower garden. The original masonry could then be finished with a gabled brick coping similar to that on the wall further south.

The layout of the garden, of which drawings will shortly be ready, provides for excavating the ground within the chapel to its former level and turfing it.

Because of limited space, it would not be practicable to expose the outer face of what remains of the chancel wall and the ground here will have to be kept at its present level. Some of it might be paved and the rest planted with flowers or flowering shrubs: it would be desirable, for example, to plant creepers against the precinct wall and the brick wall of no. 4.

Railings similar to those in the Little Cloisters will be required for the arcade on the north side and on the south side the ugly patching of the Norman pillars and arches with synthetic stone should be removed and the arches opened out. This would give opportunity to enhance the amenities of the precincts and particularly the outlook from no. 2 and 3 Little Cloister.

> S.E. Dykes Bower
> Surveyor of the Fabric

1 Edward Blore designed the quire stalls in 1848.
2 The six pre-war lancets and one in the west aisle of the transept remembered individuals killed in the Indian Mutiny.
3 Designed by the Surveyor.
4 They were bases to wooden pinnacles at the entrance to the quire – engraved by John Dart in his 1723 history of the Abbey.
5 They remained there until cleaned again and placed in the Abbey Museum in 1972.
6 The expulsion of Hagar tapestry, and a small piece depicting a flower and vase design, still remain in the inner room.
7 Repair after war damage. The flats are 2a and 2b Little Cloister.

63N. At Chapter on 10 June 1958 a letter from the Surveyor regarding rebuilding at 1–19 Victoria Street was recorded. This new structure was to have been 140 feet high and the Surveyor was able to get this reduced to 108 feet to lessen impact on the Abbey.

64. WAM S/1/104

Report of the Surveyor of the Fabric 16 March 1959

The amount of work carried out during the past twelve months was limited by the necessity of saving approximately £20,000 on the previous year's expenditure. Restoration has therefore proceeded more slowly, partly because fewer men have been employed on a particular job, such as stone cleaning, and partly because the scope of what could be undertaken has been curtailed.

Nave roof

The fourth section of the roof occupied most of the year and the temporary covering has now been removed from it and re-erected over the fifth. The old lead had been lifted from the two bays of this by the end of 1958 and eight new oak trusses prepared in readiness for fixing. The condition of the existing roof timbers shows no improvement on that of previous sections and is, if anything, worse. But the problems do not differ in kind from those already met with and there is nothing fresh to record about this work, which will continue the same for many years.

The new stone parapet on the south side can be well seen from the south cloister, now that scaffolding is no longer present to hide it.

Internal cleaning

Cleaning of the north choir aisle and of the vaulting, clerestory and triforium in the choir was completed in time for the closing service of the Lambeth Conference in August. The bridge and scaffolding were then erected in the next two bays westwards, which are now also completed. A great deal of masonry repair has had to be carried out in this section which has caused the scaffolding to remain longer than otherwise would have been necessary. The stone cleaners meanwhile have been transferred to the four bays of the south aisle of the choir, which should be finished about the end of April.

Cleaning of the Muniment Room was carried out by our staff, who also cleaned the bay of the main arcade normally covered by the two fronts of the organ. Only after the organ had been dismantled could they be reached for this purpose.

The change in the treatment of the vault between choir and nave – the one richly gilded and ornamented, the other plain – appeared excessively abrupt with the stone of the nave vault restored to its natural whiteness. The carving of the nave bosses moreover could not be fully appreciated from below for, although these are at least as fine or finer than those in the choir and transepts, the absence of paint made them look dull by comparison. It was decided therefore to gild the bosses and paint gold on the ribs, just as in the choir, but without any painted decoration on the infilling. Mr Butchart has been responsible for the gilding and the result is, I think very successful.

Monuments

The cleaning of monuments has been carried out during the year entirely by our staff, except in the last few weeks when Mr Hart of J. Whitehead & Co. Ltd, has been coming when required to repaint the lettering of various inscriptions. On many memorials the pattern of black lettering on stone or marble – an essential element in the decorative effect – has become so faint as to count for nothing. The work is necessarily slow and there is so much to do that I hope it will be possible to employ Mr Hart more fully in the future.

The monuments cleaned during the year are those in the north and south transepts and their aisles. A few in the north transept are still to be finished.

Our cleaners and polishers will next work on the monuments in the choir aisles, which are likely to absorb their time for most of the coming year, leaving the nave monuments to be finished during the next three years. To some of these monuments however I suggest that consideration should be given before cleaning starts. It would in my opinion be legitimate, and certainly desirable, to make slight alterations in the position of those that have been so fixed as to cut across the design of the building. In the north nave aisle there are two or three tablets that do this, whereas a slight change of position on to the splayed sides of the windows would obviate any damage to the architectural lines. No objection could reasonably be made, I think, to adjustments of this sort, which probably would hardly be noticed.

But there are some memorials whose right to occupy floor and wall space in the Abbey seems so slender as to call for re-examination. It would not be a question of exclusion, but of transferring them to the triforium, which already contains a sufficient number to counter any suggestion that this would be equivalent to banishment.[1]

There are obviously many factors to be weighed – aesthetic, historical, perhaps even personal. But none should be given greater weight than the architectural, which has received least regard in the past. The cleaning of the interior has in a remarkable way emphasized the supreme excellence of the design of the Abbey: the aim should now be not to lose any of the few opportunities of revealing it more clearly.

I would add one further observation in connection with the monuments. Although those in the nave will give employment to our own labour for some years, it still remains to restore the large 17th century monuments in the apsidal chapels which need specialised skill. The Hunsdon monument alone has been completed so far. These are potentially the most decorative in the Abbey and would offer scope for keeping Mr Butchart at work after the decoration of the organ cases is finished.

North west tower

Repairs were carried out to the lead flashings and the wire bands supporting the flag staff. This flag staff ought now to be repainted.

In the course of a gale this winter the hand of the clock was blown off and inspection showed that the spindle had rusted away to a thickness of only three eights of an inch. Had this historic and valuable clock been kept in going order, which would have ensured its regular inspection and maintenance, the damage might never have occurred. Estimates which I have obtained for putting the clock into order and fitting it with an automatic winding apparatus show that the cost would be comparatively moderate; but it will eventually be high if protracted disuse leads to serious deterioration of the mechanism. So famous a clock may be thought to deserve a better fate than to be doomed to perpetual silence and neglect.[2]

Glazing

The six lancet windows below the rose window in the north transept were filled with stained glass in the summer of 1958. The previous war damaged glass was not harmonious with the 18th century Joshua Price glass above and Mr Brian Thomas, in designing the new windows, took the opportunity to achieve a better relationship of style and colour.

Renewal of the clerestory windows on the north side of the choir has proceeded while scaffolding for the interior cleaning has made it possible. The War Damage Commission is contributing 50% of the cost.

Investigation of two more boxes of broken glass that have lain in the triforium has brought to light an unexpected find of old glass from Henry VII's chapel. The contents of these boxes are being laid out in the glaziers' shops and I hope in due course to submit proposals for their use.

Furniture

On the south side of the sanctuary, following replacement of the tapestry after cleaning, the picture has also been replaced in front of it.

A new walnut case to contain the Battle of Britain Roll of Honour is almost finished and will shortly replace the metal stand in Henry VII's chapel. Another case of oak will at the same time be placed in the Islip chapel to house the Obit Roll.[3]

The platform made necessary at the east end of the stalls in the choir to accommodate part of the heating equipment is to be cased with spare portions of Blore's pews, so that they will look an integral part of the choir woodwork. It has been impossible hitherto to put our joiners on to this job but I hope the unsightly appearance they have presented for too long will soon be remedied.

The bomb damage, which caused the lantern roof to fall in, left scars on the floor which have been little noticed only because the areas affected are normally covered by seating. But much of the black and white marble paving was destroyed and had to be replaced temporarily by concrete. New marble squares have now been supplied and are in process of being laid.

A framed notice, written by Miss George, has been fixed in the Nurses Chapel to record the story of its formation.

The oak cases in the Sacristy, containing frontals, banners, vestments etc. have had painted Roman numerals placed on the doors to enable them to be referred to by number in the Inventory.

The list of bishops' names under the organ loft has had further additions made to it.

A painted and gilded wrought iron notice, inscribed 'Offerings' was placed on the alms box in the north transept.

Memorials

The ashes of Ralph Vaughan Williams were buried in the north choir aisle and a design for the memorial slab, with lettering by Mr Reynolds Stone, has been approved. It should be ready shortly.

The Organ

Dismantling of the organ started in August 1958 and a small organ, erected on a temporary loft in the north choir aisle, came into use in September. The stonework of the arcade on either side of the pulpitum was cleaned before erection of the organ cases began and the north case is now in place except for the carved wings and the panelled base. The south case should be finished in about a month.

The pipes will not be replaced until Mr Butchart has carried out the gilding and decoration; extensive alteration in the lay out of the instrument, which at first it was thought would be unavoidable to enable Pearson's cases to go back in their correct position, has fortunately been avoided. Only the panelled lower sections will need some re-modelling and I hope to contrive this in such a way that it will be virtually unseen from the floor of the nave and choir.

Although the cases had been carefully repaired in the triforium over a period of many months before assembly, some difficulty was found in erection owing to shrinkages which had developed in the timber. This was perhaps inevitable seeing that the woodwork had been lying in pieces for over twenty years. The problems have however been overcome and any slight irregularities will be too small to be noticeable.

It is too early to say when the whole instrument will again be available, but I hope that substantial portions will be ready for the Purcell and Handel celebrations in June.

The Feretory [of St Edward's Shrine]

Repair and restoration has continued at the works of J. Longley & Co Ltd, and although it is impossible to be sure of a date for completion, I hope that it may be this year.

Heating

The necessity of rationing oil consumption during the first winter after the new heating system came into use made difficult a judgement on its efficiency. It has now been tested more fairly and I think the results may be considered satisfactory, though not yet perfect since inexplicable draughts persist at the east end of the stalls in the choir. The heating engineer is working on a means of rectifying this trouble and confident that it can be done.

A forced draught apparatus for lifting the fumes from the flue on the north side of the apse clear of the building has recently come into operation and this will help to prevent damage to the external stonework.

Hermeseal has been fitted to the outer doors of the north transept wind porch to make them air tight.

Fire Prevention

The installation of an automatic fire alarm system has been in progress during the year and is complete, except for two detectors still to be fixed in the organ cases. This will enable the services of a night watchman to be dispensed with and give quicker and better warning of any outbreak of fire. Arrangements have been made whereby a distinctive signal at the fire station will ensure that any alarm from the Abbey will be answered immediately, without the verbal confirmation normally required.

The London Fire Brigade, the Post Office (telephone department) and the Police have been consulted and have agreed on the drill that will be followed in the event of an alarm.

The Cloisters

Stonework repairs have been carried out to the buttresses of the east side of the garth and further repairs await attention from the masons when they can be freed from other more pressing jobs.

One of the trefoil lights in the northernmost window of the east range has been filled with stained glass composed of fragments of glass[4] from the lantern and elsewhere, salvaged after war damage. It was made up by the glaziers to demonstrate how this glass could be used, and presented by them free of charge. Now that its effect can be seen, I hope the rest of the tracery in the two northernmost windows may be filled, since the rather coarse details of these two windows would be less noticeable if they were filled with coloured glass. In continuing to store this and a great deal of other glass from the Abbey, the glaziers are, moreover, rendering a service of which we can hardly take advantage indefinitely.

A few tablets from which the inscriptions had disappeared have been removed from the walls and two more are to go from the west walk.[5] A small stone tablet has been placed under the memorial to the Services of the Crown in India recording its unveiling by the Queen in 1958.

The arch leading into the Deanery courtyard that had for some time been strutted while awaiting attention, has been secured and partially rebuilt.

Parts of the vaulting were again brushed down from a travelling scaffold and loose portions of stone removed.

It will not be possible to move the hoist from the north east corner of the cloister garth for some time since it must remain in this position till the renovation of the nave roof is completed. I propose that the south transept roof should be undertaken next, after which it can be transferred to the angle of the north transept and apse, while the roofs on those portions are dealt with. In the meantime however I suggest that the grass in the cloister garth should be kept mown as it used to be. During the last year it presented a rough and unkempt appearance, which was not made unavoidable by any building operations.

College Hall kitchen

As a result of representations by the Medical Officer of Health on the unhygienic condition of the kitchen, and because of the nuisance of the smell of cooking affecting the whole north east corner of Dean's Yard, a scheme of internal modernisation has been carried out during successive school holidays. It was timely for other than those reasons. When the ceiling was opened up the main structural beam was found to be so greatly overloaded that complete collapse might have occurred at any moment. This highly dangerous condition had to be rectified with the utmost urgency by strutting up the existing timbers while new steel joists were inserted. It was then possible to proceed with the removal of much obsolete equipment and piping, the installation of a ventilation plant, lowering the level of the ceiling, new lighting and the repair and redecoration of the walls. Two small openings in the wall into Dean's Yard are the only visible change externally.

The results have, I understand, given satisfaction to those who use it and eliminated the aroma of food from the Chapter Office next door[6]

College Hall

Recent examination of the windows has shown that their glazing is very defective and I shall shortly be submitting estimates for repairing this. Until they are weather tight it would be of no use to carry out any re-decoration of the walls. This however is badly needed, as much of the plaster is in poor condition, and in two places has had to be removed. The whole interior is extremely dirty and it would be desirable to carry out a good many improvements which are long overdue.

Choir School

New wash basins were fixed in the boys' dormitory and maids' bathroom during the summer holiday of 1958.

Dean's Yard

The lawn which has at last replaced an unsightly wilderness of earth and weeds is an improvement too conspicuous to need comment. The lamp standards surrounding it have been repainted.

Infirmary Hall

With the laying of a new floor of linoleum tiles and provision of new electric light fittings, the restoration of this hall was finally completed. In the autumn of 1958 it was opened for use as a robing room by the Brotherhoods.

Formerly the entrance hall to no. 4 it is now separate, the door to that house having been built up. In the course of repairs carried out over the last few years its roof has been extensively repaired and partially re-constructed; a corner fireplace and chimney removed: the walls re-plastered; the two windows in the east wall, one of 19th century stained glass, re-glazed; new lighting and electric heating installed and the whole interior redecorated. Some existing furniture that formerly stood in the eastern aisle of the north transept is now accommodated here and a few pictures from the Library and elsewhere have been hung on the walls.

Serving a utilitarian purpose the interior has had to be equipped simply and inexpensively, but the character and charm of this little medieval hall can at least be better seen and appreciated.

St Catherine's chapel

Work on the lay-out of this future garden has proceeded rather slowly. Excavation and levelling that would normally be undertaken in the middle of the year were made impossible by the wet summer of 1958 and periods of snow and continuous frost have been an equal hindrance through the winter.

The unexpected discovery of a stone altar at the east end of the north aisle of the nave has entailed some modification in the plan as first submitted and approved. The altar was not entire but sufficiently so to be worth retaining. Its rubble walling has been consolidated and covered with a large stone slab in place of the original mensa which was not found. All that remains of the north wall of the north aisle has been exposed and where necessary made good to form a retaining wall up to floor level of the arcade under nos. 2 and 3 Little Cloister. In one place towards the west end some of the original plaster remains with a short length of the red painted jointing that was typical of Norman decoration.

The ground has been taken down to the former floor level of the aisle, but no trace of any old pavement has been found.

Levelling of the nave and chancel will be the next stage and one that it is desirable to complete quickly if grass is to be sown in time for a lawn to get established this summer. At present shortage of labour (partly the result of sickness among the staff) and inability to put our masons, owing to prolonged occupation on the nave vaulting, to the repair of the bases of the stone pillars are making it difficult to achieve this aim. Moreover there is the top of the precinct wall at the east end to be lowered and rebuilt in continuation of the short section that was done in conjunction with the rebuilding of no. 3; also a tiled creasing to be formed over the projecting part of the west wall, which for too long has lacked this essential protection against water penetration.

Paving has been ordered for the terrace at the east end and I would urge that suitable shrubs and creepers be planted against the precinct wall, as well as flowers in the border already formed between the arcade and the retaining wall to the north aisle. Now that nos. 2, 2A and 3 are inhabited, it is more desirable to improve their outlook. The site should not be allowed to remain a wilderness through another summer and, if gardened properly from the start, ought quite quickly to become a picturesque addition to the precincts.

Houses

The tapestries formerly in St Faith's chapel have been hung in the Langham and Litlyngton rooms of the Deanery, together with the heraldic embroideries on permanent loan from the Ministry of Works. These are now protected by glass and set in specially designed oak frames. Plans for the proper furnishing of these rooms were drawn up some time ago but little progress has been made in carrying them out. I would urge that steps should be taken to provide what is necessary to fit these rooms for suitable use and in particular to improve their lighting and heating. It is, I think, regrettable that the six 18th century chairs should have been removed from them back to Jerusalem Chamber, where they do not consort well with the set of chairs specially made for it.

The walls of the staircase to Langham and Litlyngton have been hung with portraits and an early 19th century settee, formerly stored in the triforium, placed in the entrance vestibule.

Extensive cracks in the ceiling of the staircase hall in the Deanery were investigated and, though not dangerous as yet, will have to receive attention this year.

Occupation of no. 2 The Cloister was resumed in the summer of 1958 after complete remodelling of the house. The numerous structural defects, including damage by death watch beetle which came to light in the course of the work, would certainly have become much more serious had they not been discovered in time. After the departure of the general contractors, our staff carried out repairs to the old walls, previously hidden by those parts of the house that have been pulled down, and laid out a small paved garden.

No 2 Little Cloister was redecorated, following alteration and reduction in size. With the completion of the range of building on the north side of Little Cloister, nos. 2A and 3 have come into habitation – the former as a guest suite on the first floor with a small flat above and the latter as a house for the Precentor. On the north and east sides the amenities of this house continue to be impaired by the contiguity of buildings that ultimately are to come down. I hope that pressure will be exercised on the Government department concerned to ensure that their life is not prolonged.

No. 4A Little Cloister was vacated just before Christmas 1958 and is now being redecorated for a new tenant.

In no. 8 inconvenience has been experienced with smoking chimneys. A cowl fixed on one of these has not proved completely satisfactory and there is some reason to think – though it is impossible to prove – that the stage tower of Big School has aggravated the trouble. To heighten the chimney stacks would be a costly operation and might not be a sure remedy. The difficulty is still under consideration, but at present I have no recommendations to make.

After being vacated by the Precentor no. 4B Dean's Yard was redecorated and re-wired and opportunity taken to carry out various small internal improvements

College Garden

The opening made in the precinct wall to Great College Street to enable materials to be brought in for the restoration of Big School has been built up, but grass has yet to be sown along the path fenced off and used by the contractors adjacent to the dormitory.

The aspect of the garden is still marred by the lack of parallelism between the centre path and the flower borders on either side, to which I referred in my report of 1957. This could be so easily corrected – at no expense and with no more than a few hours work – that I trust it will not last through another summer.

16 March 1959 S.E. Dykes Bower, Surveyor of the Fabric.

[1] No memorials were moved to the triforium from the nave.

[2] The clock is by John Seddon 1738. After repair it chimed a little before or after Big Ben until it was finally stopped in the 1970s. This was apparently due to the bell ringers being allowed to keep the bells up between peals. The chimes could only operate when the bells were in the down position [ex info. John Nixon, Lay Vicar].

[3] This small case was later removed to the Library, as was the book containing details of burials in the vaults below the chapel. The case has since been moved to the triforium.

[4] This includes some medieval and Tudor glass. Work was by Goddard & Gibbs.

[5] Memorials to William Wynne, Thomas Jordan, William E. Gell and Anne Winchcombe (only the latter had no inscription) were taken down from the north cloister. The Walter Davis and Catherine Palmer monuments from the west walk were removed and restored but put in the triforium.

[6] This was at no 21 Dean's Yard at this period. The work was reported at Chapter on 23 June 1959.

64N.   A letter from the Surveyor regarding a new building at the corner of Great Smith Street and Victoria Street was set out at Chapter on 28 April 1959. Further discussions about its possible impact on the Abbey and the Choir School followed at subsequent meetings.

65.   WAM S/1/105

Report by the Surveyor of the Fabric 1960

Nave roof

The temporary corrugated iron roof is in position over the two bays west of the lantern and restoration of the nave roof is thus in its final stage. The time it will have taken – approximately six years – gives some measure of the probable duration of the restoration of the transept and apse roofs, the combined lengths of which are roughly equivalent to that of the nave.

The intention hitherto has been to deal with the south transept next ie. in 1961, so that, after its completion, the hoist could be removed from the cloisters and transferred to the angle of the north transept and ambulatory, where it will be convenient for the apse and north transept roofs. Owing however to the continued need to keeping down expenditure, this plan may have to be changed and priority given to the reconstruction and covering in lead of the temporary asphalte roof over the lantern. As this will be a charge recoverable from the War Damage Commission, the Restoration Fund should, during 1961, be spared having to provide for roof repairs so large a sum as hitherto.

The apse and transept roofs have been kept under monthly observations during the year, but no signs of movement in the tie beams have developed.

Internal cleaning

Stone cleaning of the triforium, clerestory and vaulting is complete except in the two west bays of the nave. The bridge cannot however be moved because of the amount of stonework repair to be carried out from it by our masons. The quicker progress of cleaning has in fact outstripped the capacity of our small staff of masons to keep up with it, and is partly due to the plainer wall surfaces – less carving and no diapering in the spandrels of the arcade. Unhappily, to neutralize this advantage, more and more places have been discovered requiring extensive stone repairs. This is the reason why scaffolding has to remain in the north aisle: there is as much to do there as at the higher level of the triforium and clerestory.

Certain defects I have had photographed, to demonstrate the danger they constitute. In the north aisle, for example, some of the lower courses of the vaulting ribs, where they descend on to the pillars and wall shafts, have bowed outwards to such an extent that it is possible to see between them and the wall of which they should be part. In their precarious condition they could easily have fallen, with consequences that may be imagined.

For some time ahead, then, there will have to be an intermission in cleaning, while the masons catch up with it. But it is important that the contractor's team of men who have become trained to the work should not be disbanded and occupation is being found for them in polishing the pillars of the north arcade. This will mean that a good deal of scaffolding will be in position throughout the summer on the north side of the nave and, in any arrangements for seating at large services, allowance should be made for curtailment of the space available.

Polishing of the purbeck marble pillars is a slow job: each one represents at least a month's work by four men. The pillars of the west bay moreover are larger than the rest and, in addition to the arcades, there are wall shafts in the aisles. It will take well over a year to finish them, independently of the cleaning of the south aisle and the west bays. Nevertheless the aim must still be to press on and endeavour to complete the nave by the end of 1961. Once that is done and payments to the London Stone Cleaning Company, which have been a substantial item in annual expenditure, terminate, there should be some easing of the financial position. Money will still of course be absorbed by many other needs, notably the restoration of stonework in the south and west cloisters; but there will not be the same race against time which is entailed when large scaffolding is on hire and has to remain while full economic use is not being extracted from it. That is why the present delay, imposed by the inability of the masons to keep abreast of repairs, is particularly inopportune.

Externally further work has been done in fixing the south parapet of the nave and restoration of the pinnacles on the north side of the presbytery. Eight new corbel heads have been carved on these.

Monuments

The largest monument that has been restored during the past year is that of the Countess of Hertford in St Benedict's chapel. It had been impaired by the loss of various ornaments, breakage of others and fading of the painted decorations. The damage has been made good and the colouring would by now have been finished had it not been for Mr Butchart falling ill and having to be away for some months. He is expected back shortly to resume this work and also the repainting of Dean Goodman's monument close by. I hope he will then be able to tackle the monument of Sir Thomas Hesketh in the north choir aisle – another 17th century monument which was originally coloured and has been repaired by our staff in readiness for decoration.

It is in the north choir aisle that our monument cleaners have chiefly worked during the year, though a start has also been made in the south choir aisle and the Stanhope and Newton monuments have been dealt with in conjunction with the decoration of Blore's pulpitum. On these the lettering has been repainted.

Mr Hart and one other helper have repainted inscriptions, where almost illegible, on various other monuments, but the time that this task absorbs makes progress very slow. That it should go steadily on is desirable because the pattern of the lettering is an essential element in the design of a tablet.

The beneficial results of employing one man full time on the use of our Sturtevant cleaner can be seen on many of the monuments that have been cleaned in the last few years and the purchase of a moveable steel tower has enlarged the range of his activities. By means of it he has recently removed a thick coating of dust from the medieval tombs on the north side of the sanctuary.

Triforium

The purchase of a second and more powerful Sturtevant for use at triforium level has given the same man opportunity to carry out excellent work in preventing the accumulation of dust in parts of the building that, having been cleaned, must be kept clean. So long as scaffolding has to be put up and taken down, dust will permeate the atmosphere. Unless speedily extracted from every lodgment that can be reached by vacuum cleaner, it soon imposes its grey film over everything.

Glazing

Reglazing of the clerestory windows of the nave has been continued while the scaffolding on the bridge has made this possible, together with attendant repairs and pointing of the stonework. The Clayton & Bell glass in the window at the south end of the eastern aisle of the south transept is undergoing repair after war damage. The glass should be in position again before the Royal wedding.

Fragments of old glass from Henry VII's chapel and of 19th century glass from some of the war damaged windows have been put together as a mosaic of colour to fill the tracery of the northern windows in the east wall of the cloister. It is hoped to have them in place in time for the Royal wedding. The cost will be recoverable from the War Damage Commission.

An offer by the Rolls Royce Company to complete the sequence of Sir Ninian Comper's windows in the north aisle of the nave has enabled execution of the work to start during his lifetime. The new glass will be placed in the window which at present forms the memorial to Richard Trevithick, the Burlison & Grylls glass from which will be transferred to the north window under the north west tower, where the cill will be lowered to receive it.

Organ cases

In June 1959 the Pearson organ cases were dedicated after re-instatement and decoration. A temporary organ, in a loft behind the north choir stalls, had been in use for about nine months while the main organ was partially dismantled and stored. The woodwork of the cases which had been undergoing repair in the triforium had to be erected in position before the organ builders could assess the full scope of any alteration in the lay out of the instrument that would be necessary. In fact their task proved to be easier than had been expected. Some re-arrangement was unavoidable on the north side but very little on the south. To obviate, however, what would have been expensive changes in the lay out of the bellows at organ loft level, I modified very slightly in the form of the lowest stage of the cases i.e. the coving and panelling. No essential parts of Pearson's design were omitted and the visible differences are negligible. But instead of the instrument having to be partially reconstructed, it was able to go back much as before, and with the benefit of tonal improvements effected by new outlets for the sound in the cases fronting the aisles. Wooden grilles have been substituted for some of the solid panels in these fronts, and pipes restored to the openings for which they were intended.

The job of piecing together the existing woodwork, repairing it where necessary and supplying and carving missing parts was carried out by J. Longley & Co. Ltd., who had previously been employed on the stall canopies of Henry VII's chapel. Throughout the long preparatory work and the difficult business of erection their craftsmen showed much patience and skill.

The cases had not previously been painted; but the colour of their oak was never the same as that of the choir seating and it was obvious that they would gain by decoration. Mr Butchart's execution of the design for this is another testimony to his skill and artistry.

The light oak of the organ console has been toned dark to match the panelling of the base of the organ cases and the list of organists, formerly painted direct on one of its panels but much worn and also incorrect, will shortly appear in incised lettering on a new framed and painted tablet, fixed centrally on the west face of the console.

Organ Screen

Since the decoration of the organ cases, the Bath stone face of the nave front of the pulpitum has looked more than ever drab and dirty, contrasting badly with the white stone of the nave where cleaned. Washing made a conspicuous change but I have always felt that Blore's design, which has never received much appreciation, would be improved by colour and might then be perceived to have not inconsiderable merit. For its date – about 1830 – it is remarkably good, being entirely correct in form and modelled on excellent precedents, such as those of Southwell and Exeter. The wedding of Princess Margaret was an incentive to expedite the task of decoration, which was started in March 1960 for completion by May. Careless treatment in the past had denuded the design (like that of the reredos in the choir) of various features that had either been broken or had fallen off and not been refixed. They have now been made good, but I have slightly altered Blore's design in two respects: by the removal of the pinnacles and substitution of gabled heads not rising above the level of the parapet, and by the reduction in size of the overlarge finial on the central gable.

Choir

Because of the changes in the design and details of the coats of arms of New Zealand, the New Zealand government requested that a correct version should supplant the existing arms on the back of the High Commissioner's stall and undertook the cost of having it made. The firm who carried out the work also supplied a shield painted with the arms of Dr Don,[1] which has been hung, but not fixed, in the stall allotted to him on the north aisle.

The platforms built over the filters to the heating pipes at the east end of the choir stalls have been cased in with spare portions of Blore's pews, so that they harmonize with the rest of the choir woodwork. The work was done by our own joiners, who also executed alterations to the oak inner porch at the north transept entrance. The alteration consisted by removing some panels in the small enclosed cupboard between the entrance and exit lobbies and fixing bronze grilles behind which an invisible heater has been installed. This heater warms the air that is blown into the building when the swing doors are opened and helps to prevent draughts in the transept. The oak of the porch, which had darkened to a nondescript brown shade, has been bleached and new leaded glass inserted in the glass panels. There is still a good deal of repair to be done to this porch, which must have been very roughly handled in the past; I hope that sometime during the next twelve months, our joiners will be free to tackle it.

Sedilia

The sedilia in the choir [sic] must once have been one of the chief beauties of the sanctuary, for close examination shows the wealth of adornment originally lavished upon it in painting and glass enamel. For generations, however, it has appeared little more than a battered wreck – many of its architectural features mutilated or missing, its coloured decoration scarcely visible except where work was done by Professor Tristram some years ago[2] in revealing more clearly those figure paintings that survive. The actual wooden structure had been crudely patched with unsuitable materials – linoleum, for example, instead of wood in the ribbed vaulting – and badly needed repair.

The opportunity to make a start on this came through an offer of the services of Miss Plummer, the post graduate student selected to study, on a grant from the Pilgrim Trust, the conservation of old painted woodwork. Having recently had experience of her work on the restoration of the Despenser reredos at Norwich cathedral, I was able to recommend her with confidence. She submitted two reports on the sedilia, in April and July 1959, and began the cleaning of the painted decoration in December.[3] The cost of her services is borne by the Pilgrim Trust and will not fall upon the Dean and Chapter; but there is a great deal of actual repair still to be done to the woodwork which is being undertaken by our joiners and will be chargeable to the restoration fund.

Both repairs and cleaning require great care and will take a long time. But the result should bring back some of the lost beauty of the sedilia and I hope that it will be possible to complement it by making good those features that through maltreatment and neglect in the past have disappeared. This would be a continuation of a process that was begun, but not carried very far some years ago, possibly under Professor Lethaby: it if could be carried to completion at least the essential form and design of the sedilia would be recovered.

Sanctuary

The five brass candle chandeliers were sent away for repair and cleaning during Lent 1960. The attachment of the arms to the stem had become very loose and a new method of attachment has been adopted.

The central chandelier is disfigured by having a spot light and a microphone linked to it, with a prominent flex passing over the altar. This makeshift expedient is extremely unsatisfactory. So fine an ornament should not have its shape distorted by two utilitarian gadgets, especially when this is unnecessary. A small microphone could stand, when required, on the altar itself where, if suitably painted, it would be virtually invisible from the choir. A spot light, if necessary at all, should be fixed on one or both sides of the sanctuary.

Feretory

After two years' absence the wooden feretory was brought back and replaced over the Confessor's shrine in February 1960. In its battered condition it had become so unsightly an object that for long it had been concealed under a pall.[4] But its interest as one of the earliest examples of Renaissance design in this country, albeit on a miniature scale, made its proper restoration desirable and the late Mr Dickens bequeathed money to enable this to be undertaken.

A measured drawing by Talman,[5] made in 1713 and annotated with descriptive notes in Latin, proved invaluable in supplementing the evidence surviving in the actual structure which, by a fortunate chance, was just enough to indicate the authentic details of all mouldings, carved capitals and such like. The feretory was taken to the works of J. Longley & Co Ltd at Crawley, Sussex and subjected to minute examination. The preparatory work, before any actual repair was put in hand, entailed enquiries in Germany, France and Italy as well as this country to discover glass that would match the limpid blue of the original. In the end this had to be specially made and a craftsman at Horsham had the task of cutting to shape as many as 10,000 tiny pieces for the pilasters, which were then gilded from behind to give richness to the colour and set in a specially prepared mastic supplied by a chemical firm at Leicester. Working under the supervision of Mr Eric White, one joiner, Mr H. Pavey, and one carver, Mr R. Bacon, gradually pieced together the innumerable new sections of woodwork and Mr G. Winder of Horsham executed the green and red porphyry marbling, both behind glass and direct on the wood, and the final gilding.

The feretory has now regained the appearance it must once have presented except that it is not known what the recess on its west face was intended to contain. Something to fill this is obviously needed. The Skilbeck rood,[6] which formerly stood over the altar of the shrine, would be incongruous in such a classical setting; a new rood to replace it and designed to fit the recess, would, I think, offer the best solution.

Beneath the colour and glitter of the feretory the defacement of the shrine itself is now more than ever obvious. I hope that steps may soon be taken to remedy the mistakes that, in past alterations, have stultified its design and bring back to it something of the beauty it has lost.

Coronation Chair

The chair has been regularly inspected for flaking of the gesso but none has been observed.

Memorials

The memorial stone to Ralph Vaughan Williams[7] was laid in the north choir aisle, the nearby monument of William Wilberforce cleaned and its inscription re-painted, and the missing brass letters on the black marble floor slab of Henry Cary made good.

In the north walk of the cloisters a mural tablet, commemorating those of British nationality who served in the Sudan, was unveiled by the Duke of

Edinburgh on March 8th 1960. It is of Roman stone with incised and painted lettering.

The new walnut desk for the Battle of Britain roll of honour and an oak desk to contain the Islip Chapel Obituary book were completed and placed in position in the summer of 1959.

St George's chapel

Tall tapering candles have been made and fixed on the top of the wrought iron screens to this chapel. To the detriment of the design they disappeared many years ago, leaving the candlesticks meaningless.

West entrance

The brass light fittings on either side of the west porch have been cleaned and lacquered. Probably designed by Blore or Sir Gilbert Scott, they are of good design and workmanship, which passed unnoticed because of the decrepit state into which they had fallen.

Vergers' Room

Alterations, decorations and the refurnishing of this room were started in January 1960 and are still in progress. Hitherto there has been no drainage for the sink and arrangements for cooking and washing up have been very inadequate. By constructing at the south end of this room an upper floor, a miniature pantry has been formed with an enclosed space for a cooker below. The new sink is connected to a drain and the roof light, which is the only window, has been fitted with wired glass in the interests of safety.

Fire Prevention system

Two new hose reels have been installed and a new opening section fitted in the clear glass window in the west aisle of the north transept. This is to give access to the Fire Brigade in an emergency, if they are unable to enter immediately by the west door. Adjustments have been carried out to the dry riser and the indicator panel under the organ loft, to meet requirements of the Fire Brigade.

Burgot alarm

The doors to the library, east cloister turret stairs, St Faith's chapel and the new fire access door above mentioned have been connected to the alarm system.

Direction signs

New wrought iron signs were designed and brought into use in June 1959 for the notices required in connection with the one way route for summer visitors.

New lavatories

After consideration of various sites it was decided that the need of lavatory accommodation, particularly by the public on the occasion of special services, could best be met by the erection of a low building in part of the mason's yard, just outside the Poets' Corner door.[8] Plans were drawn up, tenders obtained and a scheme approved, but its execution has had to be deferred till after the Royal Wedding.

Externally the only visible indication of the new building will be a stone wall instead of the wooden enclosure to the yard. The roof will be flat and the interior lit by dome lights that will not show from outside. The blocked door in St Benedict's chapel will be opened to give access to a small vestibule with a sink for washing the Communion vessels; a second door will lead to the men's lavatory. The approach to both lavatories for the public will be from outside Poets' Corner.

The Cloisters

The renewal of decayed stone in the plinth and base mouldings of the east walk facing the garth has made some progress but, owing to the continual demands of more urgent work on the masons' time, has temporarily been suspended.

In the north walk some of the flooring, which was uneven and had sunk, was lifted and re-laid. The walls and vaulting have been brushed down and limewashed. This treatment which was applied to the east walk about three years ago should help, if repeated at regular intervals, to preserve the stonework for some time. The marble shafts ought however to be re-polished as soon as possible and there is much stonework that needs repair or renewal.

College Hall

During the summer holidays, following repairs to the lead flashings on the roof, general renovation was carried out to the interior. Much of the plaster of the walls was so loose and unsafe that it had to be cut out; the stonework of the windows and the glazing were also defective.

The work comprised a thorough cleaning of walls and ceiling, making good and limewashing all plastered surfaces, repairing as necessary the stone corbels supporting the roof trusses and the jambs of the windows, inserting leaded glazing and ventilation in the roof light and fitting the side windows with new inward opening metal casements, new saddlebars and stanchions where missing, and new leaded glazing incorporating as much of the old as possible.

The hall, which had become exceedingly dirty, is now clean and in good condition, though many improvements could still be made to it. I would however emphasize that, if it is to remain in good condition, limewashing should be repeated at least every three years, the windows cleaned at regular intervals and all ironwork painted every three years. It might be advisable to enter into a formal agreement with the School to ensure compliance with these requirements.

The bookshop

Various small repairs and decorations were completed in June 1959 to the office rooms behind the shop.

Houses

No. 20 Dean's Yard. The external woodwork of doors, window frames etc. was painted.

No. 21 Dean's Yard (Chapter Office). In the ground floor room to the right of the entrance a new counter[9] was installed and the room redecorated. The stone treads of the staircase were covered with linoleum, with rubber nosings.

Choir School. The walls and paintwork were washed down during the summer holiday. A new bath and lavatory were provided in the Head Master's house and the rooms re-decorated. The railings to Deans Yard were repainted.

No. 5 Dean's Yard. The interior was re-decorated throughout.

No. 2 The Cloisters. New fireplaces were designed and made for the drawing room and the room above it on the 2nd floor.

No. 7 Little Cloister. The interior was re-decorated throughout.

No. 8 Little Cloister. The cowl fixed experimentally on the drawing room chimney did not prove satisfactory and had to be replaced by a taller one, combining higher efficiency with greater ugliness. Re-decoration has been carried out in certain rooms.

The Deanery

After this house had been vacated in July, a start was made on remedying the structural defects in the roofs of the staircase hall and drawing room. Considerable deflection had taken place and water could not drain away from the asphalte flats. These have now been re-surfaced with Paropa roofing and, internally, the cracked ceilings made good.

From the former study, now a spare bedroom, a new doorway was made between the east wall and the fireplace to what used to be an office and is now a private bathroom for this bedroom. The doorway to the staircase hall has been built up and the door itself rehung in the new opening from the bedroom. The small shuttered opening from the office to the niche in the staircase hall has also been blocked up. No other structural changes of note have been made but new lighting, from fitments sunk in the ceiling, has been provided in the first floor gallery. The re-decorated portion of the house came into occupation in January 1960, leaving only the Islip wing, which needed extensive remodelling, to be tackled as a separate building operation.

This is still in progress and will fall to be described in the Audit Report for next year. At this stage I need only say that the first part of the work has consisted of opening up the structure and rectifying the numerous hazards that exposure revealed; the second part in re-ordering what, through past alterations, had become confused and ill-planned. A single large chamber, to form the Dean's study, has been formed out of a former sitting room, bedroom and cupboard; the narrow room with the oriel window facing south will be his secretary's office; and the staircase is being enlarged and remodelled to rise direct from the Long Gallery. The main alteration is done and what remains should not take long. When all is finished, the Langham and Litlyngton rooms will be freed and I hope that their equipment and furnishing, to which I referred in my report of last year, may then be undertaken.

Concurrently with the work in the house, the Deanery garden was re-planned and laid out as a paved garden with formal borders for flowers but no grass. The white glazed bricks in the retaining wall have given place to bricks matching those at its south end. The cloister wall has been planted with creepers and flowering shrubs.

Under the archway from the cloisters to the Deanery courtyard, the medieval stonework of the east wall was repaired and re-pointed. The result shows by contrast how urgently the opposite wall cries out for similar treatment.

St Catherine's chapel

The paving of the terraces was completed early in the summer and turf laid in the area of the former nave, north aisle and chancel. The coping of the west wall in brick was completed and a section of its masonry at the south end repointed. Unfortunately it has not yet been possible to do more and the bulk of the wall, its dirty stone partly plastered and patched with brick, presents a very poor aspect.

At the east end the wall is being lowered to the same height as the rest of the precinct wall and finished in the same manner, with a gabled coping of brick. Here too a start was made but labour had to be diverted to other things and progress has been disappointing. I am anxious that the job should be resumed and finished at the earliest opportunity, since the consolidation and pointing of the bases of the stone pillars remains and had not even been begun.

There was not much opportunity to develop the planting of the garden last year, but I would urge that flowers should not be lacking this summer and that the new turf of the lawn should be carefully tended. As soon, moreover, as the garden is in a fit state to be seen, consideration ought to be given to the renewal of the wooden doors in its west entrance and the substitution of a wrought iron grille.

College Garden

The threat which for so long has jeopardised the future of this garden was suddenly and surprisingly lifted when it became known that, instead of a lofty office block rearing itself just behind the east side of the precinct wall, the land between this wall and the street was to be laid out as an open space. The Ministry of Works, responsible for this beneficent scheme, have already commenced demolition of the buildings that occupy the site and the plan (I understand) is to make the space between the road and the wall into a lawn. Because this would prevent access to the garage that was constructed in the garden, originally built as an air raid shelter, they offer to build a new garage in the extreme south east corner of the garden – a position which in every way would be preferable. The existing structure is so unfortunate in siting and appearance that its demolition cannot be welcomed too warmly.[10] The garden will gain in beauty by the exposure of the full length of the east wall and the chance this will give to form a fine border for shrub and flowers.

After building operations by the School ceased, the opening in the precinct wall to Great College Street was built up and the former path adjoining the dormitory turfed.

19 Victoria Street

The prospect of a new office block on the large site west of Deans Yard between Victoria Street and Abbey Orchard Street gave rise to apprehension about its possible effects on the Abbey and other Dean and Chapter property. When the plans were first prepared, I had negotiations with the Royal Fine Art Commission, the London County Council and the architect, particularly in respect of the height to which it was proposed to build. The architect was sympathetic to my representations and agreed to reduce this from 147 to 107 feet. But when the final plans were drawn up, it was found that the accommodation thus sacrificed was to be supplied by three basements entailing very deep excavation. This made it necessary to ensure that the water table should not be lowered, with injurious effect on the foundations of the Abbey.

A series of meetings took place with the contractors and engineers concerned and, on the advice of the President of the Institution of Civil Engineers, Mr Harding, a consulting engineer with expert knowledge of the geology of Westminster, was engaged to watch the interests of the Dean and Chapter. A trial hole was dug near the north west tower to ascertain the depth of the new foundations and the nature of the sub soil, and a pipe has been sunk 36 feet below ground level down to the clay to permit periodical readings of the water level. Very comprehensive photographs were taken of Dean and Chapter property on the west side of Deans Yard and of the Abbey itself, particularly of weak places that might be susceptible to settlement or vibration.

Pile driving on the site commenced at mid-summer in 1959 and continued for six months to an accompaniment of noise that necessitated a temporary migration from the Choir School for classes during the day. Noise of other sorts will continue while the building is going up. But it is satisfactory to record that no serious ill has come of the operations so far.

S.E. Dykes Bower, Surveyor of the Fabric.

[1] Alan Don retired as Dean in 1959. Stalls for use of the High Commissioners of the Dominions were assigned in 1944.

² In the 1920s.
³ Some reports and slides are now on the Library shelves. The Surveyor files are in WAM S/3/27.
⁴ Since 1902, at the time of the coronation.
⁵ In the Library CN collection of drawings.
⁶ Provided in 1902 and now on the nave altar. Nothing now stands in the recess.
⁷ This covers his grave.
⁸ Files on this are in WAM S/3/51. The block was demolished in 2015 in preparation for the construction of a new lift to the new Queen's Diamond Jubilee Galleries in the triforium.
⁹ This was the main reception area for the Chapter Office.
¹⁰ Files on the garden and shelter are WAM S/3/47–48. A new garage was not built. The shelter was retained and later used as a BBC studio and for Abbey storage.

65N.   At Chapter on 12 July 1960 proposals, drawn up by the Surveyor, for the commemoration of the 900th anniversary of the consecration of St Edward's original church to be held in 1965 are recorded. On 8 November his designs for stalls for use at the nave altar were not accepted and he was to prepare new ones. This was further discussed at the 13 December and 24 January 1961 meetings. His designs were finally accepted on 24 October 1961. A new scale of fees to be paid to him for new works are set out at the meeting on 22 November 1960. On 13 December his report on the future use of St John's church in Smith Square and the possibility of moving some Abbey monuments there was noted. No monuments were actually moved.

66.   WAM S/1/106

Report 1961

Nave roof

The restoration of the nave roof, which began approximately six years ago, was brought to completion in March 1961. The whole of the lead covering is new, the timber structure supporting it has been virtually reconstructed and the stone parapet on the south side rebuilt.

A wooden walk-way down the centre of the enclosed space above the vaulting has been formed in the western portion of its length, but the boarded floor, which has been in use while fixing of the new trusses has been in progress, is being retained temporarily in the eastern portion so that this area can serve as a workshop for repairing and making new trusses for the south transept roof. When no longer needed, the walk-way will be continued throughout. Its purpose is to facilitate fire fighting and future inspection of the roof timbers.

Lantern

In November 1960 work began on the outer lead covering of the Lantern roof, which has hitherto been of asphalte – a substitute material which at the time of the war damage repairs had to be used because lead was unobtainable. The asphalte is being retained and battens and close boarding have been laid on top of it to take the new 8 lbs lead, the roof therefore becoming of double construction. The gutters have also been lined with lead.

The work is now almost finished and payment for it is a War Damage Commission liability.

South transept

The roof over this transept is being undertaken next so that, when finished, the hoist can be moved from the cloister garth and transferred to the north side of the choir. The new steel tie beams have been ordered and scaffolding erected externally at the south end for repair of the stonework of the gable and its cross, which for a long time has had a conspicuous inclination to the north. Having examined it from this scaffold I find that it will be necessary to remove the cross itself but not the stones which support it. Its condition is reasonably good and, after refixing, it should be sound. The moulded stonework of the gable copings, with their crockets, is very defective. Where Portland stone has been used, decay has not proceeded too far; but many of the stones are of Chilmark and these have eroded so badly that renewal is unavoidable.

The masonry of the triangular head of the gable is also of Chilmark, now blistered and crumbled to such an extent that lumps can be lifted off by hand. The expense of renewing it would be so great that, for the present, I think the best course will be to remove all loose material and brush back to a hard surface, treating it with a silicone preservative. This will not constitute a permanent remedy but may prolong the life of the stone until large scale renewals become feasible. Scott's refacing of the south transept end dates from about 1850 and his use of Chilmark stone may have been influenced by Sir Charles Barry's adoption of it for the Houses of Parliament, where in less than a century it has all had to be replaced by Clipsham.

On elaborate mouldings and carvings, such as cover the Palace of Westminster, it fails more quickly than in plan ashlar walling. At the Abbey it has perhaps lasted longer because there is not quite so much of the former. But sooner or later the greater part will have to be replaced. The Portland stone that has been introduced marks, I assume, isolated repairs that were probably carried out by Lethaby.

Clock

Scaffolding to enable the clock face on the north west tower to be repainted was erected in June and the clock mechanism taken away to Thwaites and Reed's works in Clerkenwell for overhaul. The painting of the dials in gold, red and black follows the original colour scheme, which could be dimly made out at close quarters. The clock itself has been fitted with electric automatic winding gear and its striking apparatus, which has been out of use for some years, brought back into action. After a wayward start, when the quarter chimes and hour bell behaved erratically, timekeeping has been good. The clock has been adjusted to sound a little after Big Ben.

Stone cleaning

The bridge was moved from the third and fourth bays from the west in the nave and moved to the two west bays in October 1960. In the north aisle scaffolding remained in position until March 1961, having had to be retained long after cleaning finished owing to the extent of repairs required to the vaulting.

The contract with the London Stone Cleaning Company is now limited to cleaning, from the bridge, the triforium, clerestory, vaulting and the west wall of the nave. Their work will therefore finish fairly soon, but the scaffolding will again have to remain in place for many months while the masons execute repairs.

In the interests of economy the cleaning of the south aisle is to be undertaken by our staff, though this will limit their deployment for other tasks and slow up completion of the nave. One bay of the south aisle is well advanced and that to the west will shortly be scaffolded. But separate scaffolding will still have to be placed round each pillar for the polishing of the Purbeck marble and this is the slowest job of all. It is unlikely that the nave will be completely finished before the end of 1963.

Other work carried out by our masons has been of an emergency character. When the statue of James Watt was removed, its weight caused the ambulatory floor to sink to a depth of 6 inches over an area of 24 square feet. This had to be lifted and re-laid. Similar work became necessary in places to the paving of the nave, the Lady Margaret chapel and the north cloister.

Glazing

The clerestory windows of the nave, which were in poor condition, have been re-glazed in each bay while scaffolding has been in position for stone cleaning. All are now done with the exception of those on each side of the west bay. This pair differs from the others in being glazed with diamond instead of rectangular quarries and is, I find, in quite good condition. Since they look into the interior of the western towers and no light comes through them, it does not seem necessary to make them match the others and the discrepancy will hardly be noticeable from below.

The triangular windows of the nave triforium remain to be done but, unlike the clerestory windows, have not been admitted by the War Damage Commission to be eligible for part payment. The expense of scaffolding will however be avoided as they are easily reached from the triforium floor.

The Clayton & Bell glass in the end south window of the east aisle of the south transept has been repaired, and the two northernmost windows of the east cloister filled with salvaged glass from windows broken during the war. Most of this glass dates from the second half of the 19th century and early 20th century but some painted quarries, forming part of the original glass in Henry VII's chapel and discovered in a box in the triforium, have been incorporated. They have been placed where they can most easily be seen, in the lower part of the tracery.

The leaded glazing of the swing doors to the west entrance of the nave which had been damaged was repaired.

Glass has been removed from one of the single light windows to College Hall kitchen and wooden louvres substituted to give better ventilation.

The new stained glass for the Rolls Royce[1] window designed by Sir Ninian Comper and now being erected by Mr John Bucknall, is well advanced and it is hoped to have it in position in the later part of this year.

Arrangements have been made for the regular cleaning of all the plain glass windows of the Abbey under contract with the New Century firm of window cleaners. They will start work this summer.

Monuments

Mr Butchart was absent through illness for some time in the summer of 1960 but after his return finished the decoration of the large monument to the Countess of Hertford in St Benedict's chapel, which had had to be left incomplete. Since then, also in St Benedict's chapel, he has carried out the painting of the coats of arms on Archbishop Langham's tomb and the decoration of the south wall, including Dean Goodman's tomb. Surviving evidence of design and colour has enabled much of the original design to be revived.

In the north choir aisle he has redecorated the 17th century monument of Sir Thomas Hesketh and in the south choir aisle the tomb of William Thynne. He is now working on the monument to Thomas Owen. Much repair and making good of missing features were necessary before painting could begin and the condition of almost all the 17th century monuments in the apsidal chapels shows that similar preparatory work will have to precede painting. Mr Butchart will soon have finished the Owen monument and will then be able to work on the painting of the wrought iron gates in the choir aisles. He can continue, as he has been doing, filling in odd time (e.g. while paint is drying) by painting faded coats of arms on various monuments; but this will not keep him busy for long and if, as I hope, we are to retain his services at the Abbey, he ought soon to be given a larger job. I suggest that this might be the monument to the Countess of Sussex in St Paul's chapel, in which case its preliminary repair should be authorized as soon as possible.

The reason for selecting the Sussex monument is that it needs less repair than many others, and a risk of a hiatus in the continuity of work would consequently be smaller. There is clearly much to be done in the next few years for which Mr Butchart is pre-eminently qualified, but account must be taken of his age and health. The 17th century monuments in the apsidal chapels are one of the potential adornments of the Abbey and it will be disappointing if they cannot contribute their proper part to the effect of the interior when this, restored and cleaned, is presented to those who will come to take part in the celebrations of 1965 and see how some of the appeal money has been spent. If that disappointment is to be avoided it will be necessary to anticipate by making sure that, while one monument is being painted, the next is undergoing repair in readiness for decoration.

The lesser works that Mr Butchart has carried out in repainting arms and other coloured ornamental features on tablets in the south choir aisle call for no special remark. But mention may be made of one, the Annandale tablet, just east of the cloister door, because the treatment of its fine coat of arms (of lead) may appear surprising. The reason why it has been gilded solid is that records in the library appear to indicate that this was formerly its sole decoration. The result is, heraldically, to render the arms meaningless; and since the coat is a particularly rich one, there is an artistic loss as well. I wonder whether in such a case historical precedent should not be disregarded.

In the cleaning of monuments by our own staff good progress has been made. Those in both choir aisles are done, as well as in the east bay of the south nave aisle and three bays of the north aisle. But unfortunately progress will now be retarded, since the men who were employed on this work have had to be transferred to the stone cleaning and polishing that hitherto have been undertaken by the London Stone Cleaning Company.

Mr Hart and Mr Stenhouse continue to work part time on the re-painting of faded lettering but it is a slow task and a great number of tablets that have already been cleaned still remain to be tackled.

Organ [Quire] Screen

The decoration in gold and colour of Blore's west front of the pulpitum and the 18th century wrought iron gates to the choir was completed in time for Princess Margaret's wedding. The repair of the stonework, parts of which were broken or missing, the removal of the pinnacles and new termination of the buttresses and the alteration of the apex of the central gable were carried out by our own masons, the decoration by Campbell Smith and Company. The sculpture of the six figures was modified and improved by Mr Donald Gilbert.

Sedilia

The amount of work executed in restoration of the structure and decoration of the sedilia during the last twelve months has been less than I hope d. Difficulties that beset much work in the Abbey account for it. First the condition of the actual structure was so poor that Miss Plummer has constantly been held up until essential repairs – in this case joinery repairs – could be carried out. Secondly our skilled joiners have not always been available at the right moment to do what was required. Thirdly interruptions for services, and occasions such as the royal wedding, making all work impossible for a time, have occurred so frequently that any regular sequence of attendance has been compromised.

Despite its obvious importance as a survival of medieval woodwork and painted decoration, the sedilia had been shamefully treated in the past, even comparatively recent repairs that ought to have been in oak having been executed in inferior substitutes – deal and linoleum. To make these good in a proper manner has been not merely an intricate job, entailing most careful joinery, but has required undoing other parts to enable the new wood to be fitted in. With our limited number of men and the varied calls on their services, this has taken a disproportionate time. Miss Plummer, meanwhile, under the terms of her Pilgrim Trust studentship, has not been able to await our convenience since she has, within the year it lasts, had to carry out a certain programme of work. We were compelled to lose her to other engagements outside London that afforded her continuous occupation.

Now, after twelve months, little more than the wooden vaulting has been finished; the cleaning of the two painted figures and the canopy fronts has not started. Essential joinery repairs still to be done are considerable and, at the present rate, another year may elapse before the appearance of the sedilia is what it ought to be.

Carved finials and crockets that, before the Coronation, were taken off Blore's wooden canopies in the bay south of the sedilia have been refixed.

Coronation Chair

The chair continues to be inspected each month and no signs have been observed of the gesso flaking.

Henry VII's chapel

Convection from the radiators behind the stalls has, in the years since this chapel was restored and cleaned under Sir Walter Tapper, discoloured the stonework immediately above the stall canopies. Now that new and different heating has been installed, the stonework has been vacuum cleaned to mitigate this discolouration as far as possible. A light staging was erected for this purpose, which gave opportunity to vacuum clean also the banners and stall canopies.

St Faith's chapel

The old tiles in the floor of the east portion of the chapel were cleaned and waxed.

An estimate has been obtained for paving the west portion in Purbeck marble, to replace the small red and blue 19th century tiles.

Triforium

Old wood removed from the Deanery during its reconstruction has been used by our carpenters to repair defective places in the floor.

Vacuum cleaning

The Sturtevant cleaner has been employed unremittingly in keeping down the dust that, without such an invaluable piece of equipment, would soon undo much of the benefits of cleaning: if there were two men free to be kept using two machines they would be well occupied. Every time scaffolding is put up and, worse still, taken down, visible clouds of dust are created, that cannot be contemplated without alarm and despondency. Equally the upheaval that attends such an event as the Royal wedding exacts a severe penalty, the effects of which may not be noticeable on a casual glance but are none the less real and pervasive. The monuments, in particular, by their size and form, are of necessity dust collectors and vigilance is required to prevent this becoming too manifest. The eye familiarizes itself all too readily to subtle changes of appearance and colour; the finger is a surer register. Its impress almost anywhere would soon convince the most inveterate doubter of what is involved in keeping the Abbey clean.

Memorials

The statue of James Watt[2] was removed from the Abbey in December 1960 and conveyed to a new museum at Clapham established by the British Transport Commission. Its portentous size made it an incongruous neighbour to the medieval tombs and other mural monuments in St Paul's chapel, and the arrangement whereby the statue has found an appropriate home and been replaced by a plaster bust presented by the Institution of Civil Engineers, concludes satisfactorily negotiations that had been in progress for some years. The bust has been placed on the window ledge in the second bay from the east of the north choir aisle.

In the south choir aisle an engraved bronze plate, surmounted by a coat of arms in colour, commemorating Queen Anne Nevill, the wife of Richard III, was dedicated on October 1st 1960. Although her burial place is nearby she has hitherto had no visible memorial. The work was designed by Mr Sebastian Comper.

The floor slab in the nave marking the grave of Lord Willingdon was replaced in March 1961 by a new stone, to include the name of Lady Willingdon.

A 19th century memorial to Henry Otway Mayne in the north walk of the cloisters had deteriorated so badly that it had to be taken down about a year ago. The original inscription panel had evidently perished long before, as the new one, which was inserted, bore no relationship in style to the mosaic frame. At the cost of descendants a fresh tablet has been designed to incorporate this second panel, with the Mayne coat of arms, a brief additional inscription and the Regimental emblem of the Indian Light Horse.

A slate tablet to Enoch Hawkins, in the west walk of the cloisters, had become illegible with age and has been renewed at the expense of the Adelphi Glee Club. The design is unaltered but the wording of the inscription has been slightly changed and curtailed.

In the east cloister the Royal Army Medical Corps presented a framed notice, with lettering on vellum by Miss George, to draw attention to the Roll of Honour kept in the vestibule to the Chapter House.[3] The notice has been placed on the gates.

In the organ loft a wooden tablet has been fixed to the west side of the console with the names and dates of the Abbey organists painted in white on a blue ground.

Furnishings

New linoleum has been laid on the mosaic floor of the Confessor's chapel.

Kneeling cushions, covered in rose pink rep, have been provided for the altar rails in the nave.

Repairs were carried out to the swing doors to the inner porch of the north transept entrance.

Observation boxes for the BBC commentators at Princess Margaret's wedding were made by the Ministry of Works and have been left by them in the Abbey for use on other occasions. They are placed on runners to slide forward and project from the choir triforium.

Vergers' Room

The alteration and improvement of the vergers' room over the west porch of the nave, which was described in my last report, was completed in the summer of 1960. The work done in this year consisted of decoration, laying new linoleum flooring and furnishing.

Heating

The emission of steam which was mistaken by onlookers for smoke and caused a fire alarm to be raised prompted examination of methods to prevent similar scares being raised. A condensing cylinder has now been fixed on the expansion pipe at roof level.

A fan has been fitted to improve ventilation in the boiler house.

Fire precautions

Special fire notices indicating the position of drain-off valves to the fire hydrants have been placed in the triforium and the fire dry ring main connected to the dry riser at Poets Corner.

At the request of the Fire Brigade the lock to the east cloister turret staircase was altered so that, in the event of a fire in the library, access may be available from the cloister.

Lavatories

The erection of new lavatories in the angle of the south transept and the ambulatory was started in August 1960 and finished in March 1961. The blocked doorway just west of Dean Goodman's monument in the wall of St Benedict's chapel, has been opened to give access to a small vestibule fitted with a sink for the washing of Communion vessels. A Burgot alarm has been fitted on the new oak door.

The lavatories are top-lit and when the stone of their external wall tones down in colour will hardly be noticed as an addition to the fabric.

Architecturally, however, the scheme will remain incomplete until this wall can be continued to join the Chapter House buttress.

The Cloisters

The ironwork of the gates and grilles in the south walk was repainted. New turf was laid in parts of the garth.

The bases of the buttresses on the east side, where decayed stone had been cut away for replacement, have had to be left unfinished as work in the nave has absorbed the masons' time.

St Catherine's chapel

The lowering to its original level of the precinct wall at the east end of this garden was started by our staff who removed the unsightly brickwork that had increased its height and distorted its appearance. Owing however to more pressing demands elsewhere our men had to be transferred and the formation of the gabled coping will now be carried out by a firm of contractors.

Dean's Yard

The road was re-surfaced with tar macadam by the Westminster City Council in August 1960 and white parking lines set out afterwards. The north entrance gates were re-painted.

College Hall

In October 1960 a York stone step and new treads, made from surplus oak taken from the Abbey, were fitted to the entrance staircase, on which the existing ones had become worn and dangerous. This was done in preparation for the Queen's visit.

In March 1961 the condition of the gallery in the Hall appeared to be getting worse. It has long been precarious and tell-tales were fixed some time ago to register movement. In the interests of safety it has not been strutted with steel posts which will have to remain in position until more extensive repairs can be undertaken.

The need for complete re-modelling of the block of building south of College Hall, over the kitchen, was the subject of a report and plans submitted in the summer of 1960.

The Bookstall

A report and plans for internal alterations and extension, prepared in the autumn of 1960, showed that the need for more space could best be met by building over the narrow empty space between the existing structure and the west wall of College Hall, also over a small part of the former garden of 21 Dean's Yard. There would be no change in the exterior, viewed from Broad Sanctuary, but the internal accommodation could be doubled in size.

It was decided that detailed plans and estimates should be obtained for a first instalment of this scheme, with a view to the work being carried out in the winter of 1961.

Meanwhile, to give greater ease of circulation and improved display facilities for books, postcards etc. the long counter was removed and some new fittings purchased.

Houses

The Islip wing of the Deanery, after extensive reconstruction, was brought into use in June 1960, thus completing the work to this house except for external painting, which ought to be done as soon as possible.

The internal re-planning was described in last year's report. The three first floor windows to the courtyard were re-glazed, the old quarries, some of which are inscribed with names and dates, being re-used. The rafters of the ceiling in the study were exposed and its walls lined with book shelves. At the head of the re-modelled staircase two old wooden pillars, for long in store and the origin of which is unknown, have been used as architectural features to support the ceiling. The former bathroom has been converted into a cloak room with vestibule and a separate passage formed to the Abbot's pew. From the archway to the nave the wooden partition has been removed so that the Abbot's Pew now becomes a room which could, if desired, be fitted up as a small chapel.

Other changes are too numerous to mention but what was formerly an ill-arranged medley of rooms has become a seemly and useful adjunct to the Deanery providing working quarters for the Dean and his secretary distinct from the more domestic parts of the house.

Towards the end of the year, in readiness for the new porter, the Porter's Lodge was redecorated throughout by our painters.

No. 6 Little Cloister and the Surveyor's office were partially redecorated, following the drying out of damp in the walls.

The interior of no. 4 Little Cloister, in lieu of repainting, was vacuum cleaned throughout.

In the Choir School iron bars were fixed for protection in the windows of dormitories, bathrooms, sick rooms etc. In the bath rooms lead pipes along the wall have been cased in with aluminium sheeting for greater cleanliness and to prevent damage.

A crack which has developed over the dining room door of no. 4B Dean's

Yard would appear to be attributable to vibration from the building operations on the site of nos. 1–19 Victoria Street. I have notified the architect to the Legal and General Assurance Society and asked for a joint meeting with his surveyor.

Abbey House

The premises opposite nos. 1–19 Victoria Street, in the angle of Victoria and Tothill streets, are to be rebuilt. The proposal is to erect a large office building with a tower at the east end, nearest to the Abbey.

After inspection of plans I wrote to the London County Council expressing objection to certain features, including this tower, and suggesting ways in which the relationship of the building to the Abbey might be improved.

      S.E. Dykes Bower

¹ This only commemorates Sir Henry Royce, not Charles Rolls, in the nave.
² The immense statue by Sir Francis Chantrey from St Paul's chapel has had several other homes since then and is now in Edinburgh.
³ The RAMC rolls of honour are now in the nave.

67. WAM S/1/107

Report by the Surveyor of the Fabric 1962

Lantern

The permanent covering of the lantern roof in lead, which began in November 1960, was finished in April 1961. Lightning conductors were fixed and the scaffolding lowered in stages to permit repointing of the walls where necessary and renewal of a number of stones that had fractured on the face due to the rusting or iron cramps. It was all removed in June.

South transept

Work had meanwhile started on the south transept roof. Five steel tie beams, delivered in May, were placed in position in June. Preparation of the new oak trusses was started by our carpenters in March 1961 and fourteen of them are now completed and ten fixed. Steel channels forming the wall plates are in place and the reinforcing rods shaped in readiness for concreting to begin. The temporary corrugated iron covering previously used over the nave has been erected over the two end bays – a length of forty feet – and from the portion of roof under it the lead has been lifted by Norman & Underwood and sent to their works at Leicester for re-casting.

The stone cross on the apex of the south gable was taken down in June and after repair in our masons' yard, awaits replacement. Of twenty four crockets on the gable coping only six can be retained; the other eighteen, eroded beyond repair, will have to be new and are now being carved.

Apse and north transept

Since it was discovered a few years ago that the centre posts of the timber structure supporting the external lead covering on the south transept had dropped and were pressing on the crown of the vaulting, regular observations have been taken to see whether any similar movement was occurring in the apse and north transept. None has been found but both roofs are in the same need of repair and reconstruction as those in the nave and south transept.

Nave

Towards the close of 1961 it became possible for the first time to see the high vault throughout the length of the interior much as it must have looked when newly built and it may seem most miraculous that stone which had become so dark should, after 600 years, regain its original colour by the cleansing properties of nothing more than water.

The actual cleaning finished in May and the gilding in August. But as on the lantern, the scaffolding above the bridge could only be lowered as the masons completed numerous repairs to the clerestory walls. The small amount that remains is for repair to the triforium. Throughout the building this necessity of dealing with defective stone has occupied more time than the actual cleaning: but had the latter, with the scaffolding it has required, not been undertaken, the extent to which both wall and vaulting were in need of repair might never have been so clearly realised.

In three months' time the bridge will be dismantled and transferred to the apse and presbytery. The apse, from triforium level upwards, was cleaned nearly thirty years ago. It has been exposed since then to two abnormal increments of dust, resulting first from war damage and then from the coronation preparations, so that now it is noticeably darker than the rest of the interior cleaned since 1954. Moreover since its ribs and bosses were only washed, and not re-gilded, those in the adjacent bays of the presbytery had to be treated in the same way, which makes them look rather duller than those in the nave on which new gold leaf was used. Re-erection of the bridge in the apse will not only enable the stone to be brought up to the standard of the rest but give an opportunity to add to the gilded features the brightness which would be specially appropriate over the high altar and the Saint's shrine.

Washing of the stone here should not take very long since it is only recent dirt which has had to be removed. But there are stone repairs, omitted in the 1930 cleaning, which must receive attention.

Nave aisles

Cleaning of the north aisle was finished in April down to cill level of the windows, except in the three eastern bays where it was extended to the floor. Here the monuments have also been cleaned. On either side of the demon's door[1] two of the original wall shafts and capitals have been exposed by removal of the brickwork which concealed them.

Cleaning of the south aisle by our own staff has continued throughout the year and is now above half finished. Completion of each bay is slowed down by the lengthy operation of polishing the Purbeck marble pillars.

St George's chapel

Cleaning of this chapel, which has just begun, is being executed by the London Stone Cleaning Company under contract and paid for out of money made available for embellishment by the Royal Society of St George. Black and white marble paving to supersede the stone floor is now being prepared in readiness for laying when the scaffolding is taken down. All existing stones that can be lifted without breakage will be kept for repair of the nave floor.

The London Stone Cleaning Company will afterwards clean, as part of their original contract, the corresponding bay on the north side and the west end of the nave from triforium level downwards. This latter will have to wait until the bridge is removed.

Glazing

Although apparently sound, the Burlison & Grylls glass in the Trevithick window in the north aisle of the nave was found, on close examination, to be too full of cracks to make possible direct transference to its future position one bay further west. The glass was broken in two hundred places, no doubt due to blast during the war and the War Damage Commission, after inspecting it in situ, accepted a claim for repair and are making a payment of £706. The glass has been removed to the glaziers' works and the opening temporarily boarded up until the new Rolls Royce window is inserted. Mr Bucknell, who has been carrying out the late Sir Ninian Comper's design, expects this to be ready for fixing towards the end of this month and completed before Palm Sunday.

Before the Trevithick glass can be fixed, the stone filling which was built across the lower part of the two main lights, thus reducing their height, will be taken out by our masons. But to avoid a cause of draughts while the weather may still be cold, this will be left until the glaziers notify us that the repairs are almost finished.

A claim was also submitted to the War Damage Commission on the Vincent Novello window in the east aisle of the north transept. Here the stained glass was broken beyond repair and the window glazed in clear glass. The payment of £1,404.4s.6d allowed represents the value of the original window, measured by the War Damage Commission standard rate for stained glass, minus the cost of the clear glazing actually inserted. Instead, however, of commemorating Vincent Novello by a new stained glass window it is proposed to purchase a small eighteenth century portable organ[2] to stand at the west end of the south aisle of the nave. The British–Italian Society have issued an appeal for this object and any funds raised thereby would supplement the War Damage payment.

During the summer of 1961 all windows other than those containing stained glass were washed externally at a cost of £187, with noticeable benefit to their appearance. The triforium windows had to be omitted because they are too high up to be reached from ladders but they cannot be seen from the floor of the church and those in the nave are in any case in poor condition and due for re-glazing.

The windows in Henry VII's chapel were also omitted: they present more difficulty, particularly in the aisles, because of the closely spaced ferraments. They are however very dirty and ought, if possible, to be done this year. Very few window cleaning firms seem ready to undertake such work: either they are too busy or they do not like it. I have tried, without success so far, to get the New Century Cleaning Company, who did the windows outside, to do them inside as well and shall renew the attempt after Easter. In London, even more than elsewhere, it is important not to let a film settle for so long on clear glass that its distinctive quality of clearness is lost.

Monuments

Monument cleaning in the nave aisles has been slow because the men previously engaged on it have had to be transferred to polishing the Purbeck marble pillars. In the south aisle it has been carried to the same point as in the north aisle: but there the sudden break between the cleaned monuments in the three eastern bays and those still untreated in the rest stands out the more prominently under the white walls and vaulting above, and as soon as the new Comper window is in place and the scaffolding removed it would be desirable to get this aisle properly finished.

A year ago Mr Butchart had only just returned after an illness of many weeks. His first job was to complete the decoration of Dean Goodman's tomb and the monument of Thomas Owen in the south choir aisle, with any spare time devoted to the regilding and repainting of coats of arms, inscriptions and decorative features on other tablets in this aisle. The Annandale coat of arms, for example, that had been gilded all over was given its correct colouring.

Meanwhile in St Paul's chapel the seventeenth century monument to the Countess of Sussex was being cleaned and repaired in readiness for decoration. It was in better condition than most of the big seventeenth century monuments in the Abbey, presumably because Sidney Sussex college had itself paid for some restoration in the nineteenth century. But it is doubtful whether anything was then done to preserve or renew its colour. So dark had this become that delicate details of the design could hardly be seen and probably few people noticed the presence of three blue and gold porcupines, gaps in whose armoury our carpenters have completed with three hundred specially made new quills.

Before this monument was finished in December repair of the adjacent one to Lord and Lady Cottington began. Beyond putting back missing ornaments, the existence of which was shown by Dart's engraving[3] and confirmed by faint marks discernible in the marble itself, this did not amount to much. But the engraving served to indicate how the black marble was relieved by gilding. It has been impossible to repeat the full scheme owing to an alteration, apparently unrecorded,[4] in the form of the monument: Lord Cottington's white marble effigy was originally lower down, and rested on an arched table in front of the main structure. This at some time was removed and the figure lifted to its present level where it cannot properly be seen. The change accounts for the centre lower portion not being of black marble like the rest of the monument, but merely faced with plaster, painted to simulate marble.

When the two candlesticks on the top, of which only the triangular metal bases survived, have been recreated as Dart showed them, the monument will be complete. Its sombre black colour may hitherto have deprived it of the attention it deserves, but it is interesting as one of the many Italian contributions to the Abbey, its designer having been a Florentine, and because the bust of Lady Anne Cottington is by Le Sueur, the sculptor of the equestrian statue of Charles I at the head of Whitehall.

Two other monuments in St Paul's chapel, to Dudley Carleton and Sir James Fullerton, have also been finished. Smaller in size and comparatively well preserved, it was only necessary to clean them and paint their coats of arms.

At present work is proceeding on the restoration of the large seventeenth century monument to Sir John Puckering: enough has already been done to enable decoration to start on the upper part. In St Paul's chapel it will then only remain to treat the other seventeenth century monument to Sir Thomas Bromley.

A suggestion by the Desiderata Committee that present descendants of persons commemorated in the Abbey might be asked to contribute to the cost of repairing their memorials, brought no immediate response in the first approach made. For the improvement of the monument of the Duchess of Northumberland in St Nicholas' chapel, a sum of £50 was offered and the work has been carried out.

Brief mention has already been made of the monuments cleaned in the nave. On others in the aisles, transepts and cloisters, where fading inscriptions were gradually becoming illegible, Mr Hart and Mrs Stenhouse, working on a part time basis, have been repainting lettering.

Memorials

Only one addition to the memorials in the Abbey itself has been made during the past year – an incised slate panel, designed by Mr Sebastian Comper, in the floor of the north aisle of the nave over the grave of Sir Ninian Comper. The position was chosen for its proximity to the series of eight windows, the last of which will represent that great artist's final contribution to stained glass.

In the cloisters new tablets, both replacements of former ones that had decayed beyond repair, commemorate Enoch Hawkins and Henry Otway Mayne. The former, in the west walk, was fixed in March 1961 and the latter, in the north walk, in May. Both were described in last year's report.

In the absence of any wall space available for tablets, it has been the practice in recent years to record the names of those buried within the Abbey on inscribed stones set in the floor. But what may have seemed a sensible, indeed the only practical expedient has not in all respects proved satisfactory. The constant wear and tear of people walking over them has almost obliterated the wording of some memorials not yet of any age, and proved that very few stones and only deeply cut lettering can be trusted to survive for long. In the last twelve months it has, for example, been necessary to substitute slate slabs for the stones on the graves of Dean Ryle and Dean Foxley Norris in the nave; to deepen and partially recut the lettering of the slate slabs to Dean Bradford in the north transept and prebendary [Richard] Lucas (this was paid for by a descendant in South Africa) in the south; and to replace the fractured and illegible slab over the grave of Dr [Thomas] Willis with a new one of white [actually black] marble, paid for by the College of Physicians of Canada.

Inscriptions formed of brass letters, inlaid in the stone, give constant trouble because the letters work loose and sometimes get lost before their disappearance is noted. Those on the grave of Henry Cary in the south transept are being discarded and the inscription incised afresh in the existing slate.

In place of Chantrey's statue of James Watt transferred to the British Transport Museum, the Abbey was presented with a plaster bust by the Institute of Civil Engineers, now in the north choir aisle. But to perpetuate in St Paul's chapel, where the statue formerly stood, the epitaph composed by Lord Brougham and carved on its pedestal has been cut on a slab of slate shortly to be laid in the floor. In view of the dimensions of some of the old slate grave stones in the cloisters, is worthy of remark that the largest size in which a piece of slate could be obtained today was 6 feet x 3 feet 9 inches. There was difficulty even in obtaining this and it had to be quarried specially in Wales.

Ironwork

No great medieval church in England possesses such a variety of good ironwork as Westminster. Almost every period is represented and not the least attractive is the contribution of the eighteenth century, exemplified in the gates in the organ screen and the six sets of gates in the choir aisles. Whereas however the former have for years been painted gold and blue, the latter have been black and perhaps on that account received less notice than they deserve.

During the past year all have been painted by Mr Butchart – the middle pair on each side, in the style of Tijou, in black and gold; the western pair in blue and gold, to match those in the screen; the eastern pair all in gold.[5] This has emphasized their ornamental value and enhanced the appearance of the aisles.

Pulpits

On the Jacobean pulpit and sounding board in the choir the limited amount of gilding had become too faint and dull to have much effect from a distance. It has now been renewed, extended and burnished and the oak of the pulpit structure freshened up. The result is further to vindicate the fitness of this pulpit for the position it was designed to occupy, but to which it was only restored about twenty five years ago after a century and a half of banishment.

For the pulpit in the nave, long disfigured by a deplorable wooden staircase, a new one of wrought iron has been designed and is about to be made. Sketches for this were first prepared by Bainbridge Reynolds and something that was conceived many years ago but never realized will thus at length come to fruition.

Sedilia

Although outwardly there may seem little change in the appearance of the sedilia, making good its wooden vaulting has provided occupation for our carpenters in intervals from more urgent work. Repair of the gable crockets will similarly serve as a spare time job for many months ahead, though the real need is to resume the cleaning and restoration of the paintings. Much of the detail and colour in these, now quite lost to view, could be recovered, not in full strength but sufficiently to show better than at present.

St Edward's chapel

At the entrance to this chapel from the north ambulatory the shallow stone step had become so worn and hollowed that frequent complaints were received of people slipping on it. Some years ago the Ministry of Works made available to the Abbey a quantity of surplus Hopton Wood stone from the Houses of Parliament and this has been used to pave the narrow passage between the tomb of Edward I and the pillar east of it and make a safer arrangement of steps.

St Faith's chapel

More of this Hopton Wood stone has been laid in front of the altar in St Faith's chapel to provide a straight footpace, which had previously been very awkwardly shaped with a semi-circular projection in the middle.

Until Sir Gilbert Scott became Surveyor in 1849 this chapel was used as a lumber room, containing among other things 'an ancient oaken pulpit with diminuative sounding board', which was probably the Cranmer pulpit now in the nave. During the eighteenth century it stood in Henry VII's chapel but presumably was removed from there early in the nineteenth century and deposited in St Faith's until Scott rescued it. He cleared out an accumulation of oddments to fit this chapel for use and the two oak kneeling desks are probably furnishings of his design dating from that time. Their position has been changed to give a more orderly arrangement of the east end and new cushions supplied both for them and the stone bench on the north side. A new curtain has also been hung over the door.

The brass tablet, formerly on the wall above this stone bench, has been moved to a position west of the entrance door.[6]

Minor improvements have also been carried out in the sacristy[7] at the west end to permit freer use of its limited space and the Burgot alarm connected to the safe.

St Benedict's chapel

The small room for washing the communion vessels, opening from this chapel, together with the lavatories beyond, was brought into use in May 1961. Electric tubular heaters are being fitted in the latter to counteract condensation.

Triforium

During August and September 1961, following an inspection of the quantity of stone, marble, wood, books, war time paraphernalia and bric a brac of every description that through the years had been consigned to the triforium out of sight, a clearance was made of all that could be classified as rubbish. What remains is not negligible in bulk, but a least there is less to collect dust. A brass lectern, at present shrouded under a black cloth, might perhaps be acceptable to some church that would prize a gift from the Abbey.

Belfry

An additional chime board, designed to match the existing ones and lettered and painted by Mr Hart, has been fixed. All ironwork in the belfry was cleaned and painted and an iron step ladder provided to enable the school bell to be serviced.

Vergers' Room

Following representations about the steepness of the stairs to the upper floor on which the sink had to be placed to permit of drainage connections, a shallower staircase has been constructed. It inevitably reduces the floor space of the room but is deemed to be more convenient.

Bookstall

Plans for enlargement were referred to in last year's report. After tenders had been received, it was decided to proceed with a modified scheme by which the former manageress's office will be absorbed into the shop and a new office built in the space between it and College Hall. Entrance to the strong room will be from this room and the present doorway blocked up. The work is being carried out under contract and should be finished by the end of April.

Electric lighting

A sub-committee appointed to consider the re lighting of the Abbey invited two firms – the General Electric Company and Troughton and Young, – to submit proposals and demonstrate them in the building. Each was asked to provide general illumination, independent of desk lighting to the stalls and pews in the choir which had already been approved in principle.

The first test, of the scheme by the General Electric Company, took place in the autumn. Its intention was to show that the interior could be adequately lit from the triforium, the light being directed upwards and downwards by a disposition of mirrors. Whereas however the source of light was not directly visible when looking east and west, it could not be concealed when looking north or south and was in fact of blinding intensity.

The second test, in February this year, avoided this disadvantage by lighting the whole of the upper part of the building from fluorescent tubes laid horizontally on the edge of the triforium. Troughton and Young agree that the colour of this light would need to be improved and are confident that it can be done. But it is complementary to separate lighting by pendant chandeliers of Waterford glass and it is the latter – lighting the lower half of the building – that would inevitably be chiefly in use. These chandeliers would hang in the same positions as the existing pendants, except in the transepts where holes in the vaulting exist for two to each bay as in the nave, and were found to give excellent light for reading as well as a form of illumination attractive in itself. The design of the chandeliers could, I think, be simplified and made more graceful; but the specimen exhibited showed that such fittings would be worthy ornaments beautiful by day as well as by night.[8]

Approval had been given to the ideas that Troughton and Young's scheme embodies.

For St George's chapel Mr Sebastian Comper has provided two new pendants, to his father's design, to replace the existing pair. They will be hung when the cleaning of the chapel is finished.

Sound amplification

Approval was given to various changes in the position of the amplifiers in the transepts and new fittings to the lectern and stalls and pews in the choir. These have not yet been fixed.

The cloisters

During March and April an old boiler cellar under the west walk was cleaned out for use as a chair store.

Chapter House vestibule

Repairs were carried out to the roof as a temporary measure to prevent leakage to the vaulting beneath. The lead however is deteriorating and this roof will soon need to be renewed.

Song School

Redecoration was carried out during the summer holiday in 1961. Our carpenters effected alterations to the cassock racks.

The Deanery

The plaster on the west side of the house was lime-washed and the brickwork on the garden side painted in the summer of 1961.

The Langham and Litlyngton rooms have been somewhat improved by the hanging of pictures and better arrangement of the furniture.

St Catherine's chapel

The brick coping to the precinct wall was completed by Ward and Paterson in April 1961. It would not therefore be possible to plant creepers on this wall, the blackened aspect of which would be relieved by foliage.

General

In reviewing the work of the past year there can be reasonable satisfaction over what has been achieved internally. The end of the stone cleaning is drawing nearer and may perhaps be completed in the coming twelve months. That will not mean that the nave will then be free of scaffolding, because polishing the marble pillars will extend beyond that time. There are places too to which our masons must return to deal with localized stone repairs at levels requiring scaffolding as well as at ground level.

But as the demands of the interior on their services lessen, it will at last be possible for the masons to be employed more on the exterior and the cloisters.

Similarly as soon as marble polishing can be finished, it will be urgently necessary to put the labour that has had to be diverted to this back on to the nave monuments. Once they are done, together with those in the apsidal chapels that still await repair and decoration, there will be the chance to deploy some of our staff in new ways. It has been a serious misfortune that illness removed for several months the man who was doing excellent work with the Sturtevant cleaner, thus undoing much of the benefit of a job that, to be effective, must be continuous. When restoration of the interior is complete, keeping it clean will be a major pre-occupation.

Illness among the staff has indeed been so constant that, with so limited a number of men for such large and pressing tasks, its effect on output is disquieting. A week when someone is not away has become almost exceptional.

With the financial loss it entails may be coupled, in this past year, two others:

one the necessity of erecting scaffolding to the north transept front to remove loose pieces of stone that, had they fallen, would have been a danger to the public. It was inescapable because some did fall – fortunately without harm. The other is the repeated cost of having to make good wanton damage caused by the public in breaking ornamental features off the monuments. I think the prevalence of this abuse calls for serious consideration.

[1]   In the mid part of this aisle, by Admiral Baker's monument.
[2]   The Snetzler organ was later kept in the north-west apsidal chapel of the Lady Chapel for use at weddings etc.
[3]   In *Westmonasterium*, John Dart's history of the Abbey, 1723.
[4]   The alterations took place in 1825 (Chapter Minutes) in order to accommodate the enormous statue to James Watt put in this chapel (now removed).
[5]   The eastern pair are those to the ambulatories so are not technically in the choir aisles. These are now painted grey. The middle pair are low wrought iron gates of c.1700. Since 1924 (*RCHM Inventory of the Abbey*, plate 51) they have lost the filigree designs on the top rails, which is now flat brass.
[6]   To the American Bishop Charles McIlvaine whose coffin rested in the chapel in 1873.
[7]   Area with an iron grille under the gallery across this end of the chapel used to house some of the plate.
[8]   The sixteen Waterford crystal chandeliers for the nave and transepts were the gift of the Guinness family and designed by A.B. Read in collaboration with the Surveyor. They replaced electric chandeliers installed in 1913.

67N.   No report was given in 1963 due to illness.

He did appear at Chapter on 4 November 1963 to discuss outstanding matters, including the siting of Richard II's portrait. His radical scheme for a new floor in the nave was put forward.

68.   WAM S/1/108

Report by the Surveyor of the Fabric March 1962–March 1964

Owing to illness I was not able to submit a written report for the Audit Chapter in 1963. For record purposes therefore this report covers a period of two years, March 1962–March 1964.

Roofs

The main work has been on the south transept roof. The lead covering of the first half was finished in September 1962 and repair of the second half – nearest to the lantern – is still in progress. Four steel tie beams spanning the width of the transept above the vaulting were fixed in position during November 1962 and a temporary roof erected during the following month, so that removal of the lead for recasting could begin early in 1963.

Under this temporary roof repair and reconstruction of the timbers have continued, the last of the old oak trusses being taken out in August 1963. Twenty eight new ones have been made, out of a total of 34 required, and 23 fixed. Their great size – the timbers forming two sides of the triangle being each 37 feet long – makes the job a slow one: the time for assembling a single truss averages a little over a month. But the east section of the nave roof has provided an excellent workshop for the purpose, enabling what formerly had to be done at ground level in the cloister garth to proceed under cover in close proximity to the position for which the timbers are required. Before fixing, all new oak is treated with Wood Treat – a preparation to protect it against beetle and fungal attack.

The last two concrete wall beams are in place and the masons have been engaged on fixing the new parapet stones and working and carving stone crockets on the south gable.

In the nave roof the installation of permanent electric lighting has been completed. Pending repair, when that of the south transept is completed, a watch has been kept on the roofs of the north transept and apse, but no movement has been observed.

During June 1963 the tie beams of the roof of Henry VII's chapel were treated with a new insecticide by a Bristol firm, Timber Treatments Limited. These timbers are known to have been attacked by the House Longhorn beetle, which is even more dangerous than the Death Watch beetle because it bores along the centre of the wood and has a long life cycle. The virtue of this particular preparation lies in its capacity to penetrate the timber more deeply than any other. Even if the beetle could remain out of its reach, it is unlikely that it could survive any attempt to reach its flight holes through the thickness of the wood impregnated. This roof can now, therefore, be regarded as a cause for less anxiety. What has been done for the comparatively modest outlay of £1,371.7.0 is not so much a guarantee of safety as a form of insurance. If, after a long enough period, no fresh signs of the beetle's activity appear, justifying the assumption that its destruction may have been achieved, much greater expenditure on removing the affected beams will have been saved.

The presence of oil in the solvent used made advisable a check on the manufacturer's claim that it was inflammable. Tests carried out, first in the open air and then in the roof itself, were entirely satisfactory.

Structural repair and stone cleaning

Until the latter part of 1963 our masons were occupied almost entirely on internal stonework repairs at the west end of the nave. The vaulting, clerestory and triforium and west window were completed from the bridge, the south aisle, St George's chapel and the lower half of the nave west wall from scaffolding put up for stone cleaning. Under the north west tower they carried out the deepening of the north window to enable it to receive the Trevithick glass and much making good of the floor paving in various parts of the building as well are re-pointing those monuments undergoing cleaning and polishing. Externally a small amount of renewal has continued to the base mouldings of buttresses in the east cloister.

In proportion as it is rightly done, such work is little noticeable unless pointed out or seen at close quarters. But its extent has been considerable and a high degree of skill is evinced by masons who can tackle Gothic detail in a manner worthy of their predecessors six hundred years earlier

Cleaning of the stonework is now almost finished. For most of the south aisle our own staff were employed but the two western bays were undertaken by the London Stone Cleaning Company whose offer of reduced rates, as a way of providing a winter job for their men, was accepted.

The same firm have been responsible for the cleaning of the west wall of the nave and St George's chapel and are now engaged in the corresponding bay on the north side, which should be finished in March.

The lengthy and tedious polishing of the Purbeck marble pillars has reached the stage when only one awaits completion. It will remain to clean the monuments and lower part of the south aisle wall in the two bays east of St George's chapel to bring to a close the task which began ten years ago and may claim to have been worth the time and money that have gone into it. Those who remember the Abbey in its former darkness and now behold its walls as they cannot have been seen since first built may perhaps echo the words "And it is marvellous in our eyes".

Full enjoyment must however be deferred a little longer. The bridge, removed from the nave in January 1964, has been moved to the east end of the choir to permit of stone repairs to the vaulting and re-gilding of the bosses and ribs. The upper portion of the apse, cleaned thirty years ago, was not, for reasons of economy, done again when the appeal made it possible to start on the interior as a whole. It has looked slightly out of tone with the rest ever since. But if to make the most important part of the church glorious could be considered an extravagance at all, the absolute necessity, in the light of what has been discovered everywhere else, of attending to defects in the vaulting would justify a return to this section to ensure its safety. For a year of more the sight of scaffolding will have to be endured; by 1965 the bridge will, it may be hoped, have served its final purpose.

Externally the west porch was cleaned in time for the wedding of Princess Alexandra. Without making any charge the London Stone Cleaning Company undertook this to demonstrate how greatly the aspect of the Abbey, like that of St Paul's, would be improved if its stonework could be freed from the grime which has gradually blackened and disfigured it. I cannot but regret that the benefits of this generous gesture received rather scant publicity. Many parts of the exterior could not be washed at present because so much of the stone is in too precarious a state to be subjected to even the gentlest spray of water. But the stonework of the west front and towers, though in need of repair, is generally in better condition and might actually be saved by washing from further decay; for the best way to avoid repeated expenditure on stone renewal is to dislodge the soot and acids that are in the insidious cause of deterioration.

Monuments

Progress on the restoration of the monument has been satisfactory. Mrs Stenhouse, who had been engaged part-time on re-lettering some of the plainer mural tablets, ceased work about a year ago having finished those she could tackle at ground level. Mr Hart has concentrated on those higher up and on others of special quality such as that of Dorothy Osborne [Temple] in the south wall of the nave, for which a private donation was received. The results of his patient and careful labour are gradually becoming evident in the better legibility and enhanced decorative value of tablets throughout the nave and transepts.

Mr Butchart and his assistants have worked in the four apsidal chapels where all the 17th century monuments have now been restored and re-decorated. In St Edmund's chapel one Gothic monument, that of Sir Bernard Brocas, has also been repaired and painted. Because almost all of its stonework was in fair condition, having been renewed in the 19th century, it afforded a good opportunity to show what such medieval tombs must once have been like. The paint acts as a preservative and it was probably through failure to renew the original colour that, in the adjoining St Nicholas's chapel, the tomb of Bishop Dudley, obviously by the same architect, now presents a spectacle only of perished stone and carving mouldered beyond recognition.

For record purposes it may be noted that the two gilded candlesticks on the top of the Cottington monument in St Paul's chapel are new. When those shown in Dart's illustration disappeared is not known, but Fanelli's design was manifestly incomplete without these essential features. Two gilded flames in stone were also supplied for Bishop Nicholas Monk's monument in St Edmund's chapel, and on the large 17th century monuments missing ornaments, too numerous to specify, have had to be made and carefully re-fixed. That losses on such a scale could ever have occurred would seem incredible were it not that the same sort of thing, if in lesser degree, still happens today. Persistent damage to the monument of the Countess of Lennox is sad testimony to it.

In St Edmund's chapel the tablet to Lady Catherine Knollys, which had to be taken down for extensive repair, was re-erected higher on the wall, to be level with the similar table to Lady Jane Seymour. In St Nicholas's chapel the Bagnall pyramid tomb was moved slightly to the south east. Other such changes have been made before: indeed the more closely the monuments are studied the more doubtful it seems whether many of them are in their original positions. The sarcophagus to Lady Jane Clifford in St Nicholas' chapel is an obvious case. Designed to stand in the open, with an inscription scroll on each side, it is now placed against the screen to the chapel and its design marred by both inscriptions being hung on the same side.

I mention this because, if monuments have been moved in the past, the expediency of doing so again should not be ruled out as inadmissable. To complete the work in St Nicholas's chapel the medieval stone screen separating it from the ambulatory was washed. Its colour was previously the same as that of the bases of the royal tombs opposite, and presumably it had been similarly treated by Scott with shellac to try and harden the crumbling stone surface. Now, like the walls, it has regained its original whiteness. But I took the opportunity to open up the wall behind the Ingram monument, placed back to back with that of Lady Beverley and found, as I expected, that the hidden east bay of the screen survives between. Since this is the only surviving stone screen which remains unrestored (that to St John's chapel in the north transept was rebuilt by Scott) it would seem worth revealing it as such by transferring the Ingram and Beverley monuments to the triforium.

A few yards away, moreover, are two other instances of monuments that, because room has only been found for them by building great lumps of stone on to the Purbeck pillars, should also be moved – the tablet to Sir Robert Ayton, just east of the tomb of Queen Philippa, and that to the Earl of Stafford in St Edmund's chapel.[1]

The advantages that would accrue from a redisposition of these and several other tablets and memorials can best be appreciated in the building itself. They deserve careful consideration.

Memorials

Incised grave slabs to Mr Bishop and Dr Peasgood were laid in the west cloister and new memorial stones to Dean Ryle and Dean Foxley Norris in the nave, the former ones having become illegible. The memorial floor stone to Lord Plumer in St George's chapel had become stained by rising damp and a new one is now being provided at the expense of his daughter. A mural tablet to Dr Perkins was placed on the south wall of St Faith's chapel. In St Paul's chapel a new slate slab, laid in the floor, perpetuates the inscription on the pedestal of James Watt's statue, formerly here and now in the British Transport Museum at Clapham.

A tablet to record Britain's association with Malaya was erected in the north walk of the cloisters and unveiled by the Queen Mother on November 1st 1962. It is of Roman stone with incised gilt lettering and bears the Royal Arms in colour.

In the autumn of 1963 an alteration was made to the tablet commemorating the Civil Services of the Crown in India. The biblical quotation from which the words 'and to walk humbly before thy God' were omitted now appears in full.

Furnishings

In St George's chapel the electric light pendants presented by Mr Sebastian Comper to replace those designed by his father were hung after the cleaning of the walls was completed. Their design is unchanged.

The guidon of the Westminster Dragoons, handed over to the Dean and

Chapter for laying up in the Abbey at a service on November 25th 1961, had been framed in a wooden case, ebonized and gilded and fixed on the west wall. The lion and crown surmounting the case formerly terminated the pole on which the guidon hung.

In the nave a new wrought iron staircase has been provided for the Cranmer pulpit, replacing wooden stairs of the meanest kind.

Designs have been made for new cases to contain the Occasional Notes [Papers] and Visitor leaflets in eight languages. They will stand near the west entrance and supersede the temporary desks that have done duty for some time.

In the choir repairs were carried out by Mr Newman [Works staff] to the desks and pews in readiness for the new lighting. Although, or perhaps because, the woodwork is only 130 years old, it had been treated with very little respect: whenever alterations in the lighting were made – and they would seem to have been many – no attempt was made to make good any damage in the process. To fill the innumerable holes drilled and piece in new bits of oak where the timber had been cut into, occupied a considerable time and demonstrated how the carelessness of one generation can put a later one to much expense and trouble. Breakages and losses on the stalls and their canopies are yet more extensive. The number of angels' wings on the former and little carved heads on the latter that are missing is certainly well over a hundred and, since many are out of normal reach, it is mystifying as to how they could have been knocked off.

Even now constant vigilance is necessary. Following a recent occasion when the BBC were allowed to mount apparatus behind the choir stalls, one length of gilded moulding was found to be missing and another hanging loose. Damage was also done by our own cleaners to the desk fronts, designed by Sir Walter Tapper, to the chairs under the lantern. The constant moving of comparatively heavy things that tend to get rough treatment because they are awkward to handle, should be avoided if for no other reason than that their subsequent repair is a further drain on the maintenance fund.

For the apsidal chapels and various monuments new descriptive labels have been written on vellum by Miss Dorothy Hutton and set in blue and gold frames. I would suggest that the old notices, which look very poor by comparison, might now be removed from all other monuments.

To improve the loud speaker system the wiring to the existing fittings in the nave was renewed in April 1962. Bracket fittings have since been supplied for the north transept, improving audibility but with some sacrifice of architectural propriety.

Small box loud speakers have been installed in the choir stalls and amplifiers for the lectern.

Five hundred stackable metal chairs were purchased for additional seating in the nave, enabling a large number of wooden chairs of various types to be dispensed with.[2] They are stored in the east aisle of the north transept when not required. The normal seating of the nave is now about 340 chairs, all of one design and set out on an orderly disposition; though whether this will be maintained has yet to be seen.

Designs for new cushions for the kneeling desks and hassocks for the chairs in St Faith's chapel have been worked by the ladies of the Precincts and some outside helpers. Designs have also been made for new stall cushions in the choir, to be worked by members of the Embroiders' Guild, but beyond the submission of samples, execution has not begun.

Glazing

The window in memory of Sir Henry Royce was dedicated after evensong on October 23rd 1962. Designed by the late Sir Ninian Comper the work was carried out by his partner Mr John Bucknall and fully maintains the high standard of the other windows in the north aisle of the nave.

The Trevithick window, that had to be displaced to make room for it, has been moved one bay further west and looks all the better for a position of greater detachment. To accommodate it the two main lights have been re-opened to their full height by removal of the stone infilling which Hawksmoor inserted to make the sill level correspond with that of the equivalent window in the west front.

The stained glass was repaired by Goddard and Gibbs at the expense of the War Damage Commission, who contributed a payment of just over £700.0.0 for the purpose. Towards the cost of work by our masons a donation was received from the Trevithick family.

In both this Trevithick window and the Sir Henry Royce window, opportunity has been taken to supply the saddlebars and stanchions without which, externally, no medieval window looks complete. It is unfortunate that from some of those further east they were removed, with detriment to their appearance. The omission, which brought a protest from Lethaby at the time, ought to be made good.

In the Battle of Britain window Mr Hugh Easton carried out an alteration in the second tier of lights from the top. It was found that two squadrons that had taken part in the Battle of Britain had been given no representation and room for their emblems has been made by removing two of the winged angels. The cost of this work was met by the Air Ministry.

Lighting

I visited the Waterford Glass Works in the summer of 1963 to settle outstanding points in connection with the chandeliers for the nave and transepts. The decision to have only two chandeliers to every pair of bays, instead of each bay, disqualified the model tried out in position, because it could not accommodate enough lamps to light an area twice as big as that for which it was intended. Since, therefore, the size of the chandeliers has had to be increased, I took the opportunity to make other alterations in the design with the aim of improving its silhouette and eliminating crudities of detail.

The desk lights for the stalls and pews in the choir have been fixed, except in the pews of the singing choir, where they will have to stand on new raised desks for which money has not yet become available. After removal of the previous strip lamps and conduit Mr Newman will start again on making good the marks and holes that they leave behind. Much staining and polishing of the oak will also be needed to get uniformity of colour; on the south side for instance a whole new desk of oak is having to be made to replace one that, with scandalous indifference, had been renewed in deal.

Floors

New paving of black and white marble was laid in St George's chapel in the autumn of 1963, the cost £641.0.0 being defrayed by the Royal Society of St George. Marble was chosen because, with over four million people passing through the Abbey yearly, the prime requisite in any flooring material must be hardness and resistance to wear. The marble floors in the choir and Henry VII's chapel[3] are almost as good as when first laid; it is in the nave, aisles and transepts – wherever stone has been used – that abrasion has been getting increasingly serious.

It is serious for three reasons: 1. There is the risk of accidents because, particularly for old people whose sight may not be good, uneven paving can be dangerous, 2. Once a hard surface is lost, loose particles of stone dust circulate and make the task of cleaning more difficult. In principle the accumulated dust already in the building should, by means of the Sturtevant vacuum machines, be gradually extracted from it: what is drawn into them is removed and emptied outside. But if, all the time, fresh dust is being generated as the floor is eroded under people's feet, the process becomes endless and the benefits of cleaning never mature. 3. A point can be reached when repairs become uneconomic. Mention has already been made in this report of our masons having to spend hours, indeed days, on making good elsewhere. With so many more important jobs claiming attention, this is a waste of valuable time. If such piecemeal repairs are to continue over many years a great deal of money will be frittered away on patching up paving that is inherently unsatisfactory and can only be a source of recurrent expense.

The remedy for this state of affairs is a floor that will be durable, easy to keep clean and, of course, appropriate to the building. That marble is the only material capable of meeting these conditions is convincingly attested in the great churches of Rome, Florence and countless other places in Italy. The magnificent Cosmati pavings, for example in the Lateran, Santa Maria Maggiore and Siena cathedral, have stood the test of time so well as still to be among the glories of those buildings. Despite the vast crowds of visitors the marble floor of St Peter's Rome has not deteriorated.

Allusion to Italy is relevant for another reason. Sir Gilbert Scott in his

'Gleanings' emphasized a uniquely important aspect of Westminster Abbey: 'I doubt' he says 'whether – I will not say any church north of the Alps – but, I may almost say, whether any country north of the Alps contains such a mass of early Italian decorative art; indeed, the very artists employed appear to have done their utmost to increase the value of the works they were bequeathing to us by giving to the mosaic work the utmost possible variety of pattern'. The sanctuary pavement at Westminster for richness and intricacy is certainly not surpassed by anything in Italy and shows the kind of flooring that on a much larger scale must once have adorned the interior. Had English Purbeck marble not been used for those bands and borders that in Italy would have been of white marble this superb floor might be perfect today. The lesson is that even a material excellent for heavy load bearing use in pillars, as in the nave, may still not be hard enough for flooring. The marbles brought from Italy and used in contiguity with it for decorative patterns, are, by contrast, almost as good as new – even in those places not covered by carpet. After 700 years neither their surface nor their colour have failed in any way.

The design, therefore, which I was asked to prepare for a new pavement in the nave is based on the use of marbles selected for their durability and laid on the Cosmati principle of developing, by geometrical pattern, their maximum decorative possibilities. Such a floor would not be an innovation so much as a return to the original royal intention – the more aptly so since the Queen has signified willingness that her gift on the occasion of the nonagentenary year should take the form of that part of the paving which comprises the nave sanctuary. It would be marked by incorporation of the Royal Arms as a central feature.

All the existing brasses and memorial slabs have been worked into the scheme, though their positions have in most cases had to be changed; ample provision has been made too for the addition of future memorials. But to enlarge upon the rationale governing their arrangement would take too long. I prefer to draw attention to the peculiar place that Westminster occupies as one of the outstanding churches of Christendom. Although the supreme mediaeval embodiment of English genius in architecture, yet it is intimately linked with the greatest achievements of French cathedral buildings and the masterpieces of Rome and northern Italy.

This is a privilege never to be forgotten or betrayed. Any new work must, therefore, measure up to the standards they set; and because the nave presents the visitor with his first impression of the Abbey, here, in floor and furnishings, they should be most conspicuously evident.[4]

The Belfry

In May the walls of the belfry were limewashed and its woodwork painted white. At the time of the Royal Wedding in 1963 some fears were expressed that space for future peal boards would in time run short. I do not think this is so.

The existing boards are fixed high up on the walls and illuminated by strip lights. There are five on one wall, four on the next and none on the third. The fourth side can provide no space because of the stairs and platform leading to the clock. But whereas, on the first side, the five boards are evenly spaced and fill the width of wall without looking overcrowded, on the wall with only four boards these have been spaced at wider intervals. This does not produce a good appearance. All the boards are identical in size and collectively have the effect of a decorative frieze: the rhythm of the pattern they form should be constant.

I suggest therefore that, when the next board is added, room should be found for it by moving the existing four closer together, so that the disposition of five boards on each wall would correspond. It would be followed on the third wall when that in turn is filled.

If nine boards have been erected in the last fifty years, and there is still room for six more at the same level, it may not be till the beginning of a new century that space elsewhere will be needed. The next level down will provide it. Here, below the existing boards, the centre of each wall is occupied by the large round openings on which externally the clock faces occur. But on either side of these round openings will be space for two boards, making four on each wall and twelve altogether. Because however they will be less high up, the lettering, to be legible, will not need to be so large. Provision here might or might not be adequate for another century, but it should certainly suffice for a long time.

When still further room is required, it can be found at a third stage down ie. below the round windows. Being at eye level the lettering could be smaller still and the boards of smaller, narrower proportion, so that six could if necessary be provided on each wall.

No problem of insufficient space need be anticipated for at least another two hundred years. Meanwhile I would not favour any departure from the use of wooden, painted boards because all those that are hung at the same level must clearly be consistent in treatment.

When the next board is added on the wall that now has four, there will of course have to be a re-positioning of the strip lights: and the electrical conduit would subsequently have to be extended to the third wall, when this is brought into use. But this is a simple and minor task.

Flags

Till the summer of 1963 the flags were kept in the belfry. This was unsatisfactory because they lay on a window sill collecting dust and looking untidy, and when wet had to be laid out on the floor to dry.

The stage below in the tower ie. at nave triforium level, has not been utilized for their storage. The flags are stretched over wires so that they dry more quickly and do not need to be folded. The stonework of the walls, previously very dark and dirty, was cleaned down and limewashed and two electric light points installed to enable the flagman to see his way on dark winter mornings.

On the top of the north west tower a new flagstaff was fixed in December 1963.

[Clock]

It is proposed to make a change in the painted faces of the clock to minimize the risk of the short end of its one hand being mistaken for a separate hour hand.

Library

The electrical wiring, found to be defective in November 1963, was rectified before the end of that year. Many ornamental details of the book stacks have been repaired or, where missing, made good, and the oak balustrade to the staircase toned to harmonize more closely with the older woodwork. After vacuum cleaning both the lower and upper libraries were re-decorated and four large royal portraits in gilt frames, on permanent loan from the Weavers' Company, hung on the south wall with great benefit to its appearance.[5] A framed notice to record this loan is being written by Miss Dorothy Hutton and will be ready by March.

[General Monck armour]

The armour of General Monck after repair at the Tower of London was returned on November 19th 1963; alterations to its old wooden stand were effected in our joinery shop. As it seems likely, however, that the armour, if not enclosed, may in time deteriorate again, I am obtaining estimates for a glass show case so that exhibition would be possible in the Museum.

Museum

Five of the bronze show cases, slightly damaged by attempts to force them open, have been repaired, made air-tight and fitted with two locks each. In one of these the Essex and Courtenay rings are now exhibited.

The walls have not been limewashed since the museum was opened over ten years ago: they should certainly be done before the end of 1965.

Cloisters

The vaulting of the west walk, in view of small fragments of decayed stone falling, was brushed down and limewashed in the autumn of 1962. Limewashing was also carried out in the passage leading to the Little Cloister, but the whole of the Dark Cloister needs doing again and will remain difficult to keep clean until plaster can be restored to its walls. Some of the old plaster survives, showing that the rough stonework now exposed in places was never intended to show. The uneven surface of the walls, by affording lodgement for dust and dirt, is not merely unsightly but an architectural anachronism.

Recently some trouble has been caused by pigeons, particularly in the west cloister and it has been necessary to fix wire guards in the tracery of certain windows to forestall their being adopted as permanent nesting places. The nuisance has been mitigated but may easily recur if visitors who eat their lunch in the cloisters continue to throw food to these birds. Unlike St Paul's and many other London buildings where special deterrents have had to be installed, the Abbey has been comparatively free of pigeons hitherto. It is desirable that it should remain so.

College Hall

Oak posts were substituted for steel to support the gallery which is unsafe. Their less ugly appearance should not, however, cause the reason for their presence to be forgotten. Thorough restoration of the gallery and the kitchen offices behind, particularly in view of the fire risk which I emphasized in an earlier report, ought not to be deferred indefinitely.

Bookstall [shop]

Internal alterations, comprising enlargement of the shop and building of a new office for the manageress and store room in the open area between the book stall and College Hall, were completed in time for Easter 1963 at a cost of approximately £2,700.0.0. Various changes were made in the display cases, counters etc. and improvements carried out to the lighting.

Houses

No 20 Dean's Yard was re-decorated internally in 1962. In the same year partial re-decoration was carried out in the Choir School and 7 Little Cloister, and plans prepared for the alteration of no. 5. Designed by Sir Gilbert Scott, this house has now been completely renovated. Changes in its fenestration have restored the architectural character that earlier alterations had spoilt and internally much structural work has been carried out to remedy extensive damage by dry rot, leaking drains and other defects. The plumbing has been re-organised and new bathrooms made, the kitchen offices reduced in size and modernized, and the whole house rewired. Heating, cooking etc. are now all electric, enabling coal sheds and other small outbuildings on the garden side to be removed. The one story addition on the north front has been pulled down and the area it covered paved with granite setts formerly serving as edging to one of the borders in the garden. Without any sacrifice in the number of rooms the house has been made smaller in size and easier to run: the only addition has been a new entrance porch, incorporating oak timbers salvaged from the nave roof.

In the summer of 1963 2 The Cloisters was re-decorated; then nos. 8, 7, and 3 Little Cloister, and 4B Dean's Yard. A small structural alteration was made to one of the outbuildings in the enclosed yard between no. 4 and St Catherine's garden.

No. 1 Little Cloister was vacated late in 1963 and only as a result of opening up a stud wall, in the process of clearing out much obsolete piping and wiring, was death watch beetle infestation discovered in some structural oak posts. This necessitated rebuilding the wall between hall and kitchen in brick, the new plaster on which has been treated with emulsion paint as a temporary measure.

The house, completely re-decorated, was ready for occupation by February 1964; but further improvements to the kitchen remain to be carried out at a later date. There is also some work to be done to the garden and boundary walls, where outbuildings abutting on them have been removed.

All the houses in the Little Cloister are in need of external re-decoration, which is much overdue.

In the Deanery repair to the Abbot's Pew has been finished. While scaffolding was in position for this it became possible to examine parts of the woodwork hitherto out of reach. Holes on the top of the cornice showed that there was formerly a cresting concealing the ends of the ceiling joists behind. Before the interior of the Abbey was cleaned, the prevailing darkness may have caused these joists to go unnoticed; more recently their unsightly silhouette has been all too obvious and a new oak cresting is now being made to restore to the cornice its intended appearance. It should be fixed before Easter.

The Pew is incomplete in other respects. There is little doubt that the wide span of its opening to the north was once subdivided by posts, and the separate lights so created may well have been fitted with transomes and tracery as in the two end lights. The western of these still retains its original tracery in the upper half and thus affords evidence of how all the lights would have been treated.

Gardens

Negotiations with the Ministry of Works and the Westminster City Council over the formation of an underground car park[6] immediately east of the precinct wall were satisfactorily concluded in the summer of 1963. Their main purpose was to ensure that the safety of the wall, which is fractured in many places, should not be imperilled and to agree a satisfactory position for the ventilating plant and exhaust shaft. This will now be in the extreme south east corner of the garden, almost out of sight and enclosed in a structure faced with stone to harmonize with the wall. Regrets that it should be in the garden at all are outweighed by the undoubted advantages of the scheme as a whole which by ensuring that building can never now take place on the Abingdon street site will preserve for the future what Archbishop Lang so insistently pressed for – the unimpeded view from the Abbey to Lambeth Palace, each rising above the trees of their gardens with only the Victoria Tower Gardens and river between. Work began on the excavations in August and is expected to finish this year.

Following adoption of a report and plan for changes in the lay out of the garden, a start was made in January 1964 on re-modelling the shape of the east border. The existing wall in front of nos. 6 and 7 Little Cloister is being continued eastwards in a straight line and the path adjacent to it narrowed to the width of the steps leading to Little Dean's Yard. This entails enlargements of the lawns and certain other alterations which should give greater scope for flowers and creepers.

In the garden of the Little Cloister the fountain, whose playing had for some time been capricious, was overhauled, its jet adjusted and the basin cleaned out. Its performance has since been exemplary.

Conclusion

I conclude this report with a few observations on matters which cause me increasing concern. In my 1962 report reference was made to the man hours lost through illness. In the two years under review the position has not changed for the better. Continual and sometimes prolonged absences make the Clerk of Works' organizing duties ever more difficult: time schedules are dislocated and administrative efficiency paralyzed.

This is the more serious because our building staff is so small. The volume of work does not diminish but the number of men employed is less than when I first became Surveyor. Too much has to be attempted with too few and pressure in one important job can cause total cessation of another. Of late, for example, the carpenters who should be occupied on the south transept roof have had to be laying boarding on the bridge in the apse. Continuity and momentum are difficult to maintain when labour is having to be switched from one task to another.

Still less it is easy, when interruptions are so frequent, to inculcate a sense of urgency. Every morning from 8.55–9.20 internal work stops for the School service. But one day a week a sermon lengthens this period to ¾ hour and the music master sometimes practices with the choir for ½ hour after the service. With seven cleaners earning approximately 6s an hour brought to a halt, the financial loss in a week is not negligible. They cannot be diverted to other jobs and in practice use the spare time to make tea and smoke. From the personal angle this is demoralizing; from the financial angle it is improvident.

Illness, restriction of man power, and interrupted working hours have not been the only trouble. In some spheres work has not been organized to produce the best results, partly because of some degree of overlapping (e.g. between cleaners on the Clerk of Works' and the Head Verger's staff), partly because we were continuing to employ individuals whose physical capacity had declined. A routine was being followed but to little purpose. As recently indeed as three months ago I felt almost a sense of despair at the state of the interior. Just when the cleaning was drawing to an end, the benefits were being neutralized by layers of dust everywhere so obvious as to fill one with shame. Had the money been spent for nothing? Had the Abbey, after all, no standards to maintain and teach? There has been a marked improvement since and the establishment of a new cleaning team is proving its value. But much that ought never to have got so bad is having to be done again and tremendous leeway has got to be made up before results are what they should be.

In this connection it may be pertinent to suggest that the problem of dust is aggravated in ways that could surely be avoided. I have in mind a recent occasion when 500 chairs were set out for an occasion at which only 100 proved to be required. And why, I have often asked myself, should it be worthwhile turning blocks of chairs in the east aisle of the south transept to face north west instead of north? Such manoeuvres take time and cannot be executed without just that element of disturbance which creates dust. Is it really necessary?

Loudspeakers and amplifiers that make it possible to hear easily in all parts of the building have surely rendered some old customs stale. To ease the problem of keeping the Abbey clean it would seem to me that established regulations ought to be re-examined and, if obsolete, scrapped. I cannot help wondering whether the seating arrangements for big occasions ought not, in particular, to be revised. When was their validity last questioned? What effective difference would there be if the number of seats were somewhat fewer?

My plea is that demands on the building should be kept within bounds. For if too much has been asked of it in the past what fears must be entertained for the future? The irruptions of the BBC and ITV fill me with apprehension. Each time the facilities they claim are larger; each time the building is more disfigured by their apparatus.

There should be no doubt of the price that has had to be paid. Such damage as has been mentioned already in this report, even the breaking of newly glazed windows to admit cables, can be counted a small part of it. Much graver is the risk that gradually the efforts that have gone into cleaning will be so impaired by dust making activities that much of the good achieved in the past ten years will be undone. It is because the process will be imperceptible that an advance warning is the more necessary.

10 March 1964 S.E. Dykes Bower, Surveyor of the Fabric

[1]   None of these memorials were moved.
[2]   Examples of these various chairs were retained and are kept in the Library or Muniment Room. Others were given to Abbey livings and to St Margaret's church. The Surveyor was instructed to design the new stackable metal chairs at Chapter 29 May 1963.
[3]   Dating from 1676 and late seventeenth century respectively.
[4]   His scheme for the nave floor did not go ahead. The coloured plan for it is framed and in the Abbey Collection. The Chapter Minutes on 26 November 1963 record The Queen's interest. Some letters are in WAM S/3/34, including an estimate from Whitehead & Sons of £96,000 for the new floor, a concrete sub-floor and re-laying gravestones and brasses. On 11 February 1964 Chapter noted that an approach to Commonwealth High Commissioners for funding from their various governments for this project was not favourably received. The legal implication of moving memorials and gravestones is set out in the Minutes of 10 March 1964. On 9 October the Government agreed to give £20,000 towards the floor, and discussions also took place on 9 and 23 February and 9 March 1965.
[5]   Actually on the west wall.
[6]   Files on the car park and plans and photos of the wall are in WAM S/3/62.

68N.   At Chapter on 26 January 1965 the Surveyor's report on the proposal to move the choir pews forward was discussed but it was not accepted.

69. WAM S/1/108A

Letter from Dykes Bower to the Dean dated 29 January 1965:

6 Little Cloister Westminster Abbey Quendon Court, Quendon, Essex

Dear Mr Dean

The Nave floor

You may like to have my observations on the letter received from the Historic Buildings Council on this subject.

I would refer first to the statement 'We do not feel that renewal of the whole floor could be justified on the grounds that it is dangerous'. What was submitted by us was not that the floor was dangerous but that its uneven surface was a danger to people – which is not quite the same thing. This risk is bound to get worse as the floor deteriorates further.

Next to the statement 'We do not feel able to subscribed to Mr Dykes Bower's view that the present design of the floor does not date back further than 1835'. That the present floor was laid by Blore in that year is proved by a Chapter Minute and it cannot therefore claim historic value as an original floor. The Council notes two old illustrations of the nave – one from Dart's Westmonasterium and a drawing by T. Bowles. It is unwise to place too much reliance on the accuracy of 17th and 18th century views of this kind and, in fact neither of these agree in their representations of the floor nor with Ackerman's view of the organ screen, which shows a little of the floor just in front of it. What is certainly clear is that Blore, by omitting the longitudinal bands in the nave proper, did not repeat precisely what was there before. He simply paved the entire nave and aisles throughout in squared stone, set diamond-wise, with longitudinal bands only between the pillars of the arcade.[1]

If therefore – and it is only a supposition – the floor depicted by Dart were the medieval floor, we have not got its design now but only, in second-hand evidence, a repetition of the square stone units of which it might have been composed. To describe as 'of considerable historic interest' this 1835 floor that is no more than a copy – an inexact one at that – of its predecessor, would seem to me an overstatement.

The Council have, as I think rashly, assumed that the paving in the ambulatory is of Henry III's time and quote as authority some theories of Lethaby. Great as is the value of his researches, Lethaby, as I have had cause to discover and as his own modesty would certainly have affirmed, was not infallible. I do not feel convinced that this was the first and original floor. In the Chapter House Henry III's floor is of tiles, – very fine ones – and pavements of such tiles were a regular flooring for great churches of this time. Would Henry III have given to the Chapter House a totally different or richer floor that he would have thought suitable within the church itself? It seems to me at least open to doubt. How is it, moreover, that small portions of tiling still remain in the ambulatory?

But it may be contended, again on the strength of a rather vague statement of Lethaby, that the Purbeck stone floor in the ambulatory was enriched by a pattern. That can never now be proved because the pattern, if it existed, has been lost through the larger part of the floor being now occupied by grave slabs. There is no surviving evidence whatever that, if Purbeck throughout was the original floor, there was also a pattern in the nave which would have made it what may be called a 'designed' floor.

That Purbeck stone, used for flooring, is not sufficiently permanent to be satisfactory is attested only too obviously by the condition of that in the ambulatory. It was because of the condition of that in the nave that a new floor was laid in 1835. In the intervening 130 years this has required, and still requires, so much renewal that 'conservation repair' is completely uneconomic – a drain on the services of our very limited number of masons, when essential and urgent work on the fabric is pressing. Surely to go on replacing what is defective with the same defective material is not merely irrational but actually creating a problem for the future.

The objection to 'wholesale rearrangement' of the floor slabs is similarly based on the attribution to many of them of 'great historic interest'. To how many and which? With the possible exception of that to Isaac Newton, none are older than 1835 when, as may be verified from records in the library, new slabs were made because the old were not fit to relay.[2] Names from other previous graves were merely incised on the ordinary paving stones and are now, several of them, again almost or totally invisible. Corroborative evidence of what had no doubt become the state of the floor slabs in the nave by 1835 is today afforded by a large number of graves, in slate and stone, that survive in the south choir aisle, ambulatory and east cloister with their inscriptions completely obliterated.

With the exception of some of the 19th century brasses, few of the graves in the nave have intrinsic claims to beauty or merit. Any 'great historic interest' must now belong more to the persons memorialized than to the memorials themselves. Nevertheless, in my design for a new nave floor all the large slabs are incorporated, in many instances with no more than a slight change of position.

What innumerable changes have taken place in the position of tombs and monuments throughout the history of the Abbey is not generally realised. Yet has the texture of history been seriously compromised thereby? Can it seriously be maintained that no change must ever be permitted again?

I pass now to the Council's third objection that the design 'would be wholly out of keeping with its surroundings'. That the design should be 'inappropriate' because the nave of a great medieval church was 'traditionally a place of circulation' seems a surprising argument. By comparison with those of many cathedrals, the nave of the Abbey is not particularly large; in medieval times its floor space was smaller because the altar of the Holy Cross was west of the rood screen which occupied the second bay west of the pulpitum. When it was available for use at all – building was going on for 150 years before its completion – the nave was the only part of the monastic church in which laity could worship. Not till the 17th century did it become the empty space that, in Old St Paul's, achieved notorious fame as Paul's Walk.

But if 'a place of circulation' is not fitted for a floor of any elaboration, what is to be thought of the Cosmati floors in such churches as St John Lateran, St Maria Maggiore and others in Rome where the vast naves are empty and might legitimately be given that description. Are these floors wholly inappropriate? Do they not rather exemplify the contribution that a fine floor can make to the architectural ensemble?

It can hardly be said that the eye is 'immediately assaulted' by their colour and pattern because the essence of these floors is that, so far from being pronounced or assertive, the colour is a harmony of quiet tones and the pattern, while distinct and pre-eminently architectural, so broken down in its parts as to enhance the overall effect of scale. The whole trend of development throughout the English Gothic in particular was towards enrichment by sub-division of the parts; and if there were greater opportunity for its display in roofs, as in the choir of Christ Church, Oxford, than in the floors, the reason was that this country could only obtain the finer marbles for the latter by importing them from abroad. A royal church like Westminster, on a lesser scale an archiepiscopal cathedral like Canterbury, could afford to do so as others could not; and naturally what was perforce expensive was applied first where adornment was most fitting. But this does not warrant the deduction that there was deliberate abstention from the use of fine materials elsewhere; on the contrary the medieval mind grasped at every opportunity for ornament and sought to emulate or surpass the best that came within its purview.

In the Abbey, where marble is an integral part of the structural design and predominates in the monuments built into its fabric, why should it be assumed that Purbeck marble pillars rising from a marble floor should be deprived of their 'tranquil base line'? Do the stone Norman pillars of Durham choir suffer by rising from Scott's Cosmati pavement? Or those of the presbytery at Peterborough where Pearson surrounded his Cosmati baldachino over the high altar with a splendid floor to match? The Norman pillars of the long nave of Ely rise from a marble pavement; so do the Decoration pillars of the nave of Worcester. Is the eye assaulted by their lack of tranquillity?

To the last paragraph of the letter I can reply more briefly. The Historic Buildings Council desire not to be associated with a design representing 'a radical departure from tradition'. But tradition does not consist in never making a change and to peg history, as it were, at a particular point in time is itself unhistorical as well as sterilizing in its consequences to architecture. If a material decays let it be replaced in the same if that is efficient and will last. If experience shows that some other material would be better, it is in conformity with tradition to adopt it.

Because something is controversial it is not necessarily wrong; there might be more probability of that were it not non-controversial. The privilege of having Her Majesty as our Visitor is one that must always command our respectful regard; it is also a reminder of what is due to the church that Her royal line founded, built and so munificently adorned.

Let me summarise what has been said. Had the existing nave floor either antiquity or outstanding quality, there might be a case for considering its retention. But it is neither old nor a valuable work of art and now that its condition entails problems of maintenance and expenditure, inescapable issues have to be faced. The Purbeck stone of which it consists has proved a failure. If renewed or repaired it will, now that the Abbey is visited by incomparably greater crowds of people than ever before, certainly fail again more quickly.

Not only the paving is suffering but also the grave slabs, some of which have had to be renewed in less than 25 years.

Yet with no more wall space for future commemorations in the building only the floor is now available. Must it gradually become an agglomeration of inscribed stones, with no system in their ordering and no coherent plan for the future? What will it look like when eventually it becomes a mass of such stones? What may be the judgement of posterity on an age which allowed this to happen?

Time and use, the two tests of materials, have shown that only the finest marbles will stand up to hard wear. Fine materials should be used in a fine way and at a time when the encouragement of fine craftsmanship receives so much verbal but so little practical support there is the more reason for allowing it a chance to prove itself. No finer pavements exist than those which date from the time when Westminster Abbey was being built; the very men who laid them worked there.

I would vindicate my design as consonant with tradition, comprehended in that wider vision of Gothic art that has been characteristic of Westminster, giving it a special place in English architecture and at the same time unique links with the greatest churches of Christendom.

Yours sincerely,
Stephen Dykes Bower

[1] Arthur Penrhyn Stanley in his Supplement to *Historical Memorials of Westminster* (1869) discusses the middle tread of the nave floor, Ben Jonson's burial there, and pavements in other aisles still remaining.

[2] A book was kept of all inscriptions and positions of the old gravestones, which is in the archives. Stanley ordered the reinstatement of the original gravestones to Newton and Tompion.

70. WAM S/1/109

Report of the Surveyor of the Fabric 1965

The interior

Completion of the cleaning of the interior has been the most noteworthy event of the past year. Scaffolding was erected during February 1964 to permit the triforium, clerestory and vaulting of the apse to be brought up to the standard of the rest of the interior, and to afford opportunity for inspecting the stonework and carrying out repairs. The vault ribs were re-gilded and the roof decoration re-painted where necessary.

This work, finished in October, brought to a close a major item of the restoration programme which had been in progress for a period of ten years and cost approximately £100,000. The masons, so long occupied in dealing with defective stonework and fractures in the vaulting from scaffolding mounted on the bridge, became free to undertake repairs at lower level and have carried out a considerable amount of work in the north aisle of the nave, renewing decayed stone and pointing up innumerable open joints.

Because it reveals more of the original structure and therefore looks natural, one interesting result of their work here may pass unnoticed if attention is not called to it. Many of the mural tablets and monuments on the walls of the nave aisles had been backed with plaster or brick in a manner that was crude and unsightly. I had wondered whether this plaster in certain instances might not have been applied over the architectural details of the wall arcading behind, leaving it wholly or partially intact, and the surmise has proved correct. In every case where it has been possible to remove large fillings of plaster the condition of what has been covered and therefore protected for perhaps two hundred years, tends to be better than that of the surrounding stone that has always been exposed. The benefits are evident on either side of the Demon's Door, where whole shafts of the wall arcading, formerly buried in plaster, are now revealed; also over the Robert Killigrew tablet further west. Here the tablet proper was surmounted by a thick mass of plaster concealing the string course below the cill of the window above. Following removal of the plaster the string course has come to light, with part of its painted lettering, and a coat of arms on the wall face below. Unfortunately with typical 18th century disregard for older work an iron clamp holding the top of the tablet was driven into the wall right though this shield, an injury it may not be easy to rectify. But here and in other places further east the recovery of more of the wall arcading is not merely worthwhile in itself but has improved the appearance of the tablets and monuments by ridding them of plaster that formed no part of their design.

A similar change has been effected in the south choir aisle. Some of the monuments affixed to the stone wall behind the choir stall canopies rise above the level of the top of the masonry and had been backed with amorphous lumps of plaster as unnecessarily large as they were unsightly. This plaster has in every case been trimmed to conform to the silhouette of the monument so that its size is no more than function demands. The wall that previously looked unfinished has been levelled and capped with a simple moulding. Probably not many people notice the difference; but the cumulative effect of such minor improvements is valuable and enhances the general aspect of the interior.

It may be pertinent here to refer to the plain boarding behind the gables of the choir stall canopies above this stone wall. I have for long thought that, in both aisles, it should be made more decorative and ought to be painted with a design in low-toned colour. But meanwhile, and before 1966, it could at least be hung at no great cost with a material resembling tapestry.

On monuments in the nave cleaning and polishing by our staff has progressed fairly steadily; Mr Butchart has renewed the colour on various coats of arms and decorative features and Mr Hart continues to repaint the lettering of faded inscriptions. Earlier in the year he was engaged on tablets on the west wall of the south transept.

Some further work in the completion of monuments elsewhere may be recorded. A new nose has been skilfully grafted on to the countenance of Dean Stanley. The missing crown and other adjuncts of the effigy of the Countess of Suffolk in St Edmund's chapel have been restored. A new eagle's head on the monument to Elizabeth Russell in the same chapel has been carved in alabaster and securely fixed to replace the original, wantonly broken off and stolen. Mr Butchart has still to make two new painted shields to replace those torn from the monument to Sir Richard Pecksall within a few weeks of their being replaced in position.

This lamentable kind of damage particularly to the monument of the Countess of Lennox, shows little sign of abatement. The subject is a recurrent one in these reports and I cannot but think deserves further consideration if only on account of the needless expenditure it occasions.

The new mural tablet to Dr Perkins is finished and awaits fixing in St Faith's chapel. For St George's chapel a tablet, carrying a bust of General Booth, was designed and is now being made in readiness for unveiling on July 2nd. The bust is a replica, slightly enlarged and executed in white Palombino marble, of a bronze head in the possession of the Salvation Army and made by the General's daughter Mary Booth.

Also in St George's chapel a new floor slab was laid to replace the former one to Field Marshal Lord Plumer, which one had suffered discolouration by rising damp. The cost of renewal was borne by the family.

An offer to renew the Rudyard Kipling floor slab in the south transept was received from America and a new one in Belgian black fossil marble is now being made at a cost of approximately £50.0.0.

A similar offer to repair or renew the slate memorial [grave] to Vaughan Williams in the north choir aisle was received through Sir Adrian Boult. Consultations took place with Mr Vaughan Williams and Mr Reynolds Stone who designed it and the stone will shortly be lifted and sent to Mr Stone for re-cutting.

In the choir the last of the desk lights, at the east and on the south side, were fixed after a new length of oak had been substituted for the former deal desk to the stalls. Our carpenters have been engaged on numerous repairs to the woodwork generally, also in making good the innumerable losses of carved ornaments on the stall canopies. This was necessary in preparation for the re-decoration of the canopies by Mr Butchart which began in June at the west end and is still proceeding.

The time that this is taking causes me some concern. Mr Butchart has now only one assistant and my attempts to secure help for him from two other firms have been unsuccessful: decorators of the requisite skill for his standard of work and particularly for burnished gilding, are hard to find. Those firms that employ them are committed to work of their own: nor are they keen to take on engagements subject to the conditions that necessarily apply in the Abbey, where interruptions due to services are inevitable. If the re-decoration of the reredos is also to be done this year in readiness for 1966, it seems to me essential that some measures should be taken to reduce the loss of time entailed in breaking off for services. I recognize that normal use of the building must have first place and that memorial services make claims that cannot be refused. But the school service at 9am has tended to get longer and frequently all work has to stop not for fifteen minutes but for half an hour. Hardly has work started in the morning before this break occurs, during which men have to stand about to no purpose, which is demoralising and, from the economic angle, thoroughly unsatisfactory. Would it be unreasonable to ask that, for the limited period now needed to enable the stall canopies and reredos to be finished before 1966, the school service should be held in the nave? I doubt whether anyone, other than Mr Butchart, would accept a job subject to such distracting limitations; still more to carry it on on terms so altruistic that he has been taking less money for himself than he pays to his younger and less experienced assistant.

To complete this account of what is being done internally – and at the present juncture to get as much done to the interior is advisable and desirable because there will be little or no opportunity during the nonagentenary year – I must say something of the recently organized activities of the cleaners. The results of the routine programme for dusting, vacuum cleaning etc. have on the whole been satisfactory, though the need for constant vigilance never grows less. Nor do I contemplate with anything but apprehension any upheavals that create dust and nullify much of the benefits. But towards the end of the year efforts will have to be stepped up to deal with certain jobs that are highly necessary, the most important being the dusting of the organ cases. This will require some scaffolding erected in the organ loft. To look down on the cases from the triforium is to see how much floating dust has settled on their carving and how urgent is removal has become.

Roofs

Against this picture of what has been done internally it has to be recorded that work on the south transept roof has advanced very slowly. The last reinforced concrete wall beam was completed in May 1964 and four new oak trusses, the last of the 34 required had been made by September. But transference of the carpenters to other work, chiefly attendance on the electricians installing the indirect lighting system in the triforium, has exemplified the difficulty of ensuring continuity in fabric restoration. With limited resources of manpower any extra demands have often to be met by switching men at short notice from one job to another, a procedure which is apt to be prejudicial to those tasks that, because perpetual, may seem to be less immediate.[1]

The wooden roofs over the vaulting of the aisles in Henry VII's chapel were treated in the autumn of 1964 with the same insecticide used on the main roof in the previous year.

Lighting

Installation of the indirect lighting system by Troughton and Young started in November 1964 and the same firm have been occupied above the nave and transept vaults on re-wiring and fixing winches for the chandeliers. These are to be sent over from Waterford towards the end of this month and it is hoped to have them hung by the end of May.

Furnishings

New kneelers for the stalls in Henry VII's chapel, made by Holley & Pike, were supplied in May 1964 and two display tables for printed notices placed in the nave in October.

The sounding board over the nave pulpit, removed in May to Rattee & Kett's works at Cambridge, has been undergoing restoration and should be returned at the end of June.

A new base to hold the Cross of Westminster was fixed to the Dean's chair in the sanctuary and wired to the security system.

The door to St Faith's chapel was sound proofed on the inside and is to be provided with a studded leather covering now being prepared.

In the same chapel embroidered kneelers for the chairs have been made by the ladies of the precincts and embroidered cushions for the altar rails, clergy seat and clergy desks by Mrs Lawrence and Mrs Foord.

Designs have been prepared for new seating to replace the existing chairs and a new stone floor with the central aisle aligned on the ridge line of the vault. This would correct the optical illusion of eccentricity which is due solely to the present aisle dividing the nave of the chapel unevenly.

Clock

An estimate of £186.0.0 from Thwaites and Reed for fixing an automatic winder to the south transept clock and softening the sound of its strike was obtained in March 1964. The delay in carrying out this work has been due to the firm not being able to obtain quickly certain electric components in the mechanism. But re-instatement is now in progress and the clock should soon be going.[2]

The alteration of the single hand on the dials of the clock in the north west tower has not been overlooked but those of our staff who could be allocated to it have had to be employed continuously on more immediate tasks.

A new telephone line has been provided to the ringing chamber to enable the vergers to communicate with the ringers.

Abbots Pew

A carved oak cresting was fixed on the roof of the Abbot's Pew in April 1964. An old Italian crucifix on a black velvet background enclosed in a gilt frame was subsequently placed on the west wall in such a position as to be visible from the nave. It formerly belonged to Sir Henry Irving and its history and the manner in which it was bequeathed to the Abbey are set out in a framed notice written by Miss Hutton and hung below.

Library

A framed notice written by Miss Dorothy Hutton to record the permanent loan by the Weavers' Company of the four royal portraits was fixed a year ago.

Museum

A head of General Monk, carved in wood by Mr Albert Siegenthaler, has been made to fit the suit of his armour.

In preparation for the nonagentenary year consideration has been given to reorganizing the Museum. Mr John Lansdell, who was asked to design the exhibition illustrating the history of the Abbey, submitted his proposals in January 1965 and these show that some preliminary work would have to be carried out by our labour. A start has been made with limewashing the walls and vaulting. The blocked doorway, south of the existing entrance, will have to be re-opened, the electrical installation altered to suit the new layout and possibly a new floor laid over the existing tiles. In September a small area of these was treated experimentally with a preparation to seal the surface and prevent dust rising. Though it has proved fairly satisfactory so far, the tiles, even if so treated throughout, might not be capable of withstanding the wear to which they would be subjected in 1966 and Mr Lansdell is in favour of raising the level of the floor and utilizing the space between the tiles and the new covering for the extra electrical wiring that may be needed.

Bookstall

Plans for further enlargement by building over the open areas to the east and south were prepared in the summer and the contractors started work on the site in November. Progress was delayed by a brick shortage holding up deliveries just when bricks were needed and I do not think that completion can be expected by Easter. It has however been possible to keep a part of the shop in use and there has been less inconvenience than was anticipated.

The scheme now being carried out utilized all the space that the site affords and represents the final development that is possible. The additions not only double the previous area of the shop but provide improved office and storage rooms as well as new cloakrooms.

Houses

In July and August 1964 alterations to the lay out of the garden of no. 1 Little Cloister were carried out by our staff and Sutton's of Reading. Nos. 2 and 4A Little Cloister were re-decorated internally.

The Ministry of Works has been restoring those lengths of the precinct wall which were exposed after removal of the building between it and Abingdon House. They comprise the east and north sides of no. 3 Little Cloister up to first floor level but not the modern brick courses superimposed on the original stone wall. These have been removed by our staff and a stone cornice is now being laid in conformity with Lord Mottistone's design.[3]

To give greater security the casements were removed from the north window of the kitchen of this house. Both lights have been reglazed and bronze bars fixed on the inside.

College Garden

The path in front of the houses was realigned, reduced in width and paved in stone by Suttons of Reading. Brick terrace walls were built in front of nos. 4 and 5 continuing the treatment of the existing walls in front of nos. 6 and 7. The terrace to no. 5 was newly paved, that to no. 4 re-laid. The central path is now being paved to match.

In the south east angle of the garden the ventilation plant for the underground car park has been housed in a stone-faced structure built at the expense of the Westminster City Council. When the new masonry tones down in colour and if creepers are planted to grow on it, the addition will hardly be noticed.

Precinct wall

With the underground car park constructed by the Westminster City Council brought into use the Ministry of Works started in the autumn of 1964 on their layout of the ground[4] extending from the statue of George V, past Abingdon House and the Jewel Tower to Great College Street. Demolition of the house which abutted on the north east corner of the precinct wall left Abingdon House in isolation. The ground between it and the wall is now being levelled and grassed so that the lawn east of the Chapter House will continue south to the Jewel Tower garden, beyond which it will continue again over the car park.

Use of the former air raid shelter by the BBC necessitates access by a wide stone paved path and it was because this path will be close to the east side of the precinct wall that the Ministry made representations as to the wall's safety. The section between the air raid shelter and the north east corner is noticeably out of plant and, if not stabilized, might, it was suggested, be a danger to the public.

Since the defective condition of the wall has long been known and obvious, some measure of risk was undeniable. Tell-tales moreover showed that recent movement had caused certain fractures to open further. It was therefore decided to carry out under-pinning while this could be done on the east side in conjunction with various site excavations by the Ministry of Works and employing the same contractor. Trial holes dug to a depth of every twelve feet revealed extensive cavities at the base of the wall, caused partly by rotting of the horizontal timber plates on top of the original timber piles, but also by what were presumably drainage schemes in connection with the monastery. A sewer had been taken through the wall to discharge into what appears to have been a kind of harbour with a quay at which boats could unload. A short length, of this, projecting at a right angle from the precinct wall, was discovered intact and has been exposed by the Ministry as a find of considerable antiquarian interest. It seems to confirm that the lower part of the precinct wall (now invisible) was built of fine squared ashlar, like a modern dock wall, because water, at any rate at high tide, flowed up against.

Now that under-pinning has been carried out the foundations of this wall are secured; but the rubble masonry of the upper part needs much repair and, particularly, to be water-proofed on top. The niched gable coping, formed in the late 18th or early 19th century, has afforded no protection for years: moisture has percolated down through the open points of the niches and assisted disintegration in the interior, while the face of the wall has suffered from the extensive use of cement pointing in association with a soft and crumbling stone. During the summer it will be advisable to carry out further remedial work to check deterioration before it reaches a stage when more expensive rebuilding might become unavoidable.[5]

S.E. Dykes Bower, Surveyor of the Fabric, March 1965

[1] A short report on the timber roofs from R.W. McDowall of the Royal Commission on Historical Monuments is recorded in the Chapter Book on 22 December 1964.

[2] Chiming of this 'sermon' clock was very noisy during services and the Organist asked for it to be silenced (Chapter book 13 July).

[3] He was John Seely before he inherited his title, and Seely & Paget rebuilt war-damaged cloister houses and the Deanery.

[4] Chapter records on 9 October 1964 that the Surveyor met the Ministry of Public Buildings and Works officials to discuss the proposed exchange of land outside Poets' Corner for the George V statue and Old Palace Yard layout. The railings were to be re-set along the new boundary (originally they were level with the present gates leading beside Henry VII's chapel to Poets' Corner door). Files are in WAM S/3/63.

[5] Major work was undertaken on the coping in 2016–17.

71. WAM S/1/110

Report by the Surveyor of the Fabric for Audit Chapter 1966

To complete the restoration of the interior in readiness for the 900th anniversary year was the principal aim of work carried out during the last twelve months. Not everything has been achieved that might have been wished; but it may perhaps be claimed that changes and improvements carried out during the period under review have materially enhanced the internal aspect of the Abbey and that no other church of like size in this country is now presented to greater advantage.

Of other work, less visible but of the first importance, a different account must be given. Restoration of the fabric, the real object of the million pounds appeal, so far from making progress, has almost come to a halt. I had hoped and anticipated that the south transept roof would have been finished by the end of 1965. Yet though all the new trusses have been fixed and some work has been done by the masons on the gable end, little more, apart from minor jobs of carpentry, has been accomplished and the roof is still not closed in. In consequence the electrical wiring for the new chandeliers in the south transept remains temporary because a permanent installation is not possible until all constructional work in the roof space is finished. Conditions there have in the meantime been fouled and made highly disagreeable by pigeons, whose entry cannot be prevented.

Shortage of labour, the primary cause of this unsatisfactory state of affairs, is attested by entries from the Clerk of Works' monthly notes. In July 1965 for example he recorded 'No carpenters working in roof owing to holidays'; in August 'No carpenters working in roof due to holidays and sickness'; in September 'No carpenters working in roof owing to sickness and carpenters being employed in Headmaster's house of the Choir School'; in October 'Only one carpenter and labourer working on the roof making door frames. Other carpenters working on more urgent work'; in November 'No work in progress owing to men being employed elsewhere'; in December 'No work in progress'.

Holidays are an inevitable interruption and sickness no doubt cannot be avoided. But is incidence seems to be ever more constant. With a small staff one man's absence may disorganise operations so effectually that others have to be taken off the job in hand making continuity, let alone a sense of urgency, impossible. Weeks when there are no absentees have become so rare as to be exceptional and the conclusion that must reluctantly be drawn is that a complete change of policy is necessary.

This subject has been discussed on several occasions in the past and the present breakdown is not something that has developed through failure to recognise or to try to meet conditions that apply to the building industry generally. A firm, for example, such as F.C. Hoskins & Co Ltd, who have done much work on the Abbey houses, the bookshop etc., have found themselves beset at time by problems similar to ours, as indeed are builders of small and medium size everywhere. In spite of better terms of payment and employment generally we have not been able to recruit new labour of the right quality and, numerically, are below the strength needed to tackle what restoration of the Abbey entails. Nor are we in a position to embark on the experiment now being tried at some cathedrals of setting up 'schools' of masonry or joinery, staffed party by trained hands, but taking apprentices and thus encouraging young men to learn a craft and perhaps become permanent employees. Competition is too fierce in

London to make this practicable. The big firms, which get the labour they want by the enticement of higher wages, would soon draw off any promising material. Geographically there is no site suitable. Our masons' yard is already too small. The joinery shop is similarly restricted with no possibility of enlargement.

I can see no alternative but to revert to the practice of calling in selected firms with adequate resources for those parts of restoration that are now beyond our scope. Expenditure will be greater but at least the work will not drag on so slowly that, for lack of attention in time, deterioration will accelerate and increase the ultimate cost. Two major items of restoration ought not, I am sure, to be longer postponed: 1. the repair of the roofs ie. completion of the south transept, the north transept and the apse; 2. the renewal of decayed stone in the cloisters.

For the latter I am obtaining estimates from Rattee & Kett Ltd. of Cambridge who have their own masonry works and would shortly be able to make available a team of men from one big job in London that is due to finish soon. If satisfactory terms can be arranged with them I would recommend that a start on the south or west walk should be made as soon as possible.

For the roofs I am negotiating with Dove Brothers Ltd. who worked on them ten years ago, have the experience necessary and express willingness to consider the proposition. But apart perhaps from some prestige value, it would be a delusion to image that this kind of job has much attraction for any large firm that has not to look for work. It may well be that only at this juncture, when restrictions have been put on many large scale projects, that it is of any interest at all. Partly, therefore, for this reason the time may be opportune to see whether an arrangement can be made that would be mutually satisfactory.

There is however one other factor that, because it has come to affect more and more the deployment of our staff, must be mentioned as a matter of importance. One of the consequences of not being able to keep men continuously engaged on their proper avocation is that lesser jobs, sometimes of an emergency character, provide a pretext for giving them something else to do, even when it may be of an unsuitable, even trivial character. I am sure this is demoralizing and in the end prejudicial to the best interests of both staff and employers. With so much going on there may be some natural pressure to treat the building staff as a labour reserve whose assistance can be harnessed to the needs of the moment. Every time this happens repetition becomes easier. Energies that ought to be concentrated on the building are dissipated on day to day eventualities, till these take precedence of what is vital and almost cause it to be forgotten.

Although, after ten years, restoration of the interior is virtually finished, that of the exterior, now due to begin, will be of far larger extent and make exacting demands in labour and money for at least twenty years or more. It cannot by its nature move very fast: the immediate objective is to get it moving at all.

Lighting

From March to June preparations were made in the roof space above the vaulting for hanging the Waterford glass chandeliers, Troughton and Young being engaged both on new wiring and fixing winches on the tie beams. In July the chandeliers in the nave were hung and shown for the first time at a press conference on July 20th.

The indirect lighting of the vaulting from triforium level, on which work had been proceeding simultaneously, was also displayed on that occasion. The eight chandeliers in the transepts, for which temporary wiring has had to be provided pending completion of the south transept roof, were not hung until September.

That this new lighting, which received wide notice in the press, seems to have aroused interest and approval is gratifying because crystal chandeliers have never before been used in a great Gothic church in England and, in some quarters, apprehension was expressed as to their suitability. As so often in the past the Abbey has benefited by its tradition of independence and awareness of European precedents.

Subsequent to this reform of the main lighting, changes of a lesser kind have been made. For selected monuments concealed lighting has been provided that will display each as a showpiece when required, but not be used at other times. In each of the four apsidal chapels some of the redundant six-branch brass pendant fittings – polished, lacquered, slightly altered and fitted with new glass shades, have been hung from the apex of the vaults, spot lights not being found suitable for showing the many coloured and gilded monument at different angles to each other. Hidden illumination is thus provide d for the ambulatories, enabling the pendants in them to be dispensed with and improving the vista by day.

In the sanctuary the existing strip lights have been equipped with new and stronger lamps and concealed spot lights added to give greater intensity on the reredos when required.

In the chapel of King Henry VII lights have been placed out of sight below the west window to give a suffused glow on the vaulting. Troughton and Young are now investigating a suitable type of glass for bowls to replace the small rather vertical shades on the standards fixed to each of the stall desk ends. The aim is both to increase the spread of the light and to improve appearance. In the aisles, where a subdued light is appropriate in the relatively smaller space, wall fittings of a type that will not be too conspicuous by day have been designed to fit into the stone panelling.

The organ loft is being wired with a ring main providing twelve socket points for standard lamps that will be available for orchestral players or singers on special occasions. General illumination will also be available from reflectors in the bay of the triforium west of the screen. From adjacent positions in the triforium both organ cases can be lit, like the monuments, for display at night.

The choir stalls

The re-painting of the choir stall canopies by Mr Butchart and his two assistants began at the west end with the return stalls and continued along the north side. But before the latter was finished in August it became clear that Mr Butchart found the job too much for him and would be relieved if he did not have to continue with the south side. His health at the time was uncertain and, when he was absent, progress was not so quick was he would have wished. Arrangements were therefore made with Campbell Smith and Company to complete the job and they took over at the end of the summer.

As the result of putting on several skilled men the work advanced more rapidly and, including the decoration of the stall backs, previously unpainted, was finished by Christmas. Throughout our carpenters kept just ahead of the painters and gilders, fixing the innumerable carved ornaments missing or broken, only some of which had been saved: most had to be made afresh.

It will however be necessary for a good many places on the stall canopies to be re-touched and tidied up. Where there is so much intricate detail a painter can easily forget whether any particular spot has received two coats of paint or only one – the conditions of light not assisting visible differentiation. Campbell Smith and Company recognise that a final check of every stall is necessary and I am anxious that they should undertake it as soon as possible and make good all that has to be done before Easter.

The new decoration, while it follows in general the previous scheme, incorporates a few minor changes and some major additions. Most notably the gold has, wherever appropriate, been burnished and the stall backs have been painted with a blue diaper pattern, fulfilling Sir Walter Tapper's wish that they should be so treated. On either side of the stalls of the Dean and Sub Dean the painted canvas in the recessed panels has been taken out and a different design painted direct on the wood. Powderings have been added in the panels of the organ balustrade above the return stalls.

The Reredos

Re-gilding started in November and was finished, except for the doors, by Christmas. Here again the number of features broken or that had disappeared was astonishing, seeing that the date of Sir Gilbert Scott's restoration was only 1867: how so much injury could have occurred to what is at any rate out of reach of the public is inexplicable. The damage having now been made good, it must be hoped that vigilance will ensure better treatment in the future. Much of the detail, as in the tabernacle work above the mosaic panel, is of extraordinary delicacy – almost a tour de force of craftsmanship – and to compare this west side of the reredos (except the mosaic Last Supper) with the east is to be reminded to the value of careful restoration. The new work, clearly derived from such evidence as the east side affords, has created anew the beauty that the old has conspicuously lost, preserving as a reality what decay and mutilation would otherwise have caused to perish.

Before it became defaced the soft stone of the east side would have been protected by painting, traces of which still remain. When the paint was not renewed, decay began and the stone not merely deteriorated but became shockingly discoloured – so that here visitors can still see the shade of brown which pervaded the whole interior before its recent cleaning. For his part use of alabaster on the reredos face Scott's reason was no doubt that this material, with its polished surface, would be more resistant.

The gilding, added later and also protective, gave a two-colour scheme of decoration which it seemed to me right to perpetuate, although in a Gothic reredos of this kind a more polychromatic treatment would have been normal. But the ultimate place for colour is in the centre and will come when, as I hope, the Salviati mosaic can be replaced by a retabulum in the tradition of the smaller medieval one in the ambulatory. The reredos will never look right until this change is accomplished.[1]

But one major fault has been rectified in the recent work. The plate glass in the panels of the doors, an anachronism of the worst kind, has gone and the unpainted oak decorated to make the doors integral with the reredos as a whole. In the lower half of each door wood has taken the place of glass; in the upper half glass has been retained but decorated in blue and gold, in the distinctive Westminster tradition exemplified in the retabulum. It was indeed already present; for the upper part of the glass (ie. those portions within the tracery) had been so painted but the gold had faded and was on a blue so dark that the latter looked almost black. Some portions of this that had been broken were then merely painted black without any gold, so that there was justification for starting afresh – vivifying the blue and re-designing the gold trails in a more refined form.

The lower panels have presented a difficult problem in decoration and it has been necessary to alter the design in the light of experiment. What looks well near by, for example within the Sanctuary, may not read effectively from further away in the choir; and the difficulty is increased by variations of lighting, eg. strip lights alone, strip lights plus spot lights, or both plus sunlight. This work is still (in February) proceeding but I hope will soon be concluded.

The Organ [Quire] screen

To link the decoration of the nave front of the organ screen with that of the choir stalls, the plaster vault with its wooden shafts and capitals were painted just before Christmas. As it turned out time was too short for the tests and modifications upon which success in all such work depends and the men had frequently to carry on by candlelight because television was being installed for December 28th and electric light was intermittently cut off. What has been done represents the basic stage, to which improvements will be made as soon as the reredos doors are finished.

Monuments

Through the past year Mr Hart and his assistant have worked part-time on polishing the marble and re-painting the lettering and heraldry of the mural tablets in the nave aisles. Comparatively few remain to be finished but there are many elsewhere, in the transepts and ambulatories, that still need attention and will occupy Mr Hart, for as much time as he can give, throughout the next twelve months.

Several tablets in the west cloister have been cleaned and polished by our own staff.

The firm of W.F. Knight Ltd of Wellingborough are making good the missing portions of the bronze ornament on the monument to Sir Thomas Richardson in the south choir aisle, opposite the cloister door. As the bust of the judge is the work of Le Sueur this bronze enrichment was probably by him also and loss of a large piece of it had so injured the design as to justify the request of Mr John Parker, M.P. that the damage might be made good. The new pieces are nearly ready for fixing and the monument will then be restored.

Scaffolding has been erected to the Bourchier tomb in St Paul's chapel to enable Mr Butchart to re-paint the coats of arms and inscriptions. Full details of them are preserved in coloured drawings in the Library.

Memorials

Owing to alterations in the wording of the inscription on the first memorial a new mural tablet commemorating the late Dr Jocelyn Perkins was made and fixed in St Faith's chapel in April 1965.

To receive the lead coffin of Lady Anne Mowbray,[2] discovered in The Minories during building alterations and returned to the Abbey as her original burial place, a shallow excavation was formed in the north east corner of the chapel of King Henry VII, adjacent to the grave of Queen Anne of Denmark. The coffin was re-interred here in May and covered with paving, pending completion of the permanent memorial slab with incised inscription and three coats of arms.

In June a floor slab of Belgian fossil [marble] was laid in the south transept over the grave of Rudyard Kipling. The former stone having become illegible the cost of a new one, with more deeply cut lettering, was met by American admirers of the poet.

A memorial to Sir Winston Churchill at the west end of the nave was unveiled by the Queen at the Battle of Britain service in September 1965. The material is Italian verde antico marble and the lettering was designed and cut by Mr Reynolds Stone.

Lying centrally on the axis of the nave, the contiguity of this memorial to that of the Unknown Warrior renders more noticeable the extraordinary error by which the latter was laid just off the centre. If ever the nave can be re-paved it is to be hoped that opportunity will be taken to rectify this: the adjustment of position required would be so slight that few would be aware of any change.

The slate memorial to Ralph Vaughan Williams, cut by Mr Reynolds Stone a few years ago, was lifted in December 1965 and sent to the works of J. Whitehead & Sons who have deepened the incision of each letter and filled it with white marble. This has been done without impairing the design and, as may be seen now that the stone has been re-laid, with great benefit to legibility. The alteration was agreed with Mr Reynolds Stone, also by Mrs Vaughan Williams, who declined an offer to bear the cost made by American musicians through Sir Adrian Bout and has paid it herself.

The slate memorial to Sir Ninian Comper is being renewed for the same reason that its beautiful but delicate lettering has failed to withstand the wear to which any floor slab is exposed in the Abbey. Mr Sebastian Comper is repeating the design but in polished black granite.

Towards the end of 1965 an alteration to the memorial in the west cloister commemorating the Civil Services of the Crown in India was carried out by J. Whitehead & Sons. The Biblical text at its base has been restored to the truncated version desired by the Committee and adopted when the memorial was erected.

A new memorial to those who served the Crown in the Colonial Territories is being made for erection in the south cloister and dedication by the Queen on March 23 1966. The material is Birds-eye fossil marble and the Royal Arms in colour surmount the inscription. In readiness for its erection the wall has been re-faced by our masons in Clipsham stone – a first stage in the restoration of the cloisters which I hope will now continue throughout the south and west walks.

In St George's chapel a white marble bust of General Booth, placed over the door to the newel stairs, was dedicated at a service attended by the Salvation Army on July 2nd 1965.

Furnishings

In the chapel of King Henry VII new wooden upholstered kneelers for the stalls were made by Holley and Pike, who are now preparing test models for the stalls in the choir, where the existing ones are as shabby as they are unstable.

Our carpenters have continued to carry out repairs to the woodwork of the desks throughout the choir stalls – a seemingly endless task witnessing to the rough treatment which woodwork in the Abbey has received in the past and from which it is unfortunately not exempt even today. Open joints, breakages, missing bits and ever fresh damage tell a sorry tale and, in time spent on repairs, are as wasteful of our limited resources of labour as in the expenditure entailed.

For the desks of the men and boys of the choir designs have been approved to meet a request of the organist for slight changes in their height, inclination and position.

The open bronze desks will be superseded by oak ones, on which lights identical with those already installed in the pews can be mounted; the bronze pillars that support them will be retained but new bronze stays added to give extra strength.

I am at present considering whether better receptacles can be devised for choir books and how more comfortable conditions for kneeling might be provided.

New cushions covered in velvet to match the colour of the desk lamps are being made for the seats in the pews and stalls, also for the stall desks. The latter will be less thick than the previous ones and leave the bases of the lights unobstructed.

In the nave the sounding board over the pulpit, which had been absent for some months during restoration by Rattee & Kett Ltd of Cambridge, was re-fixed shortly before Christmas. The opportunity of being able to dismantle the existing woodwork for thorough examination and analysis was of particular value because it enabled the original form of what was missing to be ascertained and proved that this was different and perhaps more interesting than might have been guessed.

It remains to substitute wrought iron bars for the temporary steel stays attaching the canopy and pulpit to the pillar.

The new furnishings for the sanctuary of the nave altar were also placed in position before Christmas. The timber for stalls, desks, altar rails, faldstools and credence table – Queensland silky oak and maple – was presented by the Queensland government, to whom gratitude must be recorded for the care with which every separate piece, in the size asked for, was correctly cut and sent over. The cost of the actual joinery has been met privately – one half by an Australian donor who remains anonymous and the other by Dr Alan Don, whose arms are carved on the Dean's desk with the arms of Queensland balancing them on the south side.[3]

Occasions which allow woodwork to be executed in the manner which these gifts made possible for the Abbey are so rare as to be, in present times, almost unprecedented. The combination of fine timber, inlays of maple, ebony and sycamore, and gilding is in the tradition of such magnificent furniture as may be found in the cathedrals of Spain and Italy, but it hardly to be found in England. Rattee & Kett have asked permission to publish photographs of it in a brochure comparable with that they produced to show the work in the Baldachino and American Memorial Chapel at St Paul's and I hope it may be granted.

A further gift to the Abbey in the last year has been a portable Snetzler organ in its original mahogany case, presented by the Anglo-Italian Society as a memorial of Vincent Novello, to take the place of a stained glass window destroyed in the war.[4]

Two oak credence tables were supplied during the year and a teak notice board to stand within the railings facing Broad Sanctuary.

For the nave altar I have designed new candlesticks to harmonize with the Scott altar cross, with alterations to the latter to increase its height and make it suitable for use on an altar that is exposed on all four sides. The drawings are to full size but at the time of writing the estimate has not been received from Mr Welby.

Under the terms of the Hope bequest a scheme is under consideration for replacing the 19th century oak panelling that fills the inner arch of the west entrance to the nave with teak, carved on the outside with figures of Christ,

St Peter and St Edward. A model prepared by Mr Michael Clark has received provisional approval.

Kneelers

The organisation of voluntary workers for supplying embroidered kneelers has developed rapidly during the past year. From ladies of the Precincts it has expanded to include helpers all over England who, under the guidance of Mrs Lawrence, are now engaged upon a variety of tasks – from kneelers for the chairs in the transepts to long cushions for the altar rails in the choir, the latter being undertaken by a man who is both working and presenting them.

First to benefit by this generous labour for the Abbey was St Faith's chapel, which is now completely equipped with new cushions in the sanctuary and kneelers for each chair. Kneelers of slightly larger size have been provided for the front rows of chairs under the lantern and others will follow until, it is hoped, there will be enough for all the transept seating.

A kneeling cushion for the Dean is in place in the Sanctuary and a seat cushion is shortly to be started. Kneelers for the canons' and minor canons' desks are in hand.

By the summer enough should be completed to make an exhibition worth while. In view of the remarkable enthusiasm for this type of work, it should arouse wide interest.

Copes

The five Beatrice Stuart copes,[5] of material woven at Lyons, were completed by Watts and company Ltd. in time for the nongentenary year, each hood and morse being embroidered by Miss Peppiatt on specially made French silk. The cost of the making up and embroidery, exclusive of the white and gold material, was £1,834.11.4d, purchase tax by a special concession, being reduced from £122.5.0d to £0.11.4d.

The Cloisters

New stone has been worked and partially fixed in the buttresses of the east walk. The vaulting of the south and west walls has been brushed down and lime-washed – an expedient which may retard but will not cure the decay of stonework that eventually will have to be renewed.

Alterations to the cleaners' room in the south cloister were effected in the early summer of 1965 to enable the mechanical apparatus of the dimmer controlling the new chandeliers to be installed. Opportunity was taken to make other improvements at the same time and to re-decorate throughout.

The wrought iron grille at the Dean's Yard entrance to the cloisters was re-decorated in December 1965 following washing of the stonework of the archway and the window and adjacent niches above. None of this stone is more than 100 years old but black deposits that had accumulated upon it have already destroyed much of the detail of carving that, had it been kept clean by washing, would not have decayed. The two corbel heads to the hood mould of the archway to the cloister show this very clearly.

Cheyneygates

A request from descendants of the Hora family for restoration of the stained glass window formerly known as the Chaucer window revived the question of what might be done with what was salvaged from it after war damage. Though the greater part was destroyed some was saved and has been kept in store pending a scheme for re-use. It consists chiefly of small figures of kings, queens and archbishops with a certain amount of canopy work.[6] Approval has now been given to placing the glass in the windows of the Langham Room and the War Damage Commission has accepted liability for the cost.

As the Langham Room will be in use as an office until the end of 1966 fixing cannot taken place until it has been vacated. Meanwhile work is going ahead on the repair of the glass and assembling of each light.

Bookshop

Alterations and enlargement which had been in progress since December 1964 were completed in June 1965. Although it had been expected that the shop would have to close for at least a month, this did not prove necessary and business was carried on without a break.

This last and, because the site is now fully utilized, final extension has increased the size of the shop by one third and added two more rooms to the office accommodation. A rest room and lavatories have been provided for the staff.

Final settlement of the accounts showed that approximately £1,000 had been saved on the contract figure.

Museum

In preparation for the exhibition of Abbey Treasures the interior has been equipped with show cases and new lighting designed by Mr John Lansdell. The new fittings were pre-fabricated and erected in under a month before the opening day. The only structural change has been an increase in the height of the southernmost of the two doors to the Dark Cloister. This was carried out by our masons with such skill that few people would know there had been any alteration.

The Chapter House

Mr John Lansdell similarly fitted up the interior for the One People exhibition which opened in February 1966.

Choir School

The internal walls and paintwork were washed down during the summer holiday. After the Head Master's house had been vacated at the end of the summer term, the firm of F.C. Hoskins & Co started work on alterations in the basement, subsequently moving to the floors above. Owing to shortage of labour progress has been slow: it was held back also by the obsolete condition of the electrical wiring which has had to be entirely renewed by Drake and Gorham. Since the first list of requirements was drawn up many additional changes have been asked for and work is still continuing.

Houses

Internal decorations were carried out in the Deanery during May and June 1965 and re-whitening of the external south front in February 1966.

The installation of a transformer by the London Electricity Board in the cellar under College Hall entailed some minor structural alterations internally and opening a small window, to match an existing one, low in the wall facing the Deanery courtyard. Owing to electric cable having to be laid under the paving of this courtyard some excavation of its cobbled surface was unavoidable. The LEB, who are bearing the cost of the work, accepted responsibility for restoring all work disturbed to the condition in which they found it: but because this was very poor then, they cannot be wholly blamed for its being rather worse now. It may therefore be opportune to emphasize the desirability of laying out this courtyard afresh, not changing its character but with more regard for its potentialities.

In no. 1 Little Cloister an ugly window in the passage from the dining room to the octagonal room was removed and a French window made to give access to the garden.

Internal decoration of no. 6 Little Cloister and no. 16 Dean's Yard was carried out in June 1965.

College Garden

In April 1965 Sutton's of Reading finished the stone paving of the path across the lawns – greatly improving the whole appearance of the garden.

In the summer the structure in the south east angle of the precinct wall to house the ventilation plant of the underground car park was faced with stone at the expense of Westminster City Council.

Some repairs to the east side of the precinct wall were carried out by our masons.

Flood lighting

In the summer of 1965 discussions began with Westminster City Engineer's Department on flood lighting the exterior of the Abbey. Their purpose was to decide what positions on the building itself would be permissible for fittings and cable runs and to draft the general conditions within which a number of firms should be invited to tender and submit their own proposals.

When these had been received and examined three firms were selected to give test demonstrations, resulting in the choice of the Benjamin Electric Company to carry out the work.

By consent of St Margaret's Westminster and the Central Hall certain lamps have been fixed to their property and all installation charges have been met by the Westminster City Council who will also meet running costs, the Dean and Chapter being responsible for maintenance.

The lighting was turned on at a ceremony in the evening of December 28th 1965 and may be considered very successful.

Conclusion

This report may conclude with brief observations on points that cause me some concern:

1. With the new lighting and the amount of electrical equipment now installed in every part of the building, the introduction of yet more whenever television apparatus is installed increases the risk of fire about which I grow more and more apprehensive. I believe this to be real and serious.

2. I feel bound to deprecate too the effects on the building that follow from these televised services: not only the damage of some kind that nearly always occurs but also the creation of dust and dirt inseparable from erection and dismantling of such extensive equipment. Our cleaners dust only what they can reach: the great bulk of the dust merely settles out of reach, slowly and imperceptibly undoing the benefits of the internal cleaning so recently finished.

3. Reference has already been made to the recurrent damage of which traces are everywhere to be found throughout the Abbey. Within a month of their introduction, some of the new embroidered kneelers under the lantern have had their hooks pulled off. The culprits must surely have been persons attending a service, which makes such conduct even stranger. If it cannot be checked, will the labour voluntarily expended on this work seem worthwhile?

S.E. Dykes Bower,
Surveyor of the Fabric 9th March 1966

---

[1] The reredos was never replaced. The smaller medieval Retable was at this time displayed in the south ambulatory.

[2] Anne was the child bride of Richard, Duke of York and died in 1481. Her coffin was removed when Henry VII's chapel was constructed. She was re-buried on 31 May 1965.

[3] The Dean and Chapter disliked the heaviness, in appearance and weight, of the nave furnishings and wanted them removed. The Surveyor sent a protest letter and they were reinstated for a trial period and then retained, subject to the re-design of the credence table (Chapter 22 February and 12 April 1966 and 10 January and 4 February 1967).

[4] The organ was removed in 2013 and loaned. The window was the lancet over St Andrew's chapel on the north wall showing a figure of St Cecilia.

⁵   These were designed by the Surveyor (Chapter 9 October 1964). Files on kneelers and embroideries are in WAM S/3/32–33.

⁶   The inner room of Cheyneygates. It was actually a window to St Edward the Confessor in the east aisle of the south transept, which was given by James Hora in memory of his wife Marie, with glass by Burlison & Grylls. The Chaucer window, given by Dr Rogers, was over the poet's tomb, next to it. Both were damaged by blast in 1940.

71N. Dykes Bower contributed a chapter to the Abbey's official history, *A House of Kings*, published in 1966.

72.   WAM S/1/111

Audit Report by the Surveyor of the Fabric 1967

The celebrations which made 1966 a memorable year must have brought more people to see the Abbey than ever before in its history. That this might be so was realized beforehand, though perhaps the size of the crowds and their manifest interest surpassed anything foreseen. But inevitably, with the building so continually thronged and in use for a succession of special services and events, less work on it could be attempted than in an ordinary year.

After some weeks of illness in the summer the premature death of Mr Carter brought a sense of personal loss to all the building staff. Greatly liked and respected he never spared himself in loyal and faithful service to the Abbey.

In the absence of a Clerk of Works to control and supervise, day to day organization was almost bound to be less efficient and in spite of the good work of Mr Cansdale who, till the end of 1966, became acting Clerk of Works, some slackening of impetus was unavoidable.

The appointment of Mr Andrews as Clerk of Works was made at the end of November and he took up his duties at the New Year.

Stonework

The past twelve months have seen the demands of external restoration becoming predominant. The parapet on the west side of the south transept roof and the new crockets and cross on the gable were fixed by our masons, who also finished the repairs of the buttress bases on the east side of the cloister garth and of the parapet on the west wall of the west cloister, facing the Deanery. Internally they have made good the cresting of the vestry at the west end of the north aisle in Henry VII's chapel (the carving has still to be finished) but, as in recent years, have had to devote a disproportionate amount of time to the perennial lifting and renewal of worn paving slabs in the floors of the nave and transepts.

In relation to the magnitude of the task that will have to be undertaken in repair and renewal of defective stone on the building as a whole, what has been done so far is fractional. The sudden fall of a jagged piece of a window mullion from the west face of the north tower served as a reminder that the condition of much of the stone is a potential menace. Had this particular fall occurred a few yards to the south it could easily have killed one or two people.

Safety measures were at once taken – a fan scaffold erected over the west entrance and the whole west front inspected from cradles lowered from the two towers. All loose or dangerous portions of stone were removed and a complete photographic record taken. Considerable as the expense of such an operation has been, close examination was feasible in no other way. By means of it, a spire at the top of one of the buttresses on the west face of the north tower was discovered to be loose as a result of the stone being badly eroded. Since the unsafe stones were too bulky to be handled from a cradle, scaffolding had to be erected from which they could be lowered to the ground. But in order to get an estimate for replacement a second scaffold had to be erected to the corresponding spire on the south tower to enable the correct details to be ascertained. This spire had been renewed in Portland stone probably 30 years or more ago. Yet if Portland limestone were used on the north spire, it would by chemical action be deleterious to the stone below, which is sandstone. Either therefore this sandstone, still in fair condition, would itself have to be replaced by Portland thus greatly increasing costs; or any new stone would have to be sandstone causing two features identical in design to be perpetuated in different stones, at a time when the policy of using Portland, as most resistant to the London atmosphere, is that which has been followed for most of this century. Such are the dilemmas that restoration can present.

Much of the trouble that has developed on the face of the towers and that part of the west front built in the 18th century is due to the iron cramps splitting the stone. If water reaches these and they start to rust, expansion of the metal may cause the stone to spall and fracture. Where therefore loosened stone has to be removed for safety, it is the more necessary to ensure that iron is not left exposed to the weather. Such precautions as could be taken from the cradles will do no more than serve till proper restoration can be carried out and it would be prudent to begin this at the earliest possible time.

At the east end two pinnacles, which had for a long time been out of plumb, appeared to me, towards the end of 1966 to be perceptibly leaning more. Because of the proximity of one of them to the approach to Poets' Corner door, with consequent risk to the public in the event of a fall, I arranged that Dove Brothers should put up scaffolding and rebuilt the loose top courses on each. Restoration of a third pinnacle, on the north side of the apse had been begun by our masons some time ago and the requisite new stones cut in readiness for fixing. Yet it remained unfinished because other calls seemed always to supervene. With faint prospect of our labour force being able to expedite what was already overdue, I asked Dove Brothers, as soon as they had finished the other two pinnacles and the scaffolding used for each of them was free, to hoist and fix the stones already prepared and the job is now done.

At ground level the condition of the stonework in the south and west cloisters, as well as the approach to them from Dean's Yard and the archway to the

Deanery courtyard, is so decayed as to be a standing reproach. If priority has to be given to the west towers – on which the immediately necessary work might perhaps take a year – I think that the cloisters ought to rank next in importance. Here, as everywhere else, the cost would be governed by the amount of work capable of being done at a time. For though the extent of stone repair and its total financial implications are certainly serious enough, all work would have to be phased and, if a sufficient annual sum could be found to enable it to continue uninterruptedly, over a period of time a good deal could be achieved without yearly expenditure soaring too highly.

Roofs

After months of delay in which restoration of the south transept roof had virtually drifted to a halt, the conclusion that work of this kind was beyond the resources of our limited staff was inescapable. Far from showing any economic advantage, to attempt it was proving extravagant in keeping scaffolding and plant tied up unprofitably, and prolonging the job far beyond any reasonable time schedule.

After satisfactory terms had been agreed with Dove Brothers Limited the firm took over from our carpenters in the south transept and, under their foreman Mr Markham, have now finished it. Meanwhile they started in the north transept, over which a new temporary cover of corrugated iron has been erected so that all four bays can be dealt with simultaneously, instead of two at a time as previously. The rate of progress so far justifies expectation that this roof may be finished in well under two years and possibly little more than one.

The condition of the timber has proved no different from that in the nave. Though the external appearance of the rafters indicates death watch beetle attack, it can be delusive in affording little clue to how far this may have spread. The interior of many of the rafters has, in fact, been so eaten away as to become hollow, thus fatally impairing the strength of the timber.

The lead has been removed by Norman & Underwood for re-casting and it should soon be possible to start clearing the east cloister of the steel joists which had had to lie there so long. For reasons of weight it was not desirable to store them above the nave vault; but had the order for them been given only just before they were needed, there might have been the risk of non-delivery.

Stone cleaning

Estimates totalling approximately £2300.0.0 were accepted from the London Stone Cleaning Company for vacuum cleaning the interior and the work is still in progress. Expenditure of so large a sum almost immediately after the stone and marble had been cleaned for the first time in centuries was rendered necessary because of the serious access of fresh dust and dirt resulting from intensive use of the building throughout 1966. On many occasions it became virtually a workshop for the BBC and the constant erection and dismantling of their tackle, the building of platforms and stages, and mass movement of chairs, were visibly undoing much of the good that had been achieved. While loose dust can circulate and be set in fresh motion by any major upheaval, attempts to keep the building clean are in effect a losing battle. The dust must finally settle somewhere and only complete extraction can prevent this.

The quantity removed from the nave alone in the first fortnight of the present spring cleaning – it is emptied into plastic bags which permit weighing – vindicates the wisdom of what is being done. Because the condition of the nave floor, deteriorating all the time, is unquestionably one of the major causes of trouble, maintenance of the highest possible standard of cleanliness is the more important. Abrasion from the threat of people walking over it is unavoidable: but continued alterations to seating, which generate minor dust storms, should be kept to a minimum.

The chandeliers, as each section of the building is finished by the London Stone Cleaning Company, are being cleaned at night by Troughton & Young.

Externally, with the south transept roof at last closed in, the nuisance of pigeons has been abated to some extent. They still frequent congenial spots, too high up and out of reach to make dislodgement easy, as well as lower levels where conditions are not made uncomfortable or impossible for them. A full examination of the problem was carried out by the firm who have recently treated parts of the Palace of Westminster with pigeon repellent. But the estimates showed that the cost would be high without much guarantee what the results would be lasting.

Decoration [reredos and organ loft vault]

The redecoration of the reredos was completed soon after my last report was written. That of the walls and plaster vaulting under the organ loft followed, both being carried out by Campbell Smith & Co. Ltd.

Lighting

The lighting devised by Troughton and Young to illuminate selected monuments was brought into use in time for the late opening of the Abbey after Easter in 1966.

Wall lights have been provided in the aisles of Henry VII's chapel.

Brass chandeliers formerly in the nave and transcpts have been hung in the apsidal chapels, the vestibule to the chapel of Henry VII and in the Muniment Room. The chandeliers in St Edward's chapel have been re-silvered.

A Waterford cut glass fitting has been placed on trial on one of the desk lights in Henry VII's chapel and, like the experimental lighting in St Faith's chapel, awaits consideration.

Moveable standard lamps have been made for the organ loft to provide light for the players when an orchestra is accommodated here.

Furnishings

Under the terms of the Hope bequest figures of Christ, St Peter and St Edward the Confessor have been placed in the arch over the inner west door. The figures, of teak lightly touched with gold, were carved by Mr Michael Clark[1] and unveiled at Evensong on the Feast of the Epiphany 1967. Hidden lighting has been installed to give a soft illumination and each figure can be detached from the teak doors on the infrequent occasions when these have to be opened.

These teak doors supersede some 19th century oak panelling of little distinction and internally, with their massive wrought iron hinges, may be thought to present a better appearance to the nave. So markedly does their colour contrast with that of the wind-porch below – much to the disadvantage of the latter – that it would be an obvious improvement if a new porch, also of teak, could supersede what is decrepit as well as unworthy.

A new teak notice board, designed to stand within the railings outside the west front, was made by A. Robinson of Kingston on Thames and brought into use in the late summer of 1966. Behind toughened glass there are panels for four printed posters and one with magnetic letters for other announcements.

Six small bulletin boards, for use near the various entrances to the Abbey, have recently been designed and are now being made by Holley and Pike.

Internally, new wooden kneelers with red upholstery have been provided for the stalls and pews of the Choir, also for the stalls in the Nave Sanctuary. The ten previously in use there have been returned to Henry VII's chapel.

In the Choir new raised oak desks, carrying desk lights, were fixed to the boys' and men's rows. The bronze pillars of the previous desks have been re-used, with slight adaptation, and fitted with new bronze scroll supports. The troughs for holding psalters, anthem and hymn books were altered and enlarged and the construction of the seats, which had become very loose, strengthened.

In the first half of the year under review the woodwork of the choir stalls was overhauled and repaired to receive the new cushions of wine-coloured velvet made by Watts and Company. With these in place the decorative scheme for the Choir was completed.

The embroidered kneelers for the chairs in the crossing and transepts grow rapidly in number and are a remarkable token by voluntary workers of willing service to the Abbey. For much of the nonagentenary year a selection of hassocks was on exhibition in bronze show cases placed in the north cloister, where they were studied with evident interest.

In the Sacrarium kneeling cushions for the canons' and minor canons' desks are in position. The working of the long cushion for the altar rails is almost finished – a task carried out in his spare time by one man, Mr Sear of Reading, to whom tribute is due for hours of devoted labour.

An estimate of £1000 for the embroidered altar cloth for the nave altar was accepted and Miss Peppiatt of Watts and Company will begin work on it when the material, which has to be specially woven, is ready in about two months.

For Henry VII's chapel two oak kneelers, to match those existing, are being made by A. Robinson of Kingston on Thames. They will be set facing north and south, so that the sanctuary will, in effect, be extended westwards.

Two engraved metal plates, recording the gift by Lord Lee of Fareham of the Benno Elkan candelabra, have been received with a request that they be fixed to them. The only possible place is within the oval panels on the base. This will be very vulnerable to damage and may prove to be impracticable. An alternative position might be on the pillars behind.[2]

Monuments

The activities of the year left little opportunity for further work on the monuments. Decoration of the Bourchier tomb in St Paul's chapel has been held up because, after making a good start and completing two rows of shields, Mr Butchart fell ill and was only able to return intermittently. As the scaffolding has already been up for a long time and it must be reluctantly recognized that Mr Butchart's health is very uncertain, I arranged for Mr Finney to take the job over and work has now been resumed.

The mural tablets in both aisles of the nave, which over the last two years have been cleaned and polished, have recently benefited by Mr Hart's colouring of their heraldry, gilding, and repainting of the inscriptions where necessary.

Missing parts of the bronze ornament on the monument to Sir Thomas Richardson were fixed by W.F. Knight Ltd. in the summer of 1966.

Though no attempt has been made to make good broken or missing marble several tablets in the west cloister have been given attention by our cleaning staff and now look as well as can reasonably be expected after years of neglect and exposure to damp and dirt.

Memorials

In June 1966 a floor slab of Belgian fossil marble to commemorate the poet Caedmon was laid near the entrance door in Poets' Corner. The lettering was cut by Mr David Dewey.

Also in Poets' Corner, next to the grave of Tennyson, a floor slab of Belgian black marble with the inscription inlaid in white marble commemorates T.S. Eliot. It was designed and executed by Mr Reynolds Stone, who is now engaged on a slate slab to cover the grave of Lady Anne Mowbray in Henry VII's chapel.

In front of the altar of this chapel, beneath which Edward VI was buried, a black marble square with inlaid white marble lettering has been set in the floor at the expense of Christ's Hospital. Edward VI has no visible memorial in the Abbey and this stone recalls him as the founder of Christ's Hospital.[3]

In the north aisle of the nave a polished black granite stone over the grave of Sir Ninian Comper replaces the slate one on which the lettering had become illegible.

The memorial to Sir Winston Churchill was re-polished in September 1966 and its lettering silvered. In the crowds that thronged the building throughout the summer, it was inadvertently walked over so much that the finish of the marble had become dull and the incisions of the letters so filled with dust as to lose their visibility.

In the west cloister the grave of Thomas Greatorex was restored and a small repair made to the mural tablet to [Thomas] Vaughan, both former Abbey musicians, at the expense of descendants.

Crib

A gift by Lady de Grimston towards the cost of a crib more worthy of the Abbey was expended on new figures of the requisite scale and character. After much preliminary enquiry and investigation of costs, an Austrian carver[4] was commissioned to execute them in lime wood and to send them for decoration in this country. Owing to ill health Mr Butchart was unable to do any work when the figures arrived and finally, at short notice, Mr Finney of Campbell Smith & Co Ltd. had to undertake it. Partly because completion could only be just in time and partly because the position chosen, St George's chapel, presented special problems, the crib had in some degree to be an improvisation and to take a form different from anything envisaged when the size of the figures was decided. Ideally they should be on a base about three feet high and surmounted by a canopy: a crib statuesque rather than naturalistic, and preferably in a setting of architectural significance, such as on the central axis of the nave with space all round it.

In St George's chapel, in order to provide the figures with a background against which they would show, it was necessary to conceal the wall behind with greenery, making the best use possible of what College Garden would provide.

Whether the special electric lighting introduced was more beneficial than injurious to the effect and atmosphere of the crib as a whole may perhaps be doubted. It was hastily contrived and had to be, so far as possible, out of sight. But a quieter, more subtle illumination might have been preferable.

Library

In January 1967 some alterations in the position of furniture were made to provide Mr Tanner with working space in the north east corner of the main Library. I was asked at the same time to consider whether any scheme could be devised for general improvements, giving increased accommodation for books and better facilities for the storage of documents, drawings and records of various kinds.

When in 1932 the Library was altered and enlarged with the aid of a gift from the Pilgrim Trust the intention, it may be assumed, was to distinguish between an historic library, of venerable and attractive character but of which the books were only in occasional use, and a modern section, comfortable and well-fitted, that would house those in current demand. The latter had perforce to be new and, within the space available, was created with great skill. Though now overcrowded in a manner that impairs its quality, the upper library is a very well designed room, admirably equipped and – in the architectural details of its joinery and modelled plaster – of outstanding merit.

For some years now it may have fulfilled the function it was meant to serve without difficulty. But libraries are particularly prone to outgrow themselves. The more they are used the harder it becomes to prevent their intrinsic character being compromised: extra furniture is introduced, impedimenta of one kind and another inevitably proliferate.[5] The evidence of this, not only in the upper library but in the old one, cannot but be regretted. The Abbey's chronic lack of storage space has, over the years, caused the latter to become a repository for objects with which it ought not to be cumbered. Books dumped upon it lie on the floor; tin boxes, cases, pictures, add to the untidiness. The fireplace at the south end is now almost invisible because in front of it stands a massive oak table, well made and well designed, but unneeded and apparently little used. Upon it has been placed an ugly softwood shelf, the sole purpose of which is to conceal some earthenware pots which, it might be supposed, should be in the Museum, if anywhere.

Modern furniture at the north end of the room looks sadly incongruous so close to the beautiful 17th century book stacks, while wood filing cabinets of the most utilitarian kind occupy any odd position against the wall or on the floor. Even such chairs as have to be used at meetings are commonplace and incompatible.

Size and beauty ought to entitle this Library to rank with other notable examples of the period and its manner of presentation should be of first importance. Its walls have recently been enriched with the four royal portraits; the six brass chandeliers, shortly to be suspended from the hammer beams, will be handsome ornaments, greatly improving the lighting. If, so far as possible, the rest of the room could be its original self – the book stacks with the books that belong to them – free of all unsuitable accretions and supplemented only by such necessary furniture as would be appropriate, it would be what it is best fitted to be – a 'show' library of historic and architectural interest.

I must however mention the need of repairs, long known and which ought not to be indefinitely postponed. Many years ago death watch beetle was in at least one place found to be active among the books and there has been an obvious settlement under one of the book presses on the west side, the nature of which it has never been possible to investigate. Without opening the floor there is no means of verifying the trouble or how serious it may be. Moreover, although the oak ends of the presses were carefully restored about three years ago, many defects in the shelving behind need attention.

Yet if justice is to be done to this fine room and to the upper library which, as I have indicated, equally deserves to be shown to better advantage, space would have to be found for an extension that would meet immediate practical needs and make due allowance for the future. Apart from one possible alteration in the room south of the upper library, that would give slightly increased storage for books and records but be of relatively small account, there is no way in which more can be extracted from what exists.

Moreover, because of the position of the Library there is little scope for alternative schemes. The only place where a convenient and adequate enlargement could be made is over the south cloister. Built up against the Refectory wall (than which it need rise no higher) it could be designed to look as natural as the library over the perpendicular cloister at Wells. One wall only, the north, would need to be faced in stone. The roof could be a low-pitched lead flat, in the form of a lean-to against the Refectory. Such an extension could if necessary be built in stages – a bay or two at a time – according to requirements and, unless the east window of Langham[6] were sacrificed, would have to stop short of that building. To plan the interior in a way that would meet all foreseeable needs should be fairly easy, but the cost could not be small because an addition to the Abbey in this position, if not done well, should not be done at all. The exterior of the upper library, as designed by Sir Walter Tapper, because it may be said to have improved rather than impaired the effect of the cloisters, is apposite as an instance of doing the right thing in the right way.

As a footnote to what was said earlier about the furniture in the old library, it may be suggested that the oak table in front of the fireplace might find a place either in Litlyngton or the Jerusalem Chamber: in the latter to replace the rather indifferent table at the south end. If use d there, its wood should be toned to the colour of the cedar panelling.

Museum

Throughout 1966 the exhibition to illustrate the Abbey's story through nine centuries attracted continuous interest. The arrangement of all material in chronological order and Mr John Lansdell's design of the display cases and special lighting, were so widely appreciated that consideration is now being given to perpetuating them with only those modifications that experience has shown to be desirable and certain improvements such as the installation of the ventilation system.

College Hall

The desirability of improving conditions for the serving of meals would appear now to be a need recognized by the School, although its realization does not make much progress. Mr Carden, the school architect, discussed with me plans he had been asked to prepare for the re-organization of the kitchen offices, but which, since they entailed building a larger brick excrescence in the south west corner of the Deanery courtyard, I did not encourage as acceptable. Some months later another meeting took place at which two alternative schemes were submitted, each with good points but neither paying as much regard to what, if ever money can be found for this project at all, would make any substantial contribution by the Dean and Chapter worthwhile. The drawings this time were more fully developed and showed the extreme complexity of the planning problem. I indicated however where certain revisions might be tried and understand that fresh thought is being given to the matter.

Even if a solution can be agreed, it may well be that, on account of costs, no practical steps will be taken in the near future. In the meantime however it is pertinent to emphasise again the fire risk that the antiquated interior of this building represents. Is it adequately equipped with fire fighting apparatus that could be brought quickly into use in an emergency?

Cheyneygates

Throughout 1966 these rooms were in use as offices and the hanging of the brass chandeliers has only recently been carried out. The stained glass salvaged from the James Hora window formerly in the east aisle of the south transept, and restored at the charge of the War Damage Commission, will shortly be fixed in the windows of Langham.

In the two light windows of the north wall the figures will be, from west to east, King Edward VI and Queen Mary I, Queen Elizabeth I and Queen Anne, Queen Victoria and King Edward VII.

In the east window St Oswald and St Edward are at the head of two lights with, in the middle row, St Dunstan, St Anselm, Bishop Wulstan and Bishop Grosseteste; in the bottom row Alfred the Great, King Edward III, Archbishop Cranmer and Archbishop Laud. The glass has been restored by Goddard and Gibbs and, though the borders in each light are newly made up of fragments, the glass of which they are composed is all from the original window by Burlison and Grylls.

College Garden

The condition of the precinct wall has been visibly bad for so long that its progressive deterioration cannot easily be assessed. Towards the northern end of the east side some remedial work was carried out when excavations for the Ministry of Works were in progress about three years ago. But beyond repair of a short length of the brick gabled coping nothing has been done on the south side. In the summer of 1966 some of the rubble stonework near the entrance of 2 Great College Street was noticed to be loose and evidence pointed to the surreptitious formation of footholds for climbing over the wall from the street at a point where entry would be easiest. Though quickly filled up the cavities served to reveal how precarious is the state not only of the face but of the core of the wall; and it is because this has been aggravated by the penetration of moisture from above, due to the coping no longer being watertight, that repair and pointing of its brickwork has been carried on as a stop gap job for times when labour could be spared from other works. Nothing can be done at this season of the year because of the risk of frost but I hope the length of wall between the doorway to Great College Street and Westminster School may be finished in the spring. As soon as circumstances permit it would be desirable to continue eastwards, since, if water can be prevented from soaking downwards, further disintegration of the stone structure below will at least be retarded.

St Catherine's Garden

In memory of the late Lord Mottistone the empty niche at first floor level on the north side was filled with a figure of St Catherine, with a lead inscription panel fixed on the wall below. The sculptor was Mr Edwin Russell, who executed the figure in fibre glass. The unveiling ceremony took place after evensong on November 25th 1966.

Houses

Such jobs as have been done in the past year have been of a minor nature and do not require special mention. Negotiations with the War Damage Commission whereby, in lieu of payment for a central heating plant in the Little Cloister houses rebuilt after the war, an equivalent sum might be forthcoming for the installation of separate gas fired heating in each house, have been conducted over many months and will, I hope, shortly result in a satisfactory arrangement. Mr Paul Paget, who, as joint architect with Lord Mottistone for the houses, dealt with the original claim, has given invaluable help throughout.

General

A new Clerk of Works may be expected to bring a fresh mind to bear on various aspects of organization and a critical assessment of what easily become established ways will probably be salutary. Being himself a mason, Mr Andrews[7] is naturally anxious that the craft should be more strongly represented on our staff – particularly since stonework repairs are likely to be a major preoccupation for years ahead. He has already been able to recruit a new mason and urges the purchase of a larger saw for the mason's yard. I cannot yet give definite estimates of cost, but assuming that this might be in the region of £200, the expenditure would within a few years be more than offset by larger and speedier production.

In my last report reference as made to the chronic incidence of sickness among the staff and its dislocating consequences on any planned programme of work. Mr Andrews has, I think, already become aware of this but also feels that the average age of the staff is too high. Until he has been longer in the job and taken stock of conditions in London which may differ from those in the country, it would be premature to discuss what at this stage must be first impressions rather than considered ideas. But that there is scope for change and improvement he had observed and no doubt proposals will emerge.

This report cannot conclude without again drawing attention to the nuisance of litter. Within the church itself it is bad enough; in the cloisters worse; outside Poets' Corner disgusting. All service papers after use, while awaiting removal, are apparently put in a large open container which, piled high with rubbish of every kind, stands within the gates of the masons yard until the next refuse collection. The gates have frequently to be open and in a wind the contents blow about unchecked; even on a still day anyone entering from Old Palace Yard must be revolted by squalid untidiness on the very threshold of the most famous church in the land. There is an abuse here which I think calls for drastic and immediate action.

>   February 1967 S.E. Dykes Bower

1   The figures, given by Mrs Sidney Hope in memory of Martha Cavendish, were removed at the time of Lord Mountbatten's funeral in 1979 – they were on the west face of the inner west door. The following year they were re-sited on the north wall of St Faith's chapel and subsequently moved from there to the cloister entrance over the old Porter's Lodge, no. 1 The Cloister. New glass doors engraved by Brian Thomas in 1980 replaced the old wooden doors/lobby into the nave (now in reserve collection). The present glass doors date from 1990.
2   The Old and New Testament candelabra were given in 1939 and 1942, anonymously. The inscription panels were given after the deaths of Lord Lee and his wife.
3   Dean Stanley had placed a slab with a copy of his coffin plate inscription on the site of the altar after finding the grave in the mid-nineteenth century.
4   Hans and Adolf Heinzeller of Oberammergau. The crib was shown in a stable layout in front of the Choir Screen in other years. These figures replaced the set by French artist Denis Fernand Py, donated in 1939.
5   The 1932 desks in the library gallery were all disposed of in 2015 in favour of modern metal and wood.
6   The inner room within Cheyneygates. Litlyngton is the outer room there.
7   Sidney Robert Andrews served as Clerk of Works from 1967 to 1981, and his ashes lie in the west cloister.

72N.   The Chapter Minutes from 1968 onwards are not yet available for public viewing.

73.   WAM S/1/112

Audit Report of the Surveyor of the Fabric 1968

Stonework

Much of the work on which our masons have been occupied during the past twelve months has been at triforium level. Repair of the internal cills of the windows on the north side of the nave has been finished; on the south side it is still in progress. In the north aisle of Henry VII's chapel the cresting to the stone screen enclosing the sacristy at the west end has been restored and the floor inside the sacristy made good.

In the south walk of the cloisters a start has been made on renewal of the decayed wall shafts that support the vaulting. Two new moulded bases are in place; others are stored in the mason's yard ready for fixing. Some shaft stones have been prepared and the aim is gradually to rebuild each shaft on which the existing stone has perished.

As in most years a good deal of time has had to be spent on repairing worn paving stones in the Abbey; also in the Little Cloister, on taking up and relaying paving in connection with the installation of the new gas main. Labour has been allocated, on a recoverable basis, to cutting through the concrete floors of some of the Little Cloister houses, where necessitated by the gas heating.

The fixing of new stones on the buttress north of the big west window of the nave is now being carried out by the masonry firm of Bysouth, acting as sub-contractors to J.W. Gray & Sons.[1] Because of the dangerous state of portions of this buttress, described in last year's report, loose and badly decayed stone had to be taken down for reasons of public safety.

The tops of three pinnacles round the apse have been rebuilt by Dove Brothers Limited who have also partially taken down the defective east parapet of the north transept which will later be rebuilt by our staff.

During the summer of 1967 J.W. Gray & Sons finished a detailed survey of the west towers from cradles and bosun's chairs, photographing all places in which stone was defective and removing what was dangerous. An estimate of approximately £9,000 was accepted for making good what is now missing and the work that this covered would have been put in hand had it not been thought expedient, in the light of what was disclosed on these towers, to extend the survey to the whole of the rest of the exterior. On this task the firm have been engaged since, working first along the north side of the building, round the east end and back along the south side.

Loose, shaling stone has been dressed back to a sound surface and dangerous stone removed to eliminate, so far as possible, the risk of a fall. This contingency can never be wholly discounted because the causes of stone decay are still active and consequently the process of deterioration continuous. Even from one of the towers recently inspected a piece of stone broke away at the end of January – fortunately landing on the triforium roof and not doing much harm. The cause was probably the freezing of water in open joints after a spell of very cold weather (15 degrees of frost). A great number of such open joints occur on the west towers and this is a defect that would have been rectified had it been possible to tackle their repair at once.

With the general survey almost completed it has now started. Our scaffolding is in position on the south tower and work will proceed from the top downwards. Though not included in the £9,000 estimate I think it might well be an economy in the long run to wash the stone from each lift of the scaffolding. Most of the trouble that, all over the exterior, is causing even Portland stone to fail can be ascribed to one primary cause – the accumulation of acid laden deposits in any position that cannot be washed naturally by rain. They collect under every overhanging ledge, under string courses, moulding and carvings – black incrustations that may build up to a thickness of some inches. Although inaccessible to rain in wet weather they become damp and the acid moisture that trickles down from them starts decay in whatever surface it runs over.

Wherever opportunity occurs to free the stone of what is so malignant, the chance should not be lost. There is no doubt that the stone in the cloister garth, washed about 15 years ago, has had its life extended thereby: incipient decay was checked in time. In the same way if the exterior of Henry VII's chapel could be washed now further deterioration might be successfully forestalled. Already evident in places, this, if allowed to develop, would be exceedingly costly to remedy because so much of the stone is elaborately moulded. Yet in proximity to most of the downpipes the stone has been well preserved because it is cleaned naturally by rain water. During heavy storms not all the water off the flat roofs can get away quickly enough into the heads of the downpipes. Some spills over and the contrast in colour and condition of such stone as it washes is noticeable.

At roof level on Henry VII's chapel the pinnacles, except four round the apse, were taken down during the autumn of 1967, having become too precarious to remain. They have given trouble for a long time owing to the inherent weakness of a cross sectional area only 6 inches by 6 inches for pinnacles carrying relatively tall crocketed spires. In any rebuilding it would be essential to reduce the height and make some modification of the design.

Where the need of masonry repairs is ubiquitous it is hard to distinguish one job as more urgent than another. But decay and erosion have eaten so deeply into the west wall of the archway from the cloisters to the Deanery courtyard that the supporting shafts of the vaulting have become practically non-existent. With boys constantly passing to and from College Hall this is one case in which restoration cannot safely be deferred much longer.

Deterioration, too, that has recently manifested itself in the ruins of St Catherine's chapel – above two of the blocked Norman arches of the south arcade and at the base of one of the piers – will have to be dealt with to prevent the entry of water enlarging the area of damage. The old wall is capped by an incongruous brick addition that would be better removed to allow the original stone to be finished with a watertight coping.

The real needs however far transcend comparatively minor jobs of this kind and entail a programme of work that, however costly, ought to be started soon. Something may briefly be said about conditions that will affect its execution. Masonry is not only a slow job but the number of masons that there would be a reasonable expectation of obtaining for the special class of work required is likely to be limited. I doubt whether it would be possible in any one year to get through more than what, in terms of money, would represent an expenditure of £50,000. Only one section moreover of so large a building could be undertaken at a time since to incur high scaffolding charges on tackling different parts simultaneously would be uneconomic.

At the time of writing this report I have not received approximate estimates for the separate stages into which the programme would have to be phased, but on the basis of the damage shown by the photographic survey J.W. Gray & Sons inform me that their calculations of the total cost is £500,000. This figure corresponds very closely with my own forecast and, though it must not be regarded as a firm price, will be supported by a detailed breakdown of costs which I hope to have shortly.

It will be seen therefore that work could be expected to spread over at least ten years – because the £500,000 would be independent of what has started on the west towers and of what will be needed for the cloisters. If the latter, including St Catherine's chapel and the Little Cloister, are added, the total would be nearer £600,000.

The order which should be followed if large scale restoration becomes feasible will need later consideration. The state of the pinnacles on both transepts might well make it advisable to begin with their north and south fronts, working downwards on each. I think the north transept front could not take less than two years, the south transept from one. The two sides of the nave call for an almost equal measure of repair and might easily take one and a half years each, if not more. Henry VII's chapel, because of the complexity of its exterior, might also take two years and the rest of the building another two. These are the merest indications of what may be anticipated and may even be too optimistic. But they make clear the scope and duration of external restoration that is becoming imperative.

Roofs

With repair of the north transept roof nearly finished the temporary corrugated iron covering has been dismantled for re-erection above the apse so that Norman & Underwood can start stripping the lead.

On the north transept it remains to rebuild the stone parapet on the east side in similar form to that of the upper parapets of the nave. The open parapets with pierced quatrefoils,[2] which Blore substituted, have weathered very badly and the simpler original version of crenellations and plain ashlar walling is not only cheaper but more practical.

Comparing the time taken to restore the south transept roof by our own labour, the north transept work has been quick. It will have occupied about two years, as forecast by the contractors, Dove Brothers Limited; and although more money has had to be spent in a shorter period smaller expenditure over a longer time may bring no advantage if rates for labour and materials continue to increase yearly.

Mr Markham has been an excellent foreman and I hope will remain to see the work on the apse roof through to an end. In preparation for this some changes will be made. The hoist in the cloister garth will be transferred to a position on the north side, outside St Paul's chapel, enabling materials to be lifted direct to where they will be needed. The roof spaces over the nave and north transept vaults can then cease to be passageways; the south transept roof, which has good natural light because of the large window in its gable, will instead be used as a workshop, mess room and foreman's office.

I hope to arrange, in March, a meeting for various persons, who may be interested in what will have to be done to the apse roof, to inspect it again (many have seen it already) and have an opportunity of discussing the problems that its present condition presents.

In connection with the roofs – though not exclusively so because this affects the whole building – I must recall the three sonic boom tests carried out over London last summer. Any repetition of these would give cause for serious apprehension. A building such as the Abbey, held in equilibrium by a complicated series of buttressing, with every thrust balanced by a counterthrust, could be specially vulnerable to violent spasmodic shocks. If anything happened to upset the interplay of forces that are at work all the time, the result might be disastrous.

By coincidence two representatives from the City of Westminster Engineer's office were inspecting the north transept roof repairs at the time of one of the sonic booms. So great was their alarm over its effect, as felt therein, that they immediately communicated with me on the subject and on the following day I saw the City Engineer himself on the roof. He gave me his own views and urged that I should write to the Minister of Science and Technology immediately. This I did, receiving after an interval a typically evasive reply. It may be hoped nevertheless that the warning of a threat to the Abbey will not have gone unheeded.

Lighting

The nave and transept chandeliers were cleaned during 1967 by Troughton and Young. The difference, before and after, testified to the amount of dust with which the atmosphere is perpetually charged and therefore the importance of doing this at regular intervals.

No progress has been made with improvement of the lighting in St Faith's and Henry VII chapel, although trial fittings were installed in both. I think that attention might again be given to this matter.

Some of the brass chandeliers displaced by the Waterford glass chandeliers have been hung in Cheyneygates – two in Langham, three in Litlyngton and one at the foot of the stairs. Six have been hung in the Library and one each in 20 Dean's Yard, 2 The Cloisters and 16 Dean's Yard. Others have been given to various churches and of the small remaining number it has been suggested that one should be hung in the Nurses Chapel and two to give more light on the steps up to Henry VII's chapel.

Stone cleaning

At the time of my last report vacuum cleaning of the nave by the London Stone Cleaning Company had just started. It continued throughout the transepts, choir and apsidal chapels, but then had to be abandoned because of a succession of special services. This left the apse untreated which, in view of the great change effected elsewhere, was regrettable. However in January 1968 the work was resumed and is now finished. The apse was cleaned from cradles and Henry VII's chapel as high as was possible from moveable towers. This had inevitably left a horizontal line showing the limit which could be reached but the banners render it not too obvious.

Furnishings

A new teak noticeboard matching that outside the west front has been supplied for the north transept entrance and a teak case with glazed compartments to take large notices fixed to the wall by the cloister entrance from Dean's Yard.

A. Robinson of Kingston upon Thames, the firm who made these, also made two additional communicants' kneelers for the altar in Henry VII's chapel. The new ones, which are replicas of the three that existed, enclose the sanctuary on the north and south.

In St George's chapel a torch presented by the British Legion has been fixed to a wrought iron bracket attached to the west wall, with a small engraved tablet below recording the occasion of the gift. The stem of the torch is ebonized wood, the metal parts heavily silver plated and the emblem and motto of the Legion in enamel. The work was carried out by W.F. Knight of Wellingborough, the craftsmen who made the wrought iron screen dividing the chapel from the nave.

The metal plates recording the gift of the Benno Elkan candelabra by Lord Lee of Fareham were duly fixed on the base of each and have not, as yet, sustained any damage.

Work continues on the new altar cloth for the nave altar which Miss Peppiat is embroidering. Meanwhile a new altar table, slightly smaller than the existing one and with retractable wheels to facilitate its being moved when necessary, is being made by our staff.

In the general appearance of the interior during the years perhaps the most striking change has resulted from the voluntary labour of those who have been embroidering kneelers and cushions. For the chairs in the transepts as many as 900 kneelers have been worked and in the Sacrarium cushions have been provided for the altar rails, the Dean's and Sub-Dean's chairs, with kneelers for the Canons' and Minor Canons' desks. This good work, still advancing, adds a subtle enrichment of colour and attracts much notice and interest among visitors.

Two wrought iron handrails on turned and twisted balusters are being made for the steps up to the vestibule of Henry VII's chapel.

The plain boarding at the back of the choir stall canopies, seen from the choir aisles above the stone wall to which various monuments are attached, is being painted to a diaper pattern in subdued tones of red, green and black by Mr Finnie of Campbell Smith & Company.

The 19th century panelling over the west entrance, displaced by Mr Michael Clark's figures, was given to Canewdon[3] Church, Essex, where it has been used to form a screen under the tower.

Monuments

The restoration of the monument in St Paul's chapel to Ludovick [Lewis] Robessart (Lord Bouchier) which has been in progress for many months was completed early in 1968. Mr Butchart, Mr Finnie and Mr Hart have worked on it and valuable help on heraldic details received from Mr Tanner and Mr MacMichael.[4] Although the tomb itself, as well as the super-structure which forms part of the screen that formerly, as still in St Nicholas' chapel, spanned the opening from the ambulatory, are medieval (15th century), the buttresses and pinnacles on the chapel side were rebuilt in the 19th century and the slab of the tomb appears to be 18th century, replacing the original one which may have borne an effigy or possibly a brass.[5]

The monument was once very richly decorated and although the colour had become dim close examination revealed more than superficially appeared. This was aided by what must be a rare, if not unique case of early pictorial documentation in colour. In a drawing preserved in the Library Keepe[6] depicted details of all the painted shields, so that evidence for their re-emblazoning was available and made possible what otherwise could not have been authentic.

As part of the restoration opportunity was taken to repair the old wooden doors to the chapel which had been partly made up with later oak in the 19th century and to tone the wood to the grey colour which it would have acquired naturally with age had it not at some time been artificially darkened. The monument remains sheeted over until some form of rope barrier can be provided to lessen the risk of the public damaging its painted decoration which extends down to floor level.

In the nave and transept aisles many of the monuments and mural tablets attest the care with which Mr Hart and his assistant Miss Holland have worked on the re-painting of inscriptions and armorials.

The lettering on the grave of Thomas Parr in the south transept has been deepened and restored by Mr Sydney Newman, who is also cutting additional inscriptions on the Stanhope monument in the pulpitum [choir screen] to commemorate the late Earl, his father the 6th Earl (died 1905) and, to make the family record complete, the 4th Earl (died 1855).

New brass letters have been made to replace those missing on the graves of Henry Purcell and Robert Browning. The grave of Herschel has as many as 35 missing and the Rifle Brigade memorial in the north transept 153.

The memorial to Winston Churchill has been re-polished by J. Whitehead & Sons and arrangements made for this to be carried out twice a year.

In the west cloister most of the mural tablets have been cleaned and their inscriptions repainted where necessary. The next to be done is that to Benjamin Cooke, Organist 1762–1793.

In the Dark Cloister two boys from Westminster School, as a Christmas holiday occupation, re-painted the lettering on the plain mural tablets after instruction and guidance from Miss Holland.

Memorials

A slab of black Belgian marble with lettering inlaid in white marble was laid over the grave of John Masefield in the east aisle of the south transept near to Tennyson, Browning and T.S. Eliot.

In Poets' Corner a small memorial tablet to Jane Austen, with the dates of her birth and death, was unveiled at Evensong on Sunday 17 December 1967. Of polished Roman stone, it balances on the north side of the Shakespeare monument that to the Bronte sisters on the south. All costs were met by the Jane Austen Society.

Shortly before in the same month a memorial slab of Roman stone with a Latin inscription inlaid in black marble was laid over the burial place of Dean Don, close to the nave altar.

In the west cloister an incised granite slab on the grave of Harry Carter, former Clerk of Works, was unveiled on 13th October 1967.

A memorial to Ramsay MacDonald has been laid in the floor at the west end of the north aisle of the nave. Executed in Roman stone (with inlaid brass letters) it was designed by his son Alister MacDonald.

Discussions are in progress for another memorial nearby to Lord Attlee.

Preliminary designs have been made for the grave stone of Bishop Joost de Blank in front of the screen to St George's chapel.

The Crib

Three additional figures – the Magi – were carved and sent over from Germany in time to be decorated by Mr Finnie of Campbell Smith & Company before Christmas.

It was decided, experimentally, to place the crib at the east end of the nave – a position which though it gave scope for broader treatment, entailed problems both of background and lighting. The crib figures would have been lost to view with nothing interposed between them and the organ screen; and, in a brightly lit nave, extra intensity of light to make the crib of focal interest tended perhaps to diminish its sense of simplicity and mystery. Next year it should be possible to improve on the effect achieved.

Library

During the summer of 1967 scaffolding was erected for close inspection of the roof in which earlier examination from ladders had shown death watch beetle to be active. Some of the timbers were found to be badly affected by this, as well as by wet rot and extensive furniture beetle infestation, the latter now mostly extinct. While the condition of much of the oak is reasonably sound the roof as a structure disclosed weaknesses and, in places, quite considerable movement. In a previous period – which I guess may have been earlier in this century – some members had been strengthened with iron straps and new bearing ends were provided to some of the trusses. The fact that this has not prevented further trouble is therefore significant.

With the approval of Mr McKenny Hughes, the technique adopted for repair of this roof is a comparatively new one, developed by Mr Nixon-Eckersall of Thornbury, Gloucestershire, and based on the use of epoxy resins and foam to fill all cavities and gaps in joints and so restore structural strength. After the timber has been treated with insecticide and fungicide, the filling, which is very light in weight, coalesces with it in such a way that the whole becomes inert and also fire retardant.

There is virtually no outward change in appearance and the process is relatively quick. The original estimate for the job was £1,480.0.0 but further hidden decay, discovered by opening up of the wall in positions that became suspect as the work proceeded, will entail the expenditure of another £400. A definite completion date cannot yet be given but it should be well before the summer.

Museum

Under Mr Lansdell's directions a fresh air ventilation plant was installed and some minor alterations made to the show cases. The arrangement of the custodian's desk just inside the entrance was remodelled to give better vision and freedom from draught. A new case with burglar proof glass is now being made to Mr Lansdell's design for the display of Abbey plate.

Cheyneygates

In the summer of 1967 the windows of Langham were filled with the Burlison and Grylls glass salvaged from the Hora window in the east aisle of the south transept. The War Damage Commission paid the cost of its repair and adaptation to this new setting where its outstanding merit can now be appraised.

With this accomplished and the lighting improved by introduction of the two brass chandeliers, it would seem very desirable to furnish this room properly and make it, as it could be, an attractive and useful room for meetings. The big carpet, now in Litlyngton, would almost cover the floor. The walls which only need re-whitening, are already fortunate in the heraldic embroideries[7] which came to it after the last coronation. Little furniture, beyond some existing good pieces that could be moved here, is required.

It seems to me regrettable that so little should be made of two potentially fine rooms that deserve better than to be wasted as repositories of ill assorted chairs, tables and oddments. At least ten years ago I was asked to draw up plans to remedy this state of affairs but nothing has been done and the aspect of both rooms has got worse rather than better. If Langham at least could be made what it might be, one stage forward would be reached; and perhaps then the contrast would make it easier to deal with Litlyngton.

No better is the state of the entrance which for long has served almost as a lumber room that must make the worst possible impression on all who enter it.

College Hall

The inconvenient and unhygienic arrangement of the kitchens was the subject of critical comment from the Medical Officer of Health some years ago. Because of the confused and antiquated structure of what is above, much of it timber, I have also felt it necessary to stress the danger of fire.

My last report mentioned that new plans which Mr Carden, the architect to Westminster School, was preparing might embody changes that would meet some of the objections I had raised to previous schemes. These have recently been submitted and, in essentials, may be regarded as much more acceptable. The estimated cost, £45,000, though it may seem high, is not above what must be expected at present rates. In various details the scheme might require adjustment; but it does provide for the demolition of the brick excrescence in the Deanery courtyard, more appropriate architectural treatment of the wall thus altered, and internal re-arrangement that would obviate food having to be brought in to the kitchens and waste food brought out, past the Deanery front door.

Those are considerable advantages and, as a basis for discussion, the new plans represent an advance on anything previously put forward.

Turle's house[8]

The proposal to add an extra storey to this building was the subject of discussion and correspondence with Mr Mence, the architect, and the Bursar of Westminster School. The plans first produced did not seem to me satisfactory and an opportunity to suggest various changes, chiefly elevational, proved useful, since most of them were adopted. Seen from Little Dean's Yard and the garden of Ashburnham House, the greater height is not detrimental and the frontage to the latter has gained by more orderly and consistent fenestration.

The stipulation of the L.C.C.[9] that there must be an outside fire escape stair unfortunately came too late to admit of this being placed in Ashburnham garden, where it would have been out of sight. There was eventually no choice but to accept a position where it is in view from College Garden and mars the symmetry of the south end of Busby's library. The best that can be said is that the circular iron staircase, though regrettable, is relatively inconspicuous.

Houses

The installation of gas central heating in the houses in Little Cloister has continued since the beginning of June 1967 after agreement with the War Damage Commission for payment of the costs. A new gas main was brought in from Great Peter Street, parallel with the central path in College Garden and thence under the paving round the Little Cloister. No. 2 was completed first and subsequently nos. 1,3,5,7 and the flats between nos. 2 and 3. It is now in progress in no. 8 with no. 6 to follow.

Both the Gas Board, who were responsible for laying the mains, and the firm of Davey & Roberts who are carrying out the work in each house, have, I think, managed to keep the unavoidable inconvenience to a minimum and been more expeditious than might have been expected.

Over the drawing room of no. 4B Dean's Yard and also over the flat roof of the Surveyor's office trouble occurred in the asphalte roofs. The trouble at no. 4B may have been due to a war time repair of a temporary nature; that over the Surveyor's office I attribute to the rigidity of the Bison concrete construction. Both have now been put right.

At the beginning of August the Ministry of Works agreed at my request to carry out an examination of badly decayed stone on the Chapter House buttress between the gardens of no. 1 and 2 Little Cloisters. The scaffolding necessary for this was quickly extended to the full height of the building and, since it has remained in position ever since, the need of repair has been realized. I have not yet received notice of what is intended but understand that the Ministry's immediate problem is financial.

In no. 2 Little Cloister the top floor has been converted into a flat for one of the masters at the Choir School.

The porter's lodge was redecorated throughout and much work carried out at the Almshouses[10] – renewal of all windows on the north side, repairs to chimneys, slating and gutters, and re-decorating.

College Garden

Pointing of the gabled brick coping to the precinct wall has been continued throughout the year by our staff; on the south boundary it is complete, on the east boundary complete only on the garden side. By preventing water from seeping down into the masonry below and aggravating trouble in what is already none too sound, this job has been well worthwhile: it may be thought also to have improved the appearance of the wall.

Large fractures in the wall, where the greenhouse abuts on it, and in the length between the north east corner and air raid shelter, are a cause of some anxiety. Although of long standing they appeared to me last summer to be getting bigger and further tell-tales were fixed to permit of observation. A regular check on them for several months past has not in fact indicated any movement, but the wall is certainly precarious and sooner or later may have to be partially rebuilt.

In particular it will be necessary to watch the junction of the wall with the air raid shelter. Without record drawings of the latter to indicate its construction, there is no means of knowing whether it was bonded to the wall or merely built up against it. That there is a tendency for the two to pull apart, probably because the great weight of the shelter may be causing it to settle slightly, is evident in the north east corner where a wide cement joint has opened vertically. While this could be attributed to the excessive hardness of cement depriving it of flexibility and adhesive power, I think it more likely that the cause is settlement in the air raid shelter.

Staff

With the experience gained after a first year as Clerk of Works, Mr Andrews would like to be able to build up the staff to meet what will be the most pressing needs of the future. The engagement of an extra mason has already been of benefit. If it is possible to have two more he believes that they could be found.

The purchase of a larger saw, recommended in last year's report, has recently been negotiated.

The re-employment of two painters on our staff has been approved in principle and I hope it may soon be possible to act on this. There will be no difficulty in keeping them constantly supplied with work.

It would also be desirable to find extra labourers. At present the staff is overweighted with men who have to be given light jobs but whose health is too uncertain to render them fully useful. Occasions continually occur when, because of sickness, there is a shortage of unskilled men who can be deployed on tasks of a necessary but relatively simple kind.

Reports on the apprentice mason, who attends the Brixton school of Building periodically for a fortnight and for night classes, have been notably good.

Mason's Yard

As repair of stonework will in the coming years become the main occupation of our building staff, the need of a larger mason's yard grows more urgent. The present one is not only small and awkwardly shaped but, being most of it unroofed, provides little shelter for the men. For an appendage to the Abbey in a by no means obscure position the poor and makeshift appearance of the existing enclosure is unworthy.

With no other site available there is no choice but to consider such improvements as might be possible on the present one. Some increase in size could be gained if the yard were extended eastwards – to the end of the south aisle of Henry VII's chapel. This would be tolerable only if it were enclosed with a stone wall, of plain ashlar without windows, rising no higher than the high plinth of the chapel which is itself of different stone to that of the elaborately panelled walling above. Such a wall would permit the construction of a flat roof with sky lights set flush in it and thus provide a covered workshop.

Although on this side the plinth of Henry VII's chapel would be hidden, it would remain visible elsewhere; and in so far as its stone, which is deteriorating, would here be protected from the weather, its life would be prolonged.

To continue the wall built some years ago when lavatories were formed closed to Poets' Corner door would in any case be desirable. My design at that time showed it extending as far as the Chapter House buttress and its truncated length has ever since looked unfinished. A new wall flanking Henry VII's chapel would be less high but, being similarly of ashlar, is the kind of job that could be executed by our men. To any such scheme it is not difficult to anticipate objections that might be raised. But in the circumstances that exist I believe that it offers the only practicable solution.

Tidiness

The east and north walks of the cloister have been cleared of the unsightly accumulation of builders' materials and other unwanted objects that had disfigured it for too long. But the nuisance of litter, within the Abbey and outside, calls for mention yet again.

To visitors from countries where better standards prevail it must surely seem surprising that even Westminster Abbey should have to exhibit evidence of what has become one of the social sins of the English – an utter indifference to visual decency. Enjoyment of the cloisters and the Little Cloisters cannot but be marred by finding waste paper thrown down or blowing about on the grass. The approach to Poets' Corner is worse.

I realise the difficulties but still feel that a patrol at regular intervals – say three times a day – should not be impossible to arrange. One man could easily clean up round the cloisters, Dark cloister and Little Cloister in 15 minutes or less.

With this subject may be linked the growing number of pigeons that nest and roost on the Abbey. The cost of treating with pigeon deterrent the upper part of the building may for the present preclude any attempt to banish them from the innumerable ledges and recesses that they haunt; but it is becoming essential to drive them from the cloisters. Fouling of the tablets has been getting worse and entails a wasteful use of time and labour on subsequent cleaning.

Surrounding buildings

However depressing a close to this report, indignation must be expressed over the erection in Horseferry road of three monstrous office blocks that architecturally are a disgrace to London and the City of Westminster in particular. Inhuman and endlessly repetitive they have already risen so high as to dwarf everything else in the neighbourhood. College Garden not merely now seems smaller; its charm has been impaired because these horrors intrude upon the skyline. They are even visible from Old Palace Yard. That such an outrage could have been permitted, without a thought for the effect of such high buildings on a vicinity which includes the Abbey and the House of Parliament as well as the beautiful 18th century quarter of Smith Square and its adjacent streets, seems as incredible as it is shameful.

S.E. Dykes Bower, Surveyor of the Fabric

March 1968

[1]   Correspondence with this firm for 1966–72 is in WAM S/3/15–16.
[2]   Some of this was given away to other institutions, including Portmeirion in North Wales.
[3]   Canewdon is an Abbey living in Essex. The lobby doors below were also later displaced by glass doors and are in the Abbey Reserve Collection.

4   The Keeper of Muniments and Assistant, respectively.
5   This tomb received damage when the huge James Watt statue was put in this chapel in the
      nineteenth century and the tomb slab had to be replaced then.
6   Henry Keepe's manuscript, Library MS.45.
7   These were the coats of arms of the Queen, Duke of Edinburgh and Queen Mother and
      the Royal cypher, which hung in front of the Royal gallery or on the annexe table in 1953.
      They were cleaned in 2014 and are displayed in the Queen's Diamond Jubilee Galleries.
8   The house in which organist Dr James Turle lived at the north-east corner of Little Dean's
      Yard was pulled down in the 1880s, but the school retained the name in their new building
      on the site.
9   London County Council.
10   In Fentiman Road, Lambeth (these replaced some originally in the Westminster area).

74.   WAM S/1/113

Westminster Abbey – The Presbytery roof

[undated but sent to the Dean on 10 December 1968]

1. To aid their deliberations on the future treatment of this roof the Dean and
Chapter commissioned reports from four independent advisers: two architects,
with experience of old buildings, and two engineers, sympathetic to historical
and archaeological considerations. The architects were Mr Bernard Feilden,
FRIBA, architect to York Minster and Norwich cathedral and Mr Alan Reed,
ARIBA of the Society for the Protection of Ancient Buildings; the engineers
Mr P.C.G. Hausser, nominated by the President of the Institution of Civil
Engineers, and Dr Jacques Heyman of the Department of Engineering,
Cambridge University and Fellow of Peterhouse. Dr Heyman is the author of
various publications on medieval roofs of which he has made a close study.[1]

A specialist report on the use of epoxy resin repairs has been obtained
from Mr J.D.N. Shaw of Shell Research Limited. Mr McKenny Hughes,
Entomological Adviser to the Dean and Chapter and Mr Andrews, Clerk of
Works to the Abbey, have submitted memoranda on particular aspects of this
problem.

The Dean and Chapter have interviewed all those invited to submit reports,
giving them an opportunity to expound their views further, if desired, and to
answer questions.

2. That the roof over the presbytery and apse gives cause for concern may
be deduced from the following description of its condition in a report dated
November 9th 1964 by Mr McDowell of the Royal Commission on Historical
Monuments. 'The presbytery roof is of 13th century origin but has been extensively repaired. All the original tie beams have been spliced and plated with later
timber and on them have been built up trusses carrying bearers under the old
lower collars. All the original frames are leaning over westwards towards the
tower and longitudinal strutting has been introduced to counter this. All the
feet of all the frames have been patched or shortened and all the wall plates

have been renewed or reset. None of the present ashlar pieces is original. The presbytery roof has 28 full frames in which half the rafters have been extensively repaired, many with splints rather roughly bolted in, and 13 frames in a run of 15 have suffered so severely from worm in the newer wood as well as in the old that they would be quite unsafe were it not for shores under them. All the rafters are bowed either from sagging or from the feet spreading. The westward tilt has caused trouble in the apse: the collar beam across the chord which takes the lower end of the post, into which the half frames are housed, is broken, and some of the strutting to the apse rafters is either handing free or held in place by boards nailed on. Worm attack throughout the whole roof has caused quite serious damage …. With a span of some 35 feet and a pitch of 60° the frames are impressive by their size, but the carpentry is not of outstanding quality, the chief interest is in the management of the radial frames round the apse'

3. The section on The Present Condition of the Roof in the report by Mr Hausser confirms and amplifies Mr McDowell's observations.

'The roof members show very serious deterioration from the action of death watch beetle and of rot from damp unventilated positions such as at the wall plates, lower ends of rafters and the end of ties. Hardly a single rafter on the south side is sound. In addition to deterioration from beetle attack, many are fractured and with open joints at the junction of collars and scissor bracing. Wall plates, particularly the outer one, are so decayed that they are practically useless. The main tie beams show decay at their ends which has much reduced their effectiveness as ties to the walls. Inadequate support to the feet of the rafters has allowed them to spread with consequent serious bowing and splitting at the junction of scissor bracing. The extent of this bowing can best be seen by looking down the rafters from ridge level. The north side is in rather better condition than the south but suffers seriously from similar defects. The wall plates are in better condition than on the south side and appear to have been renewed. All the frames except no. 1, are about 3 feet out of plumb in their height, leaning to the west. This imposes additional stresses on all joints particularly at frame 28 which has to take the thrust westward from the framing at the curved end of the apse. The lower collar here is completely fractured just south of the king post. Due to the bowing of the rafters much firring up on their top surface has been necessary to provide a reasonably straight line for the battens and lead covering'

4. Dr Heyman is critical of the construction. 'A tie beam was provided for every seventh or eighth truss, the inner wall plate being tenoned into the ties. These ties were apparently quite inadequate, since in most of the frames the feet have spread and the rafters are bowed … The basic triangulation of the roofs was to a satisfactory pattern. The design and construction of ties to absorb the thrust of the rafters was poor. Individual joint details are not very good and there was almost complete failure to provide longitudinal bracing. This failure is evident above all in the apsidal end of the presbytery roof, where the half frames

have almost meaningless structural functions and where there is no deliberate provision for the relatively large longitudinal forces that must of necessity be engendered by the form of construction. These longitudinal forces are in fact carried, accidentally, by the sheeting battens'.

5. Mr Feilden noted 'The death watch beetle attack also seemed to be particularly bad in the structural joints. There was rot in the wall plates and ends of the rafters particularly and many cracks, splits, loose or sprung joints and fractures, all of which has been recorded'. His drawings showing the extent of defects in the timbers are valuable evidence of the proportion of unsound to sound timber.

Mr Reed on the other hand says 'I was surprised to find so little evidence of death watch beetle in a roof of this extent and age'.

6. All the lead on the high pitched roofs of the Abbey was, after more than two hundred years, due for repair and relaying. On the nave and transepts this relaying has been completed; the lead on the presbytery was removed earlier this year for recasting. Because it should last another equally long period and any need to carry out subsequent repairs during that period must so far as possible be avoided, the safety of the wooden structure that carried it should be secured before it goes back.

7. It is right first to consider whether the existing roof structure can be made sound enough to ensure that aim. What has already been quoted indicates not only that the roof has given trouble in the past, as far back as the time of Wren's surveyorship and also subsequently, but that it cannot in fact be regarded today as complying with standards of safety that should apply to a building too valuable to be exposed to any unavoidable risk. This aspect of the matter is relevant because the City Engineer of Westminster has intimated that, unless appropriate measures are taken, he might have to serve a Dangerous Structure Notice.

8. Mr Feilden outlines a scheme for laying over the rafters of the roof trusses three layers of Douglas fir diagonal boarding to stiffen and hold the structure, now all leaning westwards, in conjunction with the insertion of new concrete edge beams and ties to replace the oak wall plates and tie beams.

Preliminary measures would be the entire elimination of beetle attack; the renewal of selected timbers and joints; the consolidation and restoration of the remainder by filling them where rotten or hollow with epoxy resin; if necessary the addition of an inconspicuous steel space frame to support the trusses at mid span.

He would favour removal of the 18th and 19th century wooden members, some of them of soft wood, which have been added and 'spoil the clarity of the original structure'.

This approach he describes as 'empirical as the design cannot be fully calculated' and 'desirable on architectural, historic and economic grounds as it would retain the original structure in position'.

9. Mr Alan Reed, advocating repair of the roof in situ says 'There is no lack of mechanical strength either in the design or in the condition of the timbers and the whole could be repaired in situ without loss of its essential features. Very little splicing is needed and the few decayed joints and hollow portions in rafters etc., can be filled with polyester or epoxy resin cements … Elsewhere strength or security can be obtained by bolting mild steel plates suitably sheradized to the timbers … I assume that a reinforced concrete ring beam will be inserted in the wall tops both to strengthen the masonry of the apse and to provide a sound anchorage for the rafter feet and wall plates'.

10. Basic to Mr Feilden's proposals is the addition of longitudinal stiffening through the application of treble (or at least double) diagonal boarding to form a stressed skin on the upper surface of the rafters. Mr Reed would seem to rely on diagonal battens only to achieve that object.

11. Both are in accord on the provision of reinforced concrete ring beams (e.g. wall plates) and tie beams, and on the use of epoxy resin to consolidate decayed and hollow timbers.

12. The principle of providing firm foundations to the feet of the rafters and spreading the vertical loading of the roof evenly over the walls by means of concrete ring beams connected at intervals with ties is, indeed, common to all four reports. But neither Mr Feilden nor Mr Reed prescribe a method of inserting them with the existing roof in situ. This in my opinion would be not merely a difficult, but a hazardous operation. The stonework at the top of the walls has itself spalled in places and would have to be rebuilt before any ring beam could be placed on top. If to gain adequate access space for working an attempt were made to jack up the rafters, strain on the roof joints would be increased and, conceivably, some the rafters in their present state might break up altogether. It may be agreed that, with the triple diagonal boarding fixed first, the risk at any rate would be reduced. But still an undertaking would not be easy, nor I am convinced that it would be feasible.* see pages 5 and 6 of Mr Andrew's report.

13. If, moreover, the existing roof is to be left undisturbed, repair of its defective timbers by the use of epoxy resin would also have to be carried out in situ. Here the opinion of Mr Shaw may be quoted: 'From a close examination of the decaying beams I would consider that it is probably not practicable to carry out a structural repair on the beams in situ using epoxy resin, but without carrying out extensive tests it is not possible to give a definite opinion. A repair which would prevent further decay and give some additional strength could be carried out in situ but the work would be extremely slow and laborious … If the roof can be dismantled it should not be a too difficult job to carry out a reasonable epoxy resin repair on the individual beams'.

14. This question of what can effectively be done if the roof is not to be dismantled must be regarded as crucial. There are two processes to be taken into account. First the elimination of the death watch beetle entirely, as

recommended by Mr Fielden. On this the entomological adviser comments '(Mr Fielden) stresses that there is a very heavy attack and that many of the beams are hollow. I agree with him on this last statement but the total elimination of all grubs etc. in situ is not the easiest thing in the world. We should have to apply Flame Retardant Woodtreat in a very heavy dosage before the epoxy resin, and possibly fibre glass sheeting, could be applied. We know by experience that Woodtreat has very deep penetrating qualities entering the side grain of Henry III oak to a depth of up to half an inch with one application. Applied to end grain the penetration is near one inch. Nevertheless, it would be a very rash consulting entomologist who would predict that every single egg, grub, pupa or adult would be eliminated though it would be likely that any beetle that managed to emerge thereafter would be killed, nor would they be likely to attach such timber again'.

15. Apart from the fact that opportunities for end grain application would necessarily be few if the roof were maintained in position, this may be taken as adequate assurance that renewed beetle activity need not be a serious threat, particularly since resin filled timber is immune from it.

On the other hand the indispensable preliminary to resin repair is complete removal of all loose dust and particles of decayed wood residual in the timber that beetles have bored and eaten. This would have to be blown out with a compressed air jet through holes drilled for the purpose. Could a perfect job be ensured if this process had to be carried out to the timbers, not as separate members, but as components of a jointed structure, in which the joints themselves are known to have been weakened by beetle attack?

While the timbers would be strengthened wherever epoxy resin filled them, if at some points the degree of filling had to be uncertain, the efficacy of the treatment could not be guaranteed. A roof of such steep pitch (60 degrees) is subject to very strong wind pressure and a gale of exceptional force may cause it to flex, as did the sonic boom tests carried out over London. However tough the bulk of the roof timbers might be made by epoxy resin, if stresses occasioned by violent wind or sudden shock caused salient joints to fracture, the consequences could be serious. If movement of this kind occurred early on, during the cure period of the epoxy resin composition, the strength reinforcement of the structure would be nullified at the start.

16. There is furthermore the disadvantage that, while resin repairs are ideally carried out at a temperature of 60–70 degrees Fahrenheit and preferably not below 50 degrees F, the temperature at the height of his roof, exposed to the open air, cannot be controlled. 'At lower temperatures' to quote Mr Shaw 'the cure of resin systems is extremely slow and systems cured at low temperatures tend to have poorer mechanical strength'. If work were done in the summer this difficulty might not be insuperable. But conditions on the roof could not be as satisfactory as, for example, in the Library where epoxy resin repair was adopted for internal localized repairs on a much smaller scale, to a roof of

flatter pitch. There it was possible to control the temperature but even so the work took longer than as anticipated.

17. The alternative of dismembering the roof so that each timber could be treated individually, while it might promote the efficiency of the resin repair, would be contrary to the wish to preserve the roof intact, implicit in both Mr Feilden's and Mr Reed's recommendations. Resin repair is best justified as a serviceable expedient for restoring strength to what has lost it, where this can be done effectively without structural interference.

18. What in this instance has to be weighed is its suitability for a large steeply-pitched roof of which a long life must be demanded. The chance that in situ application might give less than perfect results has been mentioned. Speed and cost are difficult to forecast but awkward working conditions, unavoidable in this roof, would in my opinion preclude very rapid progress and the cost for that reason might prove high. I doubt whether Mr Feilden's expectation, given verbally, that the whole job would take no more than six months could possibly be realised. He is right in saying that 'it would be difficult to control costs and obtain rough estimates'.

19. It must be remembered too that, though the technique of epoxy resin has been widely used in recent years, it is still new and has not been tested over any great length of time. It may well survive that test. Yet is it possible that such a substance, in spite of being chemically inert, could alter in a hundred years or more if the future brought atomic radiation and much else besides?

20. To draw attention to practical matters that might cause perplexity in execution is not to be unsympathetic to the desire to keep the present roof. Given its present state a remedy must be sought as best it can. There must however be recognition that its defects are palpable; that they arose originally from faults of design; that expedients in the past to correct what was wrong have confused such simplicity as the original structure possessed; and that, before the lead is put back, it is essential that the roof over that part of the Abbey church that comprises the Sacrarium with its medieval tombs and sedilia, and the Confessor's chapel with his Shrine and the royal tombs, is going to be so sound as to leave no room for anxiety.

21. Historically the interest of the roof is twofold. Documentary information throws light on its beginning and later alterations. Though that portion which covers the Presbytery is in no way unique, that over the apse is the only example of its kind in England because the apses of Norwich, Peterborough and Lichfield have relatively low-pitched roofs. In France, where apses are numerous, there must be many parallels.

Yet this apse roof does not exhibit special skill in carpentry. Dr Heyman writes of it 'It would seem that the apsidal end of the roof was not considered as a separate structural problem; that is, the same design (as over the Presbytery) is applied to the trusses of the apse. Essentially, each apse truss is a standard truss cut in half, and framed in towards the centre of the last plane truss, no. 28, which is provided with a king post to receive the half collars and scissor beams. Thus the whole of the roughly semi-circular end of the roof is centred on the king post of truss 28.

If a truss is cut in half in this way then it must be propped horizontally at the apex and at the collar beam if it is to remain in position. If the rafter carried a total roof load of about 1 ton then the collar beam thrust required is about 0.30 ton, with perhaps half this force at the apex. These are figures for an individual half frame in the apse. All the half frames together will combine to thrust westward with a force of about 4 ton at collar beam level and again with about half this force at the apex. These large forces must somehow be provided by reactions from the rest of the presbytery roof.

In the original structure the force of 4 ton could only be resisted by lateral bending of the collar beams of truss 28. This collar beam, however, is a member suited only to carrying axial load, and it is no surprise to find it broken (at a section weakened by halving).

Further, the scissor beam should come into play under wind loading on the roof. The scissor beams are framed, however, into the king post, which can resist neither lateral nor vertical forces.

The whole of the framing of the apse roof is, in fact, basically unsound. The king post in particular is a ludicrous attempt to solve a structural problem (whose existence, of course, may not have been suspected); it may be unique in English medieval roofs but it is neither *bello* nor *lodevole*. There seems to have been no appreciation at all that large longitudinal forces must arise from the type of framing used. (The almost contemporary roof of Notre Dame, Paris made elaborate provision to absorb and distribute the out of balance thrust)'.

22. There is, then, this point to consider. Should what is faulty be deemed inviolate because it is the original construction? Does age warrant indefinite perpetuation of error?

Were respect for history to be interpreted, architecturally, as insistence upon the 'original' alone being regarded as 'authentic' how much would in fact have disappeared by now? Building materials, like human beings, are not immortal. Some may last a very long time; but, as age and decay taken their toll, restoration – right restoration – may be necessary to save them. Authenticity is lost beyond recall when only the shadow, not the substance survives. If all evidence of detail, all clue to what was in the designer's mind perishes, the deprivation is final and knowledge curtailed.

23. The actual materials, valuable and to be revered, tell only a part: they are the flesh, not the spirit. The inherent artistic and intellectual quality in the works of the past is what is of supreme importance. In a world where not everything can be preserved the strongest claim must always be for what was well conceived rather than for what was aberrant. The successes, not the failures, should be honoured.

24. Through lack of experience in handling something that had not been

attempted in this country before, the builder of the Westminster roof did fail in respect of the apse. His skill was not equal to the task. Elsewhere, in the words of Mr Hausser 'the present form of roof is for its purpose still 'good modern practice' and a structurally sound design'. The intrinsic scheme of trussed rafters with two collar beams, scissor braces and knee braces was well conceived but, as Dr Heyman observes, its physical construction poor. There was omission to provide enough longitudinal stiffening, some of the joints were weak in design as well as difficult to execute, the tie beams and wall plates were inadequate to prevent lateral spreading of the frames.

25. The original builder could not know that his oak wall plates might eventually succumb to rot and beetle attack. Nor could he be expected to start with such knowledge as later ages have gained through experience.

Must it now be rational for a later age to abjure what has been learnt since and to deny to what did not quite achieve success the justice of doing so fully?

26. It is first necessary to grasp what the original designer was trying to do. Second by the most appropriate means to fulfil his aim and ensure its permanence.

Stone is still stone, oak is still oak. These materials can still be used as suitably today as in the past, with only a change to something else if there is convincing reason for it.

27. Dr Heyman's conclusion is a pertinent endorsement 'In the nave the new concrete ring beams connected at intervals by steel joist ties exactly realise the intention of the medieval designers, an intention that they signally failed to realise themselves in using timber wall plates inadequately connected to timber ties. With absolutely firm foundations provided in this way to the feet of the rafters, the basically good triangulation of the trusses will ensure a satisfactory structure. Had it not been wished to restore precisely the original form of truss, then some strengthening could have been achieved by a type of joint alternative to the original halvings. There is little need for heavy longitudinal stiffening and the use of diagonal battens will have produced a far sounder structure than the original in this respect. These remarks apply equally to the transept roofs. In the presbytery the same kind of restoration can be applied to trusses nos. 1 to 27. The apsidal end, however, requires special consideration. The original framing can only be classed as amateur and there seems little point in restoring as a curiosity a roof which is structurally offensive. It would seem preferable to make a new simple design for the apsidal end in which the thrusts in the roof are self balancing. This may well involve the combination of timber compression members and light metal ties'.

28. That there are two approaches to this problem will now be clear. The care of old buildings induces a bias of inclination that is properly and almost inevitably towards preserving whatever is of worth, towards losing nothing that can fittingly be kept. Nowhere is it likely to be more impelling than at Westminster Abbey. The very sense of continuity, however, instinct in corporate bodies and

which engenders reverence for the past, also must take thought for the future. In what condition is the building to be handed on? What will be its structural safety? Should potential sources of trouble be bequeathed to successors?

Such questions demand a balance of sentiment and realism. Has this roof over the presbytery and apse, in spite of structural shortcomings, such outstanding historical worth as to justify resort to any means to retain it? Can these means be accepted as reliable for at least one or two centuries? Will the cost of preserving it, not easy to assess, vindicate the result? When three layers of soft wood are placed over its trusses, its oak members are largely filled with epoxy resin, its joints made good by the addition of mild steel plates, the oak wall plated and tie beams replaced by reinforced concrete, how far will it really be the roof as left by the original builders? If it is the stressed skin that will chiefly be holding it, will it have been preserved or mummified?

Would a new oak structure, also on a foundation of concrete ties and wall plates but conforming to the original design, be aesthetically and historically rational or the reverse? Is it wrong in the present age to do what has been done before, with only such changes as technical advances direct? May greater convenience for ease of inspection and upkeep, as well as freedom of movement for fire fighting in an emergency, be an advantage of practical benefit? Is structural simplicity preferable to the medley of struts and supports that, as a result of repairs, have confused the existing roof?

29. These are some (by no means all) of the facts of this problem which must influence decision. It is relevant to bear in mind that, being over 100 feet above ground out of sight in the enclosed space above the vaulting and under the outer lead covering, this roof is not accessible to the public and never visited except by the very occasional student.

Surveyor of the Fabric

[1] The various reports including drawings of the condition of the roof trusses are in WAM DF.3. See also WAM S/3/18–19 for correspondence on this roof and some plans.

75.   WAM S/1/114

Annual Report by the Surveyor of the Fabric 1969

Since, when the apse roof is completed, restoration will enter on a new stage and be concentrated on the exterior, I have given my report for this year a slightly different form. The first section is devoted to consideration of a problem which will be uppermost for at least ten years – the repair of the stonework. The second gives the usual, but a rather briefer, summary of work done in the past twelve months.

Part 1

Stone in the Abbey

The stone used for building the Abbey in 1245 was a green sandstone from Surrey, generally known as Reigate although the actual source of supply is thought to have been Godstone, about four miles from that town. Its choice may have been influenced by the relatively short distance for transport, as well as by two properties of the stone itself – ease of working and alleged resistance to fire. Reigate was much used for hearthstones and often referred to as Firestone.

In the same district the lower beds at Merstham yielded the chalk which, cut into small blocks, forms the infilling of the vaults of the choir, the transepts and the cloisters.

How far Caen stone, or some Normandy oolite akin to it, was introduced is not clear because in appearance it differs little from Reigate. A supply of it was ordered in the reign of Henry V and it was being used by Abbot Esteney towards the end of the 15th century. Although Reigate, together with Stapledon and Bere stone from Devonshire, was still being bought for the building of the nave, recourse to Roche Abbey stone by Abbot Litlyngton could indicate that doubts were already entertained about its weathering properties. It may be significant, too, that Abbot Islip in the 15th century employed an Oxfordshire oolite for the base of the north west tower.

What is certain is that the condition of the stone on the exterior had deteriorated so badly by the end of the 17th century that refacing was started by Wren and continued intermittently for the next two hundred years. Experience of Cotswold limestones from work in Oxford may have led Wren to believe that they could be used with equal success in London. That known at the time as Burford or Taynton was tried by him at the Abbey with results that presumably were unsatisfactory since Hawksmoor, raising the west towers from where Wren left off, changed to Portland and initiated its adoption for external renewals over the next hundred years.

Though resistant to the London atmosphere Portland, with its white colour and compact grain, is less suited to Gothic than to classical design: much of the refaced area of the Abbey manifests itself as not original through the scale of the jointing and smooth texture of the stone. But while, with so much old and perished stone to be replaced, its selection was justified and even right, the consequences were prejudicial to the aspect of the building. The exterior of the Abbey is magnificent in mass and composition but its masonry cannot compare with that of, for example, Lincoln where the original stone still remains. Beside it Westminster's would look hard and mechanical.

When in the 19th century Gothic came to be studied afresh the importance of quality and texture in materials, as well as correct detail in design, received more attention. The restoration of Henry VII's chapel was an early instance. The high plain plinth of the Chapel was built of what today is called Kentish Rag – a stone not dissimilar to Reigate. The panelled walling above was of

Huddlestone stone from Yorkshire; Caen was used for the vaulting. Because decay of these materials had progressed so far that complete refacing was essential, Dean Vincent turned for financial aid to the Government of the time. The requisite money was granted by Parliament and the work carried out by the Abbey staff under James Wyatt, the Surveyor of the Fabric, Jeremiah Glanville, the Clerk of the Works, and Thomas Gayfere, chief mason.

Careful investigation was made into the suitability of different building stone and the report of evidence quoted in the preface of Cottingham's book of measured drawings of the Chapel is of interest.[1] That Portland stone was no longer favoured and Bath (Coomb Down) selected was due to a new percipience that, for rich Gothic elaboration, the former would be less appropriate than a limestone of warmer colour and more open grain.

Aesthetically the decision was right: when new, and so long as it remained clean, the stone must have looked well. Had it been regularly washed it might also have lasted well. But not until the restoration of the Chapel under Sir Walter Tapper in 1935 was the stone as last cleaned – a timely action without which it would have been in worse state than it is, yet too late to undo the trouble that had already started.

It may have been because the refaced Chapel displayed the contrast of the new Bath stone with Portland that the latter did not return to favour for so long. Various stones tried in the 19th century gave little permanent satisfaction. Scott experimented with Tadcaster in the west walk of the cloisters, Ketton and Mansfield Woodhouse in the south. The buttresses on the north side of the nave were re-cased in Bath stone, which Pearson used also for the North Transept front. In places Tisbury, Chilmark, Anston and other stones may be found incorporated in the fabric, but rarely in a condition that does them credit.

There was nothing amateurish about Gayfere's work on Henry VII's chapel. At a time when Gothic had hardly received serious study or been recognized as an architectural language with a grammar of its own, it is remarkable that the utmost trouble should have been taken to ascertain and perpetuate the original design. This, instead of being modified or 'improved', was faithfully respected, even though the execution of much of the detail must have compelled the masons and carvers to learn almost a new technique. The spirit in which the restoration was carried out was in advance of contemporary practice so that the principles of the Gothic Revival were being put into practice at Westminster before they were formally promulgated by Pugin and others. Something similar was seen a few years later when Blore was designing the west front of the pulpitum and the choir stalls with grammatical correctness before Gothic grammar had been codified.

It was natural that later, under the influence of the Gothic Revival, the aim should have been to give back to the Abbey as much as possible of what would have been its original appearance. This meant reversing the policy of Hawksmoor and succeeding surveyors who, confronted with widespread decay, were more concerned for a sound structure than solicitous for what remained of medieval detail. In the angle of the south transept and presbytery remodelled windows and pinnacles show how crude could be the result. Such architectural solecisms must have horrified Scott and Pearson to whom, since other existing windows afforded clear evidence of the original form, they would have seemed unpardonable.

Increased care for architectural scholarship may have caused attention to be diverted from what was happening to the stone through which it was expressed. Yet, even on some of the new work, signs of trouble were developing with an alarming rapidity that could not be indefinitely ignored.

As the superiority of Portland stone for general use in London became clearer Lethaby recognized that, even at the Abbey, there would have to be a return to its use. It reappeared in the north clerestory parapet of the nave, which he rebuilt, and in some of the pinnacles of Henry VII's chapel, though these have recently had to be removed as unsafe. Tapper used it in rebuilding the east parapets of the transepts and several pinnacles and flying buttresses. The clerestory parapets of the south side of the nave and west side of the south transept and other works of the last 15 years have tended to make Portland the predominant stone of the exterior and to further its adoption for future renewals.

The existing Bath stone of Henry VII's chapel, however, does not call for wholesale replacement; and on the north side of the nave, if washed and repaired where necessary, it should last a fair time. Being chiefly ashlar, the north aisle buttresses have not suffered as severely as the intricate front of the north transept which requires such extensive refacing that a change to Portland would be advisable. The front of the south transept, it may be noted, is already of Portland.

Dirt has stained and discoloured the walls of the Abbey in a way that partially conceals variations in the stone of which different portions are built. If washed, the large amount of Portland would be more obvious and the prevailing colour more nearly resemble the whiteness of the upper part of the west towers, the central tower, the clerestory parapets and the south west turret of the south transept. This would not be uniform because some areas, chiefly on the south side, contain an admixture of other stones that might remain for years and are distinguishable by a browner tone. Greater homogeneity of colour should however enhance the architecture, just as the design would gain if black patches of decaying stone ceased to confuse the intended pattern of light and shade that it is the purpose of mouldings and projections to impart.

Condition of the Stone

What has caused the failure of the stonework, now so serious all over the exterior? The ruinous condition of the cloisters is visible at close quarters but defects higher up on so large and lofty a building are too distant to attract notice. Yet there is probably no great church in this country where stone decay is more ubiquitous.

The Reigate stone, well preserved internally, could not stand up to damp and weather externally. A little of it surviving in the sides of the north nave buttresses and eroded to a depth of four or five inches, gives some idea of why replacement was unavoidable and how it is that so little medieval masonry remains on the Abbey exterior. When London gradually spread along the north bank of the Thames and enveloped Westminster a new danger developed from domestic smoke. The growing metropolis became composed of narrow, tightly packed streets of houses and the Abbey itself surrounded, not by large open spaces as now, but by houses that on the north and west clustered close up to its walls. Scarcely had new stone taken the place of what had perished than the soot from countless chimneys must have begun to affect it. This was probably the cause of the Cotswold limestones that Wren introduced proving unsuccessful. Portland stone did not succumb so readily but from the start was subjected to conditions that ultimately could not fail to be deleterious. As the high soot content in the air begrimed all wall surfaces, danger spots tended to be obscured, for it is under the projection of string course, deeply cut mouldings and carvings, which rain water cannot cleanse, that trouble begins. Soot clings to these and in wet weather becomes damp without getting dislodged. As acid moisture slowly oozes down from it decay starts in the stone below and, all over the exterior, most of the damage originated in this way.

Despite all that was done deterioration outstripped repair. As the face of London building of any age darkened, blackened stone work had come to be accepted as normal: the different attitude of today to its unsightliness is of quite recent growth. Yet if realization of the consequences of exposing stone to what must destroy it was slow in coming, apprehension was increasing over the state of the Abbey. In 1901 a Commission consisting of the Surveyor of the Fabric, Micklethwaite, two other architects G.F. Bodley and W.D. Caroe, and two scientists was appointed to examine and report on the stonework. Their conclusion that decay was caused by acids in the atmosphere of London and becoming increasingly progressive through the liability of the partially destroyed stone to absorb them, was accompanied by a recommendation for treating the stone with successive applications of baryta water.[2]

It is difficult now to find out whether or how far this treatment was ever carried out. In view of the extent of the trouble, and since it was thought that as many as nine applications might be necessary, the probability is that it was totally impracticable.

Another report, obtained twenty years later, from Professor Desch of Sheffield university, recommended magnesium silicofluoride as a preservative. Lethaby himself experimented with limewash in the cloisters and applied it to the whole of the north transept front, which for some time stood out startlingly white against the rest of the building. Little permanent benefit seems to have accrued: disease of the stone was too advanced to respond to palliatives.

After two hundred years much of the Portland was itself suffering from exfoliation and the policy of dressing back the stone, where this occurred, to a hard surface afforded neither prevention nor cure; the cause of it still operated and the same trouble merely began again. Had it been possible to wash the stone early enough this – certainly in many places – could have been avoided. Now washing would merely cause much of the stone to disintegrate entirely and do more harm than good. If all defective stones could first be cut out and renewed washing would be a profitable sequel and prolong the life of the stone by removal of all acid deposits.

There can be little expectation that the process of decay will cease to be continuous. In spite of smokeless zones chemical impurities in the air of London are active and said to be increasing: it seems unlikely that any betterment in this respect can be looked for. The objective can only put to put the walls of the Abbey into the best possible condition so that measures can be taken to safeguard the stone from again falling victim to known causes of damage. The stonework should be kept clean by periodical washing; but it cannot be washed at all until it has been repaired.

The cloisters require separate mention because disintegration of the stone in the south and west walks is due partly to what has been described, partly to a mistake inherent in the structure. The banding of the vaulting, which is so attractive a feature of the choir and transept roofs internally, is produced by strips of Reigate sandstone set at intervals in the white chalk blocks that comprise the infilling. Protected from the weather this combination of materials has given no trouble. But, doubtless for its decorative effect, it was repeated in the cloisters where condensation is frequent. Moisture and water running over the stone are rendered chemically active by carbonic and sulphuric acids in the air of London. The interaction of sulphuric acid and chalk causes calcium sulphate to form which, percolating into the porous Reigate stone, crystallises as gypsum and causes sandstone to flake away and rot.

This accounts for the deplorable state not only of the vaulting ribs and their supporting shafts and capitals but of the ashlar of the inner walls. The former have lost all trace of their intended shape, the latter crumbles away at a touch. Restoration of glass to the tracery of the windows has been of some benefit; but the sun can never reach the south walk and the west to only a small extent, so that drying out after a wet spell is slow. On the north and east side, though much stone decay has occurred, the deterioration is not so severe and these two walks suffer less from condensation. As an interim measure limewashing was carried out in them a few years ago with results that have been satisfactory; it will have to be repeated at intervals if these are to remain so. Tests have also been carried out with various silicone treatments on portions of stone kept under observation.

The naturally porous Reigate stone has thus been subject in the cloisters not just to damp caused by condensation but to chemically injurious damp. This cannot be remedied until either the limestone or the sandstone is eradicated. In a report obtained from Professor Whittard of Bristol university in 1954 the results of tests into the properties of seven different stones were set out. One recommendation – that all the Reigate must be removed – was emphatic; the other, advocating Clipsham stone for the walling, has already been followed in the one bay where the inner wall has been refaced and will be adhered to for the others when they can be done. For the shafts, of which a good number have just been made and fixed by our own masons, Portland has been used.

In the windows to the cloister garth washing of the stonework, renewed by Blore and Scott, was carried out about 15 years ago. It has prevented incipient decay getting worse and greatly helped to preserve the stone.

Conditions in the vaulted bays leading from the main cloister to Dean's Yard and under the archway to the Deanery courtyard are generally similar. In the latter is an extreme instance of what erosion by wind and draught can do to stone.

The repair of the stone

From what has been written it will be seen that repair of the external stonework of the Abbey is essential and long overdue. The number of masons on the building staff is inadequate for an undertaking that would be uneconomic if slow progress entailed a wasteful use of scaffolding. Masonry of the kind required cannot be hurried but unless it were possible to keep enough work going continuously the job would be endless, with the probability of rising costs augmenting expenditure.

An estimate for the restoration of the cloisters, first prepared by an experienced masonry firm in 1966 and now brought up to date comes to £124,800 for the 31 bays including the vaulting. The cost of restoring the archway to the Deanery courtyard by our own staff is estimated at £1,500 but by the time the work is done may have slightly increased. Restoration of the vaulted bays between the south cloister and Dean's Yard has not been estimated but £12,000 is a likely figure.

It would not of course be necessary to do all four sides of the cloisters at the same time. Since the south and west which together comprise 18 bays would have to be tackled first and 3 bays on average might take 6 months, the work would extend over 3 years. The passage to Deans Yard, if it followed, could lengthen this by another year. At the end of that time the condition of the north and east cloisters could be re-assessed and work started or deferred as required.

Restoration of the cloisters should be regarded as independent of that of the main fabric and not necessarily carried out by the same firm. No one firm could easily handle simultaneously two jobs so large and each equally urgent.

In the last two years a thorough examination has been made of the external stonework of the Abbey and photographs taken of all major defects; these with descriptive notes to accompany them provide a comprehensive record of the state of the building. From the roofs much could previously be seen to be wrong in positions out of reach for inspection. The information gained from this survey, partly carried out from scaffolding and with the aid of steeplejacks, confirms that in almost every case even more is wrong than was suspected. One practical object of the exercise was in fact more than justified by enabling a great amount of loose shaling stonework to be removed it has reduced the fear of accidents.

The range of work that needs to be done can best be appreciated from the close up views in the photographic survey; even the briefest attempt at description would be tedious. But reference must be made to three matters of importance.

In the light of the fuller knowledge now available about the amount of restoration necessary £500,00 was in 1968 calculated to be the minimum approximate expenditure. No figure can be a firm estimate for work that cannot be measured in advance; nor could any figure given today hold good if the work were not carried out for perhaps three or five years. In that period fresh deterioration could occur and thus enlarge the scope of the job.

While, moreover, every effort has been made to arrive at a realistic assessment of cost, it is not easy to determine how the word 'realistic' should be interpreted.

If for example, on the spire of a pinnacle 100 feet above ground, 25 stones were badly decayed, 15 are sound and 10 neither perfect nor imperfect, should their possible future failure be anticipated or should they be left, because not immediately due for replacement? The former course will increase immediate expenditure. The latter may mean either that the work, when due, will not get done, so neutralizing in some degree the virtues of the other repairs; or that scaffolding will have to be erected afresh at high cost that could have been avoided. This problem, specially relevant to a building of the size of the Abbey, must be foreseen and is almost bound to occur.

Timing is a second point of importance. Masonry work is slow and the supply of skilled men who could tackle what is required limited. Were all the money available it could not be spent at once. £75,000 represents perhaps the largest expenditure that would be feasible in one year by a single firm, taking into account concentration of repairs to avoid wasteful use of scaffolding.

This again introduces a third point. The programme would have to be phased – governed to some extent by considerations of safety, to a lesser extent by the economics of scaffolding. A typical case would be the north transept front. Here is one of the main entrances to the building, extensively used by the public. The accident risk is therefore serious. Repair of the west and east centre pinnacles (those at the base of the main gable) is pressing and its estimated (1968) cost £35,000. But over the whole front very extensive repairs are badly needed. Would it be best, having erected scaffolding to the high level of the pinnacles, to use it for all the work required down to ground level, postponing thereby other urgent repairs elsewhere?

If the public liability risk from seven pinnacles on the buttresses to the north side of the nave is less, their condition is at least as dangerous. Their part rebuilding (1968 estimate) would cost £10,500. 13 pinnacles on the south side buttresses, equally bad, would cost £23,000.

On the south transept work in the sum of £58,000 is needed to three of the large top pinnacles and also due for early attention.

On a more modest scale are precautionary measures such as the removal from the exterior of Henry VII's chapel of fractured crockets and ornamental features that are loose and could fall. The estimated (1968) cost was £600.

These few instances out of many are enough to make clear that it will not be easy or wise to lay down too firm an order of procedure in advance of knowing what resources of money and labour may be available.

Last and vitally important is the basis on which the work would be done. That the execution should be worthy of the Abbey must be the primary aim. There are few firms in this country capable of undertaking Gothic masonry and fewer still with anything more than a minimal staff. For work that, much of it, is quite out of reach for measuring, the system of tendering on a priced bill of quantities would be inapplicable: such a bill, if it could be written at all, would be too hypothetical to be of value.

Careful enquiry should be made into the capacity and commitments of masonry firms with experience of the kind required and a choice made of one who could be entrusted with an agreed schedule of work, which might be the programme for the first year. Results would show in that time whether the choice was a right one. It would be inadvisable to have two different firms engaged simultaneously on the main fabric of the Abbey, though, as already observed, there need be no objection to separate firms for the main fabric and the cloisters.

The Abbey masons could still be fully engaged on routine jobs of which there is a constant succession.

Having regard to what is physically possible – the number of men and the amount of work they could get through – ten years would seem likely to be the minimum duration of the job, and fifteen not improbable.

If £130,000 is estimated for the cloisters and £500,000 for the main fabric, allowance should be made for future cost increases and an adequate contingency sum. The total might approximate to £750,000.

Part 2

Fabric

On the west front J. Bysouth Ltd. completed the restoration of the buttress north of the west window of the nave on which two spired pinnacles had to be entirely rebuilt.

During the past twelve months our masons have prepared stone for the work to the west towers now being carried out by J.W. Gray & Sons from our scaffolding. It consists in making good all places from which loose or dangerous stone was removed in 1967.

They have also been engaged on making new shafts, moulded capitals and bases for the south and west walks of the cloisters. Fixing is now in progress.

Grouting and repointing of the north side of the precinct wall (behind the greenhouse in College Garden) was carried out and completed in the late summer of 1968.

Roofs

The restoration of the north transept roof was finished and a corrugated iron roof erected over the presbytery roof prior to removal of the lead for recasting. It then became possible for the roof timbers to be inspected from above and diagrams have been prepared recording in detail the condition of every truss.

Reports on the treatment of the roof by four independent consultants revealed no consensus of opinion and Mr Marshall Sisson has now been invited to inspect the roof himself, assess the advice given and make his own recommendations. These are still awaited.

The hoist has been moved to the north side of the apse and it is hoped to clear the compound in the north east corner of the cloister garth very shortly.

Interior

[*Crouchback tomb*]

An incident at the beginning of October when a student lit a petrol bomb in the north ambulatory led to the Crouchback tomb being damaged by loss of some of its original painted decoration and a film of soot covering everything in the vicinity. The consequences could have been much worse and the carpets, brass chandeliers and other furnishing affected were successfully cleaned. The Crouchback tomb has been inspected by Dr Rees Jones of the Courtauld Institute who will supervise the preliminary cleaning of the affected areas and then advise on further treatment.[3]

Miss Plummer is reporting on the condition of the medieval paintings of the Sedilia, following tests to ascertain how far they would respond to cleaning.

Furnishings

The former nave altar, partly of plywood, has been replaced by a new one of oak made by our joiners and fitted with a contrivance for easy moving. The embroidered altar cloth of rose silk damask was dedicated at the end of September 1968.

Two wrought iron handrails on turned and twisted balusters were fixed on the steps to Henry VII's chapel. The work was carried out by Norman Furneaux, a smith at Bishop's Stortford.

Discussions have been held with Mr Freeman of the Institution of Civil Engineers on the provision of a new bridge from the Confessor's chapel to the vestibule of Henry VII's chapel. No design has yet been received.

The decoration of the backs of the choir stall canopies, following repair of the woodwork, was completed by Campbell Smith and Company.

In St Benedict's chapel a sculptured head of a Benedictine monk and a small incised tablet of Roman stone underneath have been placed over the doorway in the south wall. The sculptor was Mr A[lbert] Siegenthaler and the donor Mr Bernard Petitpierre.[4]

The teak notice board, intended for the north transept entrance, was fixed instead by the gates to Poets' Corner entrance. A new and larger board for joint use by the Abbey and St Margaret's is being designed to stand west of the church tower.

The working of further embroidered kneelers, as well as cushions for the Sacrarium, testifies to the continued enthusiasm of those who have given much generous service to the Abbey in this way. Designs have now been prepared for altar rail cushions in Henry VII's chapel.

In St George's chapel a dorsal is being made to replace that which had become worn out. It follows Sir Ninian Comper's design and the original embroidery will be re-used.

Monuments and memorials

Additional inscriptions, in lettering to match the existing, were incised and painted on the Stanhope monument. One commemorates the late Earl, the others two earlier ones to make the family record complete. The work was paid for privately.

The [John Charles] Thynne memorial in the west walk of the Little Cloisters was repaired, cleaned and the lettering and coat of arms repainted. The cost was met by the family.

A memorial stone to Bishop Joost de Blank[5] is being placed in front of the screen to St George's chapel. In Roman stone with brass letters, it has been designed by Mr James Sutton.

Through the Counsellor of India House a black marble from India is being used for the floor stone to Lord Attlee in the nave. The lettering will be inlaid in white marble.

A floor stone of white Pentelic marble with lettering of gold Sienna marble is being made at the cost of the Byron Society to commemorate Lord Byron. It will be placed on the floor of Poets' Corner.

The name of Dora Peasgood is being incised in small letters at the foot of her husband's grave in the west cloister.

The Crib

Additional figures of the Three Wise Men were made for the Crib. In place of a background of trees and greenery curtains that could be drawn to give a view into the choir during services were hung from under a wooden shelter constructed of surplus Abbey timber and thatched with straw. This has been made in such a way that it can easily be taken to pieces and re-erected each Christmas.

Burgot alarm

Following various incidents the system was reviewed and has now been extended and brought up to date.

Song School

The lighting circuits were rewired.

Choir School

A fire alarm system has been installed and an additional lavatory formed from a previous cupboard.

Houses

In the Deanery a new gas boiler has been installed and a change to gas firing made in the central heating system.

Internal redecoration was carried out to nos. 1,5 and 8 Little Cloisters and is in progress at no. 7. No. 2 was partially redecorated and the top floor converted to a flat.

In no. 4 a new gas fired boiler was installed and the panelled drawing room redecorated. Plaster repairs were made on the staircase to the top floor flat. Gas heating was installed in no. 6.

An attic room has been formed in the roof space of 4B Dean's Yard and a new dormer window made to light it. No. 16 Deans Yard was partially redecorated. At no. 2 The Cloisters the front door hood and iron railings in the garden were repainted.

Mason's Yard

Working conditions have been greatly improved by roofing over what was previously exposed to the weather. The new saw, which came into use during the year, has already proved its value and expedited the output of stone.

Tidiness

It is unnecessary to restate what has been said in previous reports on this subject. Neither within the Abbey itself nor in the cloisters or precincts does any improvement seem noticeable. Outside the Poets' Corner entrance the mess is at its worst: litter blows on to the lawn round the statue of George V and it will surely be necessary to try and preserve greater seemliness now that the bookstall, formerly in the east cloister, has been set up here.

S.E. Dykes Bower, Surveyor of the Fabric, 18 March 1969

[1] L.N. Cottingham, *Plans, elevations, sections … of the … chapel of King Henry the Seventh at Westminster Abbey … and an authentic account of its restoration*, 2 volumes (1822–29).
[2] Professor Church's memo on the treatment of stone was published in 1904 by HMSO.
[3] Tomb of Prince Edmund, Earl of Lancaster near the High Altar. The paintings of various knights on the base on the north ambulatory side were most affected. Pauline Plummer did the conservation work and her slides are in the Library collection. Also in the Library is John Carter's coloured drawing of these figures made in 1782.
[4] Letters about this memorial are in WAM S/3/22.
[5] This covers his ashes.

76.   WAM S/1/115
Audit Report 6 April 1970

Apse roof

When last year's report was submitted Mr Marshall Sisson's opinion on the roof was still awaited. He had been asked to give an independent assessment of recommendations made by the four consultants since, although there was agreement between those from the two engineers, those from the two architects were not identical and differed from the engineers'.

Mr Sisson's conclusions were embodied in a confidential report to the Dean and Chapter received at the end of June. Describing the repair of the roof as 'a most difficult problem since there are so many factors to be taken into account, and not wholly endorsing the proposals for restoration of any one of the four advisers because I am not satisfied with their practicability or with their suitability', Mr Sisson put forward suggestions of his own, influenced by consideration for 'adequate strength and stability in the restored structure; durability and freedom from serious repair for a period of at least as long as the life of the new lead covering, perhaps 150 to 200 years; retention of the maximum amount of the original structural material; reasonable economy of expenditure in relation to the importance of the building'.

Having invited him to act in effect as an arbitrator, the Dean and Chapter decided in October to adopt the policy he had outlined.

Work was started in the autumn and has continued steadily. It cannot proceed fast because, as Mr Sisson observed 'owing to decay, damage by death watch beetle, fractures and dislocation of joints, the structure is now in a precarious condition and repair must be undertaken with great caution. The consequence of any collapse or even the fall of an individual structural member would almost certainly be disastrous'.

For reasons of safety only a limited area of roof can be dealt with at one time. Within this, beginning at the west end, the first essential has been to consolidate the tops of the walls, where the stonework was loose and spalling, so that two of the transverse tie beams could be placed in position and the requisite portion of the ring beams inserted. The westernmost truss, which was of softwood and not original, has also been repaired where necessary and work is proceeding on the next two.

In accordance with Mr Sisson's observation that 'no uniform method of repair can be laid down. Each truss must be considered individually and treated according to its condition and circumstances', every section of timber is scrutinized in the light of the work it has to do. Those so badly affected by beetle attack as to be unfit for re-use are not being removed from the building but set aside in a place of quarantine where they cannot infect others. Since the real state of much of the timber is now proving to be as stated in my former reports it is important that the evidence for rejection should thus be irrefutable.

The strength of the trusses as repaired will be largely dependent on straps and flitch plates which in many instances must be of considerable size. Analysis of the old wrought iron used in the roof showed that this was of unusual quality, not manufactured today, and much care has been necessary to find the nearest equivalent, from which a long life may be expected.

Before finalizing his report Mr Sisson rightly consulted the District Surveyor of Westminster since any proposals that could affect the safety of the building must receive his approval. Throughout all previous work to the roofs the District Surveyor has made regular inspections and satisfied himself on details of the work. I have been glad to concur with such stipulations as he has made in respect of what is now in progress.

So far as can be foreseen at present there is no reason why the work should not progress steadily. Delivery of steelwork for the tie beams has so far been satisfactory; in a job of this sort the slowest stage is usually the initial one when procedure has to some extent to develop empirically. But it would be misleading to hold out any expectation that a saving either in time or in cost will be achieved as a result of the mode of repair that has been adopted. That the work will take longer and the cost be enormously higher is unavoidable: it is better to state this now than let it be realized later.

Stonework [tower and cloisters]

Preparation of the stone for the south tower, on which scaffolding was erected almost exactly two years ago, has chiefly occupied our masons during the past year. Cut and worked in our yard, it has to be supplied to J.W. Gray & Sons at a rate which synchronizes with the cutting out of defective existing stone. This firm assists our masons with the fixing, when required, and do the subsequent pointing.

Work in the present programme comprises both towers from the top down to the cornice which marks the beginning of Hawksmoor's addition to the medieval west front. The south tower, being in the worse condition of the two, is being tackled first and, if no unforeseen difficulties occur, should be finished by the end of this year. Much of the damage to the stone has been caused by rusting of the iron cramps bedded in it and which have now to be replaced in non-ferrous metal: much too by the heavy accumulation of acid deposits wherever the stone cannot be naturally washed by rainwater.

The north tower is expected to take eighteen months.

Concurrently, so far as it could be fitted in, renewal of moulded shafts, bases and capitals for the south and west walks of the cloisters has gone forward as a job carried out entirely by our masons. Fixing was kept back for the winter when weather conditions were less favourable for work high up on the tower.

The new shafts now make obvious the need for re-facing the walling between them. Such ashlar work could well be undertaken by our men, who a few years ago made and fixed that in the bay containing the Commonwealth memorial.

[St Catherine's chapel garden]

In St Catherine's Garden grouting, repair and repointing of the south wall of the former Infirmary Chapel have proceeded at such times as Mr Green could be spared to it. This too has had to be treated as a reserve job, causing progress to be slower than might be desired.

Our dilemma is the double one of having a staff too small to cope with all that needs to be done and enforced restriction on expenditure. To keep down what is now being incurred with an outside contractor, the main output of our masons for at least two years will have to be stone for the towers. This precludes their tackling, except at half strength or less, other urgent jobs such as the cloisters, which would be suited to our resources and require little or no scaffolding.

[Blackstole Tower, Dean's Yard]

With the Blackstole Tower also in a ruinous condition and long overdue for restoration the amount of work ahead is obvious. With every year that passes costs get higher.

[Chapter House]

The cleaning of the Chapter House by the Ministry of Works, recently completed in less than two months, has already brought enquiries about the cleaning of the Abbey and stimulated a wish to see it similarly transformed.

Little of the exterior of the Chapter House is more than 100 years old because Sir Gilbert Scott in his restoration of 1865 refaced it in Chilmark stone. Cleaning has shown that the ashlar is fairly good but also how much repair and renewal is needed to certain features such as the pinnacles and those parts of the flying buttresses that were not rebuilt in 1865.

The Ministry, I understand, decided to clean first because in this way all places requiring attention would reveal themselves. The next operation therefore is to make good defective stone and scaffolding has already been erected afresh for this purpose.

On the Abbey where the stone is older and of different varieties it would not be economic to work on these lines. Much of the badly decayed stone would be pulverized by the sand blasting technique and, because of the much greater size and height, scaffolding could hardly be erected twice over.

As a demonstration of how the removal of soot and stains enhances a building of Gothic design the Ministry's treatment of the Chapter House may be welcomed and it has been represented to me that, if one portion of the Abbey could now be cleaned, there would be a better chance of getting money to do more. The improvement would commend itself.

I think this point of view deserves serious thought and that, if such a start could be made, Henry VII's chapel or the south and north apsidal chapels were the masonry is relatively in better condition than elsewhere, would be the most eligible choice.

Bells [ringing chamber, clock and flag room]

At a meeting in February 1970 with Mears and Stainbank, the Superintendent of the Belfry and Mr Pitstow[1] it was agreed to recommend that the Perkins bequest should be devoted to recasting the existing ring of 8 bells (without nos. 5 and 7) to form a lighter ring of 10, hung in a new steel bell frame; 5 and 7, the Elizabethan bells, to be hung separately and chimed as service bells.

The bells at present are very high up in the tower and there would be structural advantages if the belfry were at a lower level. Acoustically this would improve the sound and carrying power of the bells although they would seem less loud in the immediate vicinity.

The alterations entailed would be the conversion of the ringing chamber to the belfry. The new bell frame would be at the level of the floor, 22 feet 8 inches below that of the belfry and the ceiling removed to let the sound escape through the louvred windows. The clock mechanism, now enclosed in a wooden enclosure on the south side of this room would have to go since the bells (12 in all) would take up the whole space available. It would be re-sited one or possibly two floors down.

What is now the Flag Room would become the ringing chamber – lighted by the three windows on the west, north and east sides and by the upper part of the clerestory windows of the nave on the south. The new Flag Room would be on the floor below which is approximately level with the nave triforium.

The entrance to the proposed ringing chamber is by a few rather awkward steps branching off the main newel staircase. These would have to be altered to give an easier approach for the ringers.

The floor (now only partially boarded) in the proposed Flag Room would be slightly lowered and boarded throughout.

The casing for the former clock weights is redundant and should be removed; all roof timbers examined and treated as necessary for insect or fungal attack; the wall faces at each floor cleaned and whitened.

So far as can be estimated in advance the cost of the works not included in Mears and Stainbank's quotation would amount to approximately £1,500.0.0. This must not be taken as a firm price but is the best assessment possible at this stage.

Crouchback tomb

Miss Plummer, after carrying out tests under the general direction of Dr Rees Jones, produced her report and estimate in May 1969. The latter came to so high a figure that it seem s inadvisable to submit any claim to the Ecclesiastical Insurance Office until further advice had been obtained. Professor Wormald and Mr A.J. Taylor, who undertook an independent inspection of the monument in the autumn, advised elucidation of certain points and a rather different presentation of the costs.

The purport of their views was that, whereas Miss Plummer's estimates totalled not far short of £30,000, it was highly unlikely that any such sum could be looked for from the Insurance company. They considered that £10,000 should be asked which represents the approximate mean between a lower and a higher figure for what Miss Plummer defines as 'basic treatment'. This would comprise fixing and surface cleaning of the parts of the monument that sustained direct damage from the petrol bomb. The seemingly high cost is accounted for by the time required for a slow and delicate task: for example, 80 weeks is quoted for the north side, 20 weeks for the vaulting and 3 weeks for the effigy and so on.

The legitimate insurance claim, if met, will not however bring back the medieval colour where it has been irretrievably lost; but Miss Plummer holds strongly that to preserve whatever can still be fixed back (even if colourless) would be preferable to stripping it off and exposing the stone on one part of the monument which is otherwise fully decorated.

The insurance claim has been delayed for so long that I think a settlement on the best terms possible must now be sought. The sum of money paid will influence the policy to be pursued. If it were enough to cover Miss Plummer's 'basic treatment', which is one stage of the work, my impression is that Professor Wormald and Mr Taylor might regard the second stage as something for which financial help could be sought elsewhere. Costing approximately £15,000 more it could cover the general cleaning of the monument and implement the findings of the committee which some years ago reported that much could be done to reveal the medieval decoration more clearly.

Were this to be the outcome some good might compensate for a deplorable act of vandalism. But if, as is possible, the insurance claim is inadequate to pay for even the basic treatment, a situation may arise in which there will not be enough to do any part of the monument properly. Could some of the money then be spent on another kindred object, such as the cleaning of the Sedilia painting which it is known will respond well to treatment?

It is fair to quote Miss Plummer on the crucial question of her estimates 'It is impossible in this type of work to be precise as to the time necessary for the various areas of treatment. One can only really discover that when working on the individual parts. Therefore all my figures can only be approximate, as I explained in my report of May 1969. In addition, they are based on the rates quoted in the report of a year ago, and would have to be reviewed in a further year. Prices appear to be rising at the rate of about 10% a year'.

It is also pertinent to take account of the time factor. Stage 1 alone would take 136 weeks; State 2 more than twice as much.

Glazing

[*Apse windows*]

For some time a white spot at the base of the right hand light of the central window of the apse stood out rather discordantly among the colours of the old glass. How a breakage occurred here is not known but examination of these three valuable windows showed about fifteen other small cracks that have now been repaired.

[*Triforium*]

When the claim for reglazing the clerestory windows of the nave was agreed with the War Damage Commission some years ago, nothing was allowed for the triforium windows because the Commission maintained that they were already defective: their condition had not been materially affected during the war. No work was done to them at the time but it was recognized that repair could not be deferred indefinitely. A fresh inspection (March 1970) indicates that it ought to be undertaken in the next three years. Apart from a very large number of cracked or missing quarries over which brown paper has been pasted, the lead cames have in places worn very thin or come away altogether.

The number of windows which require reglazing is twenty one. There are ten on each side of the nave but on the south the easternmost contains stained glass which does not need attention. The ten on the north are in the worst condition as well as one in the west aisle of the north transept and one on the north side of the apse.

Goddard and Gibbs estimate that the cost of each window would average £250, though this figure could be reduced if a sufficient number were undertaken simultaneously. Thus for twelve the cost might be £200 each. Their price allows for hacking out the existing glass and supplying and fixing the new, but not for the scaffolding or pointing up. Internally the windows are in reach from the triforium floor; externally scaffolding would have to be put up from the ground, a height of 50–60 feet. The cost of this and our masons' time in pointing up would have to be taken into account in calculating total expenditure.

The work could if necessary be divided into annual stages, e.g. first the six at the west end of the north side of the nave; next the remaining four at the east end, with the two in the transept and apse; then the nine on the south side. Goddard and Gibbs would be able to do two windows a fortnight, but pointing would extend this time to probably another week.

St Faith's chapel [*painting*]

After many delays Mrs Baker[2] has carried out the further tests needed before she could give an opinion on the chance of successful cleaning of the painting on the east wall. The results have established that this would be not only practicable but valuable beyond expectation.

In each of the small areas treated the original colour has been found virtually intact and its vividness contrasts markedly with the darkness of the painting as it has been known for so long. The importance of what transpires from what has been done so far is more than the possibility of being able to recover much of the beauty of the original colour. It is rather that the crucifixion panel in the centre of the reredos turns out to be one of the exquisitely delicate paintings of the Westminster school of which the Retabulum and the Sedilia are, on different scales, other examples. The figure of Our Lady provides a foretaste of what further beauty may be in store if all that is necessary can be done to bring it to light.

The Pilgrim Trust has so far made available £230 for Mrs Baker's investigations. She has not yet spent anything like that sum: on the other hand what is unspent would not cover the cost of what will have to be done. Professor Wormald, who first raised with the Pilgrim Trust the desirability of a fresh inspection of this painting, is being asked to come and see what it has brought forth. If he advises that the whole painting ought to be cleaned it may be hope that the Pilgrim Trust will increase their grant to meet the cost.

The time the work would take is estimated by Mrs Baker at three to four months and owing to commitments at Canterbury and Winchester she could not begin it till next winter. It should not be necessary to close the chapel; if the altar were brought forward and a curtain placed behind it to screen a sufficient working space the job could proceed without noise or mess.

Memorials and monuments

Two new memorials, described in the report for last year, were laid in the nave; that of Bishop Joost de Blank in front of the screen in St George's chapel, that of Lord Attlee at the west end of the north aisle. The latter was unveiled in the presence of the Prime Minister.

Also described in last year's report, the memorial to Lord Byron in Poets' Corner was unveiled on May 8 1969. Its cost was met by the Poetry Society.

A request for a memorial to David Lloyd George has been approved in principle. The design by Mr Clough Williams Ellis showed what appeared to be a tablet rather than a floor slab and if, since no wall space is left, a floor slab is essential the dimensions would need to be increased. In a slab only 2 feet 6 inches long the lettering, in the form proposed, would be too small to execute in inlay and certainly too small to look right.

The large slate slab commemorating Tompion and Graham in the centre of the nave is subject to heavy wear from the tread of people walking up the main aisle and because visitors stand upon it when looking at the tomb of Livingstone. At the request and cost of the Worshipful Company of Clockmakers the inscription has been made more legible by sharpening and slightly deepening the cut of the letters which, as on the Winston Churchill stone, have been painted silver.

In the Lady Margaret aisle an incised stone lying between the monuments of Mary Queen of Scots and the Countess of Lennox bears a list of those buried in a vault below. Writing from Gurnard in the Isle of Wight, Susan Green a schoolgirl aged 14 and a half protested that, having with difficulty deciphered the names upon it, she had found that of Prince Rupert almost unreadable. The interest of the Hudson Bay Company was solicited and their generous response enabled all the names on the stone to be recut.

Although the Northumberland family still have the right of burial in a family vault in St Nicholas chapel, there is not, as might be expected, any visible record of the interments on the Northumberland monument itself. The present Duke and his sister, the Duchess of Sutherland, asked permission to place in the central panel of the base of the monument the names and dates, with a brief legend above explaining the connection of the monument with the vault. A design has been prepared and approved and the work of cutting the incised letters will be carried out by Mr Sydney Newman. They follow the style of the lettering in the inscriptions above but, being in white marble, will be painted black. The cost of the work is being defrayed by the family.

On the graves of Robert Browning and Gladstone missing brass letters have been made good. Mr F.W. Wallis, who drew attention to the condition of Gladstone's grave, paid for restoring it. Elsewhere many more brass letters have disappeared notably from the grave of Herschel and from the Rifle Brigade memorial in the north transept.

However it is not only stones with brass lettering that give trouble. The incised slate lettering on the graves of Dean Ryle and Dean Foxley Norris in the nave is rapidly becoming illegible again, although sharpened and deepened within the last fifteen years. When the nave is clear of seating each stone lies in the path of crowds; when the seating is in position each is exposed to the scraping of chairs and shuffling of feet.

Another cause of many memorials in the floor being difficult to read is that dust fills the incisions of the letters and cannot be brushed out often enough. Already the delicate lettering on the tomb of Anne Mowbray can hardly be appreciated for this reason: the Caedmon stone even more so, being close to Poets' Corner entrance through which grit and dust blow in from outside whenever the doors stand open.

This is a problem for the cleaning rather than the building staff. I wonder whether sufficient use is made of vacuum cleaners and dustettes which suck out dust (which can then be disposed of outside the building), rather than sweeping with brushes that merely move it from one position to another. In the light of experience the most satisfactory type of floor slab is clearly that in which the lettering is inlaid in marble and flush with the surface. We now have six of these and they are easy to read and keep clean.

Requests received during the year for restoration of two memorials in the cloisters raised questions of a different kind. In the west walk the grave of Dr Benjamin Cooke, organist of the Abbey 1762–1793, is so cracked and damaged that any attempt to recut the inscription would be useless. The full wording of this can no longer be read and enquiry has so far revealed no record of a transcript. Unless one is forthcoming a new stone would have to be inscribed with his name, dates and whatever description may be drawn up.

The other tablet, to Pierre Courayer who died in 1776, is in the south walk. It was urged that the inscription on this, could it be legible, would have some ecumenical interest. The work required would however be more than the restoration of the lettering on the slate panel. Until the whole wall face can be renewed, as in the bay containing the Commonwealth memorial, it would be wasteful to spend money on any of the tablets attached to it. They will have to be taken down when the decayed stone is replaced by new and the right time to clean and repair them will be before they are put back.

[*Roubliac models*]

An enquiry from the Victoria and Albert Museum brought to light the existence of three sketch models by Roubiliac[3] that, as possessions of the Abbey, had passed almost out of remembrance if not out of sight. After some search they were discovered still in good condition in the west gallery of St Faith's chapel. Only one is strictly of Abbey interest – a model for the Nightingale monument; the other two are wood and plaster models for monuments in Warkton church, Northamptonshire.

Being of a specialized rather than general interest they have been loaned to the Victoria & Albert Museum for display in an exhibition of post-Reformation sculpture. Their insurance value was assessed by Mr Francis Watson, Director of the Wallace Collection, at £10,500 for the Nightingale model and £8,000 for each of the Warkton models – an indication of the surprising worth that may attach to objects of rarity value.

Furnishings

The embroidered cushions for the Sacrarium to which reference was made in the last report, were completed and placed in the Canons' stalls. The kneeling cushions worked by Mr Sear of Reading for the gap between the altar rails have been provided with wooden bases to bring the cushion level with those on either side.

The cushions for the nave altar rails, which had been damaged first by the foot marks of people standing on them and then by unfortunate attempts to remove these with a bleach, have been covered a second time in the same velvet. A rope in front now gives some measure of protection.

Kneeling cushions, embroidered to a design combining the red rose of Lancaster with the white rose of York, have been made for the altar rails of Henry VII's chapel. They are being supplemented by embroidered kneelers for the chairs placed in the chapel when required.

This represents the conclusion of an enterprise, owing much to the zeal of Mrs Stancliffe[4] and Mrs Lawrence, whereby every chair in the nave, the transepts and St Faith's chapel has its own embroidered kneeler; three sets of altar rail cushions have been worked; and the Sacrarium equipped with seat and kneeling cushions for the Dean, Canons and Minor Canons. At a time when the church is often alleged to have lost support and enthusiasm, it is worth noting that there was never any difficulty in recruiting participants ready to given their services in this way and who regarded as a privilege the opportunity to work for the Abbey.

In St George's chapel a new dorsal, on which the original embroidery has been remounted, was placed in position in September 1969. The cushions on the wall bench have been remade and covered in the same rose pink damask. The two incongruous kneelers in front continue, unfortunately, to be the one unworthy feature of this chapel.

Before its erection at Christmas the stable over the Crib was reduced in height to hide less of the organ screen behind.

A design has been prepared for a case to contain the Commando flag which the Commando Association have asked should be laid up in St George's chapel. The estimate is £225.0.0.

Following discussions on better provisions of alms boxes throughout the church a design for a new type was drawn up to requirements specified in a report by Mr Wood. This is still under consideration.

To contain the china and glass presented in the Abbey's 900th year cupboards were designed to fit the recess in the passage from Jericho to the Jerusalem Chamber. The oak joinery was made by our carpenters and fixed during the summer of 1969.

A small spot light to throw light on the steps has been fixed experimentally in the arch of the north transept entrance.

[*Purbeck marble cup*]

A marble cup to be placed on exhibition in the Museum is of interest both for its origin and unusual character. In the course of the restoration of the north transept front, begun by Scott and finished by Pearson, a piece of Purbeck marble, according to the donor's account, was found buried beneath the porch. How the idea of making a chalice out of it arose is not known, but the excellence of the mouldings points to a first rate designer, probably Pearson himself. The turned bowl is so thin and delicate that the work must have been executed by an equally accomplished craftsman.

Heating

During the late summer the two boilers, which after twenty years' service had become worn out, were removed from the boiler house and superseded by three new ones of smaller size but greater efficiency. These came into operation with the start of the heating season at the beginning of November. Except in very cold weather, when all three are kept in use, a constant temperature of 61 degrees is maintained with two only; and since this is possible with the boilers resting on average for eight hours a night there has been a saving in fuel.

Rearrangement of the boiler house, for which this change was an opportunity, has given more space and better working conditions. Ventilation has been improved and a covered shelter provided over the entrance stairs.

A crack in the outlet pipe at roof level has still to be put right and three glands in the boiler house to be repacked. These jobs will be carried out in May, after the heating is turned off.

Organ [choir] Screen

On the south side of the passage from nave to choir the two panels painted with the names of bishops consecrated in the Abbey are filled. A new panel has been added to the north side and four names inscribed on it. An old spelling mistake (1926) on the south side has been corrected.

Excavation in the south transept

A settlement in the paving of the east aisle of the south transept, west of the Dryden monument, made investigation of the sub-soil advisable. As an indirect result a burial was found for which no identification could be established. With a view to dispelling uncertainty it was decided that the coffin should be opened at night in the presence of the Dean and Chapter and officials concerned, with the Professor of Anatomy at St Thomas' Hospital to examine and assess the age of the bones. The skeleton proved to be that of a man, aged about 30 and of large stature, possibly a young monk; but no facts gave any clue as to his identity or why he had been namelessly interred here.

The bridge [to the Confessor's chapel]

By the time this report is received the new bridge, designed by Mr Ralph Freeman and Mr Whitfield and presented by the Institution of Civil Engineers,[5] will be in position. The task of contriving a structure to span from the Chantry of Henry V to the vestibule of Henry VII's chapel in such a way that it will look aesthetically satisfactory but not appear part of the fabric, has required judgement and much technical skill. The result will speak for itself but particularly acceptable are the advantages of being able to pass under it (so that the ambulatory is continuous) and ease of erection and dismantling. The time required to each operation will be a few hours only and it is hoped that an arrangement may be entered into whereby the Royal Engineers will undertake what would be the twice yearly job of putting the bridge in place for the summer months and removing it in the winter months. Its usefulness will be apparent in the former; the view of the noble flight of steps, one of the grand features of Henry VII's chapel, will still be enjoyed in the latter.

That the last has been seen of the old bridge is a cause for thankfulness: not least because its components will no longer have to be stored in the north east corner of the cloisters.

The cloisters

In the early summer of 1969 the electric hoist and compound at the north east angle were taken down and transferred to the north side of the apse. The space they had occupied was seeded, and the garth, for fifteen years curtailed, restored to its original condition.

A small shed to house the motor mower has been erected in the north east corner of the cloister garth. Being within the projection of two buttresses at right angles it will hardly be noticeable when the Portland stone of its walls loses its first whiteness.

Well [cloister garth]

Trouble caused by blocked rain water gullies in the cloister garth made it necessary to investigate the drains leading from them, which had never been charted on any plan. This led to the discovery of an old well about 12 feet 6 inches deep, approximately 6 feet in diameter and built, for most of its height, in old red bricks.[6] When it was covered in is not known: but more curious is the fact that its existence should have been forgotten. An earthenware pipe conveying water from the north east corner of the cloisters and passing across the well not far below the surface cannot be more than 100 years old. Whoever did the work, encountering the well unexpectedly and anxious not to incur expense in having to divert the path of the drain round it, may have taken the easiest course, laid the drain straight across it and said nothing. The soil once put back the well concealed, no questions would be asked. The assumption therefore must be that knowledge of the well was deliberately suppressed.

Certainly no memory has survived of what in such a position would not have been a surprising find. Medieval wells remain in the cloisters of Durham, Chester and Gloucester cathedrals; there were other examples at Sherborne, Valle Crucis and elsewhere. To obliterate a second time all trace of what chance has brought to light would, in my opinion, be regrettable. Whatever might be the attraction of a fountain, the cost – not less than £1,500 and for a more ornamental one £2,500 – is much higher than that of a well-head which could be built by our masons for about £400. There is already a fountain in the Little Cloister. The Great Cloister evidently had a well; but this would not have been a fountain.

Though now empty, because the water has been channelled into drains, the well could be made to function by the simple expedient of cutting the pipe on one side so that water from the roofs would gradually fill it. The pipe on the opposite side would act as an overflow and thus make it impossible for the water to rise above a fixed level. Nothing could be easier.

Houses and buildings in the precincts

Repainting of the external woodwork has been carried out during the year to all the houses in Little Cloister; 4B, 5 and 16 Dean's Yard; 2 The Cloister; the Choir School and the Chapter Office.

New asphalt roofing has been laid over the drawing room of 4B Deans Yard and over the Surveyor's office.

Repairs were made to the staircase of 1 Little Cloister. The Surveyor's Office was redecorated, following leaks through the defective roof; also the staircase, hall and landings of no 6 adjoining, after damage sustained in the installation of gas central heating.

In 16 Deans Yard the dining and drawing rooms were repainted and the hall and landing re-papered.

The north and south entrance gates to Deans Yard were repainted; also the gate at the west entrance to the south cloister.

Both the Bookshop and the Undercroft were decorated. In the latter alterations have been made to some of the cases and better security provided for that containing the Essex and Courtenay rings.[7]

A new lock and entry telephone have been installed in the Library.

[20 Dean's Yard]

After vacation of 20 Deans Yard at the end of October the floors were opened up in places where investigation seemed advisable.[8] This has confirmed a great deal of work will be needed to put the house into sound repair. In the back quarters particularly its state of dilapidation is obvious; but the whole building has been so confused by past alterations and additions that nothing less than radical treatment will now bring order out of chaos.

There are various possibilities, description of which would be too lengthy for this report. If money can be found, what might appear an intractable problem is not insoluble. The vaulted ground floor room (previously a dining room) should, with the present entrance hall, be separated from the house proper. This should be entered from the courtyard behind the Blackstole Tower and, apart from a hall and a waiting room or lavatory at ground level, be entirely on first and second floor levels. With the second floor continued the whole length of the Deans Yard frontage over the drawing and dining rooms (instead of half as at present) internal re-planning would give the requisite accommodation for a pleasant and convenient house without sacrifice of any of the features which give it character.

The top floor could either be converted to form a separate flat or be removed.

The two storey portion at the back, hitherto unused, might be made into a small house or rebuilt as a separate block of flats.

But if the Song School has to be enlarged the only site on which extension is feasible would be the garden of no. 20, inclusive of the ground floor of its back wing. Such a scheme would enable a new paved garden on the flat roof to be formed at first floor level of no. 20 thus enhancing the amenities of the house.

Because the site is confined and almost all the buildings on it are old, partly medieval but chiefly 17th and 18th century in date, there are limitations on what can be done. But they need not to preclude adaptation of a sympathetic and appropriate kind.

[No. 2 Abbey Garden]

Meetings have been held with the Ministry of Works who are carrying out alterations to no. 2 Abbey Gardens in preparation for its use by members of Parliament. These are all internal, except for renewal of the stone copings of the brick walls between the house and the precinct wall and improvements, in the same area, to the drainage and rainwater disposal system. In so far as these entail the clearance of much banked up earth they will be beneficial to what has been an untidy corner of College Garden.

Masons Yard

To mitigate the unsightly appearance of the corrugated iron enclosure alongside what is sometimes a ceremonial approach to the Abbey, consideration has been given to screening this with trellis on which creepers could be planted. Since however the corrugated iron would still need to be repainted at intervals, practical difficulties would arise and I think a better course might be to substitute for the corrugated iron a wall or pre-cast concrete blocks, which would be permanent and of the colour of stone. With trellis fixed to it such a wall when covered with foliage would hardly be seen. It could be built just high enough to mask the corrugated roofing which would be cut to finish against it.

Although such a wall would very slightly impinge on the working space within the yard its thickness would be only a few inches greater than that of the present enclosure. Any loss could be compensated by extending the yard a little to the east bringing it into better relationship with the buttress at this point.

The extra cost would, over the years, pay for itself through the saving on keeping the corrugated iron painted. If carried out more seemly wooden doors should take the place of the iron ones. Some improvement in tidiness outside the Mason's Yard has resulted from the container in which rubbish is stored until removal.

[Chapter House exterior]

Now that the Chapter House has been cleaned by the Ministry of Works a plea may be made for a change in the border formed two years ago between the flying buttresses on its east side. Loosely constructed of pieces of flat stone it looks untidy and is already collapsing in places. Equally bad is its shape – a meaningless curve when it clearly ought to be straight and parallel to the railing of the George V garden. This border, though on Abbey property, is semi-public in being visible from outside. It does not at all conform to what should be our standards.

General

This report gives occasion for mention of a few matters prompted by observation of the Abbey in daily use.

While the behaviour of the majority of visitors is good, the ever increasing numbers that arrive on coach parties and go round in groups cause congestion in parts of the building, such as the Confessor's chapel, where space is limited. The guides complain that visitors wedged against the south side of Henry III's tomb sometimes kick it with their heels, without perhaps realizing what it is they are kicking. This is doing damage that cumulatively could become serious. I am asked whether the tomb could not be protected on this side by an iron grate since holes in the floor show that this once existed. There can be no doubt that the medieval practice of fencing round important tombs with wrought iron railings has, wherever these have survived, a good deal to commend it. The railings are usually decorative and in no way spoil enjoyment of what they enclose. Today it might not be easy, without evoking protest of some sort, to erect new grilles to monuments that have lost them. But a case might be made for re-using the original medieval ironwork that once served this very purpose and of which we have a certain amount stored in the north triforium of the apse. The iron is perfectly sound: with straightening of some of the upright bars and overhaul by a good smith, it could be assembled to make one or more grilles of short length.[9]

A certain amount of wilful or thoughtless damage, however, continues to occur. From the former the Countess of Lennox monument suffers more than any other in the building: attempts to break off any part of it that may be carried away as a souvenir are incessant. The hands of one of the kneeling figures on the south side have gone: those of one on the opposite side damaged. The unicorn has lost its horn; two horns from another heraldic supporter, the cross on top of Darnley's crown[10] and bits of other features are missing.

Of thoughtless damage a recent instance was ten boys clambering simultaneously on to the tomb under the newly decorated Robessart monument and lying on it until an indignant spectator summoned a verger. It transpired that the boys were from a school for delinquents and no doubt their escort should have employed firmer control. But if ever visits by parties of this sort are notified in advance, special supervision by one of the vergers would seem desirable.

The perennial subject of litter in the cloisters and precincts has been ventilated before in these reports. Something this year may be said about a different kind of untidiness that requires perpetual vigilance within the church itself. The Abbey is well kept and considering the pressure upon it – of visitors, special services, activities of one sort and another – perhaps exceptionally so. Its brightness and cleanliness are frequently remarked on with appreciation. Yet small matters call for criticism. At the evensong attended by Cardinal Marty two unsightly floodlights at the ends of wooden poles had been left projecting from the easternmost bay of the choir triforium. Last year, at the reception for the Order of the Bath the view of the choir was spoilt by a temporary lamp suspended on drooping flex hung from wall to wall. With all the rest of the lighting on display, how many visitors must have wondered at their presence of this intruder? There have been many similar instances and always the reason seems the same. Put up for a special purpose, the lights are left up through forgetfulness to remove them or because trouble would be saved in letting them remain for another special occasion perhaps in a week's time. In a building of great beauty unnecessary eyesores are inexcusable. Many people, it may be admitted, do not notice such things; but some do and for them there should be no cause for offence.

Greater watchfulness might also be exerted over the quite extraordinary propensity for leaving chairs and barriers in positions from which they should be excluded. The south choir aisle is one of their most favoured resorts and at the funeral service for Lord Dowding even a ladder was unaccountably lying there. When so much care is taken over the details of important services in other ways it is unfortunate that unnecessary blemishes should be overlooked. Possibly a discipline by which at the end of each day nothing was left where it should not be might at least hinder its getting back.

In the nave sanctuary the credence table ought manifestly to stand centrally in front of the pillar. It looks perverse to place it a few inches off centre and, since photography is no longer allowed, the former reason given for this – that people reached over the rope to set their cameras upon it – no longer applies.

A last point concerns the nave altar cloth. On the few occasions when it has to be lifted off Watts and Company, who made it, say that they would gladly come voluntarily to remove, fold and replace it – an offer induced by dismay at seeing what they regard as inexpert handling. Men are perhaps less adept at jobs of this kind than women with trained experience.

An altar cloth of which the replacement value is at least £1,500–£2,000 should be treated with great care. Watts' willingness to give their services may seem to deserve sympathetic consideration.

The nuisance of pigeons in the cloisters is unabated. Their droppings have lately marred the Malaya tablet in the north walk. Is it possible for notices to be posted asking people not to feed them?

A change which has affected the interior of the Abbey in the last few years calls for some comment. A few years ago the notices on the monuments were so patently unsatisfactory that new ones, written on vellum and well framed, were provided for all the important tombs. Since the placing of these was carefully considered in relation to the architectural surrounding of each monument as well as the monument itself, this was an undoubted gain: in the labelling of monuments it was generally thought that the Abbey had set a good example. It is strange to find that notices have now multiplied again that there are as many as four on the tomb of Edward III and three on that of Richard II. These are only two instances and it may be asked whether such repetition of precisely the same information is necessary or desirable.

The return of a stall for selling postcards and literature within the building and the 'No Photography' notices, which though effective are not attractive, are held by some to have re-introduced an alien note that is to be regretted. However this may be the tendency to proliferation ought to be watched not only for aesthetic but for practical reasons. Under the Malaya tablet by the west cloister entrance there are (at the time of writing) no less than ten notice boards in a row – some of them very much the worse for wear. How many people, it may be wondered, carry away any clear remembrance of what they read when confronted with so copious a display.

S.E. Dykes Bower
Surveyor of the Fabric
6 April 1970

1   Secretary of the Ringers. Bequest from former Sacrist Jocelyn Perkins.
2   Files on this conservation are WAM S/3/23.
3   Lady Elizabeth Nightingale's monument by Louis Francois Roubiliac is in St Michael's chapel. The two from Warkton are the Duke and Duchess of Montagu.
4   Wife of Canon Michael Stancliffe.
5   The footbridge, designed to ease congestion at a time when St Edward's chapel was still open to visitors, was dismantled in 1997 when it was decided to place the Coronation Chair at the east end of Henry V's tomb. Two small floor plaques on the chapel steps record the gift.
6   The drains were altered in 1870. WAM 47808A of 1757 records digging to empty the large well. The well, for waste water, was photographed in 2006 when it was cleared and turfed over, formerly having a wooden cover. The Little Cloister fountain dates from 1871 and is on the site of a former small water tank. For the proposed fountain in the main cloister, see WAM S/3/53 (not done).
7   The Essex ring, said to be that given to the Earl of Essex by Elizabeth I, was presented to the Abbey in 1927. Bishop Richard Courtenay's ruby ring was found when his grave in the Confessor's chapel was unexpectedly found in the 1950s.
8   Photos of the house before conversion are in the Library collection. Also an archaeological report. It was never used as a house again. The Chapter Office was relocated there from 21 Deans Yard and the entrance from Deans Yard is still used.
9   The railings in the triforium came from the east end of Henry V's tomb. None were re-used.
10 Lord Darnley was one of the Countess' sons and is shown as one of the weepers. The crown is a modern replacement.

77.   WAM S/1/116

Surveyor of the Fabric Report 1971

My Audit Report is shorter this year because accompanied by one of some length on St Margaret's. Those who have not seen the Quinquennial Survey of the church made by its professional advisers in 1968 – a document of some sixty pages – may wish to be spared reading the first section of what I have written, which is in part a commentary on it. Perhaps also the second section, which is about its interior. But in the third I refer to some questions affecting the Abbey and St Margaret's jointly that may be of interest.

Stonework

Repair of the south tower, started nearly two years ago, finished at the end of 1970. That of the north tower, on which scaffolding has now been erected, is expected to take eighteen months. Cutting and working the stone for it will therefore continue to occupy much of our masons' time.

During the past year progress was made in fixing moulded wall shafts in the west walk of the cloisters and, from the beginning of 1971, in the restoration of the archway to the Deanery courtyard.

This short passage showed how stone can be eroded by wind and draught even when under cover and not fully exposed to the weather. For the shafts Portland has been used as best qualified to stand up to adverse conditions and for ashlar work Lepine, a French stone that should weather in time to much the same colour as Clipsham.

Enquiries are being made into the properties of other French stone from quarries lately opened up and apparently of inexhaustible supply. These are of high quality and, even with customs and import duties, competitive in price with English stones. It would be specially useful to find one that would be hard enough for use as paving stone. The replacement of badly worn areas of floor in the nave, aisles, ambulatories and cloisters has for years past been an intermittent job for our masons. We no longer have a reserve of Purbeck for the purpose and new Purbeck cannot be obtained. Roman stone which has recently had to be purchased for places in the nave tends to look a little prominent when new. As the number of visitors increases and there is greater need to guard against the risk of accidents, defective stones will become due for lifting more quickly – an endless process wasteful of time and money but, until the nave can be re-floored, inevitable.

Apse roof

Restoration is proceeding satisfactorily: of 28 trusses, exclusive of those to the apse itself, 14 have been repaired and work is approaching the half way stage.

An invitation to inspect it was accepted by the Duke of Grafton and Mr Marshall Sisson, who were given full opportunity to see for themselves the state of the old timbers and to discuss the modes and methods of repair being adopted. The visit appeared to set at rest apprehension that may have arisen through lack of insight into the nature of the problems that the roof presented.

Bells

At the time of writing a protective scaffold is about to be erected over the Montagu monument under the north tower so that the Whitechapel Bell Foundry can lower the bells through the aperture in the vault. As each is brought down to floor level it will, while awaiting the others, have to stand in the nave until all can be taken out through the west door for loading on to lorries for removal. Use of this entrance by the public may have to cease for one or perhaps two days.

During the past year tests were carried out on ringing days to measure oscillation within the north tower itself, on the south tower and on other parts of the fabric. The arrangement of the bells in the new frame and the direction of their swing have been partly influenced by what these tests revealed. The period during which the bells will be away is expected to be five months.

Glazing

Reglazing of twelve triforium windows on the north side was begun in the autumn of 1970, J.W. Gray and Sons erecting the scaffolding, our masons carrying out stone repairs and Goddard and Gibbs making and fixing the glass.

Four of the six windows in the west half of the nave have been completed and the other two should be finished shortly.

To forestall another price rise Goddard and Gibbs has been instructed to make the glass for the next six so that this will be ready for fixing when required.

Chapels

On November 25th 1970, at a service attended by the Queen Mother, three gifts were dedicated in the Nurses' Chapel: a plaque recording its origin and furnishing; a carpet for the altar; and cushions and kneelers for the stalls. The notice in the plaque was written and illuminated on vellum by Miss Sherley of Cobham, Kent, and framed by the Rowley Gallery, London.

A case to contain the flag of the Commando Association, which is to be laid up in St George's chapel, has been made for fixing on the west wall before its unveiling by the Queen Mother on May 1st.

A new floor in that part of St Faith's chapel at present paved in plain 19th century tiles was first proposed ten years ago. Through the Perkins' bequest[1] it is now to be provided. The paving, on which preparatory work has started in Whitehead's yard, will be of Devonshire marble from Kingsteignton.

To mark the entrance to St Faith's as a place for private prayer a lamp presented by the Patriarch of Jerusalem is to hang over the door from the south transept. The wrought iron bracket from which this decorative ornament will be suspended is being made.

Cleaning of the wall painting over the altar, which it was hoped Mrs Baker would carry out this winter, is again delayed pending approval by the Pilgrim Trust of her estimate. The result will probably be another long wait and an increase in her costs.

Crouchback tomb

The sum agreed with the Ecclesiastical Insurance Office as compensation for the damage to this tomb was £12,000. A scaffold has been erected on its north side and Miss Plummer has started work. She will be engaged on it for an indefinite period.

Monuments

On the Northumberland monument in St Nicholas' chapel the names and dates of those interred in the family vault were incised on the central marble panel of the base. Care was taken to match the new lettering to that on the main inscription panel above and probably few people would now be aware of any change. The cost of this work was met by the Duke of Northumberland and his sister the Duchess of Sutherland.

In the south transept the large floor slab commemorating William Spottiswoode 1825–1883 has been renewed at the expense of descendants in America, the inscription having become so worn as to be illegible. The original version was recorded in the Library and it seemed best to make the new stone a replica of the old despite very coarse lettering and inferior literary quality.

The worn lettering on the grave of William Wilberforce in the north transept has also been restored at the expense of Mr D. Wrangham. The incised letters have been sharpened and filled with a white mastic.

In the south cloister the very large slab which Dean Stanley believed to mark the burial place of twenty six monks of Westminster who died in the plague[2] was lifted in December 1970 and removed to J. Whitehead & Sons' yard at Kensington. The inscription had become almost invisible and the surface of the stone very uneven; but it was hoped that, if this could not be rubbed down successfully, the stone might be reversed and used the other way up. Examination showed however that this was not feasible. The thickness of the stone was not the same throughout its length and past attempts to make good hollows in its surface with cement had weakened it so much that even its handling was precarious. The stone is being 'lined' with a concrete backing which will stiffen it sufficiently to permit of removing enough of the surface to get an even face for recutting the inscription. A Countess of Bath was found to have been buried beneath the stone in a grave of which the existence was unknown.[3]

In the 1970 Audit Report reference was made to deepening the letters on the memorial to Tompion and Graham in the nave.[4] The Worshipful Company of Clockmakers have since enquired whether it would be feasible to add, at the head of the slab, the arms of the Company and the words 'Father of English Clockmaking'. Following a meeting on the site, when I explained how this might be done and what the cost would be, the matter was to be considered further by the Company. The postal strike may have held up a further communication from them.

The condition of the 19th century brasses in the nave came to notice afresh as the result of observations by Commander Theodore. He averred that the portrait of Street was losing its authenticity as a likeness and, to make comparison possible, produced a tracing of the original cartoon. Though I think that less harm has come to this and the other brasses than might have been expected, it would unquestionably be better if they were not exposed to the scraping of chairs and feet and could be properly seen. But until repaving of the nave can be undertaken, when the siting of memorials in its floor would have to be reviewed, no effective action seems possible. Commander Theodore has meanwhile allowed copies to be made of the original drawings for the brasses in his possession and these have been deposited in the Library.

On the monument of Queen Elizabeth I a new sceptre and a cross for the orb are being made to replace those long since lost or stolen from the effigy. The cost is being borne by Mr Court Mappin.

On the recommendation of the late Mr Kingsley Adams, Director of the National Portrait Gallery, Mrs Bolt was commissioned to carve a head for the effigy of Henry V. The work has been carried out in polyester resin, resembling the oak of the recumbent figure in colour but just distinguishable as not part of what is original. In the design of the metal crown, now being made, valuable advice on historical details was given by Mr J. Nevinson.

Memorials

A memorial floor slab to David Lloyd George in the north aisle of the nave was unveiled on July 27th 1970. The work was executed by Mr Jonah Jones to the design of Mr Clough Williams Ellis.

A floor slab of black marble, with the inscription inlaid in white marble, was placed over the grave of Lord Dowding north of the altar in the Battle of Britain chapel.

The memorial to Winston Churchill in the nave and the India memorial in the west cloister were re-polished.

For dedication on May 18th 1971 a tablet of Roman stone framed in Belgian fossil marble is being made to commemorate Lord Hailey. It will be placed in the fourth bay from the south of the west cloister, the wall of which is being renewed in Clipsham stone.

On the grave of Harry Carter the name and dates of his wife, Nan Carter, have been added.

At the request of the family a new stone is to be placed over the grave of William Bishop. On the new one, which will have to be of marble, the name of his wife, who died this year, will be included.

The Bridge

Early in April 1970 the bridge, presented by the Institution of Civil Engineers, was dedicated and brought into use. By not blocking the circuit of the ambulatory at floor level and thus easing the circulation of crowds it has proved a great convenience.

Yet the former steps which led up to the Chapel of the Confessor at its east end and which were made redundant by the new bridge have now unaccountably re-appeared in the north ambulatory in front of the tomb of Henry III where they serve no purposes whatsoever. I am told indeed that they represent a positive danger for small children who, not seeing that they lead nowhere, can run up them and fall off to their hurt.[5]

The Cloisters

Pending a decision on the fountain the well in the centre of the lawn has remained boarded over.

An increasing tendency for the public to enter the garth has been evident during the past year. Signs of this had been noted at the time of the last Audit Chapter and it would seem expedient to forestall any further development of it. Since it would not be practicable to glaze the openings in the north and east walks, the only alternative would be to insert simple wrought iron grilles, less elaborate than those in the south and west walks but architecturally suitable and adequate for protection.[6]

Servery

For convenience when the Jerusalem Chamber is used for dinners and receptions a servery is being made in the short passage leading to College Hall. Plans were prepared in the summer of 1970 and the fittings, made by our joiners, were finished at the end of that year. Fixing it had to be delayed until another room could be allocated as a changing room for the Stewards.[7]

College Hall

At the request of Westminster School plans are being prepared for an alteration in the kitchen which will give space for two more gas cookers, similar to the three that exist under the original stone arch in its east wall. Investigation has shown that a similar arch exists alongside, concealed by brickwork inserted perhaps 50 or more years ago. When opened out the new cookers will be set within it leaving space in the depth of wall behind for storage or other use.

The work would have to be carried out in the summer holiday and the School, who will bear the cost, have asked if it may be carried out by the Abbey staff.

Song school

Air conditioning has been installed to remedy inadequate ventilation.

Houses

No. 2 Little Cloister was redecorated in the summer of 1970. Alterations were carried out to the flat on the top floor of no. 4, including the installation of a new hot water system, extension of central heating from the boiler of no. 4 and additional radiators.

A loose chimney pot on the stack of the west end of no. 5 Little Cloisters necessitated the erection of scaffolding for its removal. Brickwork added at some time to improve the draught by heightening the chimney was found to be defective and taken off. Relieved of unnecessary weight the stack is better for being restored to the original design. It may in time become necessary to treat the other two on this house in the same way.

The west half of the Surveyor's office has been altered to provide a room for the Clerk of Works. The room previously occupied by him is to be used by the Stewards as a changing room.

In the Deanery the ceiling of the hall was repaired and redecorated. A simple wrought iron handrail has been made for the steps to the garden terrace.

An inspection of 4B Dean's Yard showed an outbreak of damp in a corner of the dining room and many cracks in the walls and ceilings. The former is attributable to a defective downpipe on the street front where there is evidence of rather inferior repair carried out after the war. The cracks may partly have been caused by traffic vibration but, in the south wall of the drawing room, to temperature changes caused by the installation of central heating by Westminster School in the adjoining premises.

A new gas fired hot water system is about to be installed in the house itself and repairs will be carried out before redecoration which will follow.

A survey has been made of no. 20 Dean's Yard and a certain amount of exploratory work carried out to the walls and floors. A meeting was held with a representative of the Historic Buildings Department of the Greater London Council to explain the scheme for using the building as a new Chapter Office and enable him to see it in its present state.

Choir School

Plans were submitted by Mr Herbert of the firm of Rogers Chapman & Thomas for replacing the one storey block facing Great Smith Street by a new building of two storeys to provide more practice rooms, a rehearsal room and additional lavatories. In view of the estimated cost – approximately £23,000 – and for other reasons it was decided to investigate alternative ways of meeting the school's needs.

Bookshop

To improve ventilation new lay-lights were fitted in the ceilings throughout.

Little Dean's Yard

Drawings by Mr Macfayden of Carden and Godfrey for a new building on the site of the present bursar's office were submitted for comment by Westminster School in December 1970. The design follows closely that of Singleton's house, demolished about 1830 but illustrated by a print in Lawrence Tanner's book on the School. Of four storeys, the top one in the roof, and faced in brick, the building should take its place in Little Dean's Yard very satisfactorily.

A scheme for commemorating the headmastership of John Carleton by a fountain in the wall alongside the gates from Little Dean's Yard to College Garden was submitted in February 1971. The design for this had been obtained from Crowther of Sion Lodge, Twickenham, who deal in antiques but presumably undertake the execution of new work as well. I have advised the Bursar that the architectural details are amateurish and need amending as shown on a drawing supplied to him. So far as I know, the matter is being referred back to the Committee dealing with it.

College garden

The ground between the central path in College Garden and the street entrance to 2 Abbey Gardens has been tidied up by the Ministry of Works in a satisfactory manner.

To meet the Ministry's request for a screen on the east side of the entrance to 1 Abbey Garden a fence of wattle hurdles is to be fixed on wooden posts attached to the brickwork of the parapet wall. This type of fencing may be seen on the wall separating the garden in front of St James' Palace from the Mall; but it has taken a great deal of enquiry to find a firm who now supply it.

St Catherine's garden

Repair and repointing of the wall on the south side has continued whenever it has been possible to spare a mason from other work. Not only on the south but on the west side there is still much to do, as well as to the bases of the pillars which need consolidation before their stone work disintegrates further.

This is a typical example of a task that ought to be undertaken and completed in one operation but, with our small number of masons, can only get periodic attention. Progress is bound to be slow.

The Chapter House

The Ministry of Works have followed up cleaning of the exterior by stone repairs to pinnacles and flying buttresses, entailing scaffolding in the gardens of nos. 1 and 2 Little Cloisters and on the path between the Chapter House and the George V memorial garden. It will no doubt be in place for some time.

In the last report attention was drawn to the retaining wall – if such it can be called – to the border between the eastern flying buttresses. I would again urge the desirability of something more creditable to Abbey property.

Masons' yard

To make possible a slight enlargement of working space the corrugated iron enclosure was extended along the south side of Henry VII's chapel and small trees planted to screen its east end.

General

To repeat what has been said so often before in these reports about tidiness would be tedious. Of more interest may be a mention of various points raised by the Lady guides when I met them for a recent tour of the Abbey.

They are set out as I noted them afterwards and on some I add my comments in brackets.

The position of the typewritten lists identifying the banners in Henry VII's chapel was strongly criticized. It was felt that they would be better at the east end of the stalls where people standing to read them would not impede movement to the same extent as at the entrance to the chapel (I agree)[8]

Some other position was requested for the framed notice on the right hand wall at the entrance to the Queen Elizabeth aisle. People stopping to read this blocked ingress and egress. (Were it moved to the only other blank wall on the left slightly further in the difficulty would remain. To place it over the wall panelling either inside or outside the chapel would, it was agreed, be wrong. The wording on the notice is short enough to be read in a few seconds. I think in the circumstances the notice is best left where it is)

The cradle tomb of the infant daughter of James I has, it seems, a great fascination for children but on dark days the reflection in the mirror needs some illumination. Could a low powered lamp be concealed in the canopy of the cradle? (This deserves consideration)

Could concealed lamps be placed on the top of the baldachino over the altar in Henry VII's chapel to give a diffused light onto the vaulting of the apse and in particular the gilded boss in its centre – much as light is diffused from concealed fittings on the west wall? (Experiments might be worth while).

Dislike was expressed of the shape of the lights on the stall desks in Henry VII's chapel in relation to the pedestal on which they stand. They were regarded as insignificant as well as inadequate and a strong preference was expressed for the trial shade on the Queen's stall (I naturally agree).

In the chapel of Our Lady of the Pew it was alleged that the single existing lamp was never turned on and that some light was necessary both to show the wall paintings and to reduce the risk of people tripping over the step in the floor. (I pointed out that the existing lamp is a naked bulb placed off centre of the vaults and totally unsuitable for the illumination of this chapel. This brought the obvious reply that it would not be difficult to supersede it by something better and better placed).

A desire that the saddle, sword and shield of Henry V should remain on the beam in his Chantry received unanimous and most emphatic expression They are apparently of unfailing interest.[9]

The need for railings to protect the south side of the tomb of Henry III as again mentioned (I wrote about this in last year's report)

Of the three tapestries[10] at the east end of the Elizabeth aisle, two have red backgrounds and one green. The green must always therefore be in the centre. The figure on it is of the Confessor holding out his ring. But as he now appears to be offering it to Henry III instead of to St John, the red panels are wrongly placed and should be transposed (This is certainly right).

A plea was made for making more legible the names on the graves of a) Robert Adam, b) Richard Brinsley Sheridan, c)Addison – where many brass letters are missing from the inscription.

> 6th March 1971
> S.E. Dykes Bower, Surveyor of the Fabric.

[1]   The western part of this chapel. Given in memory of Jocelyn Perkins, former Sacrist.
[2]   The Black Death. Traditionally this stone was known as Long Meg.

³   Henrietta Pulteney, according to the coffin plate. No other burials or skeletons were found
    beneath this stone.
⁴   This covers the graves of Thomas Tompion and George Graham, buried together.
⁵   Once the bridge was taken down these steps were used to access the chapel between the
    tombs of Edward I and Henry III, although the chapel did eventually close to the general
    public later owing to the fragile state of the floor.
⁶   This was not done.
⁷   The Honorary Stewards who assist at special and other services in the Abbey.
⁸   These were female volunteers working under the Dean's Verger. The list was moved to the
    east end.
⁹   Only the shield, helm and saddle were displayed on the beam, as the sword was in the
    Museum. The sword is now thought to be later in date than Henry V.
¹⁰ The tapestries depicting Henry III and St Edward and the Pilgrim were woven on William
    Morris looms and presented to the Abbey. They are now in the Queen's Diamond Jubilee
    Galleries.

78.   WAM S/1/117

St Margaret's Church Westminster

Feb. 1971

The comprehensive report made on this church by Cluttons in 1968 under
the Inspection of Churches Measure 1955 is based on what has clearly been
thorough and careful observation. I endorse both its analysis of existing defects
and diagnosis of possible latent trouble.

But in the three years that have elapsed since it was written circumstances
have to some extent altered. For financial reasons a start has not been made
on any of the major repairs which it recommended might be carried out in
stages; nor, until a major appeal has been organised, is there much prospect
that it could be. Such an appeal is now to be a joint one for the Abbey and
St Margaret's and at least five years may elapse before any large programme
of work becomes practicable. By that time costs will have risen and structural
deterioration increased.

There is the further consideration that as the activities of St Margaret's
become less those a parish church and more linked with those of the Abbey,
thought will have to be given to what that may imply. The use of the building,
the functions it would service in a new or partially changed life, could affect its
internal treatment. Some attempt, at least, not too constrained by memories of
what the church has been in the past, must be made to look ahead.

The purpose of quinquennial survey reports is to record the structural
condition of a building and any list of defects which have to be described tends
to seem their main content: what is not defective calls for less comment. A first
perusal is apt therefore to induce an impression of gloom is not despair, as
though so much was wrong that little could be right.

In fact the picture of the building that the report presents is not very different
from what might be expected of a large church of its type. In 500 years age takes

its toll: and having had to withstand not just the effects of London's polluted atmosphere, but in more recent times traffic vibration and war time bombing, St Margaret's has been subjected to conditions probably more severe than those affecting comparable buildings in provincial towns or the country. That many are not immune from troubles quite as numerous is in no way to minimize that these are serious but to recognize that they are by no means abnormal.

Architecturally other churches may be as fine. St Margaret's is exceptional by virtue of its position, history and associations; and an ominous precedent would indeed be created if the future of a church so famous and in a unique way of national importance cannot be assured.

Whereas a Parliamentary grant was forthcoming when the tower was refaced by John James of Greenwich in 1735, as well as on other occasions, no such aid is obtainable today. Nor, with fewer residents within the parish boundaries, can support be enlisted as formerly from those who felt a loyalty to it as their place of worship. For though the House of Commons was mindful of its obligations to the church, the parishioners were equally solicitous for its upkeep and contributed their part when intermittent repairs and restoration became necessary.

With much work carried out in the 18th and the later 19th century St Margaret's cannot be said to have suffered from neglect. Its first trouble was no doubt, as on the Abbey, the failure of the original stonework which weathered badly and succumbed to the smoke of London when houses were warmed by coal or wood fires and Westminster was a populous area. The church would not have been, as it was, entirely refaced externally if the medieval walling had not reached a drastic state of decay. What was done to remedy this accorded with the practice of the times; but it wholly changed the appearance of the building and, ironically enough, has itself proved the cause of some of the troubles that now have to be remedied afresh.

By comparison with what internally is so good the exterior is strangely disappointing. St Margaret's is inevitably dwarfed by the Abbey but it is not a small church and ought to look larger than it does. That it fails to do so is partly due to the excessive size of the stones used in the new walling and the thin joints which hardly break their smooth surface. Such 18th century masonry is alien to Gothic work in which the stones are smaller, the coursing less regular and the mortar joints wider. But architects accustomed to designing classical churches knew no other and, confronted with the wreck of the older stonework, may have been the more convinced of the superiority of the new.

A second change affected St Margaret's. It can hardly be supposed that a church designed and built by such a skilled master mason as Robert Stowell would have been so plain outside as to lack battlements, pinnacles and buttresses. These were normal elements in the architectural language of the time and would have been incorporated as a matter of course.

But if all the original stonework had after 200 years fallen into decay, carved and moulded features had probably suffered worst. In the late 18th century, when a 'neat edifice' was the ideal, there would have seemed every justification for doing away with the trappings of a style that was neither admired nor understood. The battlements and pinnacles were superseded by plain parapets and the aisle walls, instead of being punctuated by buttresses, became shadowless flat surfaces.

That the vigour of the west tower in its original form has been impoverished is obvious. As designed by Henry Redman – like Robert Stowell one of the master masons to the Abbey – this tower must have been far finer: one of a late Gothic group whose characteristics may have been derived from an unexecuted design by Reginald Ely for a tower at King's College, Cambridge.

John James' remodelling may be sufficiently acceptable as an example of 18th century Gothic but cannot be regarded as successful or particularly beautiful. The excessively large horizontal string courses in the lower half are out of scale with the west front of the church and what would seem to have been a reduction in the size of the pinnacles has weakened the tower's silhouette.

The next restoration in 1875 was much better and marked a return to architectural literacy. The windows received their correct tracery and no doubt Sir Gilbert Scott's wish would have been to go further in bringing the exterior back to its intended appearance. In the interior he was able to do more, giving it an impress which is still evident.

Twenty years later J.L. Pearson added the west and east porches and subsequently lengthened the chancel by six feet[1] – the latter so discreetly as to leave no sign of being an addition. The porches, though their detail now contrasts sharply with the coarseness of the stone above, would look appropriate if the building could ever recover its intended design, since the scale of the stonework is right and the general architectural treatment attuned to the period of Stowell's work.

St Margaret's today is a beautiful and harmonious unity within: outside a hybrid so shorn of architectural quality as no longer to be attractive. Now that for the third time, after intervals of roughly 100 years, fresh restoration is due, the question arises of how this should be carried out.

Is it rational to restore a restoration, if the latter itself is unsound? The south aisle wall provides an instance. Rusting of the iron cramps has split the stone in many places (see photograph 15) and will continue to do so elsewhere until the iron is eliminated. To take out and renew the worst affected stones would perpetuate a type of walling manifestly unsuited to the church; and the process would be repetitive as other stones demand attention. In a wall so blackened new stone would be startlingly white; yet were the whole washed to get uniformity of colour, water percolating into the stone would only accelerate rusting of the iron.

The north aisle wall is not faced with stone at all but with Roman cement, a material of limited life and that here has become stained and drab with age. Replacement by stone is overdue, not least because it is unfitting that a church fronting Parliament Square should present so mean an aspect. What then should the policy be? To match new stone, on this more important side, to that of the south side with its faults of scale, coursing and jointing; or to change to masonry that would be appropriate to the style of the church? If the latter, then the ultimate aim would have to be to continue with it throughout.

On the west wall of the nave, though the size of the stone courses is better, both corners, containing disused flues, are weak and require rebuilding. The gable parapet, of incongruous design, is also in poor order, as are the similar parapets over the aisles. Rebuilding could not be efficient if it failed to rectify the design of features, such as copings and drip moulds, that are functionally as well as stylistically defective.

A main criticism of the 18th century restoration must be that some of the classical details substituted for what were formerly Gothic are not adept for their purpose. The unsuitable formation of the cills to the clerestory (see photographs 5 and 7) is an example, and the report (Section 11.2–4) rightly emphasizes the consequential troubles caused by it.

The inadequate height of the parapets may be cited as another example. Barely sufficient to permit of the proper falls and weirs that will be needed when the lead in the parapet gutters is relaid, they are also too low for protection. Furthermore, lowering the level of what would have been the original parapets has impaired the proportions of the external design. And where, as at the east end of the aisles, battlements were rebuilt (see photograph 5) these are of insufficient height and crudely designed.

That the window tracery – almost the only part of the exterior which is architecturally correct – is generally in good order, is a cause for satisfaction because Sir Gilbert Scott's task of inserting it into 18th century Portland stone walls cannot have been easy: had he been able to rebuild these walls no doubt the windows would have received hood moulds. It is therefore essential to ensure that the windows remain in good order and any fractured mullions should, as recommended in Section 11.7, be made good at once.

Enough has been said on this particular question of faulty stone design to make clear that the major decision to be taken on future restoration is whether this should consist in repairing and making the best of what exists, or whether opportunity should be taken to eliminate inferior details and replace them by what would be structurally and architecturally more apposite. The first course is termed 'repair' because it would not, in my opinion, be effective restoration; first costs might be less but ultimate costs more, since the causes of trouble would not have been cured.

A building should not be saddled indefinitely with mistakes that were made at one point in time, even if it could be pleaded that they spoke the language of their age. The 18th century remodelling of the exterior of St Margaret's deserves none of the esteem due to so creditable an achievement as Hawksmoor's completion of the west towers of the Abbey.

To any hypothetical argument that authentic evidence for those details that would be redesigned is now lacking, the answer should be that comparative evidence could supply what would be needed. Gothic was an established language and, given a thorough knowledge of it, reconstruction of what is here missing should be neither difficult nor too conjectural.

Nevertheless in London Gothic detail must perforce be such that it offers minimum lodgement for the acid deposits that impair stone. The ornament in Pearson's porches is of high intrinsic merit; but if not kept clean by washing, its very elaboration will become a liability. In spite of being built in Portland stone and though not yet eighty years old, this is indeed already evident (Section 20.3.2 and 20.3.1 and see photograph 11 – heads of three pinnacles).

Even if cost imposed no check, nothing so intricate would be expedient in future. Nor, where some redesign is needed, would there be occasion for it.

But while there is a strong case for altering what is wrong on the church, this would apply less to the tower which, being relatively sound in itself, should perhaps continue to bear the marks of its 18th century alteration. To what is structurally an appendage, a distinct and different character may more readily be allowed.

The considerable amount of other work entailed in making good defects of one kind or another is so fully described in the quinquennial report as to call for little additional comment. I agree with the recommendation (Section 10.3.4) that lead should again be used when the roofs are relaid and that it should replace ashphalte on the vestries (Section 20.1.3); also that eventually the lead on the aisle roofs should be in shorter sheets with drips between.

With so much to do but lacking funds to begin on it the immediate question is to decide what and how much can, without undue risk, be deferred to five or more year s. Are some jobs so urgent that an effort ought to be made to tackle them if the outlay is not prohibitive?

It is difficult to give an assured answer because in the waiting period a contingency could arise that might suddenly prove serious. Complete overhaul of the electrical installation, already ordered, is certainly essential to the safety of the church. The top of the south west pinnacle of the tower that had become dangerous was removed in 1968 and has not yet been replaced. Other minor precautions of a temporary kind have been taken. But with no large works started the time and cost schedules for 1969 and 1970, as set out in the report, are already nullified.

The logical connection of one job with another inevitably augments the outlay to be faced on any one undertaking. Thus it would be desirable to deal as soon as possible with those places in the nave roof structure that have been badly affected by wet rot and beetle attack (see photographs 1–3) and to carry out such other repairs and further insecticidal treatment as would ensure safety. But to do this, or even to know precisely how much work is necessary, the roof must be laid open for examination from above. That means lifting the lead, itself due for recasting and relaying. And since the parapet gutters need re-forming, any alteration of the parapets themselves ought to be done at the same time. Thus those different tasks would have to be carried out as one joint operation and it is at least possible that its corollary might be extensive re-facing of the clerestory walls (ie. between the windows).

On such a long roof no doubt there would have to be division into stages, perhaps three bays being dealt with at one time. But even so, only a considerable sum of money could justify a start and, without that, there is no option but to wait till it can be obtained.

In so far as this procedure represents a calculated risk it is to be deprecated because there can be no certainty of the consequences. But treatment of the roof timbers with insecticide in 1961 must have afforded some protection and, although water penetration from the gutters has weakened the timbers at a dangerous point – their bearing on the wall plates – I incline to think that for some years this roof should not become dangerous.

Inspection of the nave roof timbers may make it easier to guess what the condition of the aisle roofs may be. Their lead is better than that on the nave but if any major repair of the timbers proves necessary it would probably have to be lifted and should then be relaid in shorter lengths. Again this ought to be combined with improvement of the parapets and parapet gutters.

To attempt re-facing of the south aisle will be impossible until the church has large funds at its disposal. Splitting of stones caused by their iron cramps will continue meanwhile but I would advise taking no action about it since the final aim should be to re-face this wall in better masonry without the use of iron. The unsightly rendering on the north aisle should similarly be left until it can be superseded by stone.

Earlier priority should be given to the west end of the nave where the corners will require watching. Their rebuilding in solid walling (ie. without the disused flues) would coincide with that of the clerestory walls, just as rebuilding of the gable parapet would be synchronised with releading of the nave roof.[2] The defective west and east parapets of the aisle roofs might have to wait on any work to the aisle roofs.

Danger arising from this stonework is, in my opinion, not likely to be excessive for five or more years, though deterioration caused by open joints and progressive weathering is bound to continue. On the other hand immediate attention must be given to fractures in the window mullions, if any more occur.

The condition of the tower should not cause undue anxiety provided observation is kept on those defects (eg. spalling of the stone face, eroded drip courses and splitting of the stone caused by iron cramps)[3] which are already known. Since, however, it is important that the frequent ringing of the bells should not have any adverse effect on the structure of the tower, it might be advisable to carry out such work to them and the bell frame as would ensure that they work smoothly. The cost of this – in 1968 a little over £1,000 – represents an outlay that perhaps could be afforded from church funds over a period of one or two years.

I do not know whether anything would in fact be available from these for some of the other jobs that could be tackled separately and are not of the same magnitude as those that must await the results of an appeal. If so the west and east porches merit consideration. As has already been mentioned their stonework, had it been kept clean, would still be good today. The decay which has already obliterated the mouldings of three capitals on the west porch and caused the loss of carved details on the pinnacles (one entire pinnacle on the east porch is missing) will speedily do yet more damage unless checked. For a comparatively modest sum of money spent now a great deal will be saved later and conservation of what so well deserves it is common prudence. Stone, the ironwork of the gates, the lead on the roof each call for expenditure.

Strengthening and repaving of the floor of the north porch is imperative to ensure its safety. And since the visitor forms his first impression of a church as he enters, it would be desirable to carry out at the same time obvious improvements needed to its inner doors and general decorative conditions.

In the vestries the floors are of timber, covered with linoleum, under which the condition of the boarding and joints is not known and ought to be investigated. Match-boarding, here affixed to some of the walls, was often in the past used to cover walls which tended to be damp, and for this reason apart from that of poor appearance, its removal would be advisable. The glazing in the windows, the sky lights, the plumbing arrangements and much else combine to suggest that, apart from some redecoration, little may have been done to these rooms for a long time. Modernization is overdue and their amenities made more attractive.

The interior

Passing now from the structure of the church to its contents the purpose of the second part of this report is to consider how the best may be made of the interior.

In deference to sentiment and associations as much as to expense, the aim should be to see how little alteration, rather than how much, is necessary. The right start, as in any church, is to note those good features with which it is already endowed since these are assets whose value must not be impaired.

St Margaret's is as uncomplicated in plan as it is harmonious in design. It has undergone no such structural alterations as are evident in most medieval churches and is no longer subdivided into parts by screens, although these once existed. The whole is seen at a glance, each bay identical with the next and productive by repetition of an architectural rhythm that unties simplicity with stateliness.

The focal splendour of the interior is the old glass in the east window: an impression of its beauty is probably what stays longest in the memory of most visitors.

The west window, by Clayton and Bell, has great merit but is marred by patches of plain glass in breakages caused by war damage. Such an incomprehensible failure to carry out better repair should be made good as soon as possible.

In the west window of the north aisle, nearly as good and also by Clayton and Bell, new stained glass was properly inserted to replace what was broken but the new panel is inferior in drawing and colour and does not quite blend with the existing glass.

The west window of the south aisle, by Henry Holiday, is interesting as a late example of the influence of the Pre-Raphaelite movement. The heavy opaque effect of the glass is due to dirt. Cleaning would reveal it as more attractive than a superficial glance might suggest.[4]

Apart from the relatively modern armorial window[5] at the east end of the south aisle nothing else can be praised. The two easternmost windows in the north aisle, as well as that east of the north entrance are very bad. The third from the east, of which some remains have been left in place, was similar to its neighbours and there can be no regret that the rest of it has gone.

The north aisle windows should be re-glazed throughout in plain glass similar to that in Henry VII's chapel in Westminster Abbey which is decorative through being perfectly homologous with the architecture. The quality and slightly varied tints of the glass, the proportion of the diamonds, the thickness of the lead cames contribute to its effect; but not more than the external iron saddlebars and stancheons, without which a Gothic window looks incomplete. Nowhere is this better demonstrated than at three great late medieval buildings: Henry VII's chapel, King's College, Cambridge and St George's chapel, Windsor. Because the windows of each have retained their full complement of ferramenta the effect of the glazing, within as well as without, is immeasurably enhanced.

I therefore deprecate the suggestion in Section 17.2 of the Quinquennial Report that the ironwork should be removed from windows, as was done when those in the south aisle were re-glazed in 1966. Ideally saddlebars and stancheons today should be of non-ferrous metal such as Delta bronze. But this is expensive and splitting of the stone where the bars enter the walls can be avoided by welding bronze ends on to the iron, more cheaply, galvanizing and coating the iron with bronze.

Stancheons and saddlebars should not only be retained in the north aisle but added in the clerestory of the nave where the glass inserted as recently as 1954 is already buckling in places and may have to be renewed when other work is carried out at that level. Indifferent in quality and leading, its replacement would in any case be desirable.

The numerous mural tablets deserve to rank high among the possessions of the church. Varied in style and representative of many periods they form a remarkable collection; but for two reasons it is not seen to advantage. In line with normal medieval practice the walls must originally have been plastered, and, where not decorated with wall painting, limewashed white. Stripping of the plaster in the 19th century exposed rubble masonry that was never meant to show and this was in places pointed in black cement so that the mortar joints are now unduly prominent. The rough surface of the stone, begrimed by a hundred years of London direct as well as by convention over heating pipes and radiators, has turned a grey colour that makes a drab background to anything attached to it.

Wherever decoration had faded or nearly disappeared, marble has not been polished and painted heraldry and lettering have become dim, the memorials themselves has lost their primal brightness: their effect then tends to be dull if not oppressive. Cleaning and treatment similar to that given to the monuments in the Abbey would restore the attractiveness that is their due and add to the beauty of an interior of which they have become an intrinsic feature.

Yet re-plastering of the walls would be a necessary corollary. And to ensure that the white plaster, as well as the tablets themselves, should not quickly become discoloured by convection, all radiators and pipe runs against the walls would have to be moved. That would entail so major a modification of the heating system that a new one would be likely to be more satisfactory. Although the heating engineers in 1968 did not anticipate that any early change would be necessary, a solid fuel installation of 1955 will have served twenty years at least by the time any major recommendations in this report are implemented and its efficiency and lay out may by then be out-dated.

This introduces consideration of the floor. In the south aisle, between the blocks of pews, it is entirely of slate grave stones: in the north aisle and nave only partially, though if the grave stones now concealed under the organ could be lifted, they might be enough to fill one or the other. Elsewhere, except in the chancel, the floor is of small red tiles, with iron grilles over the heating ducts. Its condition is good but a few loose tiles show that the usual trouble with tiled paving of this kind is beginning. Once several in one area loosen it is not easy to re-bed them satisfactorily and more general disintegration ensures.

Since tiles wear down and become uneven a limited life must be expected for them and replacement by stone or marble would be expedient when changes are made in the heating. A new system would almost certainly make the open heating ducts, which act as dust traps, redundant. Without the gratings over them the aisles between the blocks of pews would gain a greater sense of width.

The floor of patterned tiles in the chancel is typical work of Scott and not without decorative value. It is in good order except for a dislocation south of the altar, possibly attributable to the same settlement that caused the fracture in the east wall of the south aisle.

Looking next up to the roof, the bosses on the chancel ceiling (more elaborate than that of the nave) have been gilded so that they stand out brightly against the dark tone of the oak. This shows up their carving but weakens the organic design of the roof by giving undue prominence to what now look like applied ornaments. When scaffolding is erected for examination of the condition of the roof timbers it would be desirable at least to gild salient members of the main trusses and panel ribs so that the bosses should not remain isolated. If colour were used as well as gold, so that the roof did not assume a two tone scheme – gold and brown – the effect would be better. The logical outcome would be decoration of the panels themselves, which is what may originally have been provided. (The present ceiling cannot afford evidence, as it was virtually renewed in the 1875 restoration).

Decoration would have to be done well enough or it should not be done at all. The greater enrichment of the chancel ceiling, compared with that of the nave, might justify its being done alone; but were it possible to extend decoration throughout, would magnify the scale of the church enormously and, in combination with the right clear glass in the windows, be an adornment preferable to any stained glass.

Although Pearson [sic] lengthened the sanctuary, Bodley[6] furnished it. The reredos, incorporating as the central feature an 18th century carved panel of Christ at Emmaus which he coloured so skilfully that it looks quite in accord with the elaborate Gothic frame, is extremely good. Equally so are his altar cross and candlesticks, particularly the latter.

The standard candlesticks, given a few years ago, are posts from a four-poster bed, fixed on rather crude bases. Though incongruous with Bodley's work, they are not unpleasing in themselves and would look better if they carried tall tapering candles of smaller diameter.

The two excellent 17th century chairs on the north side of the sanctuary were – incredible as it may seem – cast out of the Abbey before the coronation of George VI as superfluous. The Abbey's loss has been St Margaret's gain.

The Bishop's chair must date from the first part of the 19th century and is not unworthy of its place. The two 'Glastonbury' chairs and fald stools should be permanently banished.

The sanctuary contains also an old and quite good credence table and two unusual mahogany altar rails. The hinged replicas, added to afford greater kneeling length for communicants, are not of equal quality and should be kept folded back when not in use.

Scott's choir stalls, which were designed to make use of three medieval bench ends, have been subjected to misguided insertion of an unnecessary step: their original levels can be seen at the ends and it may well be that the original platforms still remain, though covered over. The boys' seat now cuts across the recessed panels of its back so that their base mouldings are concealed and, in the men's rows, the seats are clearly in wrong relation with the bench ends.

At the east end of the men's seats the arms of the bench ends are missing having, by an act of inexcusable vandalism, been cut off to provide an extra seat on each side. There are no longer used and the bench ends should be reinstated. It would be extraordinary if such things could have been thrown away: there must be a chance that they lie forgotten and buried in some obscure place and a search should be instituted to find them.

To make bad worse, raising the choir platforms necessitated higher music desks which now look as ungainly as they are inelegant.

Fortunately this sorry tale of mistakes is not irreparable and could be rectified at no great cost. Restoring the correct levels would not only do justice to the choir stalls but improve the whole aspect of the chancel.

Architecturally the screens in the arches behind the stalls suffer from a certain thinness but more from the plate glass which was doubtless inserted to keep out draughts – a trouble that might be eliminated by a new heating system. Plate glass, apart from being objectionable for causing reflections, is anomalous in a Gothic screen. If there must be glass it should be leaded; much better would be the introduction in each light or iron saddlebars and stancheons such as were normal to medieval screens.

On the north side the screens were later heightened to conceal the organ. Regrettably the ends of the added portions were not properly returned and, to mask the omission, boarding painted to look like stone was inserted between the woodwork and the pillars. These bungled corners should be corrected when (or before) the organ is rebuilt.

The stone pulpit, designed by Scott and subsequently painted and decorated, as well as the polished brass lectern, are representative of their period and should not be displaced. The massive red covered step to the latter would be needed if the choir stalls reverted to their former level.

In many late Perpendicular churches of symmetrical plan, with windows in every bay, there is no ideal place for an organ. The position of that in St Margaret's, in what otherwise could have been a side chapel, is not entirely satisfactory but the only one possible even were the existing organ replaced by a smaller one. So fine an instrument, however, ought unquestionably to remain though, being now of considerable age, it may soon be due for mechanical overhaul. Whether any changes in its arrangement, permitting the addition of an organ case, would then be feasible will have to await consideration when the work is carried out. Up till 1897 the organ had two cases which, having been designed by Dr A.G. Hill [1857–1925 Westminster School and Jesus College Cambridge, organ builder and head of the firm bearing his name who rebuilt the organ in the Abbey in the time of Sir Frederic Bridge. Also a designer of organ cases e.g. Peterborough cathedral, Gloucester cathedral, Beverley Minster etc.] would almost certainly have been good; they were removed first to a church at Holbeck in Leeds and then to St George's cathedral, Capetown. Lacking a case ever since, the organ is undeniably ugly, because its frontage to the north aisle is composed of very large pipes quite out of scale with the nave pillars.

Little need be said of the electric lighting. Because the lights are sensibly placed the present lay out is not being changed in the re-wiring now being carried out.

At no great cost the existing wrought iron pendants might be retained and utilised as the basis for a more decorative scheme of illumination, if funds should not suffice for an entirely new design. Indirect lighting would not be applicable because the building is one in which there is no concealment for fittings.

The lighting of the reredos by a fluorescent tube fixed to the back of the altar, which has been moved forward to accommodate it, is effective except in respect of the altar ornaments which, silhouetted against a bright background, now appear dark themselves.

In an age unaccustomed to large congregations, the nave may look over-filled with pews. A t the time of Scott's restoration St Margaret's had become, under Farrar,[7] an exceedingly active church and its seating capacity of 950, in Hensley Henson's time and later, would not have seemed excessive. While lack of open space can be a disadvantage, the notion that there cannot be too much of it is mistaken. A building does not automatically look larger for being empty: it may look smaller. Churches for example never seem so big as when a congregation completely fills them. Repetition is a very important factor in architecture and multiplication of the same unit, whether in structural decoration (e.g. the wall panelling of Henry VII's chapel) or in pews can be of positive value in imparting a sense of scale. Moreover, depressing as may be the sight of empty pews, their presence is at least some token that churches exist not for show but for use.

Much depends of course on the nature of the seating – whether pews are good in design and colour and consistent throughout the building.

St Margaret's is fortunate: Scott's pews are respectable work of their time and will get to look better as they get older. The same design extends unchanged throughout the nave and its aisles. The colour is harmonious with the roof and other woodwork of the building and there is little trouble from beetle or worm in either the oak or the wooden platforms on which the pews are fixed.

On the north side of the nave, however, where war damage occurred in the last war, some new pews have been inserted to take the place of those destroyed or made unuseable. Their bench ends, being plain, do not match those of the other pews; in other details care was not taken to repeat these exactly; and their colour is not identical. Where all else is of one pattern they alone are different. Yet against the west walls of both aisles are some spare pews of Scott's design, serving no purpose where they are, that could be used to restore consistency. Those that now face north in the bays of the south aisle, east of the main block, could also be available.

A plea for more free space in St Margaret's is in fact justifiable and the opportunities for obtaining it are in this south aisle – behind the choir stalls – and at the west end of the nave. For reasons to be given later, it would also be expedient to dispense with the five short pews on either side of the central aisle which could then similarly be adapted to take the place of the war damage pews.

Five loose pews that were temporarily used in the nave after the damage first occurred should be got rid of as they merely add to the congestion at the west end and elsewhere.

General

From this survey of the interior it is pertinent to pass to consideration of the future of St Margaret's, after its life becomes fused with that of the Abbey.[8]

As this report has adumbrated, the exterior, apart from the tower, would appear largely new – its walls refaced and Gothic design re-established.

The interior, after structural restoration, would be no different from what it is now except that its colouration would be transformed by washing of the stonework (remains of the limewash still adhering to the stone cause much of it to look grey instead of its natural shad. They could be brushed off), re-glazing of the clerestory and aisle windows and cleaning of the mural tablets.

If circumstances were then to suggest modification of its existing arrangement, how far would this be reconcilable with a building of such co-ordinate architectural character? In what ways may its future be foreseen?

Some things may be anticipated with confidence. For weddings and memorial services the status of the church should be enhanced by the link with the Abbey. For organ and choral recitals, equally for special addresses and lectures, it has the qualifications of a good auditorium.

The close connection of the House of Commons with St Margaret's has lasted so long that its persistence can be taken for granted. On rare occasions when Parliament may gather for worship within its walls, the building could again be a setting for memorable, historic scenes.

In respect of accommodation for each of these purposes, the primary need will be an ample rather than limited supply of seating, so that no very drastic curtailment would be practicable. Its present capacity is in excess of anything that the church even of a populous parish would normally hope to use, much less one where the parish has ceased to exist. Yet St Margaret's may not be able to divest itself entirely of its birth right which, alongside the Abbey, is in some degree also its privilege. The atmosphere of a parish church is congenial to many people and, for perhaps a long time to come, the tradition of years may not be quickly extinguished. It is never impossible moreover that the unexpected happens and that a non-parochial church might develop an extra-mural ministry of its own.

On so tentative a supposition there can be no provision. Weighed, nevertheless, against stronger probabilities, too much adaptation to contemporary desiderata of parish church practice would seem inopportune.

For those who delight in the setting for worship that the Abbey provides nothing else could take its place. But if the choir services could not but continue where they are, transfer of non-statutory services such as the 6.30pm Sunday service might benefit St Margaret's by ending what is now duplicated at the same hour and at such close quarters.

If indeed the Abbey has to submit itself yet more to becoming a show place for eight instead of four million visitors a year on whose freedom of movement there must be the minimum restriction, practical difficulties such as moving chairs would not doubt be eased by transferring certain other services to St Margaret's. This might weaken its own life; but the transfer would at least be to no unworthy home – a church with its own distinguished tradition of preaching and music.

Inasmuch as a larger intake of visitors can be expected two changes in St Margaret's are likely to become imperative. Its interior could not comfortably receive far more people than the not inconsiderable number who visit it now.

The clearance of pews and radiators from the west end of the aisles, already advocated, would go a little way to enlarge the area of clear space but not far enough. With an entrance on the north, another on the west and (as will be suggested) a third on the south, adequate room in front of each will be indispensable. It can only be gained by removal of the five short pews at the back of the nave, leaving one and a half bays free of any encumbrance. Visitors arriving en masse could here get a view of the church and decide whether they wished to stay to walk round it.

Removal of the north facing fixed pews in the south aisle would yield more open space if desired but is less essential. To set back the east frontage of the nave pews by the removal of three pews would be useful in giving greater width between them and the pulpit. But it would increase the distance between the congregation and the altar and difficulties might be incurred over alteration to the Speaker's and House of Commons pews.

The other change is more far-reaching. In bad weather people are deterred from walking even a short distance and once visitors to the Abbey found that St Margaret's was in the set itinerary, a covered way from one to the other would be demanded. For clergy and vergers also it would be convenient if not necessary.

If the blocked doorway in the northernmost bay of the east aisle of the north transept were re-opened a covered way or cloister could be built to join St Margaret's through a new door cut in the west bay of its south aisle. The church does not lie parallel with the Abbey and the west side of this cloister should be at a 90 degree angle to the latter. Arched glazed openings in it would give light and protection from the weather but the east wall would be solid and might take some of the memorials which would have to be removed from the east aisle of the north transept.

In St Margaret's the new entrance would displace only three tablets for which places could be found elsewhere. It would entail also building up at least the lower half of the west window of the south wall, which would then look like those in the eastern bays and moving the Nicholas Stone font. This small but beautiful ornament ought not to be hemmed in by pews and could either be placed in the nave in the centre of the area that would be cleared by removal of the short pews, or in the south aisle in front of the north facing pews which could then become the equivalent of what in the 17th century were called christening pews.

In the Abbey the east aisle of the north transept could not remain closed to visitors to serve as a chair store. When opened up as a thoroughfare some re-arrangement of its monuments would be unavoidable. The aisle is a crowded, unsightly corner of which reform is long overdue.

The new cloister, which would have to be Gothic in design, would be quite small – its height no more than that of St Margaret's vestry – so that the Houses of Parliament would, from the west, still be seen between the church and the Abbey.

It would necessarily sever the path between them to Old Palace Yard. But this being inevitable, no hardship would be caused by building a stone wall from St Margaret's vestry to the Abbey and thus enclosing a space which would provide, for both buildings, a masons' yard of ample size. This would have road access from the east by the existing gates and shut off from view only the least attractive part of the Abbey exterior up to about ten feet from the ground. The large plane trees, whose foliage relieves the sombre shade of this north side, could remain.[9]

The acquisition of a convenient masons' yard and more adequate storage space would be invaluable. In this manner it might, without architectural detriment and at no great cost, become a reality.

With St Margaret's thus physically integrated into the complex of buildings that Westminster Abbey comprises, there will pass to the Dean and Chapter part responsibility for a building that is the very embodiment of what may be deemed the conventional conception of an English parish church. As will have been seen from the frequent mention of his name, the interior of St Margaret's owes its present form very largely to Sir Gilbert Scott. Superficial judgment, even a few years ago, would have counted that against it. But opinion, constantly changing, has now come full circle. The 18th century has passed into history and admiration for all that was expressive of an Augustan age is, for a newer generation, excited by what is Victorian. In the world of architecture – and to some extent in the Church – the best work of the Gothic revival excites enthusiastic interest. There is recognition of its great achievements and growing watchfulness over their treatment.

For probably a long time ahead the trend of this will be increasingly sympathetic to much that has hitherto been slighted; and though accepted ideas, too often swayed by fashion, need not be overvalued, they have none the less to be reckoned with as a reality of some force.

Sir Gilbert Scott was surpassed as an architect by others of the time. But no-one was more representative of it. His work was extensive, important and the best of it, notably St Mary's cathedral, Edinburgh, outstandingly good. The restoration of St Margaret's was one of his last works (he died before it was finished) and has been rated as one of the most satisfactory. In the credit due to him Bodley should have a share, since the church owes much of its beauty to his treatment of the east end.

But buildings must be taken in their completeness and St Margaret's comes to the Abbey just at a time when its particular completeness is finding esteem. Should it be accepted for what it is or is it capable of being re-fashioned to suit new ideas?

So large a church might, for example, be expected to have a side chapel. The east end of the south aisle is disqualified as suitable because of the entrance door in its end wall; the north aisle because the organ is in what was formerly the Lady Chapel. To make a chapel further west in the aisle itself, with its altar backed by the ugly array of organ pipes, could hardly be satisfactory.

Nor, if an altar were placed in the nave, could the chancel become a chapel: since there is no other position for the organ the choir must remain in it. A nave altar is not thereby precluded. But the removal of several pews, including those of the Speaker and the House of Commons, which it would entail, might impair the effectiveness of the church for uses to which it is well fitted.

The conclusion must be that St Margaret's is too symmetrically balanced to be adaptable. However different it may once have been, with a rood screen and parcloses to chapels and chantries, no such precedent could reasonably be invoked for subdividing it today. Its character is that of a 'hall' church, to be used as one whole. There would in consequence be no need to add to expenditure on structural repair yet more for internal alteration.

A church so well known must always be under public notice. Discretion and firmness will be needed to ensure that restoration of its exterior is rational, not just a repeat of what exists, for in respect of buildings conservation – a magic word today – can too easily become mere resistance to change. St Margaret's is one in which change and freedom from change can each be defended.

It remains to take a glance into the future. While over the last few years the expanding life of Westminster Abbey, which St Margaret's will increasingly share, has been evident in various ways, one manifestation of it has acquired paramount importance.

A building that becomes the greatest tourist magnet in London should be entitled to sympathetic consideration from those whom its presence benefits – the State no less than the City of Westminster. Their help will be essential to dealing with the planning half of the problem now posed by the increase of visitors. This is at least as great outside the building as within it, for the space at present available for their arrival and departure is hopelessly inadequate and not within the power of the Dean and Chapter to remedy.

When the Whitehall Development Plan was commissioned by the Government in 1965 the scope of the problem was not foreseen. Its proposals for re-routing the traffic in Parliament Square further away from the Abbey and St Margaret's were to be welcomed: not so the abolition of the Middlesex Guildhall, the erection of a huge Government Conference Centre and the substitution of an empty Piazza for the garden.

In these and other ways the plan has indeed come in for independent criticism and there would still be time and opportunity to secure its revision. The architectural merit of the Middlesex Guildhall,[10] designed to be a good neighbour to the Abbey, will, it may be hoped, secure its retention. If the road south of it can be closed to traffic the aim should be to enlarge St Margaret's churchyard by a continuation westwards of its present alignment in front of the north aisle. This would meet the south east corner of the Guildhall, whose south front would then rise direct from the churchyard lawn.

A northern continuation of the railings in front of the west end of the Abbey would form the west boundary of this enlarged churchyard. The whole of the east front of the Central Hall should remain exposed (as it is now) and the frontage line of any future building on part of the old Westminster Hospital site kept back far enough not to impinge on it. If such a building were to be a Government Conference Centre it could still be of some size without destruction of the headquarters of the Institution of Civil Engineers.

Between it and Sanctuary Buildings there would then be a rectangular forecourt large enough for all coach and car traffic to the Abbey, easy circulation of crowds and the provision of public conveniences.

As the plan appended shows the scheme in outline there is no need to describe it in detail. Apart from preserving or enhancing views of the Abbey, it would reflect the wider conception of what is due to Westminster Abbey and the place it has come to occupy not only in the national life but in worldwide fame.

All plans seem visionary when their realization cannot be immediate. Daunting difficulties and objections will always be raised to them. But this scheme is less drastic than the Whitehall Plan and it is of the utmost importance that the interests of the Abbey and St Margaret's should not be found, when too late, to have been sacrificed because, through failure to envisage and expound them, they were never fully understood.

> February 1971.
> Surveyor of the Fabric of Westminster Abbey.

1   The chancel was altered in 1905–6, several years after Pearson's death.
2   The most recent lead replacement here was in 2016.
3   This became a problem again from about 2012.
4   These aisle windows are dedicated to Milton and Lord Frederick Cavendish respectively. The west window is to Sir Walter Raleigh.
5   The Algernon Fitzroy window, which replaced the war-damaged Caxton window.
6   G.F. Bodley, who died in 1907.
7   Frederic William Farrar, Canon of Westminster and Rector, later Dean of Canterbury.
8   St Margaret's came under the care and control of the Dean and Chapter of Westminster on 1 June 1973.
9   The idea of a covered way was not taken up.
10 The Guildhall became the Supreme Court.

79.   WAM S/1/118

Audit Report by the Surveyor of the Fabric 1972

The death of Mr Hausser in January 1972 so soon after his appointment as Consulting Engineer must be recorded with deep regret. His skill, experience and understanding of the particular problems that old buildings present were of the greatest value and gave weight to his advice. Always prompt in response to technical questions put to him he won not only esteem for dealing with them thoroughly but also the personal regard of those associated with him. From the time that he entered upon his duties it was clear that a professional connection with the Abbey brought him deep satisfaction and he was proud to hold what he felt was a position of honour.

By this loss of one who served it for too short a time a gap has been left which it would be desirable to fill because the retention of a consultant engineer indicates awareness that circumstances could arise in which his services would be essential. Many points on which an engineer's opinion may be helpful are of no special complexity; but one – the actual method to be adopted for dealing with the five sided end of the apse roof – will be imminent in less than a year's time and is of a kind that, significantly, was not dealt with explicitly in any of the four reports on the roof commissioned by the Dean and Chapter.

The appointment that I should consider most apt would be Mr R.T. James (or Mr D.T. James) both partners in Mr Hausser's firm and with the right approach to buildings of the character of the Abbey. There would be further advantage that they have possession of Mr Hausser's drawings and calculations and are not unfamiliar with the matters to which he had been giving attention.

North west tower

As the level of scaffolding is lowered the progress of restoration can be observed from the ground. With the top portion of the tower done, work on the present stage below should be sufficiently advanced for J.W. Gray & Sons to move the scaffold down again before Christmas. Restoration of the whole tower above parapet level of the nave roof ought to end by June 1973.

In addition to the preparation and fixing of stone on the tower the masons have carried out further work in the west cloister, continuing the replacement of decayed wall shafts and moulded bases and capitals as in the south walk.

Refacing of one bay in Clipsham stone to receive the Lord Hailey memorial had however to be undertaken by J. Whitehead & Sons since time was short and our men would have had to be taken off other jobs.

When the north tower is finished, rebuilding of the parapet on the east side of the north transept will be the masons' next task. This should be well suited to our limited resources because ashlar can be turned out much more quickly than moulded work and the new saw enables production to be speeded.

The same design of parapet will extend round the apse so that, since the roof of the latter should be finished by the time the north transept parapet is done, the operation should continue without a break.

For periods of very cold weather when work at high level is not practicable, refacing of more bays of the south and west walks of the cloister will give our staff further scope for the production of ashlar work. Each bay that can be done is a useful step towards the eventual restoration that will be necessary.

Bells

A year ago the bells were about to be lowered. After recasting at the Whitechapel Bell Foundry they were returned and placed on the floor of the nave for a ceremony of dedication at which, in the presence of the Queen, each was sounded in turn. Well before Christmas the bells had been hung in their new steel frame in the north tower, places at a level some thirty feet below that of the previous belfry to increase the safety of the tower by reducing oscillation near its top.

This change entailed considerable internal alterations. A new ringing room has been constructed at what was previously the level of the flag room, with a dead chamber between its ceiling and the floor of the belfry. The flag room, moved down to the level of the nave triforium, with which it is connected by a door with easier access than formerly, is to be provided with a new boarded floor and then whitened throughout. Where oak beams had been badly weakened by beetle attack, steel joists have been inserted to comply with requirements of the City Engineer.

That the ring of bells, now ten in number instead of eight, sounds less loud in the vicinity, is partly because the bells are individually lighter and partly because, being so much lower down in the tower, the sound has less direct outlet through the louvred windows of the belfry. Modern practice seems to set more store on the carrying power of bells than on what they sound like nearby and there have been cases in my experience where, to achieve this, the emission of sound has deliberately been contrived through louvred openings on the top of a tower instead of through the windows in its sides. From people who do not like bell music complaints about excessive noise are frequent and bell founders, anxious not to jeopardise the popularity of bells in an age which has condemned those in far too many towers to silence, have felt forced to pay heed.

Mr Hughes, with whom I have discussed the matter, assures me that the Abbey bells are in fact heard well at a distance, though from the precincts they sound comparatively quiet. He agrees however that their tone could be intensified if the glass in the three circular windows round the clock faces were removed, giving tonal egress at the level of the bells themselves and not solely through the large windows higher up. The glass is set in quite small openings with the four spandrels of what are square windows framing the circular clock dials; after its removal, copper wire would have to be fixed to exclude the entry of birds. As results could be tested without incurring much cost in labour or materials, the experiment may be worth trying.

The Elizabethan bells, still high up in the tower, sound clearly and have not been affected. Electrical apparatus has been fitted to eliminate hand chiming.

The new ringing room has been equipped with electric heating, washing facilities, a wood partition wall behind the glass of the clerestory window in the west bay of the nave and a sound deadening floor – the latter two to exclude strains of the organ interfering with the ringers hearing their own bells. All the existing peal boards have been ranged round the west and north sides of the room and a new board, describing the changes of 1971, is being made and will be placed on the south side. For further boards in the future there will be ample room.

Apse roof

Separate repair of the 28 roof trusses up to the chord of the apse has progressed satisfactorily and, since 22 are fixed, the three-quarter mark has been passed. There will then be the apse itself, the laying of the walkways and completion of the lead covering. The roof should be finished in about eighteen months but until the stone parapets have been rebuilt round it the external appearance will look incomplete.

Crouchback tomb

In the twelve months since Miss Plummer began the rescue operation of saving such remains of the medieval decoration as were not totally lost in the petrol bomb outrage, a total of £4,946.00 has been spent to date and another certificate will shortly be due. With assistants to help her since last summer, what seemed a slow start has quickened up and the expectation is that as much as can be done to those parts of the monument that suffered damage will be finished by July.

Considering how small had seemed the chance of getting much result for the money to be spent, it may be admitted that obliteration of at any rate the pattern of the decoration has, to a surprising extent, not been total. Under the strong localized light in which this can be examined at present, a student of medieval art would see enough to form a mental picture of the original. When the scaffolding is removed and no such strong light is available it will be less perceptible to the ordinary visitor. But this gives the more reason to hope that, out of the £12,000 insurance money, something will be left (after July) that can go towards showing the original decoration on the Sacrarium side to better advantage.

When scaffolding reached to the top of the tomb the massive stone finial in the gable was found to be loose and dangerous. The discovery was fortunate because an accident could easily have happened. The stone has now been dowelled and made secure.

Retabulum

After loose fragments of glass and paint had been noted in the summer of 1971 the late Professor Wormald was asked to make an examination. He confirmed the necessity for immediate removal and preservative treatment and a temporary workshop was fitted up in the east aisle of the north transept, to which the retabulum was safely carried by our staff. With a grant of £500 from Dean and Chapter funds Miss Plummer has for four months been engaged on fixing loose fragments, removing deposits of later paint and glue, and making cleaning tests to see whether more of the original minute decoration might survive and be recovered.[1]

The Pilgrim Trust, approached about a grant towards the cost of such work, expressed reluctance to make contributions without knowing the probably total expenditure and I have since been pressing Miss Plummer to name some figure that would be approximate if not actual. She has said that only by timing sample sections of the job could this be calculated at all and there were many different ones to tackle.

Though, for diffidence over the amount, she has not yet put it in writing, the estimate arrived at is £12,000. Professor Rees Jones, who has been watching the work since it started, was present at the meeting when Miss Plummer gave this information and, at my request, has promised to endorse its formal presentation if, after studying Miss Plummer's build-up of costs, he is satisfied that so large a sum is inevitable.

Glazing

Reglazing of the triforium windows on the north side of the nave, one on the west side of the north transept and one above the chapel of St John the Baptist has been completed. To forestall price increases due this summer glass for the six westernmost windows of the south triforium of the nave has been ordered and is being made. It will be ready for fixing as soon as our scaffolders and masons are free to undertake this.

Repair of broken or cracked quarries has been carried out in various windows. But recent examination showed further instances of damage, for some of which it is not easy to account. Work in progress on the north west tower might have caused accidental damage to the old glass in the west window of the north aisle. But there is no obvious reason for a breakage in the stained glass memorial window of the British Flying Corps on the south side of the nave; still less for fractured pieces in the Comper stained glass depicting Queen Eleanor and Lady Margaret Beaufort in the triforium of the apse. This window looks into the deep pit between the apse and Henry VII's chapel and I think it must be assumed that damage is caused by pigeons hitting the glass with their beaks since the tendency of birds to collide with glass suggests that, in flight, they do not see it as a barrier. This may also account for numerous breakages in the gable lancets of the south transept, a level which pigeons haunt, as well as in the small windows of the newel staircases which they mistake for open recesses in which they might shelter.

On the most immediate repairs – to three stained glass windows – an insurance claim of £47 has been made.

Cleaning of the interior

In February of this year the London Stone Cleaning Company began work of vacuum cleaning in Henry VII chapel. They will move westwards to complete the Royal Chapels before Easter, St Edmund's chapel being undertaken first.

The work will then continue throughout the rest of the building and is scheduled to be finished by midsummer.

The last general cleaning was after the activities of 1965–66 and how much dirt can accumulate even in five years is all too evident when those parts inaccessible for ground level routine cleaning are viewed from above. The triforium in particular, being still too much used for storage, becomes a depository for dust.

The accepted estimate is £3,900.

Monuments [and graves]

Henry V

October 25th 1971, St Crispin's Day, was the occasion for a special service to mark the restoration of a head to the effigy of Henry V: Lord Olivier recited the Agincourt speech from Shakespeare's Henry V and the congregation included many actors and actresses. The best tribute to the skill of Mrs Louisa Bolt who sculpted the new head is that probably few people, unacquainted with the history of the tomb, would believe what they now see to be anything but the original.[2]

The king's accoutrements have been removed from the wooden beam above the Chantry for preservative treatment and those who are undertaking this unanimously advise that it would be unwise to replace them where they would again be exposed to dust and dirt. If in future they have to be kept under glass in the Museum the question will arise of what should be placed on the beam; should it be replicas of the shield, helmet and saddle in their present state or should it show them in whatever may be deduced to have been their original form before decay effaced so much?

Queen Elizabeth I

A new sceptre and cross for the orb have been fixed on the effigy of the Queen. Since less than £100 of Mr Court Mappin's gift has so far been expended, it will now be possible to consider adding the Garter chain and Mr Hubert Chesshyre of the College of Arms is, at Mr Court Mappin's request, to be consulted about the details of this. If, when the cost is known, there is sufficient money still available, the crown could follow.

The only other missing feature – the lion of England to surmount the monument on its south side as the thistle of Scotland does on the north side – would be of alabaster decorated in colour and therefore more expensive. Provided the bequest eventually permits its restoration, the monument will be complete.[3]

Countess of Lennox

Further damage has been done to this monument which, more than any other, seems to tempt souvenir hunters. I think the time has come to make an insurance claim for restoring all breakages in such a way that a pilferer could not attempt removal without resort to considerable violence and noise.

Tompion grave

Full size drawings have been prepared for carving in low relief the arms of the Worshipful Company of Clockmakers on a square stone to be placed at the west end of the grave. The material will be Belgian marble matching that of the grave, on the head of which will be incised the words 'Father of English clock-making'. The design and estimate (£587) have been submitted to the Worshipful Company and their approval is awaited.

Monks of Westminster [stone in cloister]

After the old stone had been removed to Whitehead & Sons' works its condition was found to be too bad to admit of re-use. There was no choice but to supersede it by a new one – not easily to be found in such an exceptional size. The first did in fact break in transit but a second was obtained and has now been safely laid.

The lettering follows that on the former stone but the wording of the inscription has been altered to make clear that the statement that twenty six monks who died of the Black Death were buried here is less historical fact than a supposition of Dean Stanley.

Memorials

In the west cloister a mural tablet of Roman stone in a frame of Belgian fossil marble, with a carved profile of the head of Lord Hailey and an inscription composed by Sir Olaf Caroe, was unveiled by Lord Mountbatten at a service on May 18th 1971.

Close by a new stone of Belgian black marble was provided at the expense of the family to enable the wife of William Bishop to be commemorated on the grave of her husband.

In the same walk of the cloisters mention may be made of three memorials on the condition of which representations have been made to me at different times. The lettering on the mural tablet to Sir Frederick Bridge was cut by Eric Gill. No doubt to give it greater legibility it was at some time painted, although Eric Gill himself may not have originally intended this. The paint is now very faded and should either be removed or be renewed. Since it is unlikely that the lettering would now be effective without the definition of paint the second alternative is likely to be best.

A complaint about the condition of the grave stones of Sir Sydney Nicholson and Osborne Peasgood caused me to examine these earlier this year. The former, which must have been laid soon after his death in 1947, has suffered some damage in one corner but is otherwise in fair condition. There is nothing wrong with the other. But both were so covered by pigeon droppings that the inscriptions were obscured and their general appearance filthy.

[Pigeons]

That pigeons used not to frequent the Abbey seemed remarkable at a time when St Paul's was so plagued with them that electrical deterrents had to be fitted on their favourite roosting places. But the immunity persists no longer. The growing tendency for people to sit in the cloisters to eat their lunch causes pigeons to come in search of crumbs or the food that some visitors so tiresomely give them. The expedient of wiring the tops of mural tablets has proved quite unavailing: the pigeons now sit on the wire almost as a nest and foul tablets only recently cleaned as well as the walls and floor around.

To check the growth of a resident population of birds that only makes more difficult the maintenance of the cloisters in seemly condition it would seem advisable to remove the wire netting and try pigeon repellent applied to the top surfaces of tablets and other ledges that they now haunt. Such repellents are effective only for a year or so and would have to be renewed periodically. But it would be useful if, in one year, they caused the pigeons to seek some other abode and not return.

At higher levels it would be impossible to apply such a remedy. At present working conditions in the apse roof are rendered by unpleasant since there can be no means of excluding the birds until the roof is finished and closed in. In the belfry and top stages of the north tower, where louvres have had to be removed temporarily for fixing of the scaffolding, pigeons have already deposited their traces all over the new bell frame and bells.

[*Elgar and Reith memorials*]

Designs for new memorials to Sir Edward Elgar in the north choir aisle and to Lord Reith outside Poets' Corner door are being prepared. The latter will entail some refacing of decayed stone, towards which it is hoped that the BBC may make a financial contribution.

Furnishings

After trial in position the offer of an alabaster statue of the Madonna and Child for the chapel of Our Lady of the Pew was accepted. Carved by Sister Concordia of Minster Abbey, Kent, from a single block of very fine alabaster, it occupies the empty niche over the pedestal facing the entrance from the aisle without concealing what remains of the original wall painting. The statue was dedicated on May 10th at Evensong which was attended by many Roman Catholics.

Two tables designed by Sir Walter Tapper for the display of carved stones and other objects of antiquarian interest, one in the Library and one in the Museum, were transferred to the south aisle of the nave in time for the re-organized arrangements for visitors. The necessary adaptations and toning of the oak had been carried out by our joiners.

New shades for the desk lights in the stalls of Henry VII chapel are being made by Troughton & Young. They follow the pattern of that on the Queen's stall but will be slightly deeper.

The Waterford chandeliers in the nave and transepts have each been lowered, cleaned and re-lamped with very noticeable benefit to their appearance. A saving in time and cost has been achieved though the task having been entrusted to our own staff.

The stock of spare glasses held by Troughton & Young has been purchased for £525 plus £157.50 purchase tax. Some have already been needed since, during cleaning, a few fractured pieces were found and even one or two missing. There is no explanation of this; but the possibility of risk from any cause of strong vibration is the reason for hesitation about the request to fire a succession of pistol shots for acoustic tests of the building's resonance.

A stock of fifty spare glasses for the brass chandeliers was bought for £66 plus £26 purchase tax.

The reprinting of Abbey notices so that all are typographically consistent will entail the provision of some new stands, capable to being moved easily but firm enough not to be knocked over in the press of visitors and taking up the minimum ground space. The firm of Hurst Franklin & Co. Ltd. have estimated £387 for making fourteen and delivering, if approved, in about three to four weeks. The material would be mild steel, sprayed matt black, and the level of the notice board supports would be 6 feet above ground and thus, in a throng, visible over people's heads.

St Faith's chapel

The new pavement of Devonshire marble in the nave [western and central part] of the chapel was laid in the early summer of 1971, the work being carried out by J. Whitehead & Sons Ltd. at a cost of £1,160. It harmonizes satisfactorily with the colour of the old tiled floor further east.

A small plaque of Roman stone has been placed below the tablet to Jocelyn Perkins to record that the paving was the gift of his son Dr Christopher Perkins.

The lamp presented by the Patriarch of Jerusalem and hung on a specially made wrought iron bracket over the entrance to the chapel from the south transept was put up in June 1971 and first lit on the occasion of a visit by its donor.

After cleaning and polishing the three brass chandeliers that formerly hung in the choir and are of different design from those now in the ambulatory and royal chapels have taken the place of the previous very poor pendants in the nave and enabled the unsightly steel conduit and wall lamps in the chancel to be removed.

The walls and vaulting of the chapel were first cleaned, the wiring overhauled and new electrical switching installed.

In place of the silver sanctuary lamp a lamp presented by a private donor who hoped that it might be acceptable in the Confessor's chapel, has been put up for two or three months' trial.

Jericho parlour [servery]

The short passage leading to College Hall, opposite the display cupboards for china between Jericho and Jerusalem, was fitted up as a servery, with sink and cupboards made by our joiners and brought into use in time for the Collegiate Dinner in June 1971.

[*Little Cloister*]

The former office of the Clerk of the Works on the west side of the Little Cloister was divided into two rooms and fitted up to provide accommodation for the Stewards and Lady Guides.

College Hall

A scheme for improvements to the interior prepared by Mr N. MacFayden on behalf of Westminster School has been approved and is to be started in the Easter holiday. It embraces strengthening and restoration of the gallery, cleaning and repair of the traceried medieval panel below, including replacement of the missing mullions, new Cedar of Lebanon panelling round the walls, provision of new heating convectors, cleaning of the painted decorations on the north wall and the royal arms under the pediment behind the high table, new lighting by pendants from the roof and re-decoration throughout.

The cost (£20,000) is being paid for by equal contributions from the Dean and Chapter, the School, the Pilgrim Trust and the Goldsmiths Company.

Choir School

Work carried out during the year comprised the installation of new central heating and hot water system and the formation of a utility room at basement level.

Chapter House

Renewal of decayed stonework in the flying buttress between the gardens of nos. 1 and 2 Little Cloister appears to be finished. Since new tops for some of the pinnacles and repairs to other flying buttresses remain to be undertaken, the perimeter of the Chapter House may not be free of scaffolding for some time.

Houses

No. 1 Little Cloister.
In rebuilding the Little Cloister houses after war damage the architects, Seely & Paget, retained in no. 1 such parts of the earlier structure as had not been destroyed: the good staircase and some panelling survive from it. At a time when building licences were in force and there were severe restrictions on expenditure, it probably seemed expedient to leave undisturbed whatever appeared serviceable. But, as so often happens, enforced economy may be regretted later. Twice in recent years there has had to be expenditure on the kitchen of this house; a few week s ago fresh trouble that necessitated opening up the ceiling disclosed that the old oak beams, dating probably from the late 17th century, had been so weakened by death watch and long horn beetle attack as to be

unsafe. They have had to be taken out and replaced by steel joists entailing reconstruction of the floor of the bedroom above. Opportunity has been taken to carry out other improvements such as casing of the hot water cylinder and unsightly pipes on the walls of the kitchen, as well as redecoration. Investigation is being made of concealed floor joists in the rest of this house lest beetle infection should have spread to them.

No. 3 Little Cloister.
During September a small aperture was formed in the precinct wall to enable water to drain from the roof flat on the north side of the house. There is no entry to this flat enabling it to be cleared easily of leaves which blow in from the plane trees in the George V memorial enclosure; and the previous method of water disposal, by an internal downpipe, allowed no means of inspection. Without a more adequate outlet the level of water in the flat could build up quickly in heavy storms and the consequences has become evident in damp affecting the walls of the kitchen and the dining room wallpaper. Both rooms have been redecorated.

No. 2 The Cloister was redecorated throughout in 1971; also 4B Dean's Yard following the installation of central heating and remedial works on the street (west) front to cure damp caused by a defective enclosed downpipe. Built in wardrobes were provided in this house; to one of the second floor bedrooms in no. 5 Little Cloister; and in the Porter's Lodge.

A shower unit was installed in 5 Dean's Yard and the hot water system connected to the same boiler as feed 4B.

No. 2 Abbey Gardens
The extensive growth of fungus round a rain water downpipe on 2 Abbey Gardens at a level of about four to five feet above ground appeared in the summer of 1971 and was at once notified to the Ministry whose responsibility it is to maintain the building in proper repair. The diagnosis could only be dry rot: but never before have I seen a case in which it manifested its presence externally as well as internally. In spite of an assurance that immediate action would be taken, almost six months' delay ensued and when, early this year, a specialist firm arrived the dry rot was found so rampant that the interior of the wing affected had practically to be gutted.

It took almost as long to get attention to other matter of routine maintenance: eaves gutters so blocked that grass growing in them could be seen from below; a small tree that had rooted itself in a rainwater head on the east side of 1 Abbey Gardens; and gullies at the base of pipes choked with silt and leaves. The houses are presumably let on repairing leases and it must be hoped that what must have had to be spent on the eradication of dry rot will cause the Ministry, from now on, not to neglect periodical inspections.

It is perhaps fair to say that defects on those sides of the houses bounded by College Garden would not all be visible except from the Garden. But entry would never be refused for ensuring proper care and maintenance and in this instance specific defects were pointed out. None of them were attributable to the spread of Ampelopsis although this rampant creeper, which had reached roof level, had to be severely cut back in the autumn, as also on no. 5 Little Cloister.

From different positions on Abbey buildings I have noted places on buildings belonging to Westminster School where inevitable trouble must be developing – on one roof from numerous missing and broken tiles and an area where the tiling appears near to collapse; a blocked downpipe, 20 feet or more high, full to the top with water that cannot get away; a gutter in which such a mountain of silt has accumulated that it must have been choked for years; and other pipes where the evidence of water spilling down from the walls indicates some obstruction at the head.

Workshop

The purchase of a planing machine in the late autumn of 1971 has been of great benefit and well worth the £150 spent on it. In saving of labour time it will have paid for itself in two years or less.

Security

An attempted burglary in one of the houses in the Little Cloister and the chance that important buildings might be exposed to bomb attacks by IRA supporters in London brought the security of the precincts under scrutiny. Two independent reports were obtained and certain of their proposals provisionally approved subject to estimates being acceptable.

These come to a formidable sum. The cost of substituting for the flat coping a gable stone coping painted with unclimbable paint on the garden wall of 2 Little Cloister would be £560 – a total made up of £300 for 91.3 feet run of stone, £198 for cutting, £21 for scaffolding, £30 for fixing and (say) £11 for unclimbable paint. An additional railing and gate in the south east flying buttress of the Chapter House, matching the existing under the north east, would cost £746 exclusive of the special lock which the Clerk of Works recommends.

The cost of building a 12 feet high brick 13.5 inch wall between no. 2 Abbey Gardens and the precinct walls, inclusive of foundations, coping painted with Camrex Ante-Climb paint would be £883; and for the wall between no. 1 Abbey Gardens and the precinct wall up to £1,000, according to the position chosen.

The addition of upper gates in the north and south archways to Dean's Yard would cost £2,750.

Whether a total expenditure that could be in the region of £3,000–£4,000 would bring enough additional security to be worthwhile is open to doubt: there would still remain places where a determined burglar would not be thwarted. But since the easiest wall to scale is that of the garden at No. 2 Little Cloister, this, the cheapest of the estimates, at any rate might to the casual burglar also be the most effective as an obstacle.

Surroundings of the Abbey

Difficulty in eliciting any information about Governmental intentions for the planning of the area round the Abbey and the Houses of Parliament has for some time been raising apprehension in circles where the subject is of interest. An atmosphere of uncertainty is conducive to suspicion – chiefly because of the fear lest plans kept secret might assume finality and be presented almost as a fait accompli. Without direct contact between the Abbey and the Department of the Environment, there certainly seemed reason to wonder whether the latter could be sufficiently apprised of what, for us, are practical needs of great importance.

The purpose of the plan laid before the Dean and Chapter in February was to show how those needs might be met and to embody proposals sufficiently positive to stimulate consideration.

The plan had been examined by the two senior planning officials of the Westminster City Council who expressed interest and a large measure of agreement with its aims.

After the meeting with the Dean and Chapter at which the Department of the Environment and the G.L.C. were represented, I was invited to a further meeting at which Mr Scott Malden of the Department presided and four other officials were present. This gave an opportunity to clarify the particular interests of the Abbey and how these became the starting point of a scheme which embraced the whole area round Parliament Square.

My exposition was followed by a wide ranging discussion. Trained not to divulge information too readily, civil servants do not give much away: quite possibly there was nothing sufficiently definite that could be said. But rightly or wrongly I got the impression that, on such an exercise as planning, it had never been supposed that the Abbey could or would have thoughts of its own. If there was surprise I think it was at least tempered with respect.

An expectation that we should wish to see the Middlesex Guildhall removed was, nevertheless, rather startling: it seemed to denote bland unawareness that the threat to this building in the Whitehall Plan bought protest from a very wide section of opinion.

I suspect that much thought has been directed to reconciling the interests of two institutions – the Civil Engineers and the Chartered Surveyors – with those implicit in a new Government Conference Centre that would partly conflict with them. The Chartered Surveyors are, I believe, strongly resisting the conclusion of the Whitehall Plan that they should not rebuild on their present site.

The inadequacy of the triangular forecourt for coaches arriving at the Abbey was agreed. But for more parking space an underground car park was evidently the solution envisaged: I was tentatively asked whether it might be placed under the lawn on the north side of the nave – a proposal to which the obvious objection would be disturbance of the water table affecting the foundations of the Abbey. In this connection and as significant proof of a genuine desire to get traffic out of Parliament Square, an alternative plan to the Colin Buchanan tunnel had been commissioned from the engineering firm of Scott Wilson. It was to divert the District Railway and convert its present course into a road tunnel. The estimate came to £36 million and the scheme has presumably been rejected for that reason.

There seemed a courteous disposition to ponder the submissions implicit in our plan and, although some copies had already been made of it, three more have been asked for since the meeting.

Before it ended I was closely questioned about cleaning the exterior of the Abbey which is of interest to the Department of the Environment in view of the intention to clean the Houses of Parliament and give a new look to Whitehall, Parliament Square and the entire Government quarter. I deduced that the prospect of a stained and blackened Westminster Abbey remaining in the centre of it would be far from congenial and there was obvious curiosity to know whether we had any intentions that would accord with what the Department hope for.

This gave an opportunity to explain the practical and financial difficulties that frustrate what we should equally like to see accomplished. Of the extent, even the existence of chronic stone decay the Department had no realization at all and, when asked the cost of such repair as would make cleaning possible, I was able to emphasize the utter impossibility of finding money for it from the Chapter's resources.

So far as could be judged the points made were taken and noted: certainly the tenor of the conservation went to show that the outcome of whatever Lord Clitheroe[4] and Lord Amulree may be able to bring about could be of great importance.

Mr West and Mr Hirsch of the Westminster City Council strongly urged that the plan should be shown to Mr Ashley Barker of the G.L.C. Architectural Department who has now been to see it. His grasp of the argument behind it was immediate and to all the proposals he gave warm approval. He asked to have the loan of the coloured plan and has taken it away to show and make known the ideas contained in it.

Since seeing Mr Scott Malden I have visited the exhibition in Westminster Hall of the winning and commended designs for the Bridge Street building. The design placed first is the best of these shown: but since the standard of the others is deplorable, that cannot be high praise.

General

I conclude this report by touching on two questions that do not record work carried out but raise issues that require forethought.

The triforium

When the Museum was reorganized as an Exhibition of Abbey Treasures[5] some objects that seemed unlikely to be of much interest to the average visitor were withdrawn. These included a number of carved stones that, for lack of any other place, have since been stored in the cellar of no. 4 Little Cloister, where they have to be piled on top of each other and cannot easily be got at.[6]

A proposal that the best of them might be placed in the Museum on tables round one of the pillars was not practicable because circulation space quite near the entrance would have been reduced. A suggestion now put to me is that one or more of the spaces in the triforium over the apsidal chapels should be fitted up as a museum for classified exhibits (e.g. of carved stone) to which bona fide students could, on application, have access.

Though this possibility was referred to in an audit report some years ago as something that might be feasible, in the light of present conditions I feel very hesitant about it. There are more students about and a position could arise in which some might seek entry to explore a part of the Abbey to which the public is not admitted. Unless an attendant accompanied everyone ascending to the triforium and physical barriers were erected to limit the area in which movement were permitted there could be a serious security risk.

There is no possibility of a lift[7] to cut out the effort of mounting the newel stairs, which could subject persons with heart trouble to at any rate some strain. Nor is there in the triforium arches protection to restrain anyone with suicidal tendencies.

It is difficult enough to keep the triforium clean: exhibits, unless protected in glass cases, would have to be dusted continually and create a further labour problem.

I think that the most suitable place for a small number of carved stones, if it is felt essential to put them on show, would be the Pyx chapel. If possession[8] of this could ever be obtained so much the better; failing that, its present custodians might be expected not to refuse room for what would be on a temporary loan.

20 Dean's Yard

The lines on which this house may be altered to serve as the Chapter Office have been agreed in principle; but these leave unused a wing at the back on which no decision has yet been taken. It consists of a small two storey building looking north into the garden of no. 20 and backing on Westminster School property on the south. Some of its brickwork, with the original windows and glazing, dates from the late 17th or early 18th century although the brickwork in other parts is probably a century later. It would be unwise to demolish it without getting formal consent first, since no. 20 is a listed building and no changes can be made to it without Ministerial approval. The former Sunday School which is not part of the house could, I think, be taken down, being partly roofless already.

Two problems are presented by this property at the back. The first is what should be done with it; the second how there could be access to the site for building work unless this were undertaken before the Chapter Office became established in no. 20. If ever the Song School is to be enlarged to provide the accommodation set out in a memorandum prepared by the Organist some two years ago, the space required could only be obtained by taking in the garden and back quarters of no. 20. The two storey block, already mentioned, would have to be pulled down and the extension of the Song School would take the form of a ground floor building, lit from above and with a flat roof.

That would not preclude the possibility of building, over the position of the present two storey block which would have to be destroyed, a small house from first floor level upwards, for which the flat roof could become a roof garden.

Such a scheme would be expensive and, unless it could be financed, might have to be deferred for years. The simplest and cheapest alternative might be to convert the two storey block into a minute house, or even to rebuild it as such if permitted, and to cede to it the use of a garden for which the Chapter Office would have no need.

The building has been so neglected that it would have to be virtually new inside. But many little houses in London have been made out of decayed property such as this and a little paved garden could enhance its amenities. The occupant would have to be someone content to live in an inmost recess of the Abbey precincts and happy to have the south side of the nave for a view.

It must however be understood that, once the Chapter Office is in occupation of no. 20 as a working concern, there could not be any easy means of dealing with property behind it if the chance to find a use for this is not taken in time.

S.E. Dykes Bower, Surveyor of the Fabric

March 1972

[1] It was at this time that the double-headed cameo from the Retable disappeared. A detailed examination was not done until 1986.

[2] The hands, holding the ends of sceptres, were also replaced in polyester resin at this time (the original silver head and hands had been stolen by the sixteenth century). The funeral armour was displayed in the Museum after treatment and no replicas were put on the beam.

[3] The new chain, crown and lion were duly made. Railings around the tomb were provided in 1983.

[4] High Steward of Westminster.

[5] Opened as such in 1966.

[6] Photo in *New Bell's Guide to Westminster Abbey* (1986), p. 19. They were all eventually moved to a Lapidarium set up in the eastern triforium.

[7] An exterior lift was built for the Queen's Diamond Jubilee Galleries display in the triforium 2018.

[8] Still under State control at this date (Department of the Environment).

80.   WAM S/1/119

Audit Report 1973

With the works on the apse roof and the north tower in their closing stages and with the restoration fund outspent, the chief preoccupation of past months has become general repair of the external stonework and the necessity of finding money for it.

The organisation of an undertaking, bound to take at least twelve years, had to be presented in sufficiently comprehensible form to enable its nature and scope to be grasped by independent advisers; equally to be planned in a way that would show readiness to co-operate with the Department of the Environment in its wish that the Abbey should be cleaned.

To frame a plan of action, definite and feasible enough to afford a basis of discussion with builders, quantity surveyors and architectural and technical officers of Government departments, has required much thought. But time spent in conducting them over the building and demonstrating the actual condition of the stone, particularly at high level, has, I think been useful in promoting a grasp of what restoration entails.

There is no need to enlarge here on what has been dealt with in reports devoted to this subject. It will suffice to say that estimates, both for scaffolding and cleaning the north and south apsidal chapels, have been accepted and the first sign of activity on the site should be in April when erection of scaffolding on the south chapels will begin. By May 1st there should be clear evidence that the official starting date has been adhered to.

The *apse roof* and *north tower* have been referred to so often in these Audit Reports that further description of the work in progress on each would be superfluous. As forecast in the report of a year ago, the restoration of the stage now scaffolded on the north tower should finish at midsummer. The last trusses, those of the apse itself, will, it is hoped, be refixed by the end of April. The lead covering can then be completed and the temporary corrugated iron roof removed.

I have told Rattee and Kett that rebuilding of the stone parapet should immediately follow this and be advanced from 1974 (as shown on their chart) to this year. Being entirely ashlar work the stone can be cut away from the site and brought ready for fixing.

The south tower

Damage by lightning to two pinnacles in the summer of 1972 was an instance of what even to a building as fully equipped as the Abbey with lightning conductors can still occur in a freak storm. Falling stone injured the lead on the roof of the Jerusalem Chamber but did not penetrate the wooden structure. This was soon put right; but the pinnacles had to be scaffolded for removal of all fractured stone and subsequent replacement of new spires made and carved by our masons. The cost was recoverable under insurance.

Cloisters

During the winter our masons resumed work in the south cloister, cutting out and renewing defective stones in the shafts opposite those already finished.

To enable them to continue on a job that can be kept separate from those that will be allocated to Rattee and Kett's masons, opportunity has been taken of a favourable chance to purchase Clipsham stone for the ashlar walling. The price of £1.50 per cubic foot is at least £1.00 below what is normal.

One of the first bays to be refaced will be that containing the panel of tracery,[1] details of which are still recognizable but would soon disappear if left too long.

Belfry

The new board recording the Perkins bequest and details of size, weight and note of the bells has been placed in position. The lettering on it was painted by Mr Hart, who executed that of the last two peal boards.

Linoleum has been laid on the floor of the ringing chamber to deaden extraneous sounds for the ringers.

Crouchback tomb

After a period that has now extended to two years restoration of this monument is nearing its end. It will automatically cease when the £12,000 insurance money has been fully expended and, since at the end of 1972 the work carried out amounted to £10,874.00, the margin will have been almost used up in the three months that have now passed. Professor Rees Jones, who throughout has supervised what has been done, is generously making no charge for his services but only for expenses (£10.20) in seventeen visits, which can be paid from the insurance money.

His advice has been invaluable – not least for its advocacy of a reasonable rather than rigid view of 'Conservation'. Had portions of the monument that fire deprived of their original colour been left to contrast two obviously with those that retained it, the visual result could never have been satisfactory. They have in fact been painted in a way that makes them harmonious with the original decoration and Miss Plummer, accepting the logic of this course, can be congratulated on the skill with which she has conformed to it.

Charts showing the sections newly painted have been kept and colour photographs taken of the whole. These will constitute a pictorial record of the very elaborate decoration lavished on this tomb and that, because of its minute scale and the subtle refinements of colour, goes unnoticed except under a strong light. An account in book form is being written by Mr Francis Kelly of the Courtauld Institute since the success that has attended what at first appeared an almost impossible task has attracted widespread, indeed international notice.

One outcome may be a new evaluation of the Westminster School of Painting which, technically as well as artistically, achieved a quality almost unique. Its delicacy and refinement revealed by the close examination of the Crouchback tomb which cleaning has made possible is, even to many versed in medieval art, something of a revelation.

Arising out of this may, I hope, come something more. With such remaining money as is available Miss Plummer is carrying out cleaning of a small portion of the south side of the Crouchback tomb to show what would be the difference in appearance of this and the two adjacent medieval tombs – that of Aymer de Valence in particular – could funds be forthcoming for complete cleaning. By getting some of the leading experts to come and see this Professor Rees Jones hopes that it may be possible to explore whether an approach for the necessary funds, such as the Dean and Chapter, with other calls on them, could not be expected to sponsor, might be made independently. Its justification would be that works of art of the highest value, now so obscured that it is hardly realized, should receive the treatment they deserve.

A paper I submitted some months ago on medieval decoration in the Abbey dealt briefly with the chief examples of it. But, apart from the painting in St Faith's chapel to be mentioned later, there is still deadlock over the Retabulum. The £500 allocated to arrest deterioration in its condition has been used up and nothing further can be done until more is forthcoming.[2] The small cleaning tests carried out on the Sedilia some years ago sufficed to show only how different the real colours are from what they have become.

The decoration on the canopy over the tomb of Richard II cannot be seen at all except in the light of a strong torch. Mrs Baker assures me that the paintings of St Christopher and the Incredulity of St Thomas in the south transept could yield far more effect than at present.

The expense of specialist preservation of works of this kind is so great as itself to be a deterrent. If it is not to remain a permanent one, the best hope may be to look to those whose influence might count in quarters from which financial aid could be sought.

St Faith's chapel

No less than for the results it is yielding, the cleaning of the painting on the east wall is therefore opportune. The recovery of the original colour is as remarkable as, on a much larger scale, the change brought about in the interior of the Abbey when its stonework was washed some years ago. Gradual darkening had so metamorphosed the painting that it bore little resemblance to what the artist intended and the transformation is significant of what might be wrought on the Sedilia and perhaps the south transept paintings.

Mrs Baker's original figure of £1,200.00 as the likely cost was given three years ago and could not, prior to starting the work, have been more than a guess. All costs have since risen and the final amount may be twice as much because the work, as more details come to light, is taking longer to carry out than was expected.

The position has been made known to Sir Edward Ford, together with two relevant points: that the Dean and Chapter cannot contribute anything to this work which was undertaken at the request of the Pilgrim Trust; and that, if work had to stop when the £1,200 is spent (as it will be by now), the result would certainly be unsatisfactory to all parties. Nevertheless it might not be convenient to resume it until January of next year.

Sir Edward will bring the matter before the next meeting of the Pilgrim Trust in May and expects, but does not promise, that the extra expense will be sanctioned. In the meantime his strong advice is that the work should continue and in the circumstances it would seem expedient to follow it. If an interim payment has to be made by the Dean and Chapter, I hope this may not be impossible.

[*Hanging lamp*]

Since the last audit report was written the level at which the brass chandeliers were hung experimentally has been altered. The silver sanctuary lamp has been rehung from the splayed wall north of the altar after temporary trial of a lamp presented by a private donor, which has now been found a place in the Confessor's chapel east of the Shrine. Its suspension is from a hole in the vault from which a light must have hung in medieval times.

Monuments

Queen Elizabeth I

With some money still unspent from Mr Court Mappin's bequest, Mr Hubert Chesshyre of the College of Arms was consulted about details of the Garter Chain as it would have been in the time of Elizabeth I. He thought that it might be difficult to establish these with certainty and said that he would wish first to consult Garter King of Arms and then conduct such research as might be necessary. A recent letter indicates that this is nearly finished and that he hopes soon to supply the information required. Strangely enough much of it has had to be sought from a museum in Denmark.

Countess of Lennox

The Ecclesiastical Insurance Office accepted a claim for making good missing alabaster hands on the kneeling figures and other features at a cost of £620.00. Casts for the hands have been approved and the work is now being carried out by J. Whitehead & Sons Ltd. The hands will be fixed with dowels in such a way that to break and remove them will be as difficult as possible.

Henry V

Within a year of the head being fitted to the wooden effigy damage was done to the metal crown. Fortunately it was slight and repaired at small cost. The crown had been made as strong as possible to guard against such a contingency and it is clear that deliberate violence must have been used.

Earl of Minto

The large stone over the burial vault of the first Earl of Minto and his brother Hugh Elliot in the north transept lies where part of it is much walked over and the other part subjected to the scratching of chair feet. The incised lettering has become so worn as in places to be practically illegible. A descendant, Mr Dominic Elliot, has asked the cost of recutting the inscription. Alternatives are being obtained for deep incised lettering and for marble inlaid letters. The latter, though more expensive, is the only type of floor memorial that has any prospect of being resistant to wear.

Tufnell monument

At the expense of Mr J.J. Tufnell of Great Waltham, Essex, this monument in the south cloister was restored and cleaned. The missing leg of the cherub is to be made good in marble.[3]

Thorndike grave

At the request of a descendant of the family in America an estimate is being prepared for resiting the large incised stone on the grave of Dr Herbert Thorndike, a prebendary of Westminster in the late 17th century, and his brother John. This has for some years being concealed under the wooden ramp to the east cloister door to the nave [choir aisle] and will be relaid to the west of it, displacing some badly worn paving stones. Since the slab will no longer be on the exact site of the grave the words 'buried east of this stone' will be added in incised lettering at its base.[4]

Herbert Thorndike was an Anglican divine to whom the Dictionary of National Biography devotes a fairly lengthy notice though the family name has become better known through Sybil Thorndike, believed to be a descendant. That of the American one, from his signature, is Nat Simpkins III.

Memorials

To commemorate Sir Edward Elgar O.M. in the Musicians' aisle a Belgian black marble floor slab with lettering inlaid in white marble was unveiled by the [Master of the Queen's Music crossed through here] Prime Minister at a service on June 1st 1972.

A Portland stone mural tablet in memory of Lord Reith was placed on the south wall outside Poets' Corner door and unveiled by his son on November 29th 1972. Owing to the decayed condition of the original stonework on this wall a small area had first to be refaced.

Henry VII chapel

In time for the Installation of Knights of the Bath in the autumn of 1972 new glass shades were fitted to the desk lights of the stalls.

An oak case to contain the new memorial book of the Order of the Bath is being made and will shortly be finished. It has been so designed that, in the winter months, it could stand in front of the altar, between the altar rails, though in summer it may have to be moved to the west end of the chapel in front of the bronze gates. At the request and at the cost of the Order it is being made by the Royal School of Military Engineering at Chatham.

Glazing

The breakages in the stained glass of the apse triforium window, the west window of the north aisle and the British Flying Corps window in the south aisle of the nave were repaired and paid for by the insurance company. Unaccountable damage however continues. Very shortly after the first of these windows had been made good, almost the same piece of blue glass was broken again, which suggests that this colour may, to a pigeon's eye, be optically delusive. Either it is mistaken for blue sky or does not appear to be glass at all.

In the gable lancets of the south transept there are now more breakages than last year, and two quarries are again missing in the clerestory window nearest to the crossing on the east side of the north transept.

Equally perplexing are fractured diamonds in one of the west windows of the Jerusalem Chamber, which look on to the roof of the Bookshop and could hardly be hit by stones thrown from the street.

If this nuisance is not caused by pigeons, it is inexplicable; and certainly the Ecclesiastical Insurance Office might be excused if it becomes impatient of repeated claims. When the Abbey is scaffolded for restoration of the external stonework everything possible must be done to render roosting places so uncomfortable that pigeons will migrate elsewhere.

A difficulty with small breakages in inaccessible positions is that of getting glaziers to attend to such minor jobs. Goddard and Gibbs have usually been prompt in attendance at the Abbey but I have had repeatedly to remind them of what are still outstanding – most urgently the removal of the glass round the clock faces in the north tower to allow better egress of the sound of the bells.

Notices

To obviate the unsightly display of notices in the west porch a two tier teak notice board with panels for ten posters has been fixed on the north wall of the Jerusalem Chamber, the stonework of which was first washed by the London Stone Cleaning Company. This has so improved its appearance that it may now be wished that cleaning could be extended along the west wall over the Bookshop.

A single tier notice board with five panels has been fixed on the wall of the Porter's Lodge, south of the Dean's Yard entrance to the cloisters.

To facilitate the circulation of visitors within the Abbey fourteen iron stands are being made to carry the new standard size notices. They have been designed to be firm and capable of being moved easily, but as unobtrusive as possible.

[Alms boxes]

Three new oak alms boxes are being supplied for use at the west and east cloister entrances and Poets' Corner door. Each will contain a metal safe fitted with devices to safeguard money inside and carry a wrought iron frame on the top for a notice inviting offerings.

As soon as the three new boxes are in use – it is hoped by Easter – the two 18th century alms boxes at the west end of the nave will be removed for repair. There will eventually therefore be, with that in the north transept, six boxes available.

Sound Amplification

The panel of scientists giving thought to the particular acoustic needs of the Abbey have been working towards the production of a new form of loud speaker sufficiently compact in size not to be unduly conspicuous but as effective in use as stock models of larger dimensions. The model that has been evolved would seem to be successful in combining efficiency with as little architectural incongruity as can be hoped for.

Technologically this may well represent an advance of general benefit and justifies the care taken to reconcile two approaches to a problem, rather than to solve it by the sacrifice of one of them.

College Hall

The internal improvements – new panelling, redecoration and cleaning of the paintings on the north wall, restoration of the tracery in the medieval panel under the gallery and of the Jacobean woodwork of the gallery itself, relighting – were completed to Mr MacFadyen's design in time for Election dinner. The results have been adjudged successful with the exception of the lighting. On proposed changes in this I have already reported.

College Garden

A new teak door, made by H.&K. Mabbitt of Colchester with wrought iron hinges by N. Furneaux of Bishop's Stortford, has been provided for the entrance from Great College Street at the cost of a private donor. There is still some work for our masons to do in repairing the badly worn stone architrave on the street side and, on the garden side, the rendering which was at some time wrongly removed from the arch and splayed brick sides will be restored to them.

Houses

The work done during the year has been confined almost entirely to decoration. The largest job was redecoration of the Choir School carried out during the summer holiday. The Porter's Lodge was redecorated in June 1972 in readiness for the new tenants and decoration was carried out to some rooms in the Deanery. The lavatories in the Chapter Office and those at Poets' Corner door, the kitchen of 5 Dean's Yard and Mrs Tidy's[5] new home at the almshouses were redecorated. Authority to engage a painter as a full time member of the

Surveyor's department may be recorded with appreciation. There is ample work
to keep him busy.

20 Dean's Yard

Preparatory study is being given to the scheme for converting this house into a
new Chapter Office and devising effective use of the ground behind it, including
the provision of two flats.[6]

Security

Wrought iron posts and wire mesh, to be fixed on the garden wall of 2 Little
Cloisters, are being made and will soon be ready for fixing.

Workshop

Useful additions to equipment have been the purchase of a Cowley Level and a
vacuum cleaning machine known as a 'Litter Gobler'. It should be particularly
useful in the cloisters, the area outside Poets' Corner entrance, on the lawns of
St Margaret's churchyard and generally throughout the precincts.

Chapter House

The Department of the Environment have completed the refacing of decayed
stonework of the buttresses but repair of the pinnacles and lead roof continues.

Parliament Square

Although the Department of the Environment vouchsafes no information about
plans which, for good or ill, might affect the Abbey, the Greater London Council
passed resolutions at a special meeting in the summer expressing appreciation
of the plan submitted on behalf of Westminster Abbey and giving instructions
for full study of it. I have since received assurances that this is continuing.

As an epilogue to this report I would make brief reference to matters that,
though they have not come to fruition in the term of my Surveyorship, should
not be forgotten or overlooked.

Some years ago I made designs for canons' stalls in the Sacrarium to
harmonize with the Dean's stall and desk, the Sub Dean's stall, the canons'
and minor canons' desks. Lethaby did not design much for the Abbey but these
furnishings have a personal touch which gives them character. It is of a kind
vitiated by association with what is alien to it. The existing canons' stalls and the
two pairs of seats for the minor canons – whether by Blore or Scott I have never
been sure – are not without merit. But they do not consort happily with the
product of a very different outlook. If Lethaby's scheme could be completed,
the canons' and minor canons' seats could be used to much better effect in place
of the church chairs on the north side which ought not to have a place here at
all.

There is still no blue dorsal for use with the Queen's frontal although a design was made for it and material specially woven and set aside for the Abbey. The blue of the frontal is the colour which, in the Choir, holds its own from a distance better than any other and it is unfortunate that on feasts when this frontal is on the altar the Salviati mosaic should be its background.

The ultimate aim should of course be to remove this mosaic – a material incongruous in a Gothic reredos – and replace it by what, in the setting, almost designs itself.

The Abbey banners are in need of immediate repair. They must be unique in this country as decorative heirlooms of the greatest value.

I never cease to regret that the nave altar which is seen by millions of people and could therefore be thought representative of the standards of the Church of England should exhibit gilded wood candlesticks[7] so unworthy of their position. The metal altar cross by Sir Gilbert Scott is in quite a different category and should certainly be retained. I hope that my designs for metal candlesticks to accord with it and the aim of making this altar what it ought to be, may not pass out of mind.

In St George's chapel the tester over the altar is overdue for renewal: the material is faded and worn out. Comper must, I think, have intended a painted wood tester similar to many that he designed but presumably funds were insufficient at the time and damask used instead. Its condition now witnesses to fifty years exposure to dust.

Although the corner stalls at the west end of Henry VII chapel lack their canopies, these are preserved in store. It would surely be desirable to put them back.

[*External works*]

Externally the following works are becoming urgent:

Replacement of the cobbles in the approach from Old Palace Yard to Poets' Corner door. Walking over them is so uncomfortable as to be almost painful.

Repair and pointing of the medieval walls on the west and south sides of St Catherine's Garden. Intermittent work has been done by our masons but much more is needed.

Plastering the walls of the Dark Cloister. This was the subject of a recent report.

Painting of the iron grilles in the cloisters. Now that a painter is permanently employed this may be easier; but if once rust starts to corrode the iron, its removal, which must precede repainting, lengthens the job and adds to its expense. For architectural as well as practical reasons I would again like to urge the need of ferramenta in the north and east cloister windows. Designs were made and estimates obtained.[8]

Improvement of the Deanery courtyard. The paving, by its mixture of materials and lack of any plan, neutralizes the effect of what, with a proper layout, could be an attractive and picturesque feature of the precincts.

The retaining wall to the border east of the Chapter House has been criticized in these reports before. Now that structurally it is collapsing would it not be desirable for our masons to rebuilt it properly on a straight instead of a curved alignment between the buttresses?

Observations on other points would prolong this report unduly. It must end by recording the appointments of Mr David James in the autumn of 1972 to succeed the late Mr Hausser as Consulting Engineer and in 1973 of Mr Peter Foster as my successor in the Surveyorship. I am confident that both will prove good choices.

In concluding, after twenty two years, my last Audit Report I am conscious that, if ever future historians have occasion to delve into them, they may be found to record some information of interest, some seemingly trivial. But in combination these serve to give a picture of one side of the Abbey's life by illuminating, at a particular period in time, the affairs, aims and actions of its Surveyor's department.

[1] Presumably the monastic towel niches near the Refectory doorway at the west end of this walk.
[2] Its conservation was undertaken from 1998.
[3] The leg is still missing.
[4] It would appear this was never done.
[5] She was the widow of the Abbey Porter.
[6] No flats were actually provided, only office space.
[7] The wooden HMS *Barham* memorial candlesticks (altar and standard) were retained for this altar. The metal cross was eventually replaced by the crucifix designed by Micklethwaite for the St Edward altar.
[8] Not done.

80N.   Dykes Bower retired in 1973 and was appointed Surveyor Emeritus. He died on 11 November 1994 and his ashes are interred in the vault of the Islip chapel in the Abbey.

INDEX

Lowercase roman figures refer to pages in the Introduction, Arabic figures to item numbers, *not* to pages. Footnotes to reports are indicated by f and notes by n. Locations are in Westminster Abbey and its precincts unless otherwise stated.